The Scapegoat Child in a Narcissistic Family

CHOKING ON SHAME

DANA S. DIAZ

Delaney's Heart Publications

ISBN (Paperback): 979-8-9881155-2-6
ISBN (eBook): 979-8-9881155-3-3

Cover design by Aaxel Author Group and Deividas Jablonskis
Interior formatting by Aaxel Author Group
Author Photo: Jenny Taylor Boudoir Photography

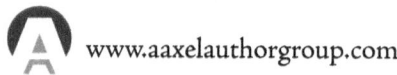 www.aaxelauthorgroup.com

Printed in the United States of America

To Gram, who gave me the foundation of knowing a mother's unconditional love and a sense of belonging I haven't felt since. I miss you every day. Rest in peace.

Foreword

Whenever Mom and I set out on a walk, I usually knew where we were going. Sometimes, we'd go to Great-Gram's. More of the time, we hopped a bus or train to my preschool and then Mom would go to work. Mom took me to the dentist a lot too. I got stickers and suckers every time, though, so I didn't mind.

One day, however, we went to a huge building downtown. The big white letters on the front spelled "Children's Memorial Hospital." Great-Gram had always been impressed with how easily I could sound out words at only three years old, even if I didn't know what they meant. That's because all she had to read at her apartment was the *Chicago Tribune*.

Thinking nothing of the ambulance that sped past with sirens blaring, I held Mom's hand as she led me inside.

"Why do I have to wear this?" I asked as Mom propped me up on the small bed on wheels and replaced my T-shirt and overalls with a light-blue gown that tied in the back.

"The nurse said you have to," she told me. Then she backed away while the nurse pressed on my shoulder to lay me down. I looked up at the lady, confused about why she didn't make eye contact with me or speak, and when she strapped one of my wrists to the side of the bed, I panicked.

"Mom?" I said as I wriggled my arm, unable to free it.

"You're fine, Dane," Mom said as the nurse restrained my other wrist.

"Mom, I'm scared!" I begged for her to soothe me. Instead, Mom followed the nurse's instruction to step back. Then, I watched in helpless horror as the nurse confined my ankles to the bed too.

"Relax, Dana. Just breathe," a blue-outfitted doctor advised as he placed his stethoscope on my chest. I didn't think he needed the earpieces to hear my heart, though; even I could hear the deafening sound of my heart pounding without them. "I'm going to need you to stay very still for me. Okay?"

Fear froze me as his strong hands held my little head still while another nurse strapped it in place. Unable to move freely, my eyes darted everywhere, desperately looking for my mom to make some sense of what was happening. I only caught a glimpse of her tight-lipped expression as I was rolled away.

Holding the rails of the bed, a group of adults took me through a hallway and onto an elevator. I looked from one to the next, hoping for some clue of what they were doing with me. None noticed me at all—not the terror I felt, the goosebumps on my skin, or the way I panted.

Once off the elevator, intermittent flashes of brights lights above made me dizzy. I squeezed my lids shut to relieve the nausea stirring in my stomach and throat. Footsteps, a clunk of two more doors, and unintelligible prompts from one nurse to another came to a halt at the same time as the rolling. When I reopened my eyes, six people stared at me with an intensity I could feel. They all wore blue head coverings and matching masks. One reached up and flipped on a bright light that blinded my wide and wild eyes. Then another lowered a clear plastic thing onto my face.

With my mouth and nose covered, I felt like I would suffocate. I wanted to scream and fight to escape, but weakness instantaneously came over me. Then my heavy lids refused to remain open. Just before they shut, I saw a long bushy beard on a fat face I knew. It was my dear dentist.

When my eyes reopened, I was somewhere else—like Dorothy when she woke up in Oz. The dimly lit room had a white tile ceiling and bare walls that seemed to be a light gray. It was quiet and still, aside from some voices and beeps outside the open door. Still, I was scared and alone.

Thinking I could get out of bed and go find someone to help me, I tried to lift my arms. They were still strapped down. A needle sticking into one connected to a long tube which I followed up to a clear pouch hanging from a metal stand next to the bed.

I gasped then cried out, "Mom?"

Standing from a chair near the foot of the bed, Mom put down her magazine and came to my side. Immediately relieved to see her, I exhaled, but my heart was still racing a mile a minute.

"You're all right, Dane. It's over," she said.

Dismissing whatever she was referring to, I averted my eyes down to the needle. "But—" I couldn't even finish my sentence because I wasn't sure what I was asking. I just cried, hoping Mom would release me from this bed and this whole situation.

"Calm down. And don't make that face. That probably isn't good for your mouth," Mom told me.

My *mouth?* Now that she mentioned it, my mouth did feel kind of weird. So, I used my tongue to feel around. There was a metallic taste, like when I put my tongue on a battery to test it, but I couldn't figure out the source of the soreness.

Distracted by a nurse who came in and checked all the machines beside my bed, and then a doctor who came in after that to talk to Mom, I lay there silently, listening for any indication of what had happened.

Using the end of what I'd thought was a pen, the doctor shined a light in my face and leaned down. "Can you say 'ah' for me? As big as you can," he directed.

I'd been to the dentist enough times to have mastered the backward tilt of my head and jut of my chin.

"Good girl," he said, sounding just like my dentist as he moved the light around the inside of my mouth before standing back up and making notes on a bedside clipboard. "We'll keep monitoring her through the night," he told my mother. "And we'll see how everything looks over the next couple of days."

Days? I hoped that didn't mean I'd have to stay *here* for those days!

"Okay, thank you," Mom said.

"Oh, one more thing—no food until tonight. Then she'll be on a soft diet. We'll bring up some applesauce and mashed potatoes and whatever else you think she might like," the doctor threw in.

"Applesauce and mashed potatoes will be fine," Mom said. Then the doctor left.

"I want to go home," I whined.

"Sorry, Dane, but you have to stay here."

"But why?"

"Because the doctor said so. They put silver teeth in your mouth, and they have to make sure they did it right before they can let you leave," she explained. Unfortunately, all I got out of that was "silver teeth," which made no sense to me whatsoever. As far as I was aware, my teeth were white like everyone else's.

"But Mom!" I whined again.

A cough and low murmurs coming from the dark corner of the room distracted us. We turned our attention to the noise and noticed a clear-sided box of sorts by the shaded window. Mom walked over, and I watched her look into it. Then a kind smile came across her lips.

"It's okay. You're all right," she said. I wondered who my mom was talking to like that, immediately envying whoever was on the receiving end of Mom's rare affection. Then I watched Mom go out into the hallway and fetch a nurse.

Mom and another female spoke in a low murmur. The only words I could make out were, "Her parents haven't been here to see her," and "She's terminal." I didn't know what that last part meant, but I was excited there was another girl here. I wished the nurses would let us out of our beds so we could play.

With creases in her forehead, Mom went straight to the other bed when she returned. I watched her lift the swaddled girl out, and then hold her in her arms like a baby.

The baby was pretty big. She didn't move much, maybe because she had a thin, clear tube attached to her arm like I did, as well as another that attached to her nose. She didn't talk either; she just made nonsensical noises. Mom seemed to like them, though. She wore a gentle smile.

Over the next few days, I remained confined to the hospital bed, though my feet and wrists were eventually freed from the straps. My dentist had come to see me and had me open wide like always, so he could look inside my mouth. He'd smiled at me and told me I'd done a good job and that everything looked just as it should.

IV

Aside from watching whatever nurse came in to fuss with the tubes and machines next to me and the mysterious girl in the other bed, the only other entertainment I had was when my mother would visit. She'd convey the well wishes Great-Gram, Grandma, and my uncles and cousins asked her to relay. Then, she'd cradle the other girl, who hadn't had even one visitor that I'd seen.

Although I felt bad for her, I struggled to understand why Mom gave her more attention than me. It's like Mom forgot I was even there or hadn't considered that I might want to be held and soothed too.

Mom had never been that way with me, though. Great-Gram was the one who rocked me and pet my head to calm me when I was upset or had a nightmare. But Great-Gram wasn't here, so I expected Mom to fill in for her, or at least divide her attention between me and the other girl. Instead, I watched Mom be more of a mother to that baby girl than she'd ever been to me.

Then one morning I woke up and saw the sun shining in, shedding light on the empty space in the corner. The girl and her clear box were gone. I wondered if she'd finally been able to go home like I was told I would be able to after this one last sleep here. So, I thought nothing of her until my mother showed up later and gaped at the vacant corner.

Without saying hello, Mom rushed out to the nurse's station.

"She passed last night," I overheard a nurse say in a hushed tone.

I didn't know what that meant, but I guessed by the ghostly expression on Mom's face when she returned that it couldn't be good.

After that, Mom was as stiff, silent, and non-present as the zombies I'd seen in *Scooby-Doo* cartoons, which didn't make sense since the doctor said I could go home. Still, I was excited. I missed Great-Gram and her white rice. I missed Uncle Juni taking me to the dime store and letting me pick a candy. I missed my cousins, especially Aaron, who was more like a big brother to me. I just wanted to go back to all the people and things that made me happy.

So, I started to skip as soon as we exited the hospital but remembered the doctor told me not to for a while. Still, I couldn't help but run straight up the stairs to Great-Gram's apartment when we arrived there. I ran straight into her cushy mass the second I saw her toothless smile.

One of my mom's brothers—my Uncle Juni—was there. "Let's see your new gear," he said. Assuming he was referring to my mouth, which had been what every doctor and nurse at the hospital focused on, I opened wide. "Man! That's a lot of metal!" he exclaimed.

Anxious to see this silver I kept hearing about, I ran to the adjacent bedroom I shared with Great-Gram when I stayed there. I heard her ask, "Que paso?" as soon as she thought I was out of earshot, and then Mom said something about someone being dead.

After leveraging myself up onto Great-Gram's dresser, being careful not to knock the figurine of Jesus and the laminated picture of Pope John Paul II leaning against it, I opened my mouth to see inside it in the mirror. It's like I'd opened a treasure chest and saw silver pieces randomly dispersed. Thinking it looked like I'd eaten a bunch of nickels, I giggled. Then I smiled, delighted at the sparkle.

Back at preschool on Monday, I was sitting at a table, coloring, when a classmate asked, "How come you got silver teeth now?"

"I don't know," I said with a shrug. "My dentist put them in."

"Well, I think they look funny," she said.

They were indeed different. But none of my family had made them seem weird. So, I didn't think much about them, either. They were just part of who I was now, and part of what made me special.

"You're No Good"

I hated it when Mom left me with her boyfriend Leo. He didn't play with me. He didn't pay me much attention at all unless it was to yell at me for something I'd done. So, I tried to fly under his radar by playing in my bedroom quietly after Mom went to work.

Bored by Barbie, I looked out of my bedroom window at the concrete and traffic, longing for someone to push me on the swing of the rusted old jungle gym behind our apartment building. I'd never ask Leo, though. I was afraid to ask him for anything.

Peering out my bedroom door to confirm his location, I saw him sitting on the dark-brown wood-framed sofa in the living room, watching some game on the console TV he'd contributed to the few furnishings here. Leaning forward onto his knees, he was too intensely focused on the screen to notice me creep past him with my back to the wall.

Once in my mom and Leo's bedroom, I released the breath I'd been holding and surveyed the room for entertainment. The queen-sized bed begged to be jumped on, but Mom had made it so nicely that I didn't want to disturb its clean lines. She always liked things to be neat and tidy, which wasn't too hard here since we barely had anything.

I looked around at the empty white walls and equally vacant space around the bed, looking for something to pass the time. Car horns and bus brakes squealing to a halt on the main traffic vein we lived on directed my attention toward the windows. I turned around and saw the twelve-inch black-and-white TV sitting on top of a wood-encased stereo speaker. I'd caught hell when I'd played with the TV antennas before, because Leo couldn't get good reception afterward. So, I knew better than to touch them. They had aluminum foil wrapped on part of them, anyway.

The knobs on the TV piqued my interest, though. Without turning the TV on, I decided to turn one of the knobs. I had no intention; it was just something to do. It took every bit of my toddler strength to turn the one knob enough to make the clunking sound of settling into the next channel position. It was a funny sound that made me giggle. I peeked into the living room to make sure Leo was still occupied. Then I decided to play a game of turning the knob without letting it go.

I turned the knob clockwise to repeat the clunking sound over and over, ducking my head under my arm so I could spin in circles to the rhythm without releasing the metal knob. I spun faster, trying to accomplish the task more quickly each time, finding amusement in the dizziness.

All of a sudden, Leo appeared in the doorway. I froze mid-clunk and stared at him with widened eyes expressing guilt and fear.

"What are you doing?!" he yelled. "You don't need to be touching my TV! Didn't you learn the last time you messed with it?"

Within a split second, Leo rushed over and gripped my left arm. I watched his fist tighten around my tiny limb then looked up at him to see if he was aware of what he was doing. His pursed lips and furrowed brows told me he did. I was terrified.

"Answer me!" he demanded.

My bottom lip trembled. My heart raced. I felt like I couldn't breathe. I was so afraid to give Leo the wrong answer that I didn't give him one at all.

Yanking my right arm to make me release the TV knob I'd held on to didn't detract from the pain of Leo squeezing my other arm.

"You're hurting me," I told him. Then I used my free hand to try to peel his thick fingers off my reddening limb. Leo stood motionless as I pulled and twisted and tried to leverage my scrawny body for more muscle, getting nowhere for all the effort. "Stop!" I ordered, still wriggling to escape his hold.

If he would just let go, I'd go back to my bedroom and sit in the corner and do nothing the whole rest of the day. I wouldn't move. I wouldn't talk. I wouldn't do anything until Mom came home. I just needed Leo to give me a chance to listen and be good.

Instead, he struck me.

The sting of his hand whacking my butt with unnecessary force overpowered the pain of his other hand gripping my arm tighter than he needed to. I was shocked into immediate tears at the unexpected assault, and the prickly tingling behind me lingered as if to exaggerate the severity of this scolding. No one had ever laid a hand on me like this.

He lowered his face to my level, making him seem that much bigger. And scarier.

I barely recognized Leo through the blur of my tears, though. I could see his black afro and thick mustache against his brown skin. The white of his eyes stood out too, because they were widened with madness.

"SHUT UP, YOU LITTLE—" he screamed in my face. His grip on my arm tightened just as he inflicted me with another whack, but on my hip this time.

"OW!" I cried out. My shoulders caved in and shook with every mournful sob. I could feel the ends of my frown falling to exaggerated defeat, as if waving the white flag of surrender, hoping my submission would end this unprovoked assault.

"I TOLD YOU TO SHUT THE FUCK UP!" he seethed.

The sheer hatred on his face made my eyes widen with terror again. I'd heard that bad word before. I was told adults only use that word when they're really angry.

"AHHHHHH!" I screamed at the top of my lungs, just because I could. The high pitch made Leo wince.

The full force of his nearly thirty-year-old masculine strength was an unfair opponent to my thirty-pound frame, but he struck me again anyway. My weeping eyes looked up at him, begging for mercy.

"What did I just tell you?" he yelled. Then he raised his free hand up in the air.

I closed my eyes as tight as I could and cowered. But then he whipped me around so fast, I had no time to brace against the repeated whacks which followed.

When he felt that I'd been sufficiently disciplined, Leo released me with a forceful fling. I pulled my assaulted arm into the embrace of my other hand, soothing my limb since I couldn't soothe my mind.

"That's what you get for not listening!" Leo scolded, waving a finger in my face. Then he retreated to the couch in the living room.

I stood in paralyzed fear, sobbing more quietly from the fear and pain simultaneously. But when he glared at me through the open doorway, I ran to the corner of the bedroom where he couldn't and curled up in a fetal position on the floor.

When Mom returned later that day, I heard Leo get up to go greet her. So, I got up too, feeling every ache and pain that Leo had inflicted on my tiny body earlier. I peeked out of their bedroom to assess whether it was safe to emerge and heard them talking in the kitchen at the back of the apartment.

With a bowed head, I went straight to my mom. "Hey, Dane," she acknowledged without disrupting her conversation with Leo. I latched onto her leg and buried my face in her thigh, finding comfort in her hand on my shoulder.

"I'll be back later," Leo finally said. The second he left out the back door, I exhaled. I didn't know if he was going to the bar, to see his two sons, or to argue with the woman he was still married to, but I didn't care. I was just glad he was gone.

"Want a hamburger from McDonald's?" Mom asked me then. "I have a little extra this week, so . . ."

Keeping my head down, I nodded. She didn't have to offer me McDonald's twice. She rarely had extra money despite working more than one job, so we rarely ate out. She wasn't much of a cook either, being only twenty years old, so anything was better than whatever she'd have otherwise fed me out of a can.

"Okay, let's go, then," she said. I followed her out the back door then took her hand as we descended the two flights of exterior stairs to the noisy street. I kept my head down, though, afraid she might notice my eyes, which were probably swollen and red from crying.

"Why are you acting so weird?" she asked on our short trek towards the golden arches.

As much as I wanted to tell her what had happened, I was afraid she might confront Leo about it, like she'd confronted the neighbor whom I had said gave me "man juice" once. She'd been angry when she discovered that the man-shaped wax figures with sugary liquid inside weren't what she thought. I didn't want to suffer the same consequence for tattling on Leo. So, I shrugged. I just wanted my forty-nine-cent hamburger, and to pretend what had happened hadn't happened at all.

After sharing the burger on the way home, I changed into my Wonder Woman Underoos and curled up on the living room sofa, where my assailant had sat just a short time before. The thick, scratchy, brown plaid fabric seemed to offer more cushion for my sensitive bum than the pile of thin blankets Mom had laid out on my bedroom floor. I never minded sleeping on the floor, like I did here and had done in the couple other apartments she'd had before. My arm and hip were sore tonight, though, so I'd have preferred to sleep on the comfortable bed she shared with Leo. Unfortunately, Leo didn't allow me to.

I slept on the couch often enough that Mom didn't question it, anyway. I wished she had, though, just like I wished she'd be more concerned about my melancholy. I wished for her to wrap her arms around me and tell me I hadn't deserved Leo's harsh mistreatment. I wanted her to promise me that she would never allow anyone to ever hurt me that way again. But she didn't know what had happened, and I don't think she'd have coddled me if she did. She wasn't affectionate like Great-Gram.

When Mom finished her random chores, she covered me with a pink blanket Great-Great-Gram had crocheted just for me. Then she kissed my forehead and went to flip off the lights. The light glared off her thick-lensed eyeglasses as she turned back and smiled softly. Then she disappeared into her bedroom for the night.

The loud metal click of the back door closing in the middle of the night awoke me. I stilled myself as I listened to Leo's heavy footsteps approach from the back of the apartment. I shut my eyes as he passed the couch, reopening them when I heard the squeak of the bed springs indicating his location and my safety.

But then the ticking sound of cockroaches scurrying around prevented me from falling back asleep. They sounded close. I held my breath for a moment to listen better when I felt something bean-shaped moving under me. Being a stomach-sleeper, I propped myself up on my hands. The silvery glimmer of the moonlight coming in through the window reflected off the backs of the few roaches crawling on the sofa. The sight didn't faze me as much as the thought of one crawling inside my open mouth as I slept. So, I had to remember to keep my mouth closed. There was no way to prevent them from getting stuck in my hair, though. I'd learned to shake my hands through my waist-long tangles before baths to make sure they fell out before falling into my bath water with me. Otherwise, I'd be scrambling as much as they did to get out of the water.

I got up from the sofa and felt a creepy crawl on my leg. I brushed my hand along my calf to flick the roach off. Then I walked toward Mom's bedroom, hoping to sneak into the bed without notice. I didn't care about Leo's rule. He wasn't the one sleeping with the nighttime crawlers, and he wasn't the boss of me.

Tiptoeing as quietly as I could, I halted as soon as I reached the open doorway. The streetlights outside shined in just enough to see Leo lying flat on his back and Mom propped on top of him. *What are they doing?* I thought as I watched her lean down to kiss him on the mouth. Leo's hands moved up and down her naked silhouette, from her hanging breasts to the curve of her bottom. Embarrassed to see Mom naked, I tiptoed back to the scratchy sofa. I brushed the few shiny tickers off then settled back in.

I laid awake, remembering when Mom had shown me the movie *King Kong*. I couldn't sleep that night either because I hadn't thought it fair for the poor gorilla to be shot at just because he wanted love. Like what had happened to me today, it didn't make sense to make someone suffer when all they longed for was to connect.

Recalling what had happened to me, I clutched the blanket tighter. I wished I was with my Great-Gram now. She'd rocked me that night I was upset about Kong. She'd petted my head and sang softly to me in Spanish, until I was soothed back into a peaceful sleep. She'd allowed me in her bed too, even though I had my own little bed at her apartment.

I knew I was supposed to love Mom, but I loved Great-Gram more because Great-Gram was the one who did all the things Mom should have been doing with me. Unfortunately, everyone thought I should be with Mom instead. So here I was, even though I didn't want to be here at all.

"Let It Be"

e went to Great-Gram's apartment the next day since Mom
didn't have to work. Although it wasn't the place where everyone
had grown up, it was the family base where relatives gathered
regularly to reconnect with each other, our Puerto Rican roots, and enjoy
home-cooked meals we couldn't get elsewhere.

For me, it *was* like going home because I'd lived with Great-Gram from
birth. Mom had taken me to stay with her on occasion, but I hadn't stayed
with her regularly until she had established income and an apartment to
properly provide for me.

Excited to be back to where my heart felt most at home, I ran up the
interior stairs of the building, ahead of Mom. Then I burst through the
unlocked door of Great-Gram's apartment, leaving it wide open behind me.

"Great-Gram!" I called out before hearing her singing "Take Me Home,
Country Roads" in the back. I once asked her why she sang that so much,
and she said it was because she missed her mother, who was in heaven now.

I rushed to the kitchen to find her standing at the stove, stirring
something in her enormous silver pot. She only cooked two foods in that
pot—white rice or orange rice with gandules, which were little brown
beans. I preferred the plain white rice, sometimes putting ketchup on it to
make it orange.

With a toothless smile and twinkly eyes, Great-Gram extended an
arm to invite me into her plump embrace. I threw my arms around my
muumuu-clad matron, closing my eyes and taking in her scent as I squeezed.
She wore Jovan White Musk. I once sprayed myself with the bottle she

kept on her dresser, just so I could think of her when I had to leave.

"Oh, hi, Ivy!" my Uncle Juni said to Mom. He'd just come down the two steps from the blacktop roof where Great-Gram kept a bunch of plants, smelling like whatever he'd just smoked. I coughed, like I did whenever Mom or my uncles puffed on those stupid little sticks.

"Hi, Juni," Mom replied as she sat.

"Got some skin for your Uncle Juni today?" he asked me, extending his hand, palm up. I released Great-Gram and wound up my arm like a fast-pitch ball player. Then I slapped Juni's hand as hard as I could. "Man! That hurt!" he pretended, shaking his hand while chuckling in chide.

Juni looked just like my grandma, with fair skin, deep-set dark eyes, and a short dark haircut to match. I didn't see my grandma much, though. She was always working.

"*Quieres arroz?*" Great-Gram asked me in Spanish. I nodded, eagerly accepting her offer of rice, then sat across from Mom at the small metal table. Aside from the clunky white stove and refrigerator, the few white cabinets with plain metal handles, and big white sink with dark rust stains around the faucet and drains, there wasn't much else in the kitchen except for a small Holly Hobbie drawing hanging on the wall. I liked Strawberry Shortcake better, though. She smiled and wore red, which was my favorite color. Plus, the strawberry print on her hat looked like little hearts, and I was obsessed with hearts.

"How's Leo doing?" Juni asked Mom as he sat on the steps.

"Okay," Mom responded. I scrunched my nose at the mention of him, glad he never came here with us.

Great-Gram set a big bowl of white rice in front of me then. Opting to pass on ketchup today, I dug right in, barely chewing before I swallowed.

My Uncle Jose walked in just then. He was the third sibling and youngest of Mom and Juni. He looked just like my grandpa, with his light brown skin and dark features. I never saw my grandpa, though. He was never around.

"Dana!" Jose called out. With a mouthful of rice, I smirked as he squatted and extended his arms to receive me. Then I abandoned my rice to hug my other favorite uncle. His deep, infectious laugh bellowed through the kitchen.

As Great-Gram, my uncles, and Mom exchanged their usual banter in a mix of English and Spanish, I thought of that baby girl from the hospital. I wondered if she had grandparents or uncles who loved her like mine loved me. Because everyone had a family. Everyone had a mom and grandma. I was lucky to have cousins and a godmother too. They were my safe place in this world, and all I'd ever need.

So, when a girl at school asked why I hadn't been at the daddy-daughter dance the teachers had put on, I matter-of-factly answered, "Because I don't have a dad."

The girl leaned away from me, like I had cooties. "What do you mean you don't have a dad? *Everyone* has a dad!"

"Not me," I said, shrugging. But then I started wondering about it.

When Mom picked me up from school that evening, I asked, "Mom? Do I have a dad?"

She slowed the pace of our walk. "Why would you ask that?" she snapped. Her scrutinous expression made me cower slightly, though she'd never hit me like Leo did.

Feeling like I'd done something wrong, I said, "I don't know." Then, just as quickly, I retracted. "It's just that everyone else has one."

"Well, you *don't*," she said as she pulled me back into her fast pace. I had to double my steps to keep up with her.

I didn't understand. Everything I'd seen on TV and learned in school said babies came from a mom and a dad. Except for Jesus. The Virgin Mary was His mother, but He didn't need a dad because God had put Jesus in Mary's womb. Joseph had stepped into the father role for Him, anyway. So, it was like He had two dads.

I glanced up at Mom, wondering if God had put me in her womb the same way he'd put Jesus in Mary's. Her furrowed brows and pursed lips made that hard to believe. The Holy Mother didn't carry the bitterness and resentment Mom seemed to, and Mary seemed to love Jesus a whole lot more than Mom loved me.

Either way, I got the clear message that Mom didn't want me asking about a dad I supposedly didn't have. Still, I wondered why. Did I not deserve one? Had I done something to make him go away? Or had Mom decided I didn't need one, since I had Leo and my uncles?

I told myself it didn't matter and cursed that mean little girl for making me feel left out because I didn't have something she did. Some of us didn't need a dad, I resolved, because the love of our family was perfectly sufficient.

Anyway, if having a dad meant having someone like Leo in my life, I'd gladly do without one.

"Hot Child in the City"

*L*eo eventually disappeared, along with the few things he had in the apartment. Mom never told me where he'd gone, nor did I ask. I honestly didn't care because Mom seemed happier. She smiled more. She was more playful and attentive to me. We laughed, which had been hard to do when Leo was always around wearing his ever-present scowl. I kind of liked life with just me and my mom, especially since I could sleep in a bed now.

Mom started a new job at a notary supply manufacturer shortly thereafter. Her administrative position replaced the three part-time jobs she'd had before, so she was excited to have evenings and weekends off for once. Plus, she said the couple who owned this company were really nice.

So, every morning, Mom would drop me at my kindergarten. Then she'd go to work and return to retrieve me before dinner. When I was sick or the school was closed for a holiday, I got to stay with Great-Gram, who lived with my godmother Sonia now. If I was extra lucky, my cousin Aaron would be home from school too, so I'd have someone to play with, even if I was more of an annoying little sister to him. Otherwise, Great-Gram and I would watch game shows on TV in the morning, the ABC trio of soap operas from noon until three, and then visit with the flow of relatives who'd come for dinner after work.

We would see our family on the weekends regardless. Sometimes, one of mom's cousins would come over to our apartment to practice the newest dance moves. They'd sit me up on the kitchen counter with the portable radio, and I'd watch them bop and turn and intertwine their arms. I couldn't wait to be grown up so I could dance like they did.

Other times, a bunch of us cousins got together at one of their houses for a sleepover. We'd lay blankets on the floor and watch scary movies like *Salem's Lot*. Then we'd be too scared to go to sleep, so we'd stay up all night watching the funny people on *Saturday Night Live* say and do crazy things until we eventually passed out from exhaustion.

Christmas was, by far, the best time of year, though. We would all get together as usual, except that there was more food, more people, loud music, and festive dancing. We'd stay up until midnight, when it was officially Christmas, and open the presents we'd anxiously awaited. No matter if it was a T-shirt or a toy, every gift was the best gift ever, because it was an expression of someone's love.

Mom was bummed this Christmas, though. Her new company was hosting an all-expenses-paid trip for every employee and a guest to go to Hawaii. I didn't know where that was, but I guessed it must have been a cool place by the way everyone gasped when Mom told them about it.

"I told them I couldn't go, though," I heard Mom tell Great-Gram.

"*Por qué no?*" Great-Gram wondered.

"Because!" Mom answered, nodding her head at me.

I couldn't understand why I couldn't just stay with Great-Gram while Mom went to wherever this Hawaii was. But I didn't interrupt their conversation. It was obvious that Mom didn't want to go and wanted me to be the reason she couldn't.

But then a week later, when Mom and I returned to our apartment one evening, the bright multicolored lights of the biggest pine tree I'd ever seen indoors greeted us in all its glory. I stared in open-mouthed awe at the shiny gold star on top and presents underneath of every size and shape wrapped in red and green paper with foil bows.

"Santa," I whispered. I had never heard of him doing something like this. But maybe it's because I'd never been on his nice list.

I looked up at Mom, who stood in the open entry with me, staring at the tree just as I had. She looked down at me, then back at the tree, then rushed to see whose names were on the tags. She checked each present, reading "Dana" on nearly every tag. My ear-to-ear grin couldn't contain the elation. I'd never been happier in my entire life.

Then Mom found a card with her first name on it. She looked at me, raised her brows, then pulled the card from the envelope. As she read the card, I watched her eyes widen. Her mouth opened. Then she rifled through the paper contents inside and reread the card again.

"We're going to Hawaii," she mumbled, still in shock.

"What?" I asked, thinking she couldn't go because of me.

"My bosses are paying for us to go there after all. Not on the adults-only trip with the whole company. Just me and you, on our own," Mom said louder. A smile began to appear on her face as she started to believe what she'd said. Then, still wearing our winter coats and with the door to our apartment still wide open, Mom took my hands, and we jumped up and down together, dancing excitedly to the music of our own joyous laughter in the red-and-yellow glow of the Christmas tree lights.

Then, shortly into the new year, we flew on an airplane for the first time. I didn't like the feeling of the plane lifting off the ground. Once the pilot announced we were at cruising altitude, though, I felt like a celebrity, being served pop and peanuts by the well-dressed stewardesses. I fell asleep after that, waking up just in time to look out the window at the sandy beaches and blue ocean below. Then I followed Mom down the stairs off the jet and squinted in the bright sunshine, amazed by the sight of palm trees and water in every direction. I was waiting for the white-tuxedo-clad hosts from *Fantasy Island* to emerge and indulge us with fruity drinks and floral leis, like they did with each guest arrival on the TV show. It didn't matter that they didn't. The trip alone was spectacular enough.

It was the first time Mom and I had ever stayed in a hotel. Located on Waikiki Beach, we had a view of a volcano from our sky-high room. The beach itself was much nicer than the beach in Chicago, where I'd spent so many summer days with my uncles. Mom tanned on the soft sand while I made sandcastles at the shore. We walked through colorful gardens brimming with exotic flowers, and I talked with a parrot. We rode a glass-bottom boat where we could see the water and fish swimming underneath. Mom was even asked on a date by a lifeguard who'd had to save me from an undertow. I didn't much like being left with the hotel babysitter for that, but the mini-modeling session Mom posed me for on the balcony made up for the slight. I don't remember ever feeling so free and so happy, and seeing Mom feel the same. So, it was a bummer to have to go back home. But I missed Great-Gram, so it was okay.

"Don't Come Around Here No More"

On a Saturday afternoon that spring of 1980, Mom put a jacket on me and told me someone was picking us up. I didn't think anything of it as she took my hand and led me down the couple flights of creaky wooden stairs. Once outside, the rush of the cars driving past chilled me. Their blaring horns didn't bother me, though; I was used to the city sounds. I looked up at the cloudy sky while we waited to cross the street, noticing the impending gloom of rain. It rained a lot in Hawaii but only ever briefly. Then the sun would come out again. I wished it was like that in Chicago.

Mom tugged at my hand to hurry me across the street to a poop-colored compact car stopped at the curb, making me forget about the island altogether. I didn't recognize the car or the man in the driver's seat. I didn't have time to wonder about any of it, though, before Mom plunked herself into the passenger's seat and sat me on her lap. She failed to notice that my head was grazing the ceiling.

"Hi, Ron," Mom said to the man.

"Hi!" The man's jovial response made me turn my attention to him. He reached behind his seat and pulled out a floppy-eared white puppet, which he put on his hand. The mouth of the puppet opened and closed in sync with this man's sad attempt to sound like a cartoon character when he said, "You must be Dana."

I giggled at the response and glanced back at Mom. She was smiling.

"Here," the man said, removing the puppet from his hand and handing it to me. "It's for you!"

Worried that I wasn't supposed to take anything from a stranger, I studied this man's face for signs that I could trust him. His cheesy smile made him seem eager to impress me, though I didn't know why. His receding hairline, which exposed a large forehead and slightly long face, made me think he was noticeably older than Mom. He still had some brown hair on his head, though. He was quite average-looking, really, except for his beady brown eyes that I didn't like for some reason.

I wanted the puppet, though, so I took it from him then turned around and looked at Mom, as if asking permission to accept the gift. She smiled at me, then at the man, which I took as a yes. Then I held the puppet closely as the man pulled away from the curb.

Mom and this man she called "Ron" conversed about the weather and people they apparently knew from work. Presuming that they met at her new job, I had no idea why we were going anywhere with him on her day off. I just knew I was getting hot and a little nauseous and needed some air.

The passenger window was cracked open a few inches, so I grabbed the glass at the top and pulled myself up to where my mouth could inhale the cool breeze as we drove. I felt a little better until I heard the man say, "Hey, don't hang on the glass like that." The sternness of his voice starkly contrasted with the cartoonish character I'd met a minute before.

I didn't move, though. I was mesmerized by the red traffic light just outside the car.

"Dana," Mom scolded as she attempted to pry my fingers off the glass.

"No," I said, grimacing at her. Then I put my mouth up to the opening again.

"Would you get her hands off there?" the man told Mom.

"Dane, please," Mom said, again attempting to peel my fingers off the window.

"No!" I refused, glancing at Mom with a scowl before turning my attention back to the traffic light.

All of a sudden, the window started closing on its own. I watched in awe, wondering how this was happening. The few cars I'd been before had windows which had to be rolled up manually by turning a knob on the door. I glanced down, seeing no knob and no hand turning anything.

"Ron!" Mom called out, just as my fingers were a quarter inch from being crushed. The window immediately stopped moving.

I tried to pull my fingers off the glass then, but they were pinched between the window and the top of the door frame. My breaths quickened as I struggled to get them out, then I turned to Mom in a panic as I burst into tears.

With a creased forehead, Mom turned to the man and scolded, "Ron!"

"What?" he said, as if innocent of any wrongdoing. Then the window slid down just enough to release its hold on my reddened fingers. I curled them up in my palms and held them close to my chest, then settled back into Mom's lap in an angry pout. I just wanted to go home, or, better yet, to Great-Gram's.

Ron parked the car outside of a white building a short time later. I gladly jumped out when Mom opened the door. Then I held her hand loosely as we walked towards the unfamiliar place.

"Look, Dana!" Ron said with exaggerated friendliness. I barely glanced at the mannequins in the store display he was pointing to. They were nothing compared to the Christmas windows my grandma took me to at Marshall Fields, anyway. Still, Ron bent to my level and put his hands on his knees to await the sudden excitement I was supposed to be tricked into exhibiting.

I turned away with my eyes closed instead, squeezing my new puppet close, worried one of them would try to take it away as ransom to induce me to express a liking for this man I didn't know.

"I'm sorry, Ron," Mom said. I opened one eye to spy on her demeanor. She was smiling politely as she excused, "She normally doesn't act like this. I don't know what's gotten into her."

What had gotten into me was that I didn't like Ron. I couldn't say why exactly, except that he didn't seem sincere. He was smiling and pretending to be nice, but I didn't think he was nice at all after what he'd done to my fingers in the car. Anyone who intentionally harmed someone, like Leo had, was bad.

I was miffed at Mom too, for letting Ron get away with what she'd witnessed. If she had really loved me like a mother should, she would have told Ron it wasn't okay to hurt me.

Instead, I'd had to endure a meal with the two. I kept my head down in an angry pout as I ate my hamburger and french fries, to make a point of my refusal to interact. Mom ignored me, laughing at Ron's audacious comments about people they knew from their work. I'd never seen her laugh like that with Leo. Still, I hoped to never see this Ron ever again.

So, when Mom dragged me out to his car another day, to be met with yet another stuffed animal puppet, I threw it back at Ron's farce of a smiling face. Mom gasped at my ungrateful reaction to the gift and then apologized profusely to Ron. He said it was fine and proceeded to drive. I noticed his side-eye, though, as well as the smug smirk on his face. And I didn't like it.

"The Great Pretender"

Mom really liked Ron. But the more Ron came around, the less I liked him, and the less we saw my uncles and cousins. I resented Ron for whatever part his presence played in their absence. I outright hated him, though, when I'd heard him refer to one of our cousins as "horse face."

Ron was in no position to comment on someone's looks. He was short and stocky, with a Fred Flintstone belly. If his hairline receded any more, he'd be nearly bald. He was old too and should have been humbled to have attracted such a young and beautiful woman as Mom. She was way out of his league.

That's why I couldn't figure out what Mom saw in Ron. He wasn't attractive. He wasn't nice. I mean, he seemed to be. However, I saw through the pretense of his affection for me as a farce to attain Mom's affection, though there was more of an effort to win me over than her. I don't think Mom realized it, though. She seemed to be pleased just to have his attention at all, for whatever that was worth.

To make matters worse, I'd overheard Mom confide to someone over the phone that she'd found out Ron had a wife whom he still lived with in the suburbs. She said she'd told Ron it was over between them unless he divorced his wife. I was proud of Mom for finally standing up for herself and happier at my assumption that that would be the end of Ron.

So, I didn't understand why he was in the audience at my kindergarten graduation, standing amongst all the other mothers and fathers. Nor why we moved in with him shortly after that.

He lived in a tiny two-story duplex just north of Chicago. It was far enough away that most of our family, who relied on public transportation to get around, couldn't easily visit us there. So, we saw them even less now.

Furniture began to disappear from the fully furnished place too, including the bed in the room I'd been assigned.

"How come I have to sleep on the floor?" I asked Mom when she came into the kitchen for her umpteenth cup of coffee one midmorning.

Forcing a weak smile while she poured it, she didn't respond. There was no way she hadn't heard me, though, unless she just didn't *want* to answer me. But I didn't mind sleeping on the floor; it wasn't like it was the first time I had. Anyway, my new room was partially carpeted, so with all the blankets she laid down for me, it was more comfortable than the hardwood floor of our last few apartments. I'd just been curious to know where the bed and everything else was going and why they hadn't been replaced.

"Mom?" I prodded between bites of cereal.

After a long sigh, she said, "Well, you know Ron was married before."

"Yeah," I said while chomping on a mouthful of sugary circles.

"So, some of the things Ron has, er, *had*, here, belong to the woman he was married to," Mom said with careful consideration.

"So, she wants her stuff back?" I asked matter-of-factly.

"I guess so," Mom said before sipping her coffee.

"Is she going to want the house back too, then?"

Mom's head shook slightly, startled by my question. She didn't know I'd overheard her through the paper-thin walls talking to someone on the phone about how Ron had fought his ex-wife to keep the duplex, even though her grandparents had given it to him and his wife as a wedding present. I thought it rude of him to take something her grandparents had given them. Then again, Ron tended to brag about duping people for personal gain.

"Well, no. It's Ron's house," Mom asserted, though I couldn't figure how. Then she added, "It's our home now too." Her weak tone failed to convince me.

To me, "home" was a place that would always be there to return to, where the people who loved you stayed. Since I expected Ron's to be as temporary as any other place we'd lived so far, I didn't plan to call his house "home" any more than I'd consider calling any other place I'd slept the same. *My* "home" was wherever Great-Gram was. I didn't get attached to places.

It was Mom who had talked about her wish to have a house, to be able to afford nice things to put in it, and to escape the city she grew up in. I guess that's why this life with Ron enticed her. His suburban duplex was bigger and fancier than any other place we'd ever lived. There was grass in front of everyone's houses, and there were no buses to catch or car horns to disturb the quiet. Mom even had a car now! So, she should have been happy. She didn't seem to be, though.

Someone who drove a pale-yellow Chevy Malibu and chose wallpaper with big yellow flowers for the kitchen shouldn't carry so much melancholy in her eyes. Yet, her movements were careful, like she was worried about meeting some standard of expectation. She dressed differently and put more effort into smoothing out her frizzy curls. She used words she hadn't used before too—*big* words meant to impress but which seemed awkward coming from an uneducated girl in her early twenties. It's like she was trying to be someone she wasn't.

Like on a midsummer morning in 1981, I came to the kitchen to find Mom scurrying around with an oven mitt on one hand. She frantically searched through spices in the pantry, opened the oven and then closed it, had a mess of things on the counter . . . She was baking! I'd never even seen her do much more than boil a pot of water on the stove or heat something from a can. Great-Gram was the one who cooked in our family, which was half the reason everyone flocked there in their free time.

"What are you doing?" I asked.

"Baking an apple pie for the block party later. So, whatever you need, get it quick and stay out of my way," she said with the same haste she expected me to have right now.

"Block party?"

"Yeah, all the neighbors here get together for a big cookout every year, and everyone brings a dish to share. So, Ron said we would bring a couple apple pies."

"How come Ron isn't making them, then?" I asked, knowing Mom had never made one.

"Because he asked *me* to do it," she snipped. "Anyway, he's introducing us to all his neighbors, so I want to make a good impression by making these pies right."

Thoughts of McDonald's handheld pastries made my mouth water. I couldn't imagine Mom, who'd only cooked noodles before this, had the ability to make that yummy treat. I hoped she could, though! Even I'd be impressed!

"Seriously, Dane. I need you to get what you need and get out of the kitchen. Okay?"

Gathering that she was nervous she'd screw up her first attempt at baking a pie (which she probably would from the looks of things), I took a can of soda from the refrigerator and went back up to my room to play.

They'd assigned me the "guest room," which I thought was appropriate for the temporary living arrangement I assumed this situation with Ron to be. I figured he'd ask us to leave when he was done with my mom, like my real dad had if I had ever had one and then Leo after.

It was a fine room for now. The sun brightened the plain white walls as it shined in from the long window that spread across the top of the back wall. It had soft carpet that felt good on my bare feet, and a foot of parquet tile in front of the long closet beside the door. What I liked most about this room was that it was clean. I could sleep without the clicking sounds of roaches waking me, and shower without shaking them out of my hair beforehand. I could play on the floor with my toys without the bother of creepy crawlies on my legs. I could even watch TV in the den across the hall without getting in trouble for bothering anyone. So, I was never bored.

A couple hours later, Mom came upstairs to retrieve me. "Let me look at you real quick," she said.

Her eyes reviewed my appearance for acceptability. I wore white shorts and a pastel-striped T-shirt that was just a little too small for me. My hair was up in the same pigtails she'd put them in yesterday, but she was more concerned with straightening my clothes than fixing my scraggly hair. I'd noticed how she ironed all our clothes promptly after removing them from the dryer since we'd moved in here. I didn't understand why it was so important when it hadn't been before, just like I didn't understand why Mom cared so much about what the people at this block party thought of us. I could understand wanting to make a good impression, but she'd never fussed this much when we went to be with our family. Why couldn't we just be ourselves?

"Okay," she said, primping my shirt at the shoulders. "When we meet these people, remember not to tell anyone we're Puerto Rican. Okay?"

I nodded, though I didn't understand why our ethnicity mattered. Everywhere we'd gone in the city, we were met with people of all colors and races. Many spoke languages other than English, including our family. Why did we have to hide who we were from *these* people?

"And Ron's neighbors know you're not his daughter, but you don't need to talk about that either."

I wasn't sure who she thought I would have a discussion with about who my parents were, but the instruction made me feel like something was wrong with me because I wasn't Ron's. I nodded anyway, to put Mom at ease. I didn't like seeing her so tense, nor the way I was feeling as a result of it.

"Okay, let's go, then," she said.

With all these things to remember, I was nervous I'd forget something. It sounded like these people wouldn't like us if they discovered our deficiencies, which made me wonder why we wanted to impress, never mind associate, with them at all.

Regardless, I glued myself to Mom's side for safety and security as she carried the two apple pies she'd made out to where Ron was waiting for us. He was drinking a beer and talking with another man at the end of the walkway to his front door.

"There she is!" he said jovially, extending his arm towards Mom.

She smiled and offered a simple greeting to the strange man, whom Ron introduced her to. It had never occurred to me until then that Mom didn't go by the Hispanic name Grandma had given her at birth; Mom went by an American name she'd assigned herself instead.

While the adults chatted, I surveyed the scene. Well-dressed women carrying casserole dishes with colorful mitts exchanged polite greetings while men admired each other's gleaming cars. The houses themselves were all brick two-stories with flat roofs and a white front door for each of the two residences contained within one. About ten of these carbon copies lined each side of the dead-end street that turned off a frontage road to a major expressway from which I could hear the swoosh of cars flying by. The only variation was in the color of the brick structures, which alternated between beige, red, and an ugly dark brown. Ron's was red, which was still my favorite color.

"Where should I put these?" Mom asked Ron, referring to the pies.

Ron excused us from his neighbor then led Mom to the row of long folding tables someone across the street had set up for food.

I followed right behind, careful not to make eye contact with any of the adults staring as we passed. I felt scorn and judgment exuding from the narrowed eyes of a group of three women huddled in a private conversation. The eldest of them, who had thick black hair styled in a half updo, made eye contact with me. Her blue eyes were stunning, but the way they looked Mom up and down didn't disguise the repulsion she attempted to hide with her fake smile. She turned back to the other two women and said, "That must be the whore he replaced Darryl with." I didn't know who "Darryl" was, but by the way they were glaring at Mom with disgust, it sounded like Mom had done something terrible to her.

I looked up at Mom for her reaction. She was smiling and nodding her head politely to all the people Ron said hello to as we passed, so I guessed she hadn't heard the comment. It was probably for the best. It didn't make me feel any better about these strangers, however.

As Ron made the rounds, introducing Mom to everyone like a show pony he'd just attained, including the woman I'd heard call her a "whore," I clutched Mom's leg for protection.

"This is Dana," Mom would nervously chuckle as she'd attempt to push me into greeting every adult who bent down to my level to ask, "And who is this?"

I'd lower my head shyly but glance up every time, to gauge whether that person was genuinely curious or just plain old nosy.

One older man (who was so tanned his skin was orange) made a funny sound with his mouth to make me giggle. He sounded like Daffy Duck, so I decided I liked him.

Another woman, however, took her cigarette out of her mouth, jutted her hip as she blew a cloud of smoke through her heavily glossed lips, and commented, "You look mighty young to have a child that age." Mom smiled instead of defending herself to the snark. It wasn't a real smile, though; it was fake, like everyone else's.

I was confused by the polite pretense, wondering why all these adults thought it a good idea to gather when some clearly didn't like others. So, I didn't think it necessary to try to remember anyone's names or answer their questions. They seemed to already know more about us than we knew about them, anyway.

"Why don't you go play with the other kids?" Ron suggested, like a father would. Fathers didn't intentionally crush their daughters' fingers in the car window, so I shook my head. I was just fine holding Mom's pant leg.

"Yeah, Dane," Mom threw in then. I looked up at her and shook my head again.

Of course, I wanted to go play with the kids. Listening to all this superficial and boring adult talk was no fun. I was terrified at the thought of having to introduce myself to them, though, as well as remembering not to let on that I was Puerto Rican. I didn't know how to explain where I'd come from either. Kids knew babies came from a mom and a dad, and we all knew Ron wasn't my father.

I looked around to assess the situation anyway, just in case Mom forced me to be social. There were two older boys tossing a football back and forth down the street. There were a few other boys that looked more my age, chasing each other in what appeared to be a game of tag.

Three little girls kneeling on someone's lawn caught my eye, though. One was much taller than the other two. The smallest looked Chinese, which surprised me since everyone there was white. I wondered if she lived on the street or was just visiting for the day. Either way, she seemed perfectly comfortable. So how come I didn't? Why did Mom want me to pretend to be just like these people, so we *could* fit in? Why did living with Ron come with so many rules and regulations? And why did Mom *want* to live like this?

Nothing made sense to me. So, as soon as Mom permitted me to, I went back to the house and up to my new room. I felt more comfortable being alone than being the odd man out. There was more kindness in the eyes of my plastic dolls than I'd seen in any human person I'd been forced to meet that day, anyway. I just hoped Mom didn't get so caught up in trying to fit in with those mean people that she became one of them. Because I would never conform. I didn't see a need to when our family thought we were just fine as we were.

"Why Can't We Be Friends?"

Despite the dismal start to life with Ron, that summer turned out surprisingly fun.

Ron had friends who'd take us out on Lake Michigan on their boat, so far out that there was nothing but sky and water in every direction. I wished Mom had come with us, to see the endless horizon or at least try the egg salad sandwiches Ron's friends served for lunch. She never did, though. She was always too busy.

But she did go apple-picking with us in Wisconsin. I'd never seen an apple tree before, so I eagerly climbed the short ladder into every tree and filled our bushel baskets to the brim. We brought home so many apples that Mom's pies were getting better with practice, since she didn't know what else to do with the bounty.

With all the cooking and baking Mom was suddenly doing, we always had ice cream and Cool Whip on hand. So, on rainy days, I'd camp out on the love seat in the upstairs den and eat one or the other frozen treat right out of the container while I caught up on my cartoons. Then I'd play my Muppet's Disco album on the record player and dance in the living room, or for Mom if she was around. She called it "The Dana Show." On sunny days, I'd practice cartwheels and handstands on the patch of grass out front or roller skate on the street in front of the house. Every once in a while, I'd look down the street at the kids playing outside, longing for their company but too shy to approach them. They eventually wandered over to meet me, though I think they were more curious about the new dog they saw me playing with. Ron got the drooly pet, claiming he loved bulldogs. Mom didn't love it as much. She wasn't much of an animal person. I think it was because she was obsessed with cleanliness, and animals didn't fit into that equation. So the bulldog, which Ron named "Bogie" after some old-time movie actor, stayed in the dark and dreary unfinished basement. I felt bad for the dog, so I took him outside every chance I got.

Bogie served as a conduit for connection, though. To pet Ron's dog, the neighborhood kids had to interact with me. Once they realized I was just like them—a kid who wanted to play tag and throw a ball around, instead of whatever rumors they'd overheard from their parents—we became friends. But when school started in the fall, we went our separate ways.

The neighborhood kids were all Jewish, including the Chinese girl who'd been adopted by the family down the street. They all attended the public grade school in the next town over. I went to the private Catholic school at the church in our town. I liked it there because the nuns and priests treated us all the same. We were all expected to wear the same black plaid uniform, follow the same rules, adhere to the same principles of servitude that Jesus taught the disciples—no one was better than or any different than anyone else. Only God could place such judgment. Ron, however, tested my ability to forgive those who had lost their way.

Mom left for work so early that Ron was left with the task of getting me ready for school and driving me there. In her absence, Ron began to treat me as cruelly as Leo had.

"Stay still!" he'd snap at me when I flinched at the sharp bristles of the hairbrush repeatedly scraping my soft scalp. I swore he was brushing my hair that hard on purpose.

He'd grab handfuls of my hair just as roughly, tying them into unreasonably tight pigtails. I'd yelp and cringe, which Ron would punish me for by whacking my head with the brush. I didn't understand why he thought hurting me more would make me stop fussing and crying. I learned quickly, though, that expressing emotions elicited punishment. So, I'd grit my teeth and bear it, just like I had to when the kids at school made fun of me for looking Chinese as a result of how tautly my hair had been fastened.

On the short drive to school, Ron often grumbled about having to bother with me at all. "I shouldn't have to waste my time doing this. You're not *my* kid," he'd once said. Crystal Gayle crooning "Don't It Make My

Brown Eyes Blue" over the car speakers seemed to echo the same despair dwelling in my heart. So much so that I hummed the tune and sang the chorus often, since Ron didn't suspect the expression of my feelings. He didn't care about my feelings, anyway. When I got out of his car at school, he tended to race away in haste, to shame me for being such a bother.

What really bothered Ron, however, was the cost of my school tuition. I'd heard him argue with Mom about it through the thin walls between our bedrooms.

"There's nothing so special about her that she can't go to public school like all the other kids on the street!" he said in a raised voice. I wasn't sure what had prompted the argument. Ron seemed to yell whenever a bill came in the mail, though. He didn't like parting with his money unless it was to buy car parts or whatever else pertained to his comfort or coolness.

"We're Catholic and—" Mom started to respond.

Ron cut her off. "I don't care what you are! I am not paying for her to go to a private school when my tax dollars pay for a school she can go to for free!"

Although I had just turned six years old, I was old enough to see Mom go to work every day to make money, and I was old enough to know that money paid the bills. So, I couldn't understand why Ron was acting like *he* was paying for my tuition or why he thought he had the right to tell Mom how to spend the money *she* made. It was Mom's decision where I should go to school, anyway. Not his.

So, I couldn't believe when Mom succumbed so easily, saying, "I guess you're right, Ron."

I panicked, wondering if Mom's relent meant I really couldn't go to the Catholic school anymore. I'd just started there this year and had made a best friend in a blonde girl named Andrea whose house I played at all the time. I didn't want to have to start over at another new school and try to make a new best friend.

But I didn't say anything, and when second grade began in the fall of 1982, Mom dropped me off at the public school Ron wanted me to go to.

I looked out the car window at the swarms of kids flooding into the metal double doors. They all wore regular clothes. Big kids trampled over small kids. There was no order or system here like there was at the Catholic school, where everyone had to wear a uniform and quietly wait in a certain line to enter.

I turned to Mom, trying not to let the tears welled in my eyes drip down my cheeks. "Mom?"

"I don't have time for this, Dane," she said with cold indifference.

Looking out the window again, trying to convince myself I'd be okay if I got out of the car, my body refused to move.

"Dane!" Mom snapped.

Upturned brows and a frown pleaded for some patience, as I hoped she'd suddenly feel inclined to park and walk me in. Even some words of encouragement or support, like an *I love you* or *It'll be okay* would have sufficed.

Instead, she scolded, "Please! I have to get to work!"

With my hand on the metal door handle, I paused, giving her one last opportunity to be a mother. Her pursed lips offered no sympathy. So, I reluctantly got out of her car, and she pulled away as soon as I shut the heavy door behind me.

Standing on the curb in my Catholic school uniform, I clutched my tote bag close as I stared at the orange-brick single-story. There was nothing inside the bag to protect, but it was the only security I had.

I wanted to cry and run away. I wanted Great-Gram. But I had no one but myself to get me through this. So, with my tears running down my cheeks, I put one little foot in front of the other, avoiding elbows, hands, and waving arms that didn't see me as I walked through them and into this strange new place.

Just inside, I met a crossroads. One hallway went straight, and another went to the left. Unsure of where I was even supposed to go, I stood still, getting pushed and shoved by older kids making their way to their known classrooms. My bottom lip trembled, and my breath quickened.

An older woman with short auburn hair made her way towards me. She bent down to my level and asked, "Are you lost, honey?"

I nodded my head anxiously.

"It's all right, sweetie," she said with a kind smile, rubbing my upper arm to soothe. "What grade are you in?"

I sniffled and wiped my face before telling her, "Second."

A bell rang then. Movement around us picked up. Older kids were saying goodbye to friends and running towards closing doors. Then the whole place quieted around us. I panicked then, knowing the ringing bell meant I'd be late, and lateness hadn't been tolerated at the Catholic school.

The woman offered me her hand and said, "Come with me, sweetie. I'll get you to the right place."

Her calmness was unusual, given the circumstances. Having no choice but to trust her, though, I let her lead me away.

We walked down the hallway to the left. Then we came upon another hallway and turned right. I quickly realized the place was shaped like a square.

An older lady who looked like a sweet grandma stood outside an open classroom door with a clipboard. She looked at us expectantly.

"I think this one belongs with you," the woman who'd led me there said to the grandma with the clipboard. "I found her in the junior high hallway."

"Oh no!" the grandma said to me. "That must've been very scary for you!"

New tears welled in my eyes as I nodded.

"You must be Dana?" she asked, referring to her clipboard. I nodded. "Welcome to second grade, Dana! I'm your teacher, Mrs. Alessi." She reached out to take my hand. "I'll take her from here," she said to the kind woman who'd brought me.

"Have a good first day of school!" the kind woman said as she released my hand and walked away.

Mrs. Alessi smiled a little bigger, making her eyes twinkle like Great-Gram's. So, I let her lead me into the classroom.

Stopping at the front of the class, Mrs. Alessi raised her voice above the chatter. "Can I have everyone's attention, please?" All the kids stopped talking and turned to look at me and Mrs. Alessi. "We have a new student this year. This is Dana Diaz. Can everyone say, 'Hi, Dana'?"

"Hi, Dana," everyone chimed in various tones and intervals.

Mrs. Alessi released my hand and stepped away then, putting me center stage. "Do you want to tell us about yourself, Dana?"

I shook my slightly bowed head. I didn't like being the focus of attention.

A few of the kids giggled, causing me to instinctively glance their way. The sea of strange faces made me even more self-conscious, so I immediately cast my eyes downward again.

"How about you tell us where you went to school before and what brought you here?" she prompted.

"Um . . . I went to 'Lad and Lassie' for preschool and kindergarten, then St. Peter's for first grade," I said in a voice barely above a whisper.

"Did you just move here?" Mrs. Alessi said, prodding me for more information.

"Kind of," I said, still not speaking loudly.

"Where did you move from?"

I looked up at the kids for a second then focused my attention back down to avoid eye contact. "I lived with Great-Gram first. In her apartment in Chicago," I muttered. "But then I went to be with my mom, who lived in different apartments until the last one with Leo."

A snort-laugh from one boy led to multiple outbursts of the same. I didn't understand what was so funny about anything I'd said, but I felt the judgment anyway.

"Well, we're glad you're with us, Dana. Why don't you choose a place to sit, and we'll begin."

Forced to look up, I didn't see any place for me. I just saw eyes, and they were all on me. I remained completely still, despite the panic I felt, scanning the room for some place to hide from the unwanted attention. To the right, along the wall where all the windows were open, I was relieved to see an open chair. A blonde girl sitting next to it motioned for me to come over. She looked like an angel with her blue eyes and wide smile, so I thought it would be okay. It was my only option, anyway.

As I made my way over, squeezing my way between the short bookcases under the windows and the backs of occupied chairs, the girls I passed took turns judging me with up-and-down looks. I made the mistake of making eye contact with one—a dark-haired girl with a darker complexion—whose return stare warned me to never approach her. Unfortunately, that empty chair was right next to her.

"I'm Kelly," the blonde girl whispered.

Thankful for the angel's much warmer welcome, I responded, "I'm Dana."

"I know," she said with a smirk. "How come you're wearing a uniform?"

"I thought I was supposed to. This is what we wore every day at my old school," I responded.

"Well, we wear regular clothes here," Kelly said in a matter-of-fact tone that didn't offend.

Class began then, making me think the kids had been laughing at what I was wearing instead of what I'd said. I wondered, too, why Mom had allowed me to dress in my Catholic school uniform when she was so concerned about us fitting in with everyone else. Had she wanted me to be the laughingstock of the school on my first day?

Either way, I was glad Kelly corrected my error. She even played with me at recess.

As we were lining up for lunch later that week, I realized that the girl who sat on the other side of me in class hadn't yet spoken to me. I'd heard her called Gail. Her darker skin and features were hard to miss. Kelly told me Gail was Mexican and had been adopted by her Jewish parents, just like the Chinese girl on our street. So, I thought that maybe Gail and I could be friends, since we were the only Hispanic kids in our class.

"Will you play with me at recess today?" I asked from behind her in line.

Gail eyed me over her shoulder before responding, "My mom told me I can't play with you." Her exaggerated snootiness made me rethink my desire to be friends with her. However, I wanted to know the reason why her mother, who didn't even know me, would tell her she couldn't play with me.

So, I asked, "Why not?"

Huffing as if I should already know my disqualifying attribute, Gail looked over her shoulder again and declared, "She said I'm not allowed to play with 'the bastard child' at school."

"Bastard child?" I repeated, confused by what she meant.

Gail turned back to me. "Yeah, bastard child," she said as her eyes scanned me up and down, ensuring I knew the reference was to me. "What's with the silver teeth too?" she asked with a snarky gloat that attracted the attention of the two girls standing in line in front of her. They all smirked before returning their focus to Mrs. Alessi, who hadn't allowed our line to move out to the hallway yet.

With my head down, I turned to Kelly, who stood behind me. She took my hand. I sensed the comfort she offered, though I didn't know why

I needed it.

"Why is she calling me a bastard child?" I whispered to Kelly when the line began to move forward. "What does that mean?"

Kelly pressed her lips together then cringed. I could tell she knew something. Then she whispered in my ear, "It means someone whose mom isn't married."

"Oh," I muttered, dropping my head shamefully.

I didn't understand why anything Mom did or didn't do reflected on me. It wasn't my fault she wasn't married, nor could I defend myself against the fact that she wasn't. I could only attest to the fact that she'd had boyfriends—married ones, granted, just not married to *her*.

"American Girl"

~~~~~~⌒~~~~~~

I was dribbling a bouncy ball by myself at recess one afternoon when a boy in my class walked up and asked, "Why do you pronounce your Rs like a drum roll?"

I shrugged, and he walked away. When I got home from school, however, I ran straight up to my bedroom, looked directly into the long mirror on the wall, and said as many words as I could think of that had the letter "R" in them.

"Recess. Rice. Read." I did trill the sound, but not as much on the last word as the first two. I opened my mouth as wide as I could and squinted to see inside. I'm not sure what I was looking for. It just seemed like the obvious thing to do since sounds came out of my mouth. Apparently, answers to life's questions did not.

So, I practiced saying different words in the mirror, forcing myself not to trill. The more I did it, the easier it was to sound like all the other kids.

When Mom and I visited Great-Gram that Sunday, my surrogate mother sounded like she was rolling down the river with Tina Turner when she asked, "*Quieres cafe? O arroz? Tenemos cerda, tambien.*"

I grimaced as I nodded. No matter how "white" I tried to sound, my love of rice would always give away my Hispanic roots.

Settling into one of the two metal seats at the tiny table between the pantry and the door to the back porch, I watched Great-Gram pour what she called a "little bit" of vegetable oil into the humongous stainless-steel rice pot. It was one of the few possessions she'd been able to bring from her old apartment when she'd recently moved in with my grandma and Uncle Juni.

"How's school going, Dana?" Uncle Juni asked as he entered the cramped kitchen. There was barely enough room for him to pass between the little table and Great-Gram's muumuu-covered bulk to get to the kitchen sink.

"Eh," I said, shrugging, as Great-Gram asked him, "*Quieres mas café?*"

"*Si!*" he responded as he washed his cup. "You don't like the new school or something?" he asked over his shoulder.

"I don't know," I said glumly. I heard Mom and grandma laughing about something in the adjacent dining room and looked over. "Mom's happy, I guess, so it doesn't matter if I am."

Great-Gram turned and eyed me.

"It'll get better, Dana," Juni comforted, patting me on the shoulder as he walked back to the dining room.

"*Que paso?*" Great-Gram asked once we were alone.

I shook my head. Then I looked towards the dining room to make sure Mom couldn't hear us.

"*Dime,*" Great-Gram said, prodding me to share.

I looked at her and sighed. "I'm just not like the other kids out there. They're always making fun of me. *If* they even talk to me," I muttered, looking down at my worn tennis shoes.

"*Por qué no?*"

Glancing towards the dining room to confirm Mom was unaware of our conversation, I whispered, "They say they're not allowed to play with me because I'm a bastard child."

Great-Gram pressed her lips together as she poured coffee into cups. Then she shook her head and said, "*No es verdad.* You have a father."

"I do?" I'd always wondered, but no one had ever let on anything about him!

"*Si, pero . . .*" Great-Gram put one finger to her pursed lips. "*No dice nada a tú madre.* Okay?"

"Okay," I agreed, nodding to confirm I understood that Mom was not to know about this conversation. But why was this a secret? I mean, I obviously hadn't been brought here like Mork from Ork on the TV show *Mork & Mindy*, so Mom had to have known who she'd made me with.

"*Ven conmigo,*" Great-Gram directed, carrying two coffee cups to the dining room table. I followed her with the other two. Then we sat and visited with Mom, Grandma, and Juni until the rice was ready to eat, forcing me to put aside my curiosity in lieu of keeping peace.

When we visited my grandmas and Juni the next Sunday, my grandma presented me with the most beautiful floral dress with short ruffled sleeves. Various shades of lavender in multiple opaque layers flared out when I spun around. That was my test for any dress I wore. The higher it flared out, the more I liked it.

"Isn't she pretty? Isn't she a lovely girl?" Uncle Juni sang his own version of the popular Stevie Wonder song as I modeled it for him and my grandmas.

"*Ay, qué linda!*" my grandma complimented as Great-Gram smiled with her twinkling eyes.

Mom half rolled her eyes, but I ignored her dismissive gesture. I looked down at the dress again, disbelieving I was wearing such a pretty thing. I rarely got new clothes, never mind a beautiful dress like this. I felt like a princess!

"Your mother said you have school pictures coming up, so I wanted you to have it for that day," my grandma said, speaking slowly to enunciate each syllable correctly. She spoke Spanish so much faster than she spoke English, but she needed to speak English for her job at the hospital.

"Thank you, Grandma," I said, looking up at her with a wide smile I couldn't contain.

"You're very welcome," she responded, rolling all her Rs. She pronounced her Vs like Bs too, making "very" come out as "berry." It always made me giggle.

"All right, Dane. Go change out of that before you get it dirty or wrinkled," Mom told me.

I scrunched my face at her then went back to Great-Gram's bedroom to do as she said.

School picture day arrived soon after. I was so excited to finally be able to wear my pretty dress. Mom even stayed home a little longer that morning, to comb all the tangles out of my long, wavy hair. Once it was smoothed, she clipped a barrette into it to hold one side partially back.

Eager to show my classmates my new dress, I went to school to find that no one else was wearing anything special. *Had Mom and I mistaken the day?* I wondered. Not that it mattered. Some of the kids were already pointing and laughing. The damage was already done.

Standing out more than I usually did, everyone's attention was on me. The anxiety made my stomach hurt so bad I couldn't concentrate in class. I thought of telling Mrs. Alessi that I didn't feel good so I could go to the school nurse and hopefully be sent home, but then I'd miss pictures altogether. So, I breathed through the pain in my tummy and kept my head down to avoid the stares.

Midmorning, while working on a lesson, Gail turned to me and snarled, "Why are *you* so dressed up today?"

I looked at her but didn't respond, because it was taking all my strength to will myself not to cry.

As if sensing I needed saving, I heard Kelly say, "I like your dress, Dana."

I turned to my friend, appreciating her kind defense. "Thank you," I muttered back. Unfortunately, it didn't change how uncomfortable I felt, mentally and physically, but it did shut Gail up, at least for the moment.

When we were lined up to have our pictures taken later that afternoon, Gail continued to harass me. "Where'd you get that dress, anyway? From the garbage?" A couple other kids turned and laughed at her comment.

"No," I asserted. "My grandma bought it for me. At Zayre."

"Why?" Gail said, crossing her arms over her chest. "She can't afford to buy you clothes at a *normal* store?" Some other girls in front of her laughed harder then.

Thinking about my school bag, which Grandma had also purchased at Zayre, I lowered my head shamefully. I knew Zayre was no comparison to Marshall Field's, or even Montgomery Ward. I didn't understand why the brand or cost of anything mattered, though. I thought my dress was pretty, and so did Kelly.

So, despite the tears caused by the insult, I wiped my eyes right before my picture was taken and smiled. It was hard to feel comfortable the rest of the school day, though, when I was desperate to go home and tear the dress off. I swore I'd never wear it again. I'd probably never wear anything my grandma sent for me from Chicago, including the T-shirt with the Puerto Rican boy band Menudo on it, even if Ricky Martin—the youngest member of the group—was cute.

"My Sweet Lord"

"Of course it's the Puerto Rican kid who has lice," the school nurse snidely remarked to her assistant while she weaved through my tangles with popsicle sticks and gloved hands. I felt the sting of judgment once again but remained unmoved as if I hadn't. It was disrespectful to speak up against an adult, even in my own defense.

When she'd finished, I was ordered to return to my classroom to collect my jacket and backpack then wait outside the principal's office for Mom to come pick me up. I hung my head shamefully while all of my classmates watched quietly, like I'd been stricken with the plague and exiled.

"We hope to see you back soon!" Mrs. Alessi said to lighten the somber mood as I left. I appreciated her effort but couldn't say I shared the sentiment.

"I can't believe this," Mom scolded the second I got in her car. "You know I had to leave work because of this?"

"I'm sorry, Mom," I mumbled as I slumped into the passenger seat. I'd been glad to see her car instead of Ron's, until she accelerated off the curb just like he would have. I already felt badly, so Mom's blame for something I had no control over just made me feel worse.

"How did you get lice, anyway?" Mom asked as she drove.

"I don't know," I mumbled and shrugged. I wasn't even sure what lice was, except that Mrs. Alessi said they were looking for bugs or eggs in our heads. "The nurse said it was because I'm Puerto Rican," I offered, hoping to deflect the fault.

Mom whipped her head towards me. "She said that?"

I nodded.

38

"Well, how would she even know we're Puerto Rican?" she scolded.

"I don't know! I think it was some of the kids on our block or one of their moms because the kids in my class call me a 'bastard child' and say I'm illeg . . ." I said, struggling to pronounce that big word.

"Illegitimate?" Mom finished it for me.

"Yeah! That!"

Mom huffed again. Then she glared at me as if I'd betrayed her.

After a silent car ride home, Mom still didn't talk to me as she scrubbed my hair with shampoo that had a skull and crossbones on the bottle. Then she appeared disgruntled while she packed my stuffed animals into large black garbage bags. I wasn't too disappointed that she did the same with the frilly yellow comforter and matching top she'd bought for my new canopy bed. I didn't even like yellow. But I also didn't like being left alone in my room with nothing but the lice in my head.

The only upside to my week of quarantine was that I didn't have to deal with Ron. My door was only opened when Mom brought me food or when I had to pee. Otherwise, I sang to myself and drew pictures of sunshine and rainbows until I was allowed to go back to school.

"Oh, look! Lice lady is back!" I heard someone say as I hung my backpack in my locker. I turned to see Gail, flanked by her two cohorts, Anna and Dawn. They stood together with smirks on their faces, waiting for me to react. I narrowed my eyes at them, though the threat I intended to convey amused them, considering how much smaller I was compared to the taller and huskier three.

"Welcome back, Dana!" Mrs. Alessi said as she walked over. The trio of terror went to their seats then. I was thankful for the save. "I hope you don't mind that we moved your locker partner to another locker. We didn't want her to catch lice from anything that you might have had in there. So, you'll have your own locker from now on!" She made this newest instance of exclusion sound so pleasant, but I felt every bit of the shame and rejection I felt in everything these days.

"Okay," I said glumly. Then I walked with my head down to my assigned seat next to Kelly. She looked at me with a sympathetic closed-mouth smile. It seemed like she was the only person who saw me as a human being instead of some alien who didn't belong.

The next day, at the start of class, Kelly passed a folded-up piece of notebook paper to me under the table. I kept my head up, turning only my eyes downward, as I opened the folds. I didn't want to get in trouble for not paying attention.

As I began to open the folds of what I thought was a note, I felt something inside the paper. I pressed the lumpy paper, trying to determine what it could be by the shape and feel. Having no clue, I opened the paper and looked down to see what Kelly had hidden in it for me.

My eyes widened when I saw a gold chain with a pendant of the Virgin Mary. I poured the necklace into my other palm then looked up at Mrs. Alessi to make sure she hadn't noticed. She had her back to the class, writing something on the chalkboard.

I took the opportunity to whisper to Kelly, "I can't take this. It looks really expensive!"

"Yes, you can," Kelly whispered back. "Anyway, you need it more than I do."

Kelly was right. I needed my faith. I'd always found soothing in praying to the Holy Mother when I'd had to go to daily mass at the Catholic school I'd attended before. Mom and I still attended mass there sometimes. We skipped a lot because Ron didn't want to go. He claimed to be Jewish.

So, I muttered a quick "thank you" and smiled at Kelly for giving me a symbol of the Holy Mother to turn to whenever I needed some compassion. Lord knows I couldn't turn to my real mother for the same solace. At least now I knew I'd never be alone.

"Voices Carry"

After the lice situation had died down, Mrs. Alessi picked me to be the "Star of the Week," which meant everyone had to write something nice about me and pin their compliments on the bulletin board at the back of the classroom.

I was excited that the kids would be forced to see something good in me, and equally anxious to know what, if anything, it would be. So, I checked the board multiple times a day to see what the kids really thought.

Most of them wrote, "You are pretty," and "You are a hard worker." Gail had written, "I like your pancakes." The reference to the recipe I'd contributed to the class cookbook Mrs. Alessi had put together—wherein we each provided the recipe for our favorite food—made me smile. Although it wasn't something pertaining to me specifically, it was close enough to count, and enough to make me feel like less of an outcast.

So, as worried as I was that the Oscar the Grouch costume Mom had bought for me to wear for Halloween would make me a laughingstock again, the other kids were too hyped up on holiday spirits and sugar to worry about me. We paraded through the hallways at school that Friday afternoon, finding more joy together in disguise than we did any other day when we were just ourselves.

The same rang true with the neighborhood kids, whom I ran from door to door with on Saturday, which was actually Halloween.

"Trick or treat!" we shouted in unison at every neighbor's door. Then we'd smile as widely as our eyes opened at the joy of seeing our bags filling with various candies and coins. One lady gave us all a new toothbrush and full-sized toothpaste, which a few of the kids groaned at. But I couldn't wait to show Mom. I went through a lot of toothpaste, diligently polishing whatever teeth hadn't fallen out yet. Mom said the adult teeth coming in were the only teeth I'd have for the rest of my life, so I needed to take good care of them to make sure they didn't fall out too.

With only two houses to go, we all raced to the next, eager to be the first to ring the doorbell. My little legs lagged behind those of the bigger kids. By the time I got there, the door was already open, and I saw the lady with the big black hair and striking blue eyes who'd called Mom a "whore" at the block party.

She smiled and said, "Happy Halloween," as she filled all the kids' bags. When I stepped up and held my plastic bag open, however, her face morphed into a scowl. My smile dissipated too at the blatant reproach.

"I don't have anything for *you*," she ridiculed.

I stood there, staring at her with upturned brows. I didn't know why this woman didn't like me. I didn't know why I was so scared of her either. All I knew was that saying "trick or treat" was supposed to result in people putting something in my bag. Not knowing what to say or do at her refusal, I just gulped.

"Your teeth are already rotted," she said with the same disgust expressed by her scrunched nose. Then she closed the door firmly in my face.

Unsure of whether she made that assumption based on the silver teeth in my mouth or the gap of missing front teeth where they'd fallen out, I nonetheless felt the shame she'd intended. So, I went home instead of joining the other kids at the last house. Half of them were already running home with their loot, anyway, for their parents to inspect the candy before they ate it.

Mom and Ron were in the kitchen when I walked in. Mom was making something to eat while Ron sat at the table expectantly. I slumped in the chair across from him.

"Hey, Dane! How was trick-or-treating?" Mom asked. Her calm demeanor and interest in my life were unusual but welcome. I saw it as an opportunity to get the comfort I needed for the way that mean lady had excluded me from having candy.

I sniffled. "Good, but . . ."

"But what?" Mom said, looking concerned. She glanced at Ron as she dried her hands with a towel and walked over to me.

"Well, that lady with the big black hair a couple doors down—the one whose son lives with her, who has lots of big muscles and that sports car he's always outside washing?" I started.

"Yeah," Mom said, at the same time Ron asked, "What about them?"

I looked back and forth between Mom and Ron and whined, "She wouldn't give me any candy."

Ron rolled his eyes and sighed. Mom gave him a wide-eyed scold then suggested, "Maybe she ran out."

"No. She told me she wouldn't give me any. Because my teeth are rotted," I said. Then I pressed my lips together tightly, so even Mom couldn't see the atrocity my mouth was.

"She wouldn't say that," Ron dismissed with arrogant assurance.

"I'm sure she had a reason," Mom said, shrugging and shaking her head as if I'd misinterpreted the situation.

But I hadn't. Mom had done something I was paying the price for, and it wasn't fair. I couldn't say that to Mom, though, because the nun who taught Catholic catechism classes said that we were supposed to honor thy mother and thy father.

So, I muttered, "Yeah, maybe," to avoid a sin and went up to my room. I dumped the bag of goodies I *had* been given out onto the floor and immediately gorged on the chocolates. They did their job of soothing the sting to my self-esteem while I separated the rest of my booty into "keep" and "give away" piles. I'd "keep" all the chocolates and coins, and "give away" the licorice, "Dots," and candy corn.

When I came out of my bedroom later, I overheard Mom talking to Ron downstairs.

"Hopefully, once we're married, people will stop talking about how I broke up your marriage and had Dana too young," Mom said in a regretful tone.

The sound of my name piqued my curiosity, but the talk of marriage made me crouch at the top of the stairs to hear more. I mean, I'd always assumed Ron would eventually disappear like Leo had. Then we'd return to Chicago, to our family, and resume our lives until the next man interrupted us with his wooing. So, I didn't like this talk of marriage.

"Things will get better," Ron soothed. I hadn't thought him capable of empathy, so I was surprised at his softness towards Mom. Then he said, "It's just a shame we have to deal with the *burden* of what he did to you at all."

Who was "he" and what had "he" done? And what was a burden? Had something happened to Mom that I didn't know about?

"Well, there's no way to change the past," Mom said. "We just have to—"

"I know," Ron cut her off. "But it hurts me to see all the problems having her has caused you."

"She's my daughter, Ron," Mom lamented.

Wait a second! Was *I* the burden he'd been referring to? Was *I* the cause of whatever problems they were talking about?

"Yeah, but it's not right that you have to deal with something you didn't ask for, and that I have to pay the price for it now too."

"Ron!" Mom weakly scolded.

Assuming they were talking about me, I'd have expected a better defense from Mom. I mean, aside from eating directly out of the Cool Whip tub while watching Saturday morning cartoons, I did as I was told—usually.

"What do you want me to say, Ivy? I want to be with you. I want to marry you. I just never asked to be a father to a kid that's not even mine," Ron said snidely.

"I have no *choice* but to take care of her," Mom responded. It was hard to unhear how she didn't seem to want to.

"But it shouldn't be my responsibility to deal with her too," Ron continued. "I'm not the one who got you pregnant and then left you to raise the child yourself!"

The chorus of the Human League's "Don't You Want Me" played in my head to replace the hurt of knowing my real dad hadn't wanted me either. Applying songs to unpleasant people and situations was a little game I'd begun playing with myself, to take the edge off the intense emotions associated with them.

Ron's words replayed through my mind on an endless loop for days after instead, though, trying to make sense of the random bits of information. All I kept coming back to was that Mom and Ron wanted to get married but that they didn't want a future with me.

Mothers couldn't choose whether to care for their children or not.

Could they? Could they shake their kids if they decided they didn't want them anymore? Because I thought mothers were supposed to love and protect their children above and before themselves. At least Great-Gram would have. I couldn't be so sure Mom felt the same, especially after what I'd heard. So, I owed it to myself to demand some answers, since Mom obviously wasn't willing to give them freely.

"Mom?" I asked after eating a bowl of macaroni and cheese for dinner one night. Ron wasn't home, which was a rare opportunity to talk to Mom about this wedding she hadn't told me about.

"What?" she asked from the kitchen sink.

"Can I talk to you about you and Ron getting married?"

"What about it?" she responded emotionlessly. I was surprised at how unfazed she was that I even knew.

"Well, I . . ." I started, struggling to find the words. "I guess I just don't *want* you to marry him."

"Where is that coming from?" she asked, glancing at me as if there were no reason for such a bold assertion.

"I don't know. I mean . . . I do know. I just don't wanna say." I dropped my head shamefully, though I wasn't sure why I felt bad acknowledging something that was true.

"You're the one who came to me, so just say it, Dane."

I looked back up at Mom, hoping she'd be receptive to my feelings this time. "Well . . . I've heard Ron say a lot of bad things about me, like how he didn't want to 'pay for' me because he's not my real dad." I paused. "And I don't like him either. I've never liked him, honestly. So, I don't want you to marry him, because I don't want him to be my dad." I averted my eyes then to avoid her reaction.

Mom huffed. "I don't know what you *think* you heard, Dane, but Ron would never say anything like that."

I know for a fact what I'd heard, and that Mom had heard him correctly too. It's not like the conversation I'd overheard had been the first time he'd said those things, anyway.

"You haven't even given Ron a chance," Mom continued before I could respond. "He's given you a nice place to live, clothes, food . . . I don't understand why you two just can't get along."

I thought about what she'd said for a moment. We did live in a much nicer place now. She kept it very clean. There were no bugs here, so I could sleep with my mouth open without worry. I had grass to play on outside. We always had food to eat now.

"But dads are supposed to love their kids," I deduced. "And Ron doesn't even *like* me!"

Mom tilted her head sideways. "He doesn't like you now?"

"No!" I asserted. "Because if he did, he wouldn't be so mean to me!"

"He's mean to you?"

"Yeah!" I insisted, before telling her about all the times he hit me with a hairbrush or yanked my pigtails too hard. I told her how he called me a bother and a burden, and how he scared me with hateful glares.

"That's just how he is," Mom defended. "Anyway, he wouldn't be that way with you if he didn't care so much about you."

Great-Gram cared about me, and she didn't treat me like Ron did. My uncles, my cousins, Kelly . . . they cared about me. Ron clearly did not.

"Who is my real dad, anyway?" I blurted, suddenly thinking my real dad probably wouldn't treat me like Ron did either.

Mom whipped her head towards me. I'd apparently caught her off guard. "What?" she asked as if she hadn't heard what I'd had the audacity to ask.

"My real dad," I repeated. "Who is he? And *where* is he?"

Mom turned her attention back to her dishwashing. "You don't need to worry about any of that. Okay?"

"I just wanna know—"

"You don't need to know anything! Okay?" she said, cutting me off.

"But—"

"DANE!"

I stared at Mom, angry that she wouldn't answer my simple question. But seeing as she wasn't, I turned to leave.

"His name is Dan," I heard Mom say behind me.

Pausing mid-step, I repeated, "Dan?" That was a letter short of my name.

"Yeah," she said. "I thought you were going to be a boy, so I was going to name you after him. But you came out a girl, so . . ."

"You named me after him?" I confirmed with wondrous joy, ignoring my error in being born the wrong gender.

"Yes," she said. "I was going to name you 'Prudence' after the Beatles' song I liked. Then I thought to name you Danielle, since it's the female version of Daniel. But I wasn't sure you'd be able to spell a name that long. So, I shortened it to Dana."

Standing in the doorway between the kitchen and foyer, I silently evaluated each new piece of this puzzle of my life.

I'd never liked my name. It was dull and uninteresting for someone as strong-willed and feisty as I was. It wasn't girly either. I'd have much preferred a name like Bianca—something with pizzazz. Knowing my father and I shared a name, however, made me appreciate mine a little more, for at least the sentimental value.

What I didn't appreciate, though, was Mom's assumption that I'd be dumb. "Why would you think I wouldn't be able to spell 'Danielle'?" I asked, hoping for some other reasoning.

"Well, your, uh . . . Dan," she said, emphasizing his name instead of just calling him my dad, "was into a lot of drugs and alcohol. They say that stuff kills off your brain cells. So, I didn't know if it would affect yours too."

Although I didn't miss the hidden insult to me and my dad, I had seen commercials on TV about what drugs do to your brain, so I couldn't dispute her logic.

"I'm glad you didn't name me *Prudence*," I remarked as I turned to go up to my bedroom. That just didn't sound like a nice name, and I could imagine the kids calling me "dense" as a mocking nickname on top of everything else I was singled out for.

After Mom had tucked me into bed that night, I prayed for my real dad—this *Dan*—to come rescue me like Daddy Warbucks had saved Annie from Mrs. Hannigan in the movie.

My dad didn't have to be rich or have a mansion, though. He didn't have to have a house and a car like Ron did either. Being my dad and loving me like Daddy Warbucks loved Annie would be enough. And I, his daughter and namesake, would be enough for him too.

"A Little Bit of Soap"

Christmas had always been my favorite time of year. Our family would have a huge celebration that lasted from the afternoon of Christmas Eve until the wee hours of morning on Christmas Day. Then we'd sleep for a bit, until I couldn't wait any longer to open my presents from Santa, who I still believed in. Fortunately, Mom and I were early risers, so I'd never have to wait too long.

This year, I was doubly excited because my new school held a Christmas bazaar where students were allowed to purchase gifts for family and friends. Everything was priced from a quarter up to five dollars. So, I had enough change in my piggy bank to buy something for everyone I loved. I bought my grandma a cobalt-blue crystal ring for only fifty cents, since she loved jewelry and blue was her favorite color. I purchased a little toad figurine for Mom for a dollar, to match some other green frog décor she had in the kitchen. I bought lavender soaps shaped like flowers for Great-Gram. I even bought Ron a gift, thinking he would make more of an effort to be nice to me in response to the kind gesture. If nothing else, it would show Mom I was doing my part to make my relationship with him better.

So, on Christmas morning, I knelt at the base of the decorated evergreen standing between the combination living and dining room, wearing my yellow Minnie Mouse nightgown. Although I was anxious to open the pile of presents before me, I admired the tree first, recalling what a fun night the three of us had had decorating it together. Ron had popped the fresh popcorn, which I then alternated with hard cranberries, stringing each piece onto the sewing needle and thread Mom had held. We'd worked for hours until there was enough popcorn and cranberry garland to layer around the tree. Now I wondered if I could eat the popcorn.

"Ready, Dane?" Mom asked as she emerged from the kitchen with a garbage bag.

I nodded eagerly.

"Then, go ahead! Start unwrapping!" she permitted.

Ron sat at the end of the sofa, wearing elastic-waisted shorts and sipping his coffee while Mom stood over me, waiting to collect the wrapping paper I tore off each present. I wished she'd sit down too and be more present in the moment. She seemed more concerned about the garbage, though, than seeing my exuberant reactions to getting everything I'd wished for.

"Oh my god! Look what I got, Mom!" I hollered and squealed when I opened my last gift. I never thought I'd have my own Cabbage Patch Kids doll. She was beautiful too! I held the box on my lap, staring at the doll's big blue eyes and blonde yarn hair. I'd heard these dolls were impossible to find, so I thought I must have been really good this past year for Santa Claus to make sure I got one.

Ron had bought me a knock-off doll at a swap meet he'd dragged me to over the summer, but she hadn't come in a package like a real Cabbage Patch Kid, nor did she have adoption papers. Plus, it had red hair and green eyes, and the face was kind of misshapen, so you could tell it was fake.

Anxious to tear this authentic Cabbage Patch doll from its packaging, I was equally eager to give Mom and Ron the gifts I'd gotten them first.

"You're next, Mom!" I said excitedly.

"What?" my mom asked with surprise. I reached under the tree for the small box I'd wrapped in paper I'd drawn a Christmas design on with markers.

Mom put the garbage bag down and took the box. "Is this for me?"

I nodded, watching her smile wider as she peeled back the paper. She placed the paper on the dining room table behind her. That meant she was going to save it in that special box where she kept pictures I'd drawn and other things I crafted for her.

"You like it, Mom?" I asked, eager to know she was pleased with me.

"I haven't even opened the box yet, Dane!" she said, laughing. She glanced over at Ron, who appeared disinterested in our joy as he sipped from his mug.

"Well, open it, then!" I urged.

She chuckled and then opened the top flap of the box to reveal the small green frog figurine.

"Do you like it? It has a daisy in its mouth, like it's giving you the flower! And it matches the other frog stuff in the kitchen!" I pointed out.

"Thanks, Dane," Mom said, placing the frog back in its box. She said it was for safekeeping, until she found just the right spot for it.

"Now it's your turn, Ron!" I said, scrambling under the tree again with my "skinny butt" in the air. That's what he called me when I streaked down the hall from the bathroom to my bedroom after a shower.

I pulled out another small box, which I'd wrapped in yellow legal pad paper and hidden near the tree base. "I wrapped it the best I could," I said, excusing what Ron would deem to be beneath appropriate expectations before he ruined the moment with a mean comment. He didn't say anything, though his unemotional indifference to the gift made me doubt myself nonetheless.

Once he opened it, though, he'd be happy. So, I knelt on the floor in front of him, bouncing my bottom off my bare feet and clapping my hands with excited anticipation of the praise he'd bestow upon me when he saw what I'd gotten him.

I looked over at Mom to make sure she was watching as Ron peeled back the yellow paper. She smiled at me, which I took to mean she was happy that I was making the effort to get along with Ron like she wanted me to.

"Hmm. What is it?" he asked, turning the cardboard box back and forth to see if it said what was inside.

"Open it!" I encouraged.

Ron scrunched his brows as he did. I sat in front of him with wide eyes, waiting for him to realize what it was. Once he did, he'd thank me for being so thoughtful, and Mom would be happy to see the family she wanted us to be.

Unable to contain myself another second, I blurted, "It's soap on a rope! Like the one Mom bought you before that you said you loved! It smells like cologne too!"

Ron emptied the square of soap into his hand and sniffed it while I looked at Mom to ensure she was watching. I wanted her to witness Ron's reaction. She was busy picking up wrapping paper and ribbons from the floor, though. So now we'd both missed seeing Ron's face.

"What am I supposed to do with this?" Ron asked, sounding confused and annoyed.

I looked at Ron and then at Mom with a worried frown. That hadn't been the reaction I'd expected.

"Ron . . ." Mom said with a cocked head and raised brows.

I looked back to Ron, expecting a proper "thank you" now.

"What?" he said to Mom with a shrug, as if he'd done nothing wrong.

"Ron!" Mom said more firmly.

"Well, what do you expect me to do with this cheap piece of crap?" he said, tossing the little box and the soap onto the floor with the rest of the garbage.

If I'd had the audacity to throw a gift from him onto the floor like that, I'd have been spanked, yelled at, and forced to offer an apology. He should have to follow the same guidelines for appropriate behavior and be disciplined just the same too.

All Mom did was shake her head, though. Then she returned to her task of cleaning up.

So, I made a dramatic scene of standing up, grabbing the *real* Cabbage Patch doll Santa had brought me from the North Pole, and pounding up the stairs in a pout.

Once in my room, I locked the door. Then I stopped and stilled when I heard them arguing in the living room below.

"Ronald!" my mother scolded.

"What?" he retorted with justified snark. "It was cheap soap!"

"But she's six!"

"Yeah, well, she . . ." Ron rambled some lame excuse.

I covered my ears so I didn't have to hear it. I already knew how this would end, anyway—with it somehow being my fault.

"You Dropped a Bomb on Me"

Instead of going to Great-Gram's to eat leftover ham and pasteles like we'd always done on Christmas Day, we went to Ron's family's Christmas. Considering what had happened with the soap, I was obviously less than enthused.

Ron's family consisted of his three sisters, one brother, their spouses, and children. Assuming what Ron said was true, his father had been a fire-thrower and acrobat with the Vaudeville entertainment group, which travelled all over to perform. His mother had abandoned the five children when Ron was barely a toddler, leaving them to fend for themselves until they were separated into foster homes. The kids reunited as adults, however, and seemed to be closer than ever.

Mom and I had been around them a time or two before. She seemed uneasy, like she felt as out of place as I did when we were around them. So, I wondered if that's why she became quiet as we got ready to go there and then sat in the car with a flat expression.

I'd once overheard Mom complain to someone on the phone, early in her relationship with Ron, that one of Ron's siblings had insulted her about having me so young. But, according to her, everyone made that judgment. So, I wasn't sure why it was any more impactful coming from one of his family members, unless it was because she took it as a sign of not being accepted.

Either way, she did what she always did and put her polite smile on when we walked up to Ron's sister's door. I could tell the smile was fake by the deadness in her eyes. Clearly, she didn't want to be here any more than I did. I was always bored, listening to the adults talk and joke, since there were no kids my age to play with.

Ron rang the doorbell. After waiting a few seconds, he glanced at his watch and said, "We're late." We were always late, though it only upset me when they made me late to something at school.

When Ron's sister finally answered the door, Ron chimed, "Hey!" He threw one hand in the air and waved it in sync with whatever silent song he was bopping around to in his head, expressing the same enthusiasm Santa Claus would when arriving with presents on Christmas Eve.

I discreetly shook my head at this happy version of a man I only saw when he had an audience, wondering where he'd been that morning.

"Come on in," his sister said with a closed-mouth smile.

"Thanks," Mom offered in a mousy tone as soon as we stepped inside the dark living room. "You remember Ron's sister, Anne?" she asked to remind me of my manners.

I nodded as I stepped in, eyeing Anne cautiously. She had curly brown hair that barely grazed her shoulders. It was pinned back at the sides, to show the green Christmas tree earrings dangling above her equally festive sweater. She had small beady eyes like Ron's and a fresh face free of the blue eye shadows and pink lip glosses most women wore to look like the desirable actress Morgan Fairchild.

I remembered meeting Anne one time before, but because I didn't like Ron much, I just assumed not to like any of his family either. I think I'd like Anne, though. She seemed *genuinely* nice.

"The boys are somewhere around here," she said, referring to Ron's nephews who were all older than me.

"You want to go find them, Dane?" Mom asked.

I shook my head frantically, hoping she wouldn't make me. If they were anything like Leo's boys, who'd played tricks on me and then laughed at my gullibility, I wanted nothing to do with them.

"That's okay," Anne said with a kind smile. "Let me at least take your coats for now."

Ron set his armful of presents beside the others near the Christmas tree. Then I followed Mom, who followed Ron, to the back of the house where we heard loud chatter.

As soon as we entered the well-lit kitchen, where the adults were all already gathered, Ron stopped mid-step and threw his arms in the air. "Hey!" he hollered to get everyone's attention. Then he remained there with his mouth wide open as if surprised, and his brows raised up to his receding hair line.

Everyone proceeded to exchange boisterous greetings while Mom and I stood by watching. I looked up at Mom, whose leg I clutched for security, for a sense of how I should feel. Her weak and meek smile didn't fool me like she was trying to fool the others. Not that they noticed. They were a loud and animated bunch who were more interested in exchanging snarky one-liners and rude jabs than acknowledging Mom and me at all.

Ron carried on joking and drinking with his family, seemingly forgetting we'd come with him. So, we sat at a folding table in the corner, watching him talk over everyone and use showy antics to ensure he was the center of attention. Mom shyly chuckled at something he said now and then but otherwise didn't attempt to mingle with the group. I didn't know if she was intimidated by them because they were all so much older, but it made me sad to see her clear separation from them. I also thought it rude that they made no attempt to involve her in their conversations. Our family would have never made anyone feel so unwelcome.

Mom wasn't withdrawn like this around our family. She was normally very eager to be part of conversations and gossip, often interrupting or talking over others like Ron did, to share whatever she couldn't wait to divulge. She could be funny too, in an awkward way, and her silliness was always followed by her distinct laugh, which sounded like the Count's from *Sesame Street*.

So, I was thankful when Anne announced that it was time to eat. It gave us something to do other than sit in the corner by ourselves. We even moved together in the line around the kitchen counter, where all the food was put out. One of Ron's other sisters, whom I'd heard called Marie, was in line ahead of us.

"How are you doing?" she asked Mom while spooning mostaccioli onto her plate. Aside from her pointy chin, she looked quite different from Anne and Ron. Marie was heavier, wore thick glasses like Mom's, and had short, light, feathered hair. "Having a good Christmas, Dana?" she added before Mom answered.

I nodded, more entranced with the strings of mozzarella cheese stretching from the large glass baking dish to the serving spoon near her plate. She looked at me and giggled as she pulled the cheese until it finally surrendered to one or the other.

"We're good," Mom responded politely. "And you?"

"We're great!" she said louder than she needed to, though I was learning that was the normal volume with which they all spoke here. "The boys got everything they wanted. You know, skateboards and walkie-talkies ... How about you, Dana? You get everything you wanted?"

I nodded and smiled.

"Tell her what you got, Dana," Mom prodded, shaking her head and rolling her eyes. I was irked by her embarrassment of me. Had she forgotten we were on the same side here?

"A Cabbage Patch doll," I said, barely above a whisper.

"A Cabbage Patch doll?" Ron's sister repeated with fake disbelief. "Well, you must have been a *really* good girl to get that!" She nudged Mom with her elbow and winked. In response, Mom gave that same weak smile she'd had plastered on her face all afternoon.

"How about you? I heard *you* were a good girl!" Marie said to Mom next as she moved along in the line to where beef and bread rolls awaited.

"Yeah," Mom said, making me wonder what she'd gotten that I'd missed. I found out quickly, when she lifted her hand slightly for Marie to see the modest diamond ring on it.

Where the heck did that come from? I wondered. *Does that mean Mom and Ron are getting married after all?*

"Well, good for you!" Marie exclaimed before making a scene of leaning in and squinting at the ring. Despite my upset at finding out about this over a tray of noodles, I almost burst out laughing at the implied insult.

Unfortunately, I couldn't get past how betrayed I felt. After telling Mom all the terrible things Ron had said and done to me, it didn't make sense that she would agree to go ahead and marry him. So, I gaped at her, wondering how she could do this to me and to us.

"I gotta say, though, I am surprised," Ron's sister remarked. "Ron's always been more of a boob guy!" She cackled as she walked away, leaving Mom frozen with embarrassment. Having been the butt of enough teasing myself, I felt bad for Mom. So, I put aside my resentment. This wasn't the time or place for it, anyway.

We returned to our corner seats, where Ron's sister-in-law and niece joined us and exchanged pleasantries while we ate. Afterwards, I watched as Ron's nieces and nephews opened presents, surprised that Santa had left a couple there for me too. Then we packed up to leave. When we got in the car, though, I immediately sensed tension.

Mom's lips were pressed together tightly, as if physically restraining herself from speaking up about something. Ron seemed oblivious, mumbling about how slow the heat was to warm us.

"Ron?" Mom finally said with a seriousness that caught my attention.

"What's up?" he said cheerfully, still on a high from being the life of his family's party.

"Did you hear some of the comments your family made to me today?"

"No. Why?" he asked. I moved forward and to the center of the back seat to hear better.

Mom huffed. "Well, your brother asked me if I was old enough to have that Kahlua and cream I was drinking," she said.

I must have missed that comment in the two minutes I was gone to the bathroom. I didn't understand why it bothered Mom so much, though.

"He was just joking," Ron dismissed. "I mean, you do look young, even for twenty-three."

"You don't think that was rude?" Mom persisted.

"No," Ron answered firmly. "I think you're just sensitive about people calling attention to the fact."

"Of course I am," Mom responded. "Because there's always some judgment about having had Dana so young."

"You took it all wrong, Ivy. He was probably complimenting you. You are an attractive woman."

"What about your sister's comment about my breasts?" Mom snarked back.

"Your breasts?" he said, glancing at her with a creased brow.

"Yeah. She said she was surprised you were with me because you were more of a 'boob' guy."

Ron's lips twitched between a smirk and a frown. Mine couldn't help doing the same. I'd never heard Mom say the word "boob."

"Well, I didn't think it was funny," Mom said, swiping her finger under her nose.

Ron glanced over at her again and saw her visible sadness. "What do you want me to do? Tell my family they're not supposed to joke with you?" Ron said harshly.

Mom bowed her head. She was normally so unemotional that her sadness felt that much more significant. I expected Ron to notice this and try to mitigate it, especially if he was going to be her husband.

"Why won't you defend my mom?" I blurted.

"Dane!" Mom scolded under her breath.

"No! You never stand up for yourself. You're telling him you're upset about stuff his family said to you, and he's not doing anything to make you feel better! Just like he doesn't say anything to his family to make them treat you better," I asserted for her.

"Dane, this isn't—" Mom said at the same time Ron grunted and reached back at me with his small stubby hand. I jumped back to avoid it.

"Don't you talk to me that way!" he growled as he moved his hand every which way, reaching and clutching but missing me every time.

He almost got a hold of me, so I pulled my legs up onto the seat. All of a sudden, the car swerved to the right, knocking me off balance. I caught myself before I fell to the left.

"Ron!" Mom cried out mercifully. She grabbed the handle of her door to steady herself.

The car came to a stop at the side of the road. Within the millisecond that curiosity made me look out the window to see where we were, the upper half of Ron's body came from between the two front seats. I scrambled to get out of his reach when I felt his hand squeeze my ankle as tightly as he could.

"Stop! That hurts!" I cried, trying to wiggle my ankle out of his grasp. He wouldn't let go. The skin around his grip was reddening to purple. I was afraid he'd tear my foot off if he didn't let go. So, I clawed at his hand, whimpering with worried frustration as my unmatched strength left me no choice but to admit defeat. "I'll stop! I'll stop! I swear! Please! Let me go!"

"Ron!" Mom snapped at him. I was glad for her attempt to cease the assault. But when he didn't release me, she made no other motion for him to let go of me. I felt disloyalty more than I felt the pain in my strangled limb.

"Mom, make him stop!" I begged, crying tears of physical pain now. "Mom! Ron! Please!" I sobbed, making guttural noises that sounded like they should be coming from the depths of hell instead of a little girl's mouth.

"You better watch how you talk to me!" Ron threatened, bubbles of spit oozing out of his clenched bite. Then, with a last tight squeeze, he released me.

I curled up in the corner of the back seat behind Mom, though it was no use hiding behind her. She'd done nothing to stop Ron. She didn't tell him he wasn't allowed to hurt me like that. She didn't even ask me if I was okay! She might as well have given him permission to do what he'd done!

So, if she wanted to marry him, that was her choice. But I clearly saw where I stood. And it wasn't with them.

"White Wedding"

On June 25, 1983, I stood in the unlit second-floor hallway of Ron's duplex, staring at myself in the full-length mirror that leaned against the wall between the two smaller bedrooms.

I should have been smiling at my reflection. I looked like a princess in the floor-length, off-the-shoulder peach gown Mom had bought for me to wear. It had ruffled chiffon trim along the top, a thin satin ribbon above the waist that tied at the back, and larger ruffles along the bottom of the A-line. The opaque material was lined with satin, which felt luxurious and silky against my bare legs and skinned knees.

My long brown hair, with blonde kisses from the early summer sun, had been pulled back from my tanned face, French braided on either side, then joined together into one long braid that fell to the middle of my back. A delicate crown of baby's breath laid upon my head to match the white flowers I'd carry down the church aisle in a basket.

I looked over my shoulder into the master bedroom, where my grandma and her sister—my Godmother Sonia—were busy fussing over Mom's white lace dress and floral headpiece. She didn't even look like my mom today. Her dark, tightly curled hair had been straightened and pulled back into a low bun. She wasn't wearing her thick-lensed glasses either. Someone had said she got contact lenses to put into her eyes, allowing her to see without her black frames. She wore makeup too, which I wasn't used to. The natural peaches and light browns complemented her beautifully, though. She was stunning. I just didn't understand why she was trying so hard to look so different than she normally did.

I didn't look like myself either, I supposed. I normally wore elastic-waist shorts and raggedy T-shirts that matched my scraggly hair. Yet, today I looked like royalty, so we could present as the perfect family we weren't about to become.

The whole day seemed like a farce, beginning with the wedding ceremony. It was held at the Catholic church where I'd attended first grade. Ron had always claimed to be Jewish, so I didn't know how they'd gotten the church to agree to marry them without Ron becoming Catholic. I can't say I'd ever *seen* Ron wear a beanie like the Jewish boys and men in our neighborhood did when they went to temple, nor did Ron ever light a menorah at Hannukah. Come to think of it, I'd never witnessed him worship God at all. So, as far as I could tell, he was no more Jewish than Catholic. As a matter of fact, I think he thought he *was* a god by the way he sought everyone's admiration and praise!

This was what Mom wanted, though. All I had to do was walk down the aisle on cue and stand up at the altar with Mom and her friend from work, who she'd asked to be her maid of honor.

My tummy began aching as I waited to enter the ceremony. One of Ron's nephews, who was the ring bearer, silently stood next to me in a light-gray tuxedo. He never did talk much, so I didn't try talking to him either.

I glanced back at Mom for some reassurance, but she looked tense as ever with her straight lips pressed together. I wondered why she wasn't smiling like brides I'd seen in movies and on TV. Her father was. Mom's arm was looped through his, but it didn't seem to comfort her in the least. I didn't know much about their relationship, though, because I didn't really know him. I'd only heard my grandma say stuff about him being a "drunk."

Suddenly, organ music began to play. Mom's friend from work, who stood directly behind me, softly prodded me to walk down the long red-carpeted aisle. I looked at Ron's nephew, whose expressionless face made me wonder if he was even human. But then he shrugged, and we stepped forward in offbeat unison.

The church was glorious with its heavenly high rafters. The stained-glass windows seemed taller than the Sears Tower. Despite all there was to admire, everyone turned to stare at *us* as we approached the altar. I didn't like people staring at me, so I bowed my head to avoid eye contact.

"Dane." I heard a loud whisper up ahead. I glanced up to see Sonia pointing at her cheesy smile. I wanted to follow her direction, but I didn't feel like smiling right now. I was too scared by being the focus of everyone's attention to pretend. Anyway, I didn't like having to pretend. It made me even more uncomfortable when Mom made me.

The priest kindly pointed to where I should stand at the altar and directed Ron's nephew the other way. Mom's coworker from the notary supply company stood next to me soon after, in a simple floor-length chiffon gown that matched the peach color of mine. Then everyone stood as the organ music triumphantly announced Mom's entrance.

Maintaining her straight-lipped restraint, she made her way up the aisle. Her father was smiling. Our family was smiling. Even Ron's face lit up like he was watching everything he'd ever wanted walking towards him.

I looked out at Great-Gram, hoping for reassurance that Mom was happy. She met my gaze with a twinkle in her eyes, not heeding my worry. I looked at Sonia and my uncles, who were enthralled with the vision of Mom, making me question whether I was seeing the situation for what it really was.

The ceremony itself was boring. I just stood there, holding my basket of baby's breath and carnations while the priest droned on about unions and whatever else the Bible had to say about love.

The rest of the day passed quickly, every aspect of it requiring me to pretend to be happy about all that had happened. But I wasn't. I was having a hard time observing all these people who had said this or felt that, coming together as if the world were right. It didn't make sense to see Ron and our cousin he'd called a "horse face" laughing together at the bar. It didn't make sense to see Ron's sister, who'd said he was a "boob guy," congratulating Mom and welcoming her to the family. Everywhere I turned, I felt like I was witnessing some dishonesty I couldn't make sense of. Overwhelmed with emotion, I ran out to the lobby. I wanted to leave this reception, leave this building, and any memory of this occasion altogether.

"Dane? What's up? Where are you going?" a familiar voice asked from behind me. I turned to see my godmother, Sonia. She was one of the few people I trusted because her actions always matched her very direct, no-nonsense attitude. So, I turned around, knowing it was safe to expose the angst begging to erupt out of me.

"I . . . uh . . . I . . ." I couldn't stop crying and sniffling long enough to get a word out.

Sonia squatted to my level and put her hands on my shoulders. "Okay, breathe, Dane," she said as she stared into my eyes. Then she breathed in deeply through her nose and out her mouth. Her deep-set dark eyes entranced me. They matched her dark bob, which shined as much as her tanned skin glowed. She was so beautiful, like a fairy godmother. Her voice was calming too. So, I followed her instructions, though short breaths and sniffles interrupted my inhales. "Okay, good. Now, whatever it is, it'll be okay. Just calm down and tell me what's going on."

I smeared the mess of tears on my face with my hand, sniffled some more, then said, "I . . . I don't like him. I just wish my mom hadn't married him at all!" My shoulders shook in Sonia's hands.

"Well, Dane, I don't know what to tell you. Getting married was your mom's decision, and we have to respect it."

"But everyone is lying! I don't understand why they're all acting like they like each other when they don't. And it all started when Ron started coming around!" I said before weeping even louder.

Sonia sighed. "Listen, we're going to wipe these tears off your face and go back in that room and show your mom we support her. Okay? You just hold your head high and ignore whatever you see or hear that bothers you. You don't need to get worked up like this. You're only hurting yourself when you do. You understand?"

I was little, but I understood what respect and self-discipline were. So, I nodded while I wiped the last of the tears from my face. Then I took Sonia's hand and returned to the reception with my head held high like Sonia had said. She walked me to where Great-Gram sat overlooking the dance floor.

Great-Gram had a twinkle in her eye as I approached. She patted her lap, inviting me to sit with her, like she always did to soothe me. I climbed up onto her cushy body, feeling even more comfort in the way she held me. She was my constant because her love was consistent. It never wavered.

So, I laid my head on her shoulder and watched as Sonia bounced around the room with the rest of the guests, singing along to "The Loco-Motion." I still didn't like that everyone pretended everything was fine when it wasn't. Then again, maybe this was how people worked things out. Maybe people moved forward without holding each other accountable or forgiving, just to keep the peace.

I wasn't sure I could do it. It felt ingenuine to pretend I liked Ron when I didn't. It felt wrong to ignore his mistreatment of me too. I couldn't see how pretending we got along could influence real change.

From the way this crazy train of people looked as they pranced by me and Great-Gram, though, I knew I'd better try to hop on board with all of them. Otherwise, I'd get run down or passed by. By everyone, including Mom, who was one of them now too.

"What's Your Name"

Mom and I were singing along to the oldies station like we usually did when it was just the two of us in the car. We both knew every word to every song, and we belted them out like we were the famous singers themselves, performing on stage. I loved seeing Mom carefree and happy, and I loved how close I felt to her in those moments even more.

When a commercial came on, she turned down the volume. "I have to talk to you about something, Dane." Her serious tone distracted me from strategizing about how to convince her to allow me some treat at the grocery store we were on the way to. I mean, what could be more important than deciding between a pound of gummy worms or chocolate nonpareils (assuming she'd let me get any of it)?

She and Ron had had several serious talks since returning from their honeymoon. From what I could gather from the stairway where I spied, the company they were both employed at had shut down while they were gone. I'd overheard Ron say they only had five hundred dollars in the bank, and that it would run out within a short month, or less if an unnecessary expense arose.

With his sixth-grade education and her General Education Diploma—which I'd determined to be my fault since she often commented about having to drop out of high school to avoid judgment for becoming pregnant with me—neither qualified for any decent-paying jobs. So, they decided to start their own notary supply company in our basement. Until it took off, money was tight.

"Now that Ron and I are married," Mom started, glancing over to ensure I was paying her due attention, "we've decided that you should have the same last name as us—Ron's last name."

"Why?" I asked, surprised a name could even be changed. I'd never heard of such a thing.

"So nobody will know we're not a real family."

"But we're *not* a real family," I responded.

"Well, Dane, he's my husband now, which makes him your dad. So, we are. And having the same last name will—"

"But I don't want his last name," I said, cutting her off. I didn't want to live with him, be associated with him, have Mom married to him . . .

"Look, it's hard enough with people whispering about us all the time. So, it's just easier if people think you're really his daughter." Finally, the truth.

I was seven and a half years old, but I wasn't stupid. This had been Mom's idea, not Ron's. He could care less about me, never mind want me to have his name. Kids required time, money, and attention that he wasn't willing to share. He was only good with kids, including me, when there was an audience to praise him for his efforts.

That's why I was waiting for my real dad to find me. I had to believe that anyone with a child would want to know where their child lived, and that the child was okay. So, I knew he'd come looking for me someday. He'd have a tougher time finding me if my name was changed, though.

"I don't want his name, Mom. I mean it," I asserted.

Mom looked to her left and made a sharp turn into an empty parking space. Then she turned off the ignition and looked at me sternly.

"Well, you don't have a choice, Dane. We've already filed the paperwork for him to adopt you, so when you go back to school after Labor Day, you'll have the new last name."

I crossed my arms and sulked. I wasn't happy.

How would I explain this to the kids at school? Some were still bothering me about being "illegitimate" and Hispanic. Now I'd have to answer questions about why my last name was different? The last thing I needed was to call any more attention to myself. I'd have expected Mom to understand this, considering how much she worried about what other people thought about us.

Instead, she added insult to injury when she said, "And from now on, we want you to call him 'Dad,' not Ron. 'Dad.' Okay?"

"No!" I protested, hitting the bench seat with my fists. "I have a dad, and it's not Ron!"

Countering my tantrum with dismissive calmness, she said, "You don't even know him, Dana. You probably never will . . . and you're better off."

Infuriated that she would talk about my dad so negatively, I defended, "I will too meet him someday! And I will be better off!"

Staring at me with a cross expression, it was like she was trying to decipher whether I really believed that. "You need to start being more grateful," she scolded. "Ron doesn't have to put a roof over your head or feed you or buy you clothes. But he does. Because that's what fathers do. So, you better start showing him some respect. Now, let's go." She opened her door and got out of the car.

As I remained with crossed arms and a pout, I realized Ron and I had something in common. We had no choice but to comply with the situation Mom had unwillingly sucked us all into. So, I had no choice but to unstick myself from the fake leather seat of her car and follow her into the store. Needless to say, I didn't get gummies or chocolates that day. I didn't seem to get anything I wanted anymore.

"Help"

"**Y**ou look just like your father," a saleswoman at a department store commented while Ron and I waited for Mom to come out of a dressing room.

Ron bent down, put his face next to mine, and gave the lady a cheesy smile. She gazed at us affectionately, as if witnessing an adoring father so lovingly endeared to his daughter. Mom came out then, happy to see her husband and her daughter playing along with this farce of a family she wanted us to be.

We weren't a real family in any sense of the word. Yet, according to my new birth certificate, which had come in the mail recently, Ron was my biological father. It had angered me to find out that she hadn't just changed my last name to his, as she'd let on. She and Ron had outright lied and claimed Ron was my real dad. I couldn't believe some amount of money and a few signatures could just erase who I was and just as easily create a fraudulent past that better suited Mom's ego.

What could I do about it, though? I was only a kid. I didn't have a job to afford a fancy lawyer to change my name back to what it had always been. So now, legally, I was someone else—someone who didn't even exist—and I was expected to uphold this new persona.

Fortunately, the new last name didn't draw any attention from kids at school when I started the third grade in September. I was just "Dana" like I'd always been, though it took some time to stop writing "Dana Diaz" on top of my schoolwork.

School had started on a better note overall. I'd even befriended another girl named Miranda. She'd been in my class the year before, but I hadn't talked to her until recently because no one else did, and I'd been afraid to be made fun of more than I already was. I rethought that when I realized Miranda was ostracized just the same as I had been. I never wanted anyone to feel left out like that.

Miranda was really good at doing the cooperative hand-clap routine to the tune of "Miss Mary Mack." So, we sang and clapped to the tune over and over at recess one day, speeding it up more each time, then laughing and starting over the second we faltered.

When Gail and her sidekicks walked up to us, we dropped our hands and smiles, knowing the sneer on Gail's face meant she intended to ruin our fun.

"Oh, look—the loser is playing with the bastard," Gail snarked, crossing her arms. Anna and Dawn looked at each other, snickering at the insult.

Miranda frowned and looked down. Her clothes were dirty and sometimes too small for her chubby belly. Her straight auburn hair was greasy and stringy. That didn't make her a loser, though. She was a nice girl if anyone had bothered to get to know her.

"Just leave us alone, you big meanie!" I hollered. I wouldn't let her make Miranda feel like any less than the rest of us.

"What did you say?" Gail asked, moving her hands to her hips. Dawn and Anna exchanged knowing glances behind her.

I looked to Miranda, hoping she'd join me in the rebellion I'd initiated, but she shook her head anxiously, warning me to relent. Although I was as scared of Gail as she was, I took a deep breath, gulped a dose of courage, and turned back to the three bullies with clenched teeth. "I said leave us alone!"

Without warning, Gail charged me. I cowered, but it was too late. She grabbed a big wad of my long hair in her fist, causing my eyes and mouth to widen in shock. Then she yanked me back hard enough to make me fall to the ground. Before I could even think about my next move, she began to drag me away, using my hair to pull my lightweight body across the grass and away from the crowd.

"Help!" I cried out, hoping someone would come to my aid. No one heard me over the crowd of kids squealing and hollering around the few teachers who were too involved in their own gossip to care. Miranda made no move to get help or intervene either, instead turning her back to what was happening to me.

Realizing that Gail and her friends could do anything they wanted to me, and that no one would stop them, made me panic even more. I clawed Gail's hands frantically, trying to pry them off, while simultaneously kicking and digging my heels into the grass to stop, or at least slow, the drag.

When we were far enough away that Gail felt confident she could get away with whatever punishment she intended to inflict, she finally released her hold. I pulled my knees up and placed both hands on my head, as if they had healing powers to make the pain go away. My back and bottom felt moist too—the result of the morning's dew having been brought to the surface of this otherwise undisturbed field behind the school. Mom wouldn't be happy about the grass stains, and I would surely cry more tears defending myself to her later.

Gail moved to the front of me, and the other two girls stepped in behind her. I looked up at them with teary eyes, feeling both hatred and worry about what she'd do to me next.

"Wah, wah," Gail said, mocking me. Her cohorts snickered, so she threw in, "Crybaby."

I wiped the tears off my cheek with my soiled palm. Then I exhaled sharply.

"What're you gonna do? Huh?" Gail taunted.

I narrowed my eyes and pressed my lips together tightly. Then I pushed myself up with the skinny twigs I had for arms and grunted as I charged at her.

Dawn and Anna stepped away from their leader, their arms in the air, gaping at my rageful reaction. Gail's smug expression fueled my adrenaline. I wanted to wipe that arrogant grin right off her hateful face, to make sure she knew she was no better than anyone else.

Shoving her as hard as I could, she didn't move except for the slightest bit at the shoulder where I'd bounced off of her. My mouth fell open in shock. I'd known my tiny frame and shorter height were no match for her, but—

The sky was a bright light blue. The sky? How had I gone from standing to laying on my back on the grass again?

Laughter brought me back to reality. I propped myself up on my elbows to see the three girls celebrating their handiwork with high fives. Gail had pushed me down, hadn't she?

Despite being much smaller and outnumbered, I was determined to stand up and stand against them again. I'd been pushed around by a bigger girl in kindergarten because a teacher had allowed me on the only swing on the playground instead of the other girl. Then a girl in my first-grade class had put chewed-up bubblegum in my hair because I liked the same little boy she did. Then I'd come to this school in the second grade, to be made fun of for how I looked and talked. So I was about done being everybody's punching bag, tired of forced apologies being the only consequence anyone had ever had to suffer for what they'd done to me. These three would pay the price, though. No one else would get away with the injustices I'd endured.

As I took a moment to catch my breath and simultaneously summon up the gumption to stand up and defend my own honor, Gail kicked my shin.

"Stop it!" I shouted, kicking back at her. She jumped to avoid contact. Then, before I could get up, all three girls crowded around me, using their feet to assault me—in the side, in my legs, in my back. Anna, the tallest girl among the three, picked up one of my feet and wiggled it just to taunt me. Then she laughed, looking at Gail, who looked on with that smug grin that reminded me so much of Ron's.

"Stop!" I screamed again. I sobbed as I pulled my knees up and wrapped my arms around them to avoid any more pain. "I'm gonna tell on you!" I lamely threatened, knowing it would have no effect.

"Who you gonna tell—your whore mommy?" Gail said, kicking me even harder. I didn't defend Mom, nor myself. I couldn't think of anything I could say that would make them stop. So, I buried my face in my knees to hide my crying.

"She won't be able to tell anyone after I knock those silver teeth out of her mouth," Anna commented as she delivered the most painful kick to one side of my gut, which was already aching.

"She doesn't need our help looking stupid! She looks like a hillbilly with all those missing teeth!" the third girl added. Dawn was one of the two in my class but by far the largest of all the boys and girls by weight alone. So, I was thankful that she didn't kick me anymore. Her words hurt just the same, though.

The obnoxious ring of the school bell signaled the end of recess. The three girls immediately retreated to the school, laughing as they looked back to where they'd left me curled in fetal position in the grass.

I watched as they and everyone else funneled towards the front entrance of the school to go back inside. Then I got up, brushed the grass off the back of my light-colored shorts, and walked swiftly to catch the tail end of the line to get back in, despite the aches and pains all over my body.

At the risk of being late to class, however, I stopped in the restroom to wash the dirt and tears off my face. I didn't want Mrs. Alessi or any of the other kids to ask questions I didn't want to answer. I was afraid of what Gail, Anna, and Dawn would do to me if I got them in trouble.

"Are you okay?" I heard a familiar voice behind me. I turned to see Kelly. My quick, successive sniffles answered her question.

With a compassionate smile, Kelly handed me a paper towel to wipe my face. I was grateful to her for recognizing my angst and for caring about me enough to risk being late to class too. She made me feel less alone in that moment, which was a true testament to the fact that there were still caring and considerate people in this world. I just wished I had more of them around me, to protect me from all the others.

After I'd dried my face and hands, I checked my reflection to ensure I'd removed all the visible evidence of the scuffle. Then I turned to Kelly and released a long exhale. She extended her hand, and I gladly took it. Kelly didn't let go until we were settled back in our seats, instead squeezing it tighter as we walked past Mrs. Alessi and then Anna, Dawn, and Gail—none of whom said a word.

"Mama Said"

I hadn't wanted to tell anyone what had happened, but I thought Mom might console me if she knew what I'd been through that day.

So, while I sat at the kitchen table with my homework spread before me, I said, "Some girls in my class beat me up today, Mom." I took a bite of my after-school snack while I awaited her reaction to my nonchalant mention.

"What?" she said. She stopped washing dishes for a moment, scrutinizing my outward appearance to decipher whether I was telling the truth.

I looked as scraggly and dirty as I always did, though, so she had no way of knowing that the bruises on my legs and arms hadn't come from acting like a spider monkey on the jungle gym at the school playground. There was no way for me to show her the aches and pains on the inside either.

Compelled to explain, I said, "Yeah, a few girls in my class dragged me out to the field by my hair." Then I relayed the details of the attack.

"Why did they pick on you in the first place?" she asked, as if it were my fault they had.

I wrinkled my forehead, disgruntled that she hadn't even asked if I was okay. "Well, they called me and this other girl a loser, and I told them to stop."

"You must have done something else for them to react the way they did, Dane," Mom said.

"I swear I didn't!" I insisted. "They've been mean to me ever since I started school there. Remember I told you they called me a 'bastard child'? And they said they couldn't play with me because you aren't married to Ron or something."

"Yeah," Mom said with tight-lipped disapproval—of me, I assumed.

"Well, that's why!" I said, hoping Mom would see it was actually *her* fault I'd gotten beat up.

"I don't know, Dane," Mom responded with a shake of her head and a sigh. "You say Ron is rough with you . . . now girls at school . . . Are you sure you're not just making up stories to get attention?"

"No!" I shouted, frustrated that she didn't believe me. "Anyway, you've *seen* Ron do mean things to me!" I reminded her.

With her lips curled in and a hand on her hip, Mom turned and stared at me. I stopped eating, nervous that my big mouth had gotten me in trouble again. It didn't take long for her to break the standoff. "Every time you come to me and say he did or said something to you, I confront him about it because you're my daughter and that's what I'm supposed to do. And every time, we end up arguing because Ron says he didn't say or do whatever you claimed. So, I'm sorry, Dane, but I think he's right. I think you're lying because you're jealous you're not getting my attention."

"That's not true, Mom! Girl Scout's honor!" I offered, holding up the three middle fingers of my right hand as proof of my oath.

Ignoring my plea, Mom said, "Despite what you think, I do get it. We just got married, and you feel like he took me away from you . . ."

"But Mom—" I whined.

"But nothing. Finish your snack so I can clean the table up," she ordered.

So I did. Then I took my schoolwork to my bedroom. It was better to be alone than to feel invisible in Mom's presence, anyway.

A week later, Gail approached me at my locker at the end of the school day. She didn't have her two cohorts with her. Still, I pushed my hair behind my shoulders and stepped back.

"I'm sorry," she said, prolonging the latter word to express her annoyance at the obvious coercion. Her eyes rolled so far up in her lids that I thought her head would start spinning as a consequence of the kind act.

Caught off guard by her ability to say those words, specifically to me, her forced delivery implied an insincerity I wasn't sure how to respond to.

"Well, aren't you going to say something back?" she asked with offense.

"I don't know what you want me to say," I said with a shrug.

"You're supposed to say, 'thank you' or 'it's okay.' At least that's what my Mom told me," she said, jutting her hip as she waited for me to comply.

"Your mother?" my scrunched face asked.

"Yeah, why?"

I shook my head and shrugged again. Then I fessed up. "Well, I just didn't know your mom knew what happened."

Gail huffed and rolled her eyes again. "She didn't. Until *your* mom called her."

"*My* mom?" She didn't go anywhere but to work, Great-Gram's, and the grocery store. So how did she know Gail's mom?

"Yeah. She got our number from the class phone list Mrs. Alessi gave us. Duh!" Gail explained with bulging eyes.

"Oh," I said, dropping my head, embarrassed for being stupid. But then a light bulb went on in my head—Mom had decided I'd been telling the truth! "Oh!" I repeated, raising my head and spirit with sudden zeal. "Well, thank you, then," I said to appease Gail for an apology she'd never have given without our mothers' involvement. I didn't want any more trouble with her, anyway. I didn't think I'd have any, now that I had a mother who would defend me.

She walked away, looking back snidely. But I didn't care. I'd been waiting for the day when I felt important to Mom. There was something empowering about having her support too, like nothing could touch me. I was on top of the world. Nothing could bring me down from that high. Not the class bully. Not even Ron.

"You Don't Own Me"

We rarely ate out, so I was thrilled when Mom said Ron was taking us to the Ponderosa restaurant for dinner one night. Now that their notary business was taking off, I guessed we could afford the luxury. So, I sat on my knees in the sticky vinyl booth, relishing the thick steak-cut fries that came with the huge hamburger I had only taken a bite of. Half of the ketchup I drowned them in ended up on my *Punky Brewster* T-shirt. I could tell by Mom's reproving glances that she wasn't too happy with the mess I was making. So, I was sure she wouldn't like me using my red knickers as a napkin either.

"I know you had your tubes tied after having Dana," Ron said to Mom in the midst of our meal, "but it would be nice if we had our *own* biological child."

My eyes widened. He'd never mentioned wanting a child. He hadn't even wanted me! Plus, Mom couldn't have any more babies. I'd heard her talk about having her "tubes tied" immediately after my birth. She said it prevented her from being able to have any more babies. So, how did Ron expect her to have *his*?

Mom seemed unfazed by Ron's idea as she pushed her food around her plate with her fork. So, it was hard to tell if he'd mentioned this before, or if she was just really that unenthused with the idea.

"Is this because you saw your ex-wife is pregnant when she came by the house that day?" Mom finally responded with a tinge of attitude.

This was new and interesting information! I acted like I was completely unaware of their conversation, though, looking around as I chewed another french fry, wondering if she'd returned to take more of our furniture. I hoped not. I didn't want to have to sleep on the floor again!

"No!" he snarked back. I didn't believe him, though. Mom was on to something. Ron always wanted what everyone else had, especially if it was something he *didn't* already have.

"Well, I guess it's something we need to talk about after we look into whether we can reverse the tubal ligation," Mom said with the calm and restraint of a robot.

Her emotionless face made me wonder whether she understood that we were talking about a human being—one that she would carry in her belly and then take care of like she had gotten stuck taking care of me.

I mean, I'd never heard Mom say she wanted another baby or that she wished she and Ron would have one together. She just wasn't the motherly type, unlike Great-Gram, some of my teachers at school, and Kelly's mom, who were all encouraging and supportive.

"I've read about some advancements that have been effective in reversing tubal ligation. It's not easy or cheap. There's surgery involved and . . ."

Thinking I could prevent Mom from being lured into something she didn't seem to want to do, I intervened despite my mouthful of french fries. "I thought we didn't have much money, Ron."

Mom glared at me with wide eyes at the same time as Ron snarked, "Shut up, Dana. We're not even talking to you."

"You can't tell me what to do, Ron." I bobbed my head in a taunt.

"I told you to call him 'Dad,'" Mom scolded.

"But he's not my dad!" I argued.

Ron leaned down to my eye level and waved his finger at me. "You better start listening to your mother!"

I sat back with a pout and arms crossed over my chest, almost daring him to come at me in public. Ron pierced me with his squinty little eyes instead, to impress his authority over me. I averted my eyes to avoid him altogether.

"Ron," Mom reigned him back in. He settled back in his seat but held his glare.

"Anyway," he said, "there's a doctor in Indiana—a gynecologist—who's familiar with the procedure. I think we should make an appointment to talk to him."

Worried that she'd agree to something she didn't seem to want just to make him happy, I watched Mom closely. She cast her eyes down to her plate. She pushed her food around some more. She clearly had some feelings she was struggling with or hiding. But then she muttered, "Okay."

Ron smiled widely, satisfied he'd gotten his way, like he always did. Then he took up a forkful of his steak.

Mom, on the other hand, looked terribly sad. I thought people were supposed to be excited about having babies, so it didn't make sense to me that she would agree to something just to make Ron happy. Immediately thinking of Bogie—the poor bulldog that was now banished to the basement—I recalled how Ron *had* to have the dog, just like Ron had to have Mom, and now both seemed utterly miserable.

For once, I was glad Ron didn't want any part of me. He seemed to have a ruinous effect on all his heart's desires.

"Out of Touch"

*T*hat Christmas, Ron had a full-size Ms. Pac-Man arcade machine delivered to the house as a present to Mom. The thrill of having the machine in our dining room distracted me from all else from then on, including Mom's consultation with the doctor in Indiana to start the process of getting Ron his baby.

I played Ms. Pac-Man from the second I was done with my homework after school until the latest I could get away with playing it at night. It was impossible to tear me away from the game. I was very competitive, so no score was high enough, despite having all the high scores the machine displayed.

So, I didn't think anything of it when I was told Mom was having a medical procedure one day. I was more excited about going home with my newest friend, Jenny, after school, anyway. She'd moved here from Switzerland and didn't know much English. The other kids made fun of her accent and her struggle with our language. It certainly took the attention off of me, but I felt bad for her. So, I befriended her, helping her learn our language. Reading and English were my best subjects.

Although Jenny lived only two blocks away, Ron picked me up after dinnertime that night. Strangely, he wasn't mad about the inconvenience of carting me around. He wasn't happy or nice either. He was something between sad and indifferent. He didn't even talk until we walked into the dark and quiet house.

"Where's Mom?" I asked. I was so used to her being in the kitchen, washing dishes.

"Sleeping," he said.

I creased my brow, thinking it was too early for her to be sleeping. I thought to ask Ron why, but he went upstairs after locking the front door. I didn't know whether he'd gone to the bathroom or gone to bed too, but the whole vibe of the house was weird. I shook it off, though, as hungry to play arcade games as Ms. Pac-Man was for those white dots neither of us could get enough of.

I pressed the button to power the machine on. The *wocka-wocka* sound of the bowed yellow circle eating dots echoed through the duplex, then Ron's heavy feet on the steps followed. I froze and turned toward the stairway.

"Not tonight," he said sternly, waving his finger. Worried for the consequence of not listening to him, I immediately turned the machine off. I watched TV in the living room instead, keeping it low enough to avoid another interaction with Ron.

The next day at school, my teacher asked me how Mom was doing.

"Fine," I said with a shrug. I hadn't seen her that morning, though. She hadn't gotten up earlier than the rest of us like she usually did. Her bedroom door remained closed after Ron had woken up. He'd told me to stay quiet because she was still sleeping, which I'd thought strange because Mom never slept in. Her car was still in the driveway when I left for the bus stop too.

So, my teacher's question made me worry that I should be more concerned about Mom's well-being. I decided I'd go into her bedroom when I got home from school, even if the door was still closed. I needed to see her for myself, to see that she really was okay.

As soon as I got off the school bus at the corner, I ran full speed down the block. Upon approaching the duplex, I noticed Mom's car in the driveway. I guessed she hadn't gone to work, which was also unusual. She never missed work. No matter what.

The house was still and quiet when I entered, just like it had been the night before and that morning. I dropped my bag on the floor and cringed at the thumping sound, hoping it hadn't woken Mom if she was still sleeping.

I opened the door to the basement and saw Bogie lying on his blanket on the landing. He raised his head hopefully. "I need to check on Mom first. Okay? Then I'll take you out," I said. He lowered his head as if he understood. I hoped he did. I felt bad that his existence had come to this.

"Mom?" I instinctively called out as I started my ascent to the second floor.

Mom came out of her bedroom, wearing a thick white robe. Her frizzy black hair was disheveled, and the purple bags under her dark eyes dimmed them even more.

"I'm sorry, Mom. I didn't know you were still sleeping," I said, even though I'd suspected she had been.

"Do you need me for something?" she muttered.

"No," I said, wondering what this slump-shouldered imposter had done with Mom. "Are you okay?"

"Yeah," Mom grumbled. Then she shuffled past me to the bathroom, her head hung lowly.

Mom had never had more than the sniffles, so I was worried about her. I went to my bedroom and tidied it while I waited for her to come out.

When she finally did, I stopped her before she closed herself back into her bedroom. "Mom?" She halted mid-step and looked up at me with a dead expression. "Are you sick or something?"

"No."

"How come you didn't go to work, then?"

A long exhale passed her lips. "The doctor is fixing me so I can have another baby—*Ron's* baby."

"Oh," I said, recalling when the subject had come up before. I guess I hadn't realized that they were actually going through with it. Then again, I didn't realize doctors could do anything to prevent or allow pregnancy at all. I thought all women could have babies when they wanted to.

"Do you need anything else before I go back to bed?" Mom asked with drowsy eyes begging for sleep.

"No," I said. I was used to being alone after school, to take the dog out and do my homework. I'd officially become a latchkey kid when I'd started at the public school, since the school bus service relieved Mom and Ron of the job.

"Okay," Mom said. Then she disappeared for a few more days.

"Little Lies"

Mom bounced back soon enough. Then she had another procedure, which she seemed to struggle to recover from just the same as the first, as well as the one after. I heard the words "reverse tubal ligation" and "D&C" too often in conversations between Mom and Ron when either of them talked on the phone or with each other. I didn't know what those were, chalking it all up to having this baby Ron suddenly wanted.

In between these procedures, Mom was pulling double duty working an office job Ron wanted her to get while simultaneously building their notary supply business, which they'd recently moved out of our basement and into a nearby strip mall. The expense of that new space added more pressure to their already stressful lives.

So, by late night, Mom would come home, lay in bed, and fall asleep to whatever was on the TV. I couldn't tell if she was that tired, or if she was in that much pain. I imagined she was a bit of both, so I didn't bother her. She'd be gone too early in the morning for us to interact. So, I pretty much never saw her anymore, except when she took me shopping with her on Saturdays and then to visit my grandmas and Juni on Sundays. The rest of the time I was usually left with Ron.

Every morning with Ron seemed to start and end in conflict.

"What are you doing?" he snarked from the kitchen table one morning.

"Making breakfast," I responded. I'd just come downstairs dressed for the day, teeth brushed. I'd even managed to tie my hair back into a low ponytail so Ron wouldn't have to do it.

"Bread?" he said with a judgmental tone. He didn't remove his stare as he sipped his coffee.

"No, French toast," I said as I slathered butter on the bread and then sprinkled cinnamon and sugar on top. I slid the two slices into the toaster oven to brown and glisten into deliciousness.

Ron set his coffee mug down but kept his fingers around the handle. "That's not how you make French toast," he said arrogantly.

"It's how *I* make it," I said, shrugging. I knew Mom made it on the stove with eggs. I was too young to use the stove, though, so I improvised.

As soon as the toaster oven dinged, I set the sweetened toast on a plate then squeezed the bottle of syrup until the bread was drowning in brown glory. I had planned to sit at the table to eat but opted for the counter instead, to avoid Ron.

"You shouldn't even be eating bread," Ron said, just as I'd taken my first bite. "It'll make you fat like your grandmas—like all Hispanic women get."

I whipped my head in his direction. I was eight years old, but I shouldn't have to tell a grown man that it was rude to insult someone's grandmas.

"Well, you're not the one eating it, so you don't have to worry about it," I said, staring right at him while I stuffed a huge forkful of my French whatever into my mouth.

"Are you talking back to me?" he asked, sitting up more erectly.

His sharp tone put me on edge. "No," I retracted. "I just—"

"You just what?" he shouted as he stood.

I swallowed my food quickly but tried not to move otherwise.

"You don't have anything to say now, huh?" he poked.

"Just leave me alone," I said, taking another bite of my toast and looking out the window over the sink so I didn't have to see the smug look on Ron's face.

"What did you just say to me?"

My body tensed while I thought about whether to repeat myself or ignore him. I knew he'd heard me, though.

"I shouldn't even have to *deal* with you!" Ron grumbled as he stood up to leave.

"Well, you don't have to, because I'm not your daughter!" I snarked back, slamming my fork down.

"You better watch your mouth!" Ron threatened, coming towards me. I backed away from his waving finger. "You're only here because your *mother* is here, and *she* doesn't even want you!"

"She does too!" I defended.

"No, she doesn't. And neither do I. So, I'm not going to tolerate your disrespect when *I'm* the one putting a roof over your head and paying for you to eat. Do you understand me?"

"My mom is the only one I have to answer to! Not *you!*" I retorted. Then I cowered to avoid the backlash, which I expected to be physical.

Ron's nostrils flared. "No wonder your mother didn't want you," he sneered before storming out of the house.

Frozen by the hateful comment, I struggled to understand how toast turned into tears. Then, as soon as I heard the rev of his engine as he accelerated down the street, I released the breath I'd been holding. I exhaled again before heading out to the bus stop at the end of the street, abandoning the toast altogether.

Even though I told myself Ron was wrong about what he'd said, his words replayed through my mind on an uncontrollable and endless loop. I couldn't dismiss the fact that Mom had never shown me the same love and affection Great-Gram always had. I'd also heard her refer to me as an "accident" before—and more than once. So, as much as I didn't want to believe Ron, the very real possibility that he was telling me the truth made me wonder why Mom couldn't love me.

"Mom?" I asked on the way to the store with her one Saturday.

"What?" she said without looking my way.

"I need to talk to you about Ron."

She huffed. "What now?" she asked, clearly tired of my complaints.

I looked down at my lap and began to pick out the dirt from underneath my fingernails. Then I gulped, recalling the words I didn't want to speak. "He, uh . . . he said you don't want me, and you don't love me, that nobody will ever love me . . ."

With upturned brows begging for her to tell me he was wrong, I looked at her, waiting for reassurance that she did love me.

"You must have misunderstood," she responded, sounding just like Ron did when he told her she was misinterpreting his family's jokes about her. "He wouldn't say those things to you."

"But he did, Mom! Those were his exact words!" I insisted.

"Dane, please. I don't need you causing trouble for me and Ron. Okay?"

"But I'm not, Mom! I'm—"

"Don't I tell you I love you almost every night before bed?"

She did say the words, but she didn't hug me or give me any other indication that she actually *felt* love for me. That's why Ron's words bothered me so much.

My other issue was that Ron lied all the time, especially if it benefited him in some way. But he spoke the truth sometimes too, like when he said he didn't want me. It wasn't a nice thing to say, nor did I like hearing it, but at least his actions followed his words, allowing me to tell the difference between his truth and his lies.

"But Mom, he—"

"But nothing!" she said sternly, cutting me off. "I'm tired of hearing about how you two can't get along!"

I slumped back into my seat with furrowed brows. I wished there was something I could say to appeal to Mom. It seemed to be a lost cause, though. She didn't want to believe me. Or maybe she did believe me and was okay with Ron treating me badly. If so, I didn't know how to feel about that. I mean, how was I supposed to love a mother who didn't love me back?

That night, I lay in my dark bedroom awake, hearing the low murmur of a conversation between Mom and Ron in their bedroom next to me.

"She said you told her I didn't want her and that I don't love her," I overheard Mom tell Ron.

"You know she's lying," Ron responded. "Like I told you before, she's probably jealous of the relationship you and I have, and . . ." I didn't hear the rest of his phony explanation over the imploring defense I imagined in my head. I couldn't make out Mom's mumbles after that either.

But I hoped she was setting him straight, telling him that she did, in fact, love me, even if she couldn't tell me the same. I hoped she could see him for the liar he was too, so he couldn't continue weaving this web of mistrust between us. The way I saw it, it was Ron that was jealous of Mom's relationship with me! It's like he wanted her all to himself! Mom had to see that for herself, though; she wouldn't accept it coming from me, being that I was a jealous liar and all.

The next day, we were driving to my grandmas' apartment in Chicago for our Sunday visit when Mom said, "I talked to Ron about what you said yesterday."

"You did?" I said as I turned down the radio, pretending I knew nothing about it. I didn't want to miss any part of her telling me she'd finally put an end to Ron's mistreatment of me, or the end of her relationship with Ron altogether.

"Yeah. And he said he never said those things to you." She looked over at me with reproach.

"Well, he did. He's lying to you," I asserted.

Mom tilted her head and looked at me with pressed lips. "Ron wouldn't lie to me," she said, apparently forgetting about Ron's first wife, whom he'd forgotten to mention to Mom for the entire first year they'd dated.

"Well, he did," I repeated. I knew what I'd heard. I'd been there. She hadn't. And I stood firm in my truth.

"I know I'm busy with work and everything," she lectured, "but it's not okay for you to tell lies like that. And it's not okay for you to call your dad a liar either."

"But I'm not lying, Mom! You have to believe me!" I said with increasing frustration at her refusal to side with me on anything. "And he's not my dad!"

"That's enough," she said harshly.

Frustration silenced me for the remainder of the ride. I was just a kid, but even I could see how he was manipulating her into believing what he wanted her to think. I didn't understand why, though. What was he trying to gain? What would Mom loving me inhibit in his life? What would happen if this baby they wanted ever came? Would he be jealous of his own child too?

I told myself to stop asking so many questions, like the nuns at the Catholic school demanded when I asked who God's mommy and daddy were. I didn't have any reasonable answers, anyway, and neither had they. They'd told me I just had to accept what was. I couldn't accept Mom believing Ron, though. Then again, lying was a sin, and sinners went to hell. So, I guessed I just had to have faith in God to do with Ron what He would. And not ask questions about it.

"Say It Isn't So"

Ron continued to berate me with his negative assertions every morning, adding that my real dad didn't want me any more than Mom did. He'd say no one would ever love me, and that I was stupid, incompetent, incapable, and every other diminishing insult in between.

The upset of Ron's words, or simply being in his presence anymore, was causing me chronic headaches and stomachaches. Sometimes they were so bad I'd ask my teacher to go to the nurse, instead of sitting in class with my hands on my stomach or holding my head in my hands at my desk. The nurse would give me a peppermint candy to calm my stomach, but she couldn't give me anything for my head without permission from Mom. The one time I had insisted the nurse call her to come get me, I'd been sent back to class without resolve. I guessed Mom had told the nurse it was all a ruse to get attention, like Ron had convinced her. So, I learned to deal with the dull pains instead of dealing with the consequence of my constant complaints.

It angered me that everyone believed Ron, especially Mom. He had a way of speaking like he knew everything, so people mistook his arrogance for intelligence. Mom was a lot younger than him too and had little education and life experience, so I think she assumed he was older and wiser, since he carried himself that way. And I couldn't compete with that—any of it.

Nor could I let go of the feeling that I hadn't been meant to exist. Maybe that's why I felt so out of place, why I didn't belong. It also made sense of why Mom never got too close to me. But she was my mother; it was her job to love me, even if no one else ever did.

So, on a Saturday morning, when I knew Ron was off to wherever he disappeared to, I came out of my bedroom in search of my maker. She had just begun her weekly house cleaning in the dining room. I sat on the landing of the stairway, which overlooked the combined living and dining rooms. With my chin in cupped hands and elbows on my knobby knees, I waited for her to notice me.

"What's up, Dane?" she said, pushing her frizzy bangs out of her face.

"Did you want me?" I blurted.

"What?" she asked, having been caught off guard by my frankness.

I straightened up then and fumbled my fingers nervously in my lap. "Ron said you didn't want me. Is that true?"

"Ron said that?" Mom asked with a tilted head.

"Yes," I stated with firm resolution.

"I'm sure he didn't—" She stopped short of whatever excuse she was about to offer and released a lengthy sigh. She sat back on her heels and looked at me with a seriousness I heeded. "Okay. Look. It's not that I didn't want you, Dane. I just didn't . . . I was young. *Too* young. To have a baby, at least," she said.

"Why *did* you have me, then?"

"I didn't have a choice," she said.

"You could've given me up for adoption. The Chinese girl down the block said her real mom didn't want her, so she was adopted."

After a long pause, Mom admitted, "I thought about it. There was a couple who wanted you, and when I went to the hospital to have you, I was ready to give you to them."

I gulped. That was hard to hear, especially when she still didn't demonstrate any particular fondness for me. "Why didn't you?" I asked.

Mom huffed. "Because your grandma and Great-Gram wouldn't let me," she finally admitted. "You were the first grandchild and great-grandchild to them, and they said no child in our family would be raised by strangers."

I perked up. "*They* wanted me, then?"

"Yeah," Mom said, nodding. "Your grandma said she'd get a job to pay for you, and Great-Gram agreed to take care of you, since she was already helping Sonia with Aaron anyway."

My eyes widened and brightened as everything began to make sense to me. I was meant to be here, even if I was an "accident." I was wanted. I did belong, at least with my grandmas. All of which meant, to a certain extent, that Ron was wrong.

"But what about my real dad?" I wondered out loud, recalling Ron saying he hadn't wanted me either.

"You don't need to worry about him," Mom said in a forbidding tone. "And don't bring him up again. Okay? Especially not in front of Ron."

She penetrated me with a stern stare. I nodded but kept my head down, feeling ashamed for having trodden on what was obviously a delicate subject. I couldn't help but wonder what it was about my real dad that had to be hidden, though. Especially from Ron. As far as I was aware, the two had never met.

Assuming it was just another one of Mom's attempts to pretend Ron was my real dad, I accepted the situation for what it was. Her happiness seemed to hinge on my cooperation with the facade, anyway. So, I stopped asking questions and kept my big mouth shut. That seemed to be the only way to ensure peace around here.

"Our Lips Are Sealed"

Aside from a fishing trip to Ontario, Canada—where I'd caught the biggest walleye with my little Snoopy fishing rod—Mom and Ron were always working. So, by the time I started fourth grade in the fall of 1984, I had learned to take care of myself. I got up, brushed my teeth, dressed, ate, and made it to the bus stop at the end of the street on time. I'd even convinced Mom to let me get a boy-short haircut, relieving us all from having to deal with my long locks anymore. Then, I let myself in after school too.

I'd take Bogie out for a walk or leave him in the small side yard to get some fresh air. Then I did my homework on the living room floor in front of the T.V. I'd make myself a cup of hot cocoa (the kind with the tiny marshmallows in it) and maybe grab a cookie or two (or three) and turn on cartoons for background noise. I'd usually finish my homework by the time *Benson* or *WKRP in Cincinnati* came on. Benson made me laugh, and Lonnie Anderson's beautiful blonde hair made me envious for the same luxurious look. She and Tom Selleck made the most handsome couple. I had a crush on Corey Haim, though. I had a poster of him on my bedroom wall, right next to the one with "The Karate Kid."

If Mom wasn't home to make me something to eat by then, I'd heat up leftovers (if there were any), or boil and butter noodles since that was all I knew how to make on the stove. But if Ron came home first, I'd just go up to my bedroom and lock the door to avoid him altogether, thereby protecting my newfound peace.

It was lonely, though. Every once in a while, I got to go to Kelly's house to play. She lived too far away to walk there, so we had to plan in advance. The girl from Switzerland was always too busy. I played with one of the neighborhood kids a lot. I couldn't go there until my homework was finished, though, and the girl's family was usually eating dinner by then. So, I often wondered if Mom would ever have a baby, so I could have a little sister to play with. I'd have no use for a little brother, though any company would be welcome.

As such, I looked forward to shopping with Mom on Saturdays and visiting Great-Gram on Sundays. On our way to Great-Gram's one weekend, the song "Sister Golden Hair" came on the radio. Mom scrambled to turn the knob. Her furrowed brow relaxed once she settled on a popular song by Prince.

"You didn't like that other song, huh?" I joked as I moved my shoulders to the catchy beat of the guitar riff playing now.

"It just . . ." Mom hesitated.

"I didn't like that song either. It doesn't even sound like all the other oldies on that station," I commented.

"It's not that," Mom said.

I looked over at her, expecting her to elaborate. She didn't, looking out at the traffic ahead of her instead with glazed eyes that seemed to be somewhere else.

"What is it, then?" I prodded.

Mom came out of her trance and sighed. "That song. It just reminds me of . . ." She shook her head, as if doing so would erase the memory from her mind like an Etch A Sketch.

I sat there wondering how a song could so quickly change Mom's mood from carefree to somber when, just a minute before, she'd been smiling and laughing while belting out "Rockin' Robin" with me and the radio. So, what was it about that old seventies song?

"That song reminds me of your biological father," Mom muttered, answering my unspoken thought. I was surprised she'd brought him up at all but took her initiative as permission.

"I know you told me not to talk about him, but . . ." I started, treading lightly.

"That song was playing one of the last times he was supposed to come see you," she offered.

"Supposed to?"

"He never showed up." I didn't miss the resentment in her tone.

I'm sure he'd had a reason, though. Something had to have happened that Mom just didn't know about.

"I wonder if I'll ever meet him," I accidentally said out loud. Mom scowled at me. "I'm sorry," I said. "I can't help but wonder about him!"

I cringed at how Mom pressed her lips together. Then I looked down and fumbled with my fingers. I hadn't meant to make her upset. I just didn't know how to tell her how confused I was about how I fit into the world. I mean, I wasn't like her. We didn't connect. Nothing about us made sense of her being my mother. And I wasn't Ron's daughter. That had been made clear to me in every way possible.

After a long moment of silence, Mom finally said, "You look a lot like him. I see him in your eyes, the color of your hair, your smile . . ."

I turned my head slightly to hide my smirk. Those superficial similarities made me feel like I was a part of him, even if I didn't know him.

"He is very tall, though," she shared. "And his eyes are green."

These few details were like puzzle pieces I could put together to form a clearer image of him. Up until now, he'd been an abstract idea. But the more I knew, the more real he became.

"He was into drugs, though," Mom continued. "He tried to tell everyone his dad was killed by the mob. Everyone knew he was lying, even though his dad was from Italy."

I dropped my head in disappointment. Our school had a "Say No to Drugs" program wherein a policeman would come talk to us once a week about how bad it is to take drugs. He said it messes up the way your brain works and makes you do things that will get you locked up in jail. So, I guess I'd built my dad up so much in my head I thought he could do no wrong. But then again, if he was so bad, why did Mom make me with him? So, I asked.

Mom looked at me sternly. Then she said, "We weren't *trying* to make you." The frustration and scorn in her tone was hard to miss. "What he did . . . well . . ."

"What?" I pressed.

Mom gripped the steering wheel a little tighter. Something was clearly upsetting her. He must have done something really awful. I wasn't even sure I wanted to know anymore. I didn't want to think my dad was capable of making Mom feel like this.

"There was a party . . . and some drugs . . . he'd been drinking . . ." she said. Tears welled in Mom's eyes as her words drifted into thoughts she wouldn't speak. Then she instantly returned to reality and said, "No more questions, Dane."

For once, I listened. I looked back down at my fumbling fingers and kept my mouth shut.

No one in the family ever spoke of my dad. It's like he'd never existed. Great-Gram was always honest with me, though. So, I decided to ask her about him when I sat with her in her bedroom that afternoon.

"Great-Gram? Can I ask you something? About my real dad?"

"*Pues . . .*" she said, elongating the word as she always did. "*Qué quieres saber?*" Great-Gram's round glasses took up nearly the top half of her face, but somehow her skinny gray brows rose above them.

"It's about my dad," I said, scrunching one side of my face before proceeding. "Did he ever come around after I was born? I mean, did he even know about me?"

"Oh, yes!" she responded with a certainty that surprised me.

"Really?"

"He came to visit you *many* times. From the time you were born until you were about one and a half years old!"

"Hmm," I sounded, resenting that nobody had told me this before.

"He'd put you up on top of his shoulders and carry you around. It would make your grandma so nervous because she thought he would drop you. He was so tall, that man," she said, giggling at the memory. Imagining the scenario in my head softened the upset I'd felt a moment before.

"What happened to make him stop coming to see me, then?" I asked, recalling Mom's claim that he just hadn't shown up that last time.

Great-Gram put her finger to her pursed lips and nodded toward the dining room.

"Mom?" I mouthed for confirmation. Great-Gram nodded.

I hadn't figured the deterrent was a "who."

"*Entonces . . .*" Great-Gram said, hinting that it was time to change the subject. So, I dropped the interrogation. Yet, I couldn't help but think there was a big secret about my dad that no one would tell me.

Later that evening, I was in my room getting ready for bed when Mom knocked lightly before opening the door just enough to poke her head in.

"Here, Dane," she said in a low voice.

"What?" I asked, staring at the small white envelope she offered through the cracked door.

"Just take it," she said hurriedly. Then she looked over her shoulder at nothing and no one.

Taking the hint that whatever was in that envelope was to be kept secret from Ron, I took it before we could be discovered. Then she closed the door and left me to myself.

I looked down at the mysterious envelope, wondering what it held that Mom was so worried about Ron knowing about. I wasn't sure I even wanted something that *she* was fearful of him seeing, not if it could get *me* in trouble too. That just made me want to open it even more, though!

I stared at it first, noticing how worn and slightly yellowed the exterior of it was. It had been opened long ago and torn slightly as it had come unglued from where it had been sealed. There were no words written on it, which meant Mom hadn't wanted anyone to ever suspect it of being anything but some old and unimportant remnant she hoped no one would think anything of.

Carefully opening the triangular closure, I saw an old wallet-size photo inside. Although tattered and out of focus, like the envelope it had been stored in, two unrecognizable teenage boys stared back at me. Wearing jeans and T-shirts and long hippie hair, they looked like they were just hanging out, without a care in the world. I had no idea who they were, though.

Recalling that Mom always put names and years on the back of any photos she developed, I turned the photo over. It read: *Dan—1975.*

Dan was my biological father's name. And I was born in 1975.

Gasping as I frantically flipped the picture back over to see which of the two boys was my dad, I focused on the boy who was significantly taller than the other. That had to be him!

I held the photo up to my face, squinting to clarify his blurry image. I needed to memorize every detail of him. I also wanted to see what parts of myself were visible in him, to know for sure that he was real and that I'd come from him.

Aside from his tall stature, he was lean and lanky. His hair was just as thin, falling straight to his shoulders. It was the same light-to-medium brown as my hair, though mine was wavy. He wore a shy grin, as if he'd just made a snide remark he thought funny. With his shoulders slumped forward, I could tell he was easygoing and relaxed. He had a twinkle in his eyes that endeared me to him. They were the same shape as mine too.

This *is* my dad, I thought. He looked like the kind of man I could love. Better yet, he looked like the kind of dad who would love *me*.

But then I wondered if the similarities in our appearance the reason Mom couldn't love me. I mean, I was the physical manifestation of her biggest regret in life, her biggest mistake, the hindrance to her happiness. So, how *could* she love me? And if she didn't love me, why would Ron?

Suddenly feeling lowly about myself, I tucked the picture back in the envelope and put it away where no one would ever find it. As much as I'd wanted to see him, to know who he was and that he'd even existed, I couldn't look at him. I couldn't even look at myself right now.

"You Can't Always Get What You Want"

I couldn't let go of the feeling that there was still some big secret about my real dad or the past that no one wanted to talk about. So, while Mom folded laundry in the living room a couple weeks later, I plopped on the bottom stair, hoping to find the last few pieces to the puzzle of my existence. Ron wasn't home, anyway.

"What's up, Dane?" Mom asked as she shook a towel and brought the corners together. She wore her black cropped 97.9 "The Loop" radio station T-shirt, which was the only piece of clothing she still had that was true to who she really was. She never wore it out, though; she dressed much more conservatively when Ron was around.

"Nothing much," I said, resting my chin in my hands, bony elbows on skinned knees.

Mom eyed me sideways.

"Okay," I said since my cover was blown. "I feel like there's some secret about you and my real dad and how I was made that makes me different, and I want to know what it is."

"Why does it matter?"

"I don't know. It just does," I said with a shrug. "Like, were you two boyfriend and girlfriend? Or were you . . ." I stopped talking when Mom stopped folding.

"We knew each other from school," she said shortly.

"But did you date, or were you just friends?"

"We dated," she said like I was stupid for not assuming the obvious. "But when I found out I was pregnant, my dad—your grandfather—

thought *your* dad should marry me to make it right."

"Okay . . ."

"Your dad and his mother didn't agree, though," she said with high-browed expectation I didn't understand. I thought people got married because they loved each other. Why would she want someone to marry her out of obligation?

"What did *his* dad think?" I asked, since I'd only heard my dad's mother mentioned.

"He died when your dad was ten or eleven."

"Oh," I said with regret, instinctively dropping my head in respect.

"That's why your dad did drugs and drank so much," Mom stated as if it were fact only those close to my dad would have been privy to.

"So, you and my dad knew each other from school. You dated. Ended up at a party together, where he did drugs and drank alcohol—which you're saying he did all the time," I summarized to see if it made sense I couldn't see. "The two of you made me. He wouldn't marry you . . . I still don't get what happened that was so bad that you hate him so much."

"Hate him?"

"Yeah," I said.

"I've never said a bad word about him!"

"You've never said a nice thing about him either," I snarked back with a raised brow.

"You know, Dane," Mom said with a tone accusing me of betrayal, "I was the one who suffered. I was the one who had to drop out of high school because everyone was calling me a whore. I was the one who got kicked out of my house and—"

"You got kicked out of the house?" I asked, disbelieving that my grandma would do that to her only daughter and that Great-Gram would allow that to happen at all. I couldn't know whether my grandfather would do that because I didn't know much about him, aside from being told he was a drunk who had supposedly left me in a bar by myself when I was three years old to leave with a woman who wasn't my grandma. Still, I couldn't imagine anyone throwing their pregnant daughter out to fend for herself.

"Yes! I had to live in a shelter when I was pregnant with you," she said with a slight whimper, "while he got to go on and live his life like nothing happened!"

I thought of the movie *Trading Places*, in which Eddie Murphy played a beggar on the streets of New York. I'd never imagined that Mom had ever had to live like that. When I thought of her cold and starving and having no place to go, however, it made me sad. I dropped my head, wondering if she blamed me for having to endure that.

"You were born at the Salvation Army Hospital in Chicago," Mom continued. "If it weren't for them, who knows what would have happened?!"

I'd have probably ended up dead or in a dumpster, I guessed. I made a pointed decision right then to put all my extra change in those red buckets the Salvation Army had people ring bells at during the holidays.

"I'm sorry, Mom," I mumbled. I hadn't meant to bring up all this sorrow.

"I hope you are, Dane," Mom said, "because you have all this curiosity about your real dad. But he's not who you think he is. He's no one you want to know. Trust me."

I wished I did trust Mom, but her inconsistent behavior didn't make me feel like I could. This wasn't the time to talk about *that*, though.

"His friend even offered to marry me since he wouldn't," Mom went on. "Even he saw that I'd been wronged by your father."

"Why didn't you marry *him*, then?" I asked.

"Because your *father* should have been the one to take responsibility for what he did," she said. "I guess I should be glad we didn't get married, though. He probably still drinks and does drugs."

I ignored the presumption, instead asking the only other question I had. "I've heard you talk about 'what he did' to you before. So, is that why you hate him so much? Because he didn't marry you like you thought he should?"

Mom whipped her head towards me. Her narrowed eyes held a scathing I cowered from. "You really want to know? Will that satisfy you, so you stop asking all these questions?"

I nodded my head slowly.

"Fine. I'll tell you, then. When your biological father and I . . . got together . . . well, let's just say it's not what *I* wanted."

I think I understood what she was saying. I'd seen enough R-rated movies and TV shows to know that men sometimes forced women to do things in private that the women didn't want to do. But if that had been the case with Mom, then why would she think marrying my dad was a good idea?

I needed to know the truth, though. So, with fearful reluctance, I dared ask, "Are you saying you were—?"

"I'm saying, Dana, that sometimes drugs and alcohol make people do things they shouldn't do."

Mom wasn't making sense, which made me wonder whether she even knew what really happened the day I was conceived. "Was it just him using the drugs and alcohol at that party?" I asked with a cringe.

Mom's huff and stare, implying my audacity to have even thought her capable of either, was blatant.

"So, you were aware of what was happening," I stated, trying to make sense of her vague and confusing implications.

"That doesn't mean I *wanted* it to."

The sound of the front door opening and closing shut us up. Mom gave me an intense look too, conveying that the conversation was over now that Ron was home. So, I never got my answer, nor did Mom give me that last piece of the puzzle I so desperately needed to complete the story of my existence.

"When Doves Cry"

few months later, I was drawing in Mom's office on a Saturday morning. Ron had taken Bogie to some game at his eldest niece's high school, to serve as the mascot for the Bulldogs. I thought it odd that he hadn't invited us to come—unless he had, and Mom declined like she often did whenever something came up with his family anymore. She said she had some office work to do anyway, so I'd tagged along with her to avoid the boredom of being home alone.

There wasn't much excitement at Mom's office either. They'd rented two offices and an industrial space in the rear of a barber shop. Two wood-laminate and black metal desks were crammed into this office—one for Mom and one for the blonde woman they'd hired to help her. The other office was filled with multiple metal shelving units containing papers, stamp pads, chubby neon highlighters, and other office supplies I used for whatever entertainment they could provide to pass the time.

Mom and I were listening to a cassette tape she'd bought me because the rapper's name was Dana Dane. It wasn't bad, but I didn't mind her turning it down to take an incoming call.

"Hello and thank you for calling . . ." Mom answered with her cheery well-rehearsed greeting. She introduced the company name and hers with exactly the same intonation every time. I usually heard an "uh-huh" or "I can help you with that" afterward. So, when I heard silence, I turned to look at Mom, whose grim expression made me think she'd just seen a ghost.

"Hold on," she murmured to whomever was on the other end. Then she turned to me and ordered, "I need you to leave the room while I take this." Her seriousness told me not to question her, so I took my papers and a handful of markers to the hallway, wondering what I wasn't supposed to hear.

"I'm back," I heard her say from the other side of the wall. "No, I don't want anything! . . . Well, what do you want me to tell her? . . . I *didn't* bring anything up. She's been asking questions, and—"

This obviously wasn't a business call.

"I am not trying to get money from you!" I heard her raise her voice. "I'm married now and have my own business," she continued, "so I don't need anything from *either* of you!"

No one in the family had any money she could take. She didn't have any friends either. She barely said hello to *my* friends' parents when dropping me off or picking me up from their houses. The last time I'd seen her socialize was when we hung out with the lady she worked with at the office where she'd met Ron. That lady had been her maid of honor in their wedding. Since the wedding, however, Mom hadn't seen her or anyone else in any social capacity.

"I wouldn't have contacted you at all if it were up to me, but she keeps asking about him, and I'm the one who has to deal with her curiosity!"

Oh my god! Was that my dad on the phone? How did he have Mom's office number, unless she'd given it to him? Have they been communicating all this time without me knowing it? Why would mom keep that from me? I went to the doorway of her office, hoping to confirm whether it was him, because if it was, I wanted to talk to him myself!

When Mom saw me, she extended the phone cord across the room and slammed the door in my face. I didn't miss her teary eyes and accusing glare. So, I couldn't help feeling like it was my fault that she was upset. The yelling I only heard parts of didn't help ease the guilt. Nor did the sound of the phone being slammed down into its receiver.

The office door burst open then. I looked up at Mom, who stared back at me with contempt.

"I don't ever want to hear about your biological father again! Okay?" she yelled. Then she went back into the office.

I rushed in after her, intent on lashing back about my right to know my dad but halted when I saw her sitting at her desk with her face in her hands. "Mom?" I asked warily. "Was that him? Was that my dad?"

She turned her head towards me, with painful slowness reminiscent of the possessed girl in *The Exorcist*. Then, with narrow-eyed scorn, she said, "No. That was his *mother*."

I had another grandma? Mom had mentioned my dad's mother before, but I never considered her relation to me. Realizing it now, though, it was like I had a whole other family! I mean, if I had a dad and a grandma, I probably had aunts and uncles and cousins, maybe even siblings I didn't know about! So, now I wanted to know all of them that much more!

This discovery circled my thoughts back to how my new grandma had the phone number to Mom's office. And how had she known Mom would be here today?

I asked the most obvious question of all that begged to be answered. "What did she call you for?"

After a huff and a shake of her head, Mom looked at me with narrowed eyes. "She called because of *you*."

"She did?" I said, twisting my fingers in the bottom hem of my fitted T-shirt. I'm not even sure why I was nervous. I hadn't done anything to deserve Mom's blame.

"Yeah," Mom reproached. "I got in touch with her because you keep asking all these questions about your real dad. And I thought that maybe if you met them, you'd see what kind of people they are and just drop it already."

"So, do they? Do they want to meet me?" I asked, raising my brows as high as my hope.

"Do you see me right now?" Mom said nastily.

I nodded slowly.

"Well, then, it's obvious that they don't, isn't it?" she reprimanded. "According to your biological father's mother, I'm just a whore looking to pin her son as your father to get money out of them. Do you understand now why I don't want anything to do with him?" she shrieked.

Open-mouthed and afraid, my tensed body cowered from her harsh words. I'd never seen Mom so angry. So, I couldn't be sure she wouldn't hit me like Ron did when he was mad.

"I'm sorry, Mom!" I pleaded. "I didn't mean—"

She cut me off. "You never mean anything, do you?"

Repetitive sniffles, quick matching breaths, and salty tears felt every bit of her scathe. "I don't understand why you're mad at *me*, Mom."

"You don't understand anything. You don't understand what I went through when I got pregnant with you! You don't understand how it felt when your dad denied he was your father and when his mother accused me of sleeping around and trying to pin the pregnancy on him. You don't understand the humiliation I felt when everyone at school called me a whore after that! It was awful, Dana! It was—"

Mom broke down into tears then. I didn't know what to say. I was inclined to go to her, to hold her, to tell her I was sorry again. She wasn't much for affection, though. Not like me, who was starving for some right now.

Instead, I retreated to the hallway and sat on the floor. I pulled up my knees, laid my head in them, and cried, careful not to be heard. I doubted Mom could hear me over her own sobs anyway. I couldn't compete with that kind of pain.

"We're Not Going to Take It"

Mom didn't speak to me for a few days. Not unless she absolutely had to. She wouldn't even look at me. Ron ignored me too, except that he shot me hateful glares of disapproval at every opportunity, to ensure I knew that Mom's upset was my fault. So, for all our sakes, I spent most of my time locked in my bedroom, where I couldn't affect anyone.

That's when I fell in love with music. I'd always loved dancing to it. I liked singing too, but my choral skills were as good as the sounds I'd croaked out of my squeaky recorder in second grade. The lyrics were what really spoke to me, though; I was intrigued by how skillfully artists could craft words into conduits for emotions that couldn't otherwise be explained. I even started writing my own, using verbiage, word play, and symbolism to express my feelings about the tense relations at home. It was the only safe outlet I had since I was scared Mom and Ron would punish me if I'd spoken to anyone about my feelings instead. From all appearances, we were as normal a family as anyone else, despite the fact that we weren't.

So, I was thrilled when my fifth-grade class was introduced to different musical instruments, in case we wanted to take lessons at school and participate in the school band or orchestra.

After the music teacher demonstrated the variety of string, percussion, and wind instruments, I was firmly set on playing the cello. The deep tones bellowing through the wood expressed a bold but agonizing lament that resonated with me. It sounded like I would sound if I were an instrument.

The music teacher said I was too small to handle even the smallest size cello, though. I sat with one between my legs, willing my tiny fingers to stretch around the neck enough to reach all four strings, desperate to prove her wrong. She maintained her position and recommended I try the viola instead. Probably the most unpopular and unknown orchestral figure, it was small like a violin and held just the same. It had the deeper tone of the cello, though, sharing strings with it and the violin. I could easily wrap my fingers around its skinny neck to play it. It was much easier to carry around too. So, I decided it would suffice and took the permission slip home to Mom.

"No!" Ron said after I gave Mom my sales pitch to sign the permission slip that evening. I glared at him, suddenly annoyed by how he always sat in the wooden kitchen chair as if it were his throne.

"Why not?" I asked, challenging his authority.

"Because I said so!" Ron responded.

He wasn't my father, so he didn't get to decide anything about my life for me. I hadn't asked him to sign the permission slip, anyway. I'd asked Mom, who'd gone to the adjacent foyer. I went out to appeal to her.

"But everyone else is gonna play in band or orchestra," I whined as I watched her straighten the pile of shoes by the front door.

"So, if everyone else jumped off a bridge, you would too?" Mom asked me.

I pressed my lips together and tossed my head and hip to one side. "But Mom!" I whined, as if those two words would beg her to take this more seriously. She had to understand that this was about me being a part of something and finding my place somewhere.

The creak of Ron's chair warned me to stand down. I stepped back towards the stairway as he approached.

"What did your mother just tell you?" he scolded, waving his finger near my face.

"Mom?" I begged for her intervention. She had moved to the coat closet to put her purse and jacket away, acting as if she was completely oblivious to what was happening just a foot behind her. Even the mirrored closet doors called her bluff.

"Mom!" I shouted to get her attention.

At that, she turned and reproved, "What do you want me to say, Dane? If Ron says no, then—"

"I don't care what Ron says!" I boldly asserted. "*You're* my mother. It's *your* decision, not *his!*"

"Dane . . ." she said, her eyes darting to Ron and then back at me. I took that as her discrete way of warning me not to provoke Ron's anger any more than I already had. Then she threw in, "And I told you to call him 'Dad' from now on."

"Maybe if he acted like one . . ." I started to threaten. But then Ron seized my upper arm and wrenched it around like he was trying to rip it out of its socket.

"OW!" I screamed as I tried to wrestle myself out of his grip.

"You . . ." he seethed.

"Get your hands off me!" I shouted as I writhed in Ron's iron grip. I looked around for Mom to save me, but she was gone.

"You better—" Ron began to threaten before I cut him off.

"Just stop!" I shrieked. Then, by some grace, he released me.

I scrambled up the stairs on all fours, so fast that I tripped down a couple. Once in my bedroom, I slammed the door shut. Then I stood with my back against it, breathing hard and fast.

"No! I won't allow her to talk to me that way! This is *my* house!" I heard Ron holler below. Mom had obviously found some decency within her to say something to him. I'd just wish I'd heard her defense of me, since I didn't think she'd ever had one.

They went back and forth for a few minutes. Mom rarely raised her voice, so I only heard the murmur of it, followed by Ron's loud retorts, which all sounded the same. When they'd finished to seemingly no resolve, I heard Ron's heavy feet pounding up the stairs. I pushed the button on my doorknob to lock it, thinking he was coming for me. Then I stood still, instinctively holding my breath, as if doing so would prevent him from detecting my presence.

The sudden blare of the "Where's the beef?" commercial coming from the TV in their bedroom disrupted the silence. My chest heaved as I exhaled. Then I listened a few seconds more to make sure I was safe.

I crawled into bed, hoping to calm down. I nodded off but woke up intermittently. The slightest shudder of wind against the window or click of the furnace igniting would startle me awake then leave me lying there with anxious anticipation that the next sound would be Ron coming to punish me. So, I couldn't sleep too deeply or too well. That's how it was most nights now, though.

When I went down to the kitchen the next morning, I noticed the permission slip on the counter. Mom had signed it! She'd gone against Ron, making her own decision for once. I was thrilled with the favor and proud of her independent move, and I exhibited the same confident pride when I turned the form into my teacher with the majority of my class that day. For once, I wasn't the odd man out.

But then my music teacher asked, "What's that bruise on your wrist?"

Averting my eyes to the same place the kids sitting around me stared down at, I saw a dull purplish-brown oval covering the entirety of my wrist like a watch. I had felt the soreness earlier but had been so caught up in the excitement of having my mom's permission to play viola that I hadn't noticed the imprint Ron had left on my pale skin.

Embarrassed at the unwanted attention and worried my teacher would ask more questions, I said, "I put a watch on too tight, and . . ." Then I pulled the cuff of my pink shirt over the mark.

"Oh, goodness!" she said. "Better be more careful next time!" Then she went about her task collecting the permission slips.

Relieved at the close call, I exhaled but remembered to hold my shirt cuff with my fingers the rest of the day to prevent anyone else from noticing the mark.

The school had arranged for everyone to rent their instrument of choice from a particular music store. So, Mom drove me there the next evening. She was quiet and expressionless. She didn't sing along with me to the songs on the radio. She didn't seem to be too happy at all.

Although I assumed her decision had caused an issue with Ron, nothing could dispirit me. I was all smiles as the man at the shop measured the length of my arm and placed different-sized violas under my chin to assess my ability to reach across the four strings comfortably.

Once a suitable size had been determined, the man put a long bow in my other hand and positioned my fingers in a particularly strange way at the base. Then he placed the horsehair on the strings and moved my hand like a puppet to make the instrument bellow. I smiled widely and wondrously at the sounds I'd made with this scrolled-end hollowed wood. I looked at Mom excitedly, hoping she'd witnessed my first notes. She looked on disinterestedly, which was disappointing, but I was getting something I wanted, which I wasn't accustomed to. So, I accepted her presence for what it was, holding my chin higher than usual as she signed the rental agreement.

Despite our strained relationship, that viola represented our united front against Ron. It proved we still had a connection too, even if it was just by a (horse) hair.

"One Thing Leads to Another"

Ron gave me the silent treatment again. He glared at me whenever we crossed paths, to make me fully aware of his disdain. It was a welcome change from the usual snide remarks about what I ate for breakfast or what a nuisance I was, so it didn't bother me as much as it usually did.

It was a sign that I'd won this battle too. It just made me sad that we were at war at all, because we didn't have to be. Ron could sometimes be really funny, like the time he'd put two of his birthday candles in his nose and made a face that made me keel over laughing. He and Mom had taken me to Disney World over a school break too. He'd let Mom buy me a Minnie Mouse sweatshirt, and then I hit the jackpot when I had my picture taken with Cinderella when we visited her castle!

Seeing as Ron could sometimes be a fun and loving father figure, I couldn't understand why he chose to diminish me at every opportunity. I would have respected my doting stepfather and been eager to achieve all I could to make him proud of me. Instead, I was overachieving, hoping something I accomplished would qualify me to be *enough* for him and Mom. Maybe then they wouldn't need to keep trying to have a baby of their own.

Ron's approval was the key to getting Mom's, and that approval was what I understood to be essential to securing my position as their daughter in our family. With that goal clearly in focus, my viola became my new best friend. Mastering it would make Ron and Mom see that I was worthy of their pride, and that I was a daughter worthy of their affections. In the meantime, it gave me a sense of achievement when I could correctly read the notes on the pages of music and use my fingers and bow strokes to successfully bring the black dots to life. So, I spent most of my fifth-grade year practicing my new craft but only when no one was home. I didn't want to hear Ron's rude remarks about my elementary level of musicianship, and Mom seemed indifferent to any talent I exhibited.

My diligent efforts paid off at school, though. The lady who gave lessons there would sometimes play duets with me. It was just like dancing in the way we had to be cognizant of the other's next move and timing, to create interactive melodies and harmonies that swelled with emotion. It made me feel connected to another person in a way I didn't feel in real life. At least not at home.

Participating in the school orchestra took that feeling to the next level. Instead of just two, dozens of us had to play off each other in a certain sync to make Bach and Beethoven's artistic ensembles transform from scribbles to correlating chords that whispered or roared depending on the conductor's instruction. It was almost magical.

Despite Mom's disinterest, I was eager for her to see me play with the orchestra at the 1986 spring music concert. Once she saw what I could do and what the lot of us accomplished together, she would recognize my talent and praise me for it.

Unfortunately, she'd got caught up at work that night. We arrived at the school so late the orchestra was already playing when we walked in. I halted as soon as I heard the familiar music, thinking I'd missed the opportunity to perform what I'd spent so much time practicing to perfection.

The principal—a kind older man with white hair and thin gold-framed glasses—was standing just outside the full gymnasium, watching the performance. He glanced to greet whoever had come into the school. When he saw me wearing a white button-up shirt and black skirt and holding my viola case in my hand, it immediately registered that I was supposed to be part of the orchestra playing.

So, he waved me over, led me into the gymnasium, then walked me up to the stage. The entire place watched me take out my instrument, tune it, and then wait for the principal to bring a chair out for me to sit in. The concert resumed then, but the embarrassment of having so much attention focused on me and my lateness overshadowed any sense of glory I'd had before. I just wanted to crawl into a hole and die.

After playing the one and only song I'd been present to participate in, I put my viola back in its case at the side of the stage while my classmates filed out into the hallway. I had to elbow my way through the band kids and their much more cumbersome instruments to escape the scrutiny of the hundreds watching from the bleachers.

"You ruined the whole thing!" one boy said, sneering as he passed me in the hall to catch up with his friends.

It was bad enough I was the only Hispanic kid and illegitimate bastard child born to an unwed mother who was now wed to an older man who'd divorced his wife to marry his young mistress. I'd recently been labeled "poor" as well, since a popular girl asked where I'd gotten an outfit I'd worn, and I'd made the mistake of telling her it was from Kmart. And now this.

I kept my head down to avoid eye contact and interaction, taking my time to help return the music room to its usual order until the concert was over. Then I exited the school in search of Mom, hoping to make a quick escape from the glares, comments, and snickers I could hear behind me.

Thankfully, spinning blue-and-red lights in the parking lot across the street captured everyone's attention instead, including mine. Ron had parked in that lot.

"Dana!" I heard. I turned to where I'd heard Mom call for me. She rushed over and took my free hand with an urgency I didn't comprehend. "Come on," she said, practically pulling me directly towards the police cars.

No, no! I thought, worried more about my perceived connection to the crime scene than whatever the cops were there for. I could only imagine what would be said about me if my classmates and their families thought we were criminals too! I pulled on Mom's hand, but she tightened her grip on mine, leading me directly to Ron, who was talking to two police officers next to what was left of his precious Nissan 300ZX.

The windshield and windows of Ron's prized possession had taken a beating they hadn't survived. Shattered glass lay all around the car, reflecting like crystals off the police officers' flashlights and spinners. Their lights showed the leather interior of the car too, scratched and torn and piled with shards.

Ron looked like he was going to cry as he discussed the timeline between arriving at the school and discovering this mess. As terrible as it was, I felt an evil satisfaction in seeing the thing he loved most destroyed. It wasn't nice, but it was about time he suffered just as much as I had at his hands.

I'd only seen Ron this panicked once before. Mom had a radio station prank him with a phone call pretending to be the police, telling him his new Corvette had been found all smashed up on the side of some road. I'd laughed my ass off when he'd gone to the garage of their business, where it was usually kept, to find it missing. He hadn't known that Mom had moved it. He also hadn't found the prank funny.

"Wait here," Mom instructed me when Ron waved her over.

I nodded then overheard Ron tell her, "It's going to be a while. I have to file a report. They're trying to find evidence in the meantime. Then they'll clean it up enough for me to drive home."

"Oh, okay," she said. I looked at the car while he caught her up on the presumed theories of what had happened. I couldn't imagine the car was even drivable in the condition it was in, at least not without Ron getting cut from all the broken glass.

Just then, a familiar convertible pulled up.

"Do you need a ride home?" my friend Jenny's mother asked through the lowered car window.

"If you don't mind," Mom responded, looking to Ron for permission like she always did. He nodded. I climbed into the back seat with Jenny almost instantly, grateful for the dissociation from the scene. Mom sat up front.

"What happened?" Jenny's mother asked mine as she pulled away.

"The police think it was just a couple of drunks or homeless people hanging out in the park who might've thought they'd find money or something of value in the car," Mom said.

I was surprised to hear her speak so many words to Jenny's mother. She never had before. She did like gossiping, though. Grandma told me everyone used to call Mom "Parrot" when she was younger because she repeated everything she heard to everyone who'd listen.

"Ron's flashy car does attract attention," Jenny's mom said.

That's exactly why he bought it, I thought.

"Are you okay?" Jenny asked. That was always a loaded question.

"Just been a weird night," I said with a shrug. I never knew how to sum up all the thoughts swirling through my head and the tangents that stemmed from them. Even I had a hard time keeping them all sorted.

Of course, I was nervous about the scandalous rumors and questions I would face at school the next day, as well as the blame I expected for what happened to Ron's car. I even woke up with a pain in the pit of my stomach the next morning.

So, when I trudged down to the kitchen, I ignored Ron altogether. I didn't have the interest or energy to deal with whatever diminishment he decided to start our day with. It was taking everything in me to go through the motions of pouring the bowl of cereal I wasn't sure I could eat. As I forced the first spoonful into my mouth, I made the mistake of peeking out the curtains to see the status of the ZX.

"What are *you* looking at?" Ron asked sharply.

I immediately flattened my feet and snarked back. "Nothing!" Then I refocused my attention down to my bowl of cereal.

"You're looking out the window at nothing?" he accused.

"I was just curious to know if you were able to get the car home last night. Okay?"

"So *now* you're worried about the car?" Ron said as he stood. I immediately tensed, holding my spoon halfway between the bowl and my mouth. Even the air around me stilled for my sake. "You know, none of this would've happened if it weren't for you!"

"What are you talking about?" I said with furrowed brows. "*I* didn't break into your car!"

"No, but you told your mother the wrong time for the concert!"

"No, I didn't!"

"If we'd been on time, there might've been room to park in the school parking lot instead of the parking lot across the street."

"I gave Mom the flyer for the concert and *told* her I had to be there earlier! It's not my fault she was late getting home from work," I asserted.

"Are you calling your mother a liar, then?" he asked.

"No, but . . ." I lied to protect myself from the consequence of telling the truth.

"But what?" Ron asked, attempting to provoke me into more argument.

I opened my mouth to retort, but nothing came out. There was nothing I could say to win or end this argument anyway. So, I pressed my lips together, choosing not to engage at all.

"This is why nobody can love you," Ron said as he returned to the table. "You're a *liar*. You're *defiant*. You're nothing but *trouble*."

Tears welled in my eyes, but I wouldn't let them fall. I wouldn't give him the satisfaction of knowing his effect on me. I just wished his words didn't hurt me as much as they did. Yet, every time he repeated them, they cut just a little deeper.

"Why do you hate me so much, anyway?" I begged through the blur.

"*Why do you hate me so much?*" Ron mocked in a high, whiny pitch.

My trembling lips and hands turned into shoulder-shaking sobs. Ron just stood and watched me drown in his hurtful words. In an attempt to hurt him back, I lashed out. "You're not my father, so you don't get to talk to me like that!" I jutted my chin to gulp then sniffled repeatedly in my attempt to calm myself.

"I'm not your father? Well, then I shouldn't have to pay for you to live here and have all the things you have, should I?" he said before exiting to the foyer to get his jacket from the coat closet.

I picked up the phone on the kitchen wall and started dialing Mom's work phone number. Before I punched the last number in, Ron returned and snatched the phone out of my hand. I froze, stunned by his aggression.

"Who are you calling?" he shouted an inch from my face.

"MOM!" I yelled in his, giving him a taste of his own medicine.

Ron clenched his teeth and raised the phone over his head. I cowered slightly. Then he hit me with the receiver. The shock of the blow paralyzed me despite my inclination to put my hand where I felt the immediate pain.

Rage revived me before I could consciously subdue it. I went at him with both hands, pushing, pinching, grabbing, hoping anything I did would hurt him like he'd hurt me. I heard myself grunt as I attacked, but I didn't recognize the sounds as my own. It's like he'd summoned some monster that dwelled deep within me.

Having no other defense, Ron hit me with the phone again.

"STOP!" I screamed so loudly that the rasp in my throat would remain long after.

But Ron didn't stop. He grabbed a wad of my hair from the back of my head and banged my head against the wall, over and over. Helpless to stop him, I moaned, "Why? Why are you doing this to me?" All I could see was Mom's happy yellow-flowered wallpaper through the assault. It was no wonder I hated yellow.

When Ron finally released me, he left. I hid my face in my hands and crumpled to the floor, crying. I hated Ron. I hated Mom. I hated my life. I just wished I hated myself enough to end it altogether. But for some reason, I didn't.

So, I had no choice but to keep playing my role in this facade. Just like I had no choice but to go to school now.

My classmates whispered behind my back all day, just as I thought they would. Then a nerdy boy approached me at recess. "What happened to your forehead?" he asked matter-of-factly.

"What?" I responded. Then I glanced at my friend, Jenny, who stood beside me. She offered a weak smile.

"Looks like a bruise or something," he pointed. "Did you hit your head?"

My hand immediately flew up to my forehead.

"Oh, yeah. I forgot!" I said, holding my hand there. Then I faked a laugh. "I accidentally walked into a door this morning. Stupid me!"

"That is stupid. Klutz!" the boy said before walking away.

"Is it that noticeable?" I asked Jenny, slowly revealing my forehead to her.

"Yeah," she said with a cringe. "Did Ron—"

"I don't want to talk about him," I cut her off, scrambling to pull my bangs over my forehead.

"Okay," she said. "But if you change your mind . . ."

I nodded. Then I went to the girls' restroom before going back to class after recess. A pinkish-purplish bump gave away the rough start to my day. I poked it then winced, wondering why I was compelled to produce a pain I knew I'd feel. Then I covered it back up with my hair and kept my head down the rest of the day. I'd rather seem withdrawn, thereby disinviting interaction, than have anyone else notice and suspect anything other than clumsiness.

As soon as I got home, I went straight to the bathroom and opened the medicine cabinet. Remembering that Mom had something called concealer, to hide the dark bags she had under her eyes, I patted the skin-tone liquid onto the bruise repeatedly, watching its prominence diminish a bit more with every coat.

It was enough to fool Mom that evening, so I used it again before school the next morning. I resented that I had to do something other kids didn't have to. But a little makeup and effort was a small price to pay for my peace.

"It's a Hard Knock Life"

I was glad that my friends never questioned me about anything. They didn't call attention to any marks on my body or any moodiness I exhibited. They weren't offended if I became withdrawn. They treated me as if none of that ugliness at home happened at all, like I was a regular kid living a regular life, even though we all knew I wasn't.

I preferred it that way too. I didn't want any attention called to anything that made me or my life different. I didn't want to acknowledge it myself, which was why I went to my friends' houses to hang out instead of having them come to my house. Being in sixth grade now, Mom decided I was old enough to ride my bike further than the end of our block.

It was good for me to see how other parents were and how other families operated. Aside from the fun of dancing with Kelly to the music videos on MTV, I enjoyed being at her house to experience the care and consideration her parents exhibited to us and each other. They were kind, affectionate, and respectful in a way I'd never seen Mom and Ron interact with me or each other. Kelly's parents treated me just the same as they treated their daughters, even asking me about school and orchestra and whatever else they knew I was involved in.

Hanging out at Jenny's condominium was more fun, though, because her mom was the coolest. She'd talk with us about boys and makeup. She'd blast the music in her pink Chrysler LeBaron convertible while cruising down Lake Shore Drive in downtown Chicago with the soft top down, so Jenny and I could sit on top of the seats in the back. She walked around their condominium naked, claiming everyone in Europe did the same because they weren't ashamed of their bodies like Americans were. It embarrassed me at first, to see her private parts. She didn't make a big deal of it, though, so I became just as unfazed. I actually admired her confidence. I'd never seen someone feel so comfortable with who they were, aside from Jenny, who was encouraged to be as confident as her mother was.

That's why I felt comfortable being so forthcoming with them.

"I feel like I just can't win," I said, glancing at Jenny's mom, who was the spitting image of the *Three's Company* actress Suzanne Somers, with her thick blonde hair and tanned skin. "I mean, all Ron talks about is lifting weights and eating protein. So, I thought he'd be impressed when I told him I eat two peanut butter and jelly sandwiches for lunch every day. Because peanut butter has a lot of protein."

"It does?" Jenny asked.

"Yeah. I read it on the container," I told her. "Anyway, he said the peanut butter is going to make me fat."

"What're you, a hundred pounds?" Jenny's mother said from where she sat naked on their couch.

"Barely."

"Hmm," she said, pressing her lips together. "Does he talk to your mother about what she eats too?"

I shrugged. "I don't know. She has quite a collection of Jane Fonda exercise videos, though. And she joined Women's Workout World for a while."

"I hope I'm not overstepping my bounds," she said, "but Jenny has told me about some of the stuff going on at your house."

"Mom!" Jenny scolded.

"It's fine," I said. I wished more people would overstep their bounds where my home life was concerned. Maybe then I'd be taken to live with people who actually *wanted* me around.

"Okay, good. Because I have to ask you something," her mom said.

"Okay . . . ?"

"Does Ron hit her too? Your mother, I mean," she said with her usual frank candor. I swore nothing fazed this woman.

Something about the calm and direct way she'd come right out and asked the question put me at ease, though. There was no judgment in her tone, no blame. She just simply wanted to know. Truth be told, I wanted somebody to know what was going on in our house too. Better yet, someone I knew and trusted, who might be able to help me get out of the situation.

Unfortunately, I couldn't answer her question. I mean, Mom was submissive to Ron. She allowed him to dictate everything about everything. But did I ever *see* Ron hit Mom? No. But that didn't mean he didn't either.

So, as much as I wanted to confess that he beat Mom to a pulp every night, I couldn't. "I don't know," I said. "He is controlling. And he'll lie to anyone about anything if he has something to gain. But he seems to just take his anger out on me." Kind of like my Mom did, now that I thought about it.

Jenny and her mother lowered their heads, as if mourning.

It made me sad too, because there was nothing I could do about my situation. What Ron did to me was physically rough enough to call abuse, but I didn't feel like it was extreme enough to be considered any more than harsh discipline. Yes, I had bruises and hand marks. But I didn't have black eyes. Yes, he hurt me and behaved aggressively towards me when I angered him. But as damaging as the hateful glares, silent treatment, demeaning insults were to my psyche, there was no visible, quantifiable, outward evidence with which to hold Ron accountable. So, my suffering flew under the radar.

"Well, honey, I have only spoken to Ron enough to say hello or goodbye during pick-ups and drop-offs, but I am fairly perceptive when it comes to men who abuse women, seeing as *I* was one of those women." She paused when I bulged my eyes at the shock of this new information. I mean, Jenny had mentioned her parents arguing a lot before they'd divorced, but I'd never realized her mom had been hit too. It didn't even make sense because of how strong and independent she seemed to be! "And what I see . . . well . . ." she continued before stopping again, as if being careful not to say anything that would upset me. She didn't have to, though. Just knowing another human being understood my plight, even if she could do nothing to change it, made me feel better.

"Like you said, Dana, he's a jerk," Jenny interjected.

I snort-laughed at the simple summary to what was a complex topic of conversation. Then Jenny suggested we show her mother some dance moves we'd practiced the last time I'd been over. She played the Madonna song "True Blue" on their stereo, and we sang and danced for her mother, who stood and cheered us on. For that little bit of time, I forgot all about

Ron's abuse, Mom's submission to it, and my abhorrence of my home life altogether. Because for that little bit of time, I was safe, and I was free. I could just be.

"Go Your Own Way"

One early evening over the winter of 1986 to 1987, I was revamping the lyrics to an oldies song I'd heard when Mom knocked on my door. "Can you come out here, Dane?" she said before opening the door wider. I saw Ron walk into the wood-paneled bedroom across the hall, which we used as a den. "We have to talk to you about something."

Now I was leery. I ran through every recent memory of what I'd said and done that might have provoked the necessity of a talking to. Nothing specific came to mind, though, since everything seemed to be an issue around here. The pressure of Mom standing at the door with an impatient grimace told me I'd better get up and get this over with regardless.

"Okay," I said, taking my time to put my pencil and notebook aside. Then, with slumped shoulders, I followed Mom into the den.

Ron was sitting on one end of the beige Berber sofa, his arms folded across his bulky chest. He glanced up at Mom as she passed him and sat on the opposite end. With no place for me but between them, I plunked down where I always found myself anyway and where all the tension could be felt.

For a long moment, no one spoke. I looked at Mom, expecting her say something, since she had been the one to summon me. Mom was side-eying Ron with her usual stone face but averted her gaze when she noticed me looking. So, I turned to Ron, who leaned back with high brows and pursed lips, as if passing the buck back to Mom. Whatever they weren't telling me felt big, and I got the sense it had to do more with them than with me.

"What's going on?" I finally asked, looking at Mom again.

She dropped her head. "Ron and I . . . well, Dane . . . we've decided to separate."

I could feel the gravity of what she'd said by the sadness in her eyes. I also noted that she referred to Ron by name instead of calling him my dad, as she usually insisted. She didn't look at Ron either, which I thought odd, since she rarely said or did anything without first looking at him for approval. Still, I didn't know what any of this meant.

The only time I'd ever heard about a couple separating was in the movie *Kramer vs. Kramer*, wherein the husband and wife broke up and then fought relentlessly in court and in life to win custody of their son. They'd divorced, and the dad had ended up with his son in the end.

Mom didn't say they were getting divorced, though. Nor would I ever believe they would fight over who gets to keep me. So, since I still didn't understand what any of this meant or how it pertained to me, I just said, "Okay . . ."

"Do you know what that means?" Mom asked with tear-filled eyes that almost accused me of not feeling a devastation I was apparently supposed to.

She looked to Ron for help, but he raised his brows and looked up, avoiding the situation altogether. So, I looked back to Mom, wondering what the big deal was.

"Ron and I will be living apart, Dane," she finally said, "until we figure some things out." She stared at me then, awaiting my reaction. But I didn't know what to say!

On the one hand, I was thrilled! I'd been waiting for the day that she'd finally realize what a jerk Ron was and get us out of here already. On the other hand, I'd finally made some friends and loved playing in orchestra. I didn't want to have to start over somewhere else.

Plus, living apart brought to mind a million other questions. I mean, was this going to be temporary, or was it permanent? Was one of them going to stay somewhere else until they figured out whatever they needed to, and then come back? Or did Mom and I have to go somewhere until they decided what to do?

"Where am I going to live, then?" I asked, being it was really my only concern.

"I've secured an apartment for us nearby. I was planning to take you to see it after school tomorrow," Mom told me before looking back down shamefully.

"An apartment?" I repeated. I scrunched my face, recalling all the apartments we'd lived in before, where I'd slept on the floor and roaches got stuck in my hair. I didn't want to return to that kind of life. I didn't like Ron, but at least his house was clean, and I had a bed. I wondered if he'd let me take it with us.

It didn't make sense to me that *we* had to move out, anyway. The neighbors down the street had divorced recently, but it was the dad who'd moved out so the mother and two girls could remain in the house. The older girl told the rest of us that her parents said it was to maintain their stability, which sounded like a grown-up's responsibility to their children. So, how come I wasn't being granted the same consideration? Was it because I wasn't Ron's biological child? Did that make me undeserving of this stability other parents wanted for their kids?

Then it hit me. Was this about the biological child Ron wanted? Mom hadn't given him one yet. I hadn't heard much talk about it either, though Mom still often seemed to be sad, tired, and in some sort of pain. Were we being booted out because she couldn't have his baby?

"If you don't want to move to the apartment with your mother, you can stay here with me," Ron intervened.

Mom and I both whipped our heads towards him, stunned by the offer. Why would this man who complained about bearing the cost of my food and shelter suddenly *want* to keep me?

Before either of us responded, he smugly enticed, "We can repaint your room like you've been wanting."

Despite our mutual dislike of each other, I surprised myself by considering the offer. I imagined my bedroom painted light blue like one of the neighbor girls had. Or maybe pink. I liked pink. My bedroom was yellow now, which had been Mom's choice. The ruffled comforter, the wallpaper, the furnishings—everything was that god-awful yellow.

"I'm sure she'll be coming with me, Ron," Mom argued. I assumed the same, even though I didn't want to live in another apartment. So, I was ready to refuse Ron's offer in defense of Mom, until she said, "It's up to you, though, Dane. If you want to stay here . . ."

I gaped at Mom, insulted by the choice.

She should have assumed we'd go together. I mean, I was *her* daughter, not *his*. Why was she giving me the option? Had she been waiting for an opportunity to shake me, like she'd pawned me off to Great-Gram and Leo before? Is that why she'd had Ron listed as my biological father on my birth certificate? To stick him with legal and financial responsibility for me, so she didn't have to have any?

With the pressure of having to choose between the lesser of two evils, I sat in an open-mouthed daze, unsure of what to do. Ron mistreated me, but he was predictable, whereas Mom could laugh and sing with me one day and then clam up and close off the next without reason or warning. It's like she couldn't decide whether to love me or hate me. Ron never wavered in his dislike for me, and I preferred knowing what to expect, even if it wasn't always good.

But how could I tell Mom I wanted to stay with Ron? Would she even care? Or would I be doing her a favor?

"Dane?" she pressed.

I didn't want to have to point it out, but this life had been her wish, not mine. She couldn't fault me for wanting to stay. Still, I didn't want to hurt her. So, I shrugged and said, "I don't know."

"What do you mean you 'don't know'?" Mom scolded.

"Well, I'd rather live in a house than in an apartment," I answered, focusing on my reasoning for the "where" instead of upsetting her with my reasoning for the "who" in this situation. "Especially if I can redo my bedroom."

"Whatever you want!" Ron said, sitting straight up and wearing a satisfied smirk. I was too, honestly. As much as I hated Ron, it seemed like Mom was the one who had things to figure out, and I didn't want to be dragged through any more of her mistakes when I could stay here and resume life as usual.

"We'll look at the apartment tomorrow first," Mom insisted. "Then you can decide."

"Okay," I said, unable to understand why she wouldn't take no for an answer. I mean, Ron and I were both giving her what she seemed to want, so why wouldn't she just go live in her apartment and get on with her life?

"Well, I've got to get to the gym," Ron said as if it were any other night. Then he stood up to leave.

Mom looked up at him with sorrowful eyes and slumped shoulders, like a puppy who'd angered her owner. It was pathetic and made me wonder what she'd done. I was just glad it wasn't me for once.

"Can I go back to my room?" I asked with the same normalcy Ron had.

"Yeah," Mom mumbled without looking at me.

I hesitated for a second, feeling like I should soothe her instead. I didn't like to see anyone hurting. Mom wasn't emotional and affectionate like I was, though. So, I assumed she was better left to herself, to process her emotions on her own.

The next evening, I stood in the doorway of the apartment Mom had secured. It was across the street from the Catholic school I'd attended with the church Mom had married Ron in, above some local business that was currently closed.

The walls were white and chunky, showing the layers of paint that had been slopped on over the years. The windows looked old too. I wasn't sure they'd even open in case of an emergency. Normal kids probably didn't notice things like that. I did only because I'd examined the windows in my bedroom and in the upstairs bathroom at Ron's so many times, trying to figure how to escape out of them safely so I could run away. At least Ron's walls were clean and flat, though. His house was immaculate compared to this old, used-up apartment, which looked like every other apartment we'd ever lived in before.

"So?" Mom asked from the middle of the living room. "Aren't you going to come in and look around?"

I shook my head. I'd already pictured myself sleeping on the splintered wood floor of this place. I didn't want to worry about cockroaches and have back aches every day because Mom couldn't afford a bed for us. Not when I had a perfectly comfortable bed at Ron's.

"Help me out here, Dane," Mom said, jutting her hip.

"I don't like it," I said with a fearful cringe.

"I know it's not the best, but it's all I can afford. Ron said he'll help me out with money, but—"

"I'm sorry, Mom. But I'd rather stay with Ron." I lowered my head slightly, afraid to see her reaction.

"You know, *you're* the one who doesn't like Ron. *You're* the one who's been telling me how horrible he is to you," she accused, crossing her arms. "I wouldn't be going through all of this if it weren't for you and your constant complaining about how he treats you."

When did the demise of their marriage become *my* fault? She was the one who'd decided to move us to the suburbs with him. She was the one who'd chosen to marry him and let him control her every thought and action. And now that we were finally settled in his duplex, after I'd changed schools and finally fit in with some friends, after she'd legally bound us to Ron by name and settled into some normalcy, she wanted to up and change everything again?

"You're right, Mom. I don't like him," I said, "but I don't want to live in this dumpy apartment with you either."

"What?" Mom gasped.

I shrugged. I hadn't meant to offend her. I was just being honest because she'd called me a liar so many times that I upheld the truth with more loyalty than the truth had ever given me.

But yes, truth be told, I was done being the scapegoat for all Mom's bad decisions. It was time for me to stand up for myself and make decisions that were best for me, since she couldn't be trusted to do the same for either of us.

"I don't get you, Dane," Mom said, shaking her head.

I could have said the same to her. Mom couldn't handle that truth, though, so I withheld it.

"I'm sorry," I said, barely above a whisper. I really was too, for both of us.

Mom huffed as she brushed past me. I followed her out and endured the silent ride back to Ron's.

Days went by without any indication of "separating." Mom and Ron continued to sleep in the same bed. Nobody packed their clothes or possessions. No one ever moved out. Nor did anyone ever say why not. Everything just went on like it always had.

In fact, I was the one sent packing, when Mom and Ron sent me to Puerto Rico with Great-Gram and Uncle Juni the next summer. She'd said

Great-Gram needed travelling companions, though I begged to differ by the way Great-Gram chugged several of those little bottles of tequila on the airplane. She ate the worms on the bottom too!

The entire trip had been just as relaxing and laid-back. Relatives I couldn't understand my relation to welcomed us with a lobster boil and music. They toured us through El Morro and the brick-paved streets of Old San Juan, which I appreciated despite my young age. We went on day trips to the beach, where men hacked the tops off fresh coconuts and stuck straws in to drink from them for just a buck. We took boats out to Vieques, where I played in the clear water with my Spanish-speaking "cousins," and enjoyed the plantains and pork the elder women cooked in a little bonfire in the sand. Other days, Juni and I went for long walks through our family's mountain hometown, crossing streets with chickens and goats, and buying handmade souvenirs from straw-covered huts. By night, we slept in the tropical cross-breeze of the open windows, soothed by the sound of the island's coquis.

I didn't think I'd ever felt at such ease being among people who didn't judge or single me out for anything. Then again, I wasn't different than anyone else there. Some of my relatives were white, some were dark-skinned. Some had black hair, some had light. Most of them had curly hair like me. But none saw me as anything other than family, which was such a stark difference to how I felt at home.

"Hip to Be Square"

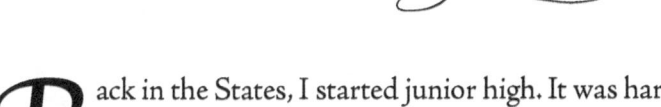

Back in the States, I started junior high. It was hard enough without having to get braces on the buck teeth Mom said I got from my biological father. Getting food stuck in them wasn't as bad as the headgear I had to wear at night, though. It was like medieval torture to have to sleep with an elastic band tightened around my head to pull the metal insert that fit into the back of my mouth. Between the soreness in my jaws and the pain of pressure in my skull, it was no wonder I had headaches more often.

I suffered for my future smile, since it seemed to be the only physical attribute I had going for me anyway. Other girls my age were developing curves in places I wasn't and had boyfriends who held their hands in the school halls. I, on the other hand, was the same annoying little ragamuffin everyone tolerated—chasing boys at recess, challenging them to belching contests, and saying, "I know you are, but what am I," in response to anyone who called me "railroad tracks."

Mom would scold me for leaving the house in something wrinkly or dirty, though her need to iron every piece of clothing (including socks and jeans) seemed a bit excessive. She even ironed my hair straight a couple times, since it had become curlier and more unmanageable almost overnight. The curls were undoubtedly characteristic of Mom's Puerto Rican roots, though she denied her heritage as usual, saying my changing hormones were to blame.

To appease Mom's constant argument about how I needed to start considering how I looked because I represented our family in public, I started experimenting with makeup in seventh grade. Jenny's mother took us to the drugstore and treated us to whatever we wanted. Unfortunately, Mom didn't like the black eye shadow and eyeliner I'd chosen.

I thought the smoky look made my golden-brown eyes pop, until a classmate said I looked like a gothic vampire. In defense, I said it was "new wave." But when I told Mom about the rude comment, she took me to Marshall Field's for a lesson with an aesthetician in the makeup department. She even bought me an eighty-dollar Marcella Borghese eye shadow compact with shimmery purple and rose tones. I left there feeling like a million bucks, but when I tried to replicate the technique at home, I looked like someone's cheap date instead. I appreciated Mom for trying nonetheless.

None of the boys at school could've cared less about my hair and makeup, though. I had been placed in the "gifted program" anyway—a class of eight of us who'd scored significantly higher than the rest of our class on the assessment tests we'd taken at the beginning of the year. So, we were separated from the others and encouraged to nurture and explore our personal passions and interests, mine being writing, music, and speaking. Aside from me, Kelly, and Miranda, however, the other five kids were total nerds, and the nerds didn't pay attention to anything except for their grades.

So, although I thrived in the more self-directed educational atmosphere, I still struggled to fit in with all the other kids, who we still took math and music classes with. Thinking they might want to hear about the trip I'd taken with Mom and Ron to Mexico, I told them about the ancient ruins I'd seen. I was called a braggart and shamed for boasting. I thought having Ron pick me up or drop me off from orchestra practice in his shiny red Corvette would catch everyone's attention. It did, but then I was called a show-off. Even wearing expensive clothes from boutiques like United Colors of Benetton and Esprit didn't earn me recognition, because my flat chest and butt didn't fill them in like Mom did when she borrowed from my closet.

I wanted so bad to be "cool," though, that I observed the so-called "cool kids," hoping to mimic whatever qualities would earn me the same regard. They acted indifferent, like nothing was deserving of their acknowledgment. When something was deemed worthy of comment or notice, a snide or outright mean remark followed. They were judgmental and rude. They reminded me too much of Ron. So, I eventually determined that "cool" wasn't for me.

Anyway, I'd heard one of the popular girls was having sex with her boyfriend. I didn't even know a girl could do that at thirteen years old! I was fully aware, however, that I wouldn't. I'd punched a short redhead in the nose when he'd stuffed a dead frog down the back of my shirt in science class, and I'd run screaming from a Filipino boy who wanted to play "Two Minutes in a Closet" at a party at Miranda's house and used the time to put his hands inside my shirt.

But a Czech boy who was new to our school was really nice to me. We got along really well, so we called ourselves boyfriend and girlfriend. Our relationship mostly involved riding bikes and listening to the latest hair bands. His favorite was Def Leppard. I was more of a Mötley Crüe fan. Our musical tastes weren't what ruined us, though; it was me. I had decided to cut my hair boy-short at the beginning of eighth grade, after which he said he didn't know if he was kissing a boy or a girl anymore. I was heartbroken by the error.

I'd tried to impress a cute Romanian boy who was new to our school by joining the eighth-grade girls' basketball team. I'd learned the hard way, though, that the basket I was supposed to throw the ball into changed after halftime. I'd been the laughingstock of *two* schools after that mistake.

Seeing how everyone fawned over the cheerleaders, I saw that as being my ticket to notice. Unfortunately, every single girl who auditioned made the squad except for me. I think it was because I couldn't do the splits. Kelly could just drop into them with ease, so she'd earned her place on the squad. The coaches asked me to be the school mascot instead. I knew it was just a consolation prize, but I agreed anyway. I was assigned to wear a Native American costume to games instead of the short skirts the cheerleaders got to wear. My low self-esteem prevented me from being peppy enough to rally the crowd's excitement, though, so the coaches fired me from that and gave me a cheerleading uniform after all. I should have been excited, but it didn't feel good to wear it knowing I hadn't earned it in the first place. Everyone else knew it too, which made it that much worse.

So, I returned my focus to my forever fallback—music. It was my prowess. It was my reliable old friend who was always there for me, no matter how much I tried to replace it or deny it. No matter whether I was playing it, dancing to it, or singing it, music gave me a safe outlet to express myself. It didn't judge. It didn't reject. It never abandoned me either. In fact, it made me forget about all else.

I thought very seriously about studying music beyond high school and earning my own place with the prestigious Chicago Symphony Orchestra, whose performances I attended on school field trips. Maybe then, Mom and Ron would see how talented I really was.

In the meantime, I practiced my viola diligently. Mom even hired a private instructor, who pushed me to new heights I would have never achieved if she hadn't taken me under her wing. The instructor encouraged me to audition for the area's youth symphony orchestra, because she believed I was talented enough to earn a place in it. And I did. In fact, I earned the same first chair distinction as the school orchestra, which meant I was considered the best in the section and expected to lead the other violists in rehearsals and performances.

I thought I'd made Mom proud. Instead, she sighed when I told her the good news. So, I tried harder.

I taught myself to play piano on the small electric keyboard I had in my bedroom. Since Mom loved the Beatles, I learned to play "Strawberry Fields Forever" to perfection and then performed it for her. After I learned "I Think We're Alone Now," Mom commented that she'd always wanted to learn how to play piano. The next thing I knew, she and Ron had bought a real upright piano!

I couldn't believe Ron approved of the expense, considering how much he complained about the cost of my viola lessons. I didn't ask any questions, though. I just took to the keys, learning songs on my own and eventually teaching myself to read sheet music I bought at the music store.

When Mom let me perform the songs I knew for Ron's family and their few employees at a holiday party they hosted in our duplex, I felt glorified in a way I never had before. Guests praised me for my talent. One even put a wine glass on top of the piano to serve as a tip jar. I was glad to make some money to spend at the school Christmas bazaar. I bought Ron a "Best Dad" trophy for a dollar, since he'd spent so much money on that piano.

I wasn't stupid, though. He hadn't bought that piano for me. Mom's constant comment about wanting to take lessons might have triggered it, but Ron's motivation to buy the piano stemmed from the sense of prestige it conveyed. Because when anyone commented on how talented I was, Ron twisted the conversation to focus on how much money the piano had cost. He wanted people to think we had more money than we did and uphold a status we didn't have. And it was annoying.

The upside to the piano, however, was that the Ms. Pac-Man machine was demoted to the basement Ron had recently finished, after giving our dog, Bogie, away to a family who lived on a farm where he could run freely. How I got piano lessons from the lady across the street out of the deal was another win I couldn't explain. But I didn't argue with the good favor.

"Mr. Big Stuff"

D ancing was my second love in life. So, I was excited when Mom registered me in the same dance classes Kelly was in. I tried ballet and tap, but I didn't like the stiffness and perfection required of ballet, and Ron didn't like the sound of my tap shoes scuffing the black-and-white tile floor I practiced on in our foyer. I eventually found my niche in jazz dance, which also prevented the fights with Ron and the floor he fought so hard to protect.

On a Saturday morning just before class, I went down to the kitchen to get a bowl of cereal. Mom was washing dishes, as she always seemed to be doing.

"Hey, Dane," she greeted.

"Hey," I responded as I took a box of Apple Jacks from the pantry and poured them into a bowl. "Are you driving me to dance today?"

"No, Ron is taking you."

"Oh," I said, wondering where he was. He wasn't sitting in his throne with his morning coffee like he usual was.

"He's on his way out anyway," Mom said. She rarely drove me anywhere, so the excuse was unnecessary.

"Where's he going so early?" I asked with a mouth full of crunchy loops. My eyes had already completed the maze on the back of the bright-green box.

"He's going golfing with his brother and sisters and all their spouses," she said as drearily as I'd felt about Ron driving me to my dance class.

I looked at Mom quizzically. "You're not going?"

"No . . ." she prolonged. "It's okay, though. I've never golfed."

Even still, I thought it rude of Ron to go without her and wondered whether she'd even been invited. "But if everyone else is bringing their spouse, why isn't Ron bringing you?"

From what I'd heard in the past, they did more gossiping and drinking than swinging clubs at balls, anyway; and since they weren't on the course already, I suspected that was exactly the agenda for the day.

"It's okay," Mom said, shrugging in a lame attempt to act like she really was. "I guess they invited another woman to be his golf partner today, anyway."

What? My appalled expression asked.

"What?" she reacted.

"You don't see anything wrong with that?" I asked with an offense she should have taken to the blatant disrespect.

"It's fine, Dane. It's not worth—" She stopped short of finishing her sentence when Ron came into the kitchen. "Hey, can you do me a favor and take Dana to her dance class on your way out today?" she asked him as if it were just another day.

I saw the pleasant expression fade from his face as he poured coffee into his mug. I felt the same repulsion, particularly since he hadn't thought to refuse the female golf partner his family had arranged for him.

"If I have to . . ." he said as he sat across the table from me.

Our eyes met. I hoped he sensed my judgment.

"She has to be there in fifteen minutes," Mom urged, just as I shoved the last of my loops into my mouth and carried my bowl to the sink.

"I just sat down with my coffee!" Ron complained.

Mom shrugged. Ron groaned. I just walked out to the foyer to put my shoes on, shaking my head at how miserable we all usually were together. Then I followed Ron out to his newest sports car and jumped into the passenger's seat.

I stewed the whole way to dance, biting my tongue about the female Ron was ditching Mom for. I glanced over at him once, cursing him up and down in my head.

"What?" he snipped when he noticed.

"Nothing," I mumbled to avoid confrontation. But out of the corner of my eye, I could see Ron glance at me again.

"What are you wearing, anyway?" he asked snidely.

I was confused because he could obviously see my attire. "What do you mean?"

"What do you mean what do I mean? Are you stupid or something? I asked what you're wearing."

Glaring at him with resentment, I struggled to determine whether he wanted me to actually answer his question, or if he'd call me stupid again for answering a question for which the answer was so obvious. I opted for the truth. "A leotard and tights?"

Ron shook his head. "Well, you look like a whore."

I huffed and shook my head, dismissing the insult. Ron had once said Jenny's mother was a whore because she'd picked me up to go shopping with them, wearing a short, fitted skirt and tube top. I thought the outfit was cute and flattered her slender figure. But Ron went on about it when I returned home that evening. He'd even told Mom that Jenny's mom offered to have sex with him! If only that lying piece of shit had been so lucky!

"I can't believe you walked out of the house like that," Ron continued.

"I'm going to dance class. What am I supposed to wear?" I snarked back.

"Clothes that cover you up! Because right now, you might as well not be wearing anything! Or is that what you want? You *want* everyone staring at you?"

"Well, no," I said, suddenly doubting my choice of activewear. I never liked being the center of attention. I didn't even like having my picture taken, since I'd heard the camera adds ten pounds to a person's appearance. According to Ron, I was fat and had the hips of a middle-aged woman. "But I'm going to dance class," I lamely defended once more.

Ron pulled up to the curb of the building where my classes were held. I stared at him, waiting for a response, an apology, anything. He stared straight out the windshield as if I weren't even there. So, I got out of his car. He barely waited for me to close the door before pulling away, leaving this stupid, attention-seeking whore in a leotard sulking on the curb of the street.

"Everything She Wants"

I was surprised when I walked into the kitchen one late winter evening in early 1989 and saw Mom smiling. I looked over at Ron sitting in his chair, looking very casual with one arm over the back and the other elbow on the table. He was chuckling about something one of them must have just said.

"Hey, Dane!" Mom said with rare enthusiasm. I felt like I was in some alternate universe where Mom and Ron were the positive and attentive parents I'd always hoped for.

"Hey," I said warily as I walked past her to the refrigerator.

"What?" she asked, giggling.

"Nothing," I said, shaking my head. I poured some milk for hot cocoa then put it in the microwave. I noticed Mom glance at Ron. He smiled. Then she looked back at me with that same weird smirk. "What's going on?" I blurted, anxious to know why everyone was in an unusually good mood.

Mom turned to Ron and asked, "Should we tell her?"

"Tell me what?"

"Yeah, go ahead," Ron said with a flip of his hand.

"Well," Mom said, "we're having a baby!"

I stared at Mom, trying to determine whether she was joking. I knew they'd been trying to reverse her tubal ligation since I was in third grade. But I was in eighth grade now. I hadn't even realized they were still trying.

The microwave beeped to let me know my cocoa was ready, but I remained unmoved. I didn't know what to say or how to feel about this. I mean, I'd always wanted a big sister. I'd have even settled for a little sister. But

I was thirteen. I'd be almost fourteen when the baby came. The age difference alone would prevent closeness with any sibling at this point. I'd be out of high school and out of the house before the kid was even in kindergarten!

Thinking about how my half-sibling and I would essentially be only children, I decided that it almost didn't matter that they were having a baby. It wasn't going to affect *my* life any.

"Did you hear what I said, Dane?" Mom asked.

"Um, yeah," I said, finally coming out of my trance.

"Well, what do you think about it?"

I reached into the microwave for my chocolate fix and took a sip before answering. I didn't want to hurt Mom's feelings by saying I didn't care. She seemed happy. So, I wanted to be happy for her, despite the slight of knowing she hadn't expressed the same joy when finding out she was pregnant with me.

"I think I don't need to think anything about it," I finally said. "I mean, you've had your tubal ligation reversed so you could have a baby. And now you're pregnant. So . . ."

"Yeah, the doctor says this fetus is viable, so it looks like you'll have a baby brother or sister around the first of September!" she said excitedly.

This fetus? As opposed to what *other* fetus? Had there been another they hadn't told me about? More than one? Maybe that's why she'd been so distant and moody and tired all these years. Maybe she'd been so consumed with being pregnant and then devastated at the loss or losses she suffered that she hadn't had the energy to mother me like I needed her to. I had more questions than feelings now but didn't want to ruin the mood by calling attention to the secrets that had obviously been kept from me.

"Do you know if it's a boy or girl?" I asked to be polite.

"We won't know that for a while," Ron said.

"I'm hoping for a boy, though," Mom chimed in. She'd once told me she'd expected *me* to be a boy. I guessed being a girl was just one more thing I'd screwed up for her. Hopefully, *this* kid would get it right. "I have some names picked out already, either way."

Intrigued enough to sit at the table with my cocoa, I took the bait. "Well, then. Let's hear 'em!"

Mom rambled some strange names, like Zoe for a girl and Jared for a boy, giving reasons why she liked this one or that.

"Those are weird, Mom," I said. Ron cracked up too. "Did you have any input on those, or did she come up with them all on her own?" I asked.

"Those were all her idea, but I'm not messing with a woman whose hormones have been as all over the place as hers have been!" he chuckled, throwing his palms up as if he were under arrest.

"Ronald!" Mom playfully scolded. It was gross to see them laughing and joking.

This whole scene was weird, really. The three of us rarely sat and talked or shared anything, never mind laughter or life stuff. So, I guessed this pregnancy and the joy they were expressing wasn't so bad. Maybe this baby was what we all needed, to bring us together as a family. I'd never wanted anything more than that. I just hoped it would last.

Unfortunately, the only thing that lasted was Ron's excitement about the pregnancy. He seemed to be glowing more than Mom! He bragged to anyone and everyone about Mom carrying *his* baby, as if he were the sole creator of what was expected to be this most magnificent being the universe would ever know. It was almost insulting to the narrative of nothingness he created about *my* existence, as well as the fact that it was Mom's body doing the hard work of housing and growing this extension of him.

As annoying as he was about making everyone aware that the next Messiah was coming, and that this greatness was the spawn of his loins, I had to credit him for his extraordinary consideration and gentleness with Mom. He was softer with her, physically and verbally, treating her like the most precious and fragile being that walked the earth.

I'd thought Mom would be happier now that Ron was treating her with such exceptional regard. Plus, she was *voluntarily* knocked up this time, in the societally appropriate marriage to the father of her baby, as opposed to the circumstances of her pregnancy with me. Instead, she looked haggard and miserable all the time. It made me question whether she really wanted this baby, or if she was fulfilling some obligatory duty to Ron. Regardless, this baby was coming, and, to my dismay, the tensions between us all grew in concordance with Mom's expanding belly.

"Don't You (Forget About Me)"

As if things couldn't get any worse, Jenny informed me that she was moving to Arizona after eighth-grade graduation because her mother's long-time boyfriend was being transferred there for work. I was devastated. I couldn't imagine starting high school, becoming a big sister, and having boyfriends and going to dances without Jenny and her mom.

"I wish you didn't have to go," I told her just before she left for the sunny state. Her mom was preparing for the move with a last-minute tanning session at a nearby salon, so I'd met them there for our final goodbye.

"We'll keep in touch!" Jenny said with an enthusiasm I believed. "I'll call you as soon as we get there so you have my new phone number."

"Promise?" I asked. "Because I expect a call from you every single day."

"Promise," she said.

"Really, I want to hear about every boy you go out with and every dance you go to and—"

"I want to hear all that stuff from you too. You're always going to be my first best friend," she told me. Then she took my hands and held them in silence. With dropped heads, we mourned the end of this phase of our lives.

"Ready?" her mom said as she approached us after paying for her time there.

Looking up at Jenny with teary eyes, I didn't know what to say. I didn't want to say goodbye, but "see ya later" didn't seem appropriate for what could potentially be the last words between us. So, I threw my arms around her and squeezed, hoping we'd find a way to see each other again soon.

"I'm going to miss you," she said when she released me. Her sparkly smile made her blue eyes light up, so I couldn't help but smile through my tears too.

Jenny's mom took me into her skinny little arms then. "You'll be okay, Dana. Just stay strong and know we'll be a phone call away," she told me. Then she pulled away and said, "This is just goodbye *for now*."

"Yeah," I said, wiping my eyes as they returned to their Chrysler LeBaron to take off on their long road trip. Then, with a drooped head, I walked home. Because no matter what she'd said, I knew better.

I had other friends, like Kelly and Miranda. But there would never be another Jenny. They were busy with interests I didn't share, anyway. Like softball. I wasn't interested in the sport, or any sport for that matter, nor did I have any athletic ability. Since there was just nothing else to do, though, I went ahead and joined the team Kelly's dad was coaching, at him and Kelly's urging.

Mom was too busy working to take me to practices and games, but she didn't want me riding my bike both ways either. She was afraid someone would snatch me if I rode home in the dark, though I wouldn't have minded if anyone did. Either way, I was often stuck relying on Ron to take me to or from the ball field, unless I could arrange a ride with someone else.

On one particular night, Ron scowled at me the second I sulked into the passenger seat of his red Corvette. He even reversed out of our short driveway with greater acceleration than necessary, to make sure we were all aware of his dissatisfaction with having to chauffeur me.

"Once my baby comes," Ron started before we even got to the end of our street, "things are going to change around here."

I raised my brows, unsure of where he was going with this. "Okay . . ."

"Me, your mom, and our baby . . . we're going to be our *own* family . . . just the *three* of us," he said.

My head dropped. His hurtful words, spoken aloud to confirm what I'd already inferred from his mistreatment of me, successfully stuck the proverbial dagger deeper into my heart. He knew it too. Or at least he knew how to get to me.

All I'd ever wanted was to be Mom's daughter. I wanted a mother who was proud of my talents and achievements, and who I could turn to when

I needed advice or had a bad day at school. I wanted her to be the person who'd hold me when I cried and remind me that I deserved better. She wasn't any of those things, though. She never had time to be, nor would Ron allow her to be. He'd only allowed her to be his wife. He might have allowed me to be his daughter too, if I'd been as compliant as Mom. I apparently had a stronger will or sense of self than she did, though, because I refused to bow down to a man who didn't deserve the honor and respect he felt entitled to.

"Are you listening to me?" Ron asked with a raised voice, attempting to bait me into a reaction I wouldn't give him.

I looked at him with narrowed eyes instead. It was taking every bit of self-discipline to hold back tears, but I let his ego take a ride on the high of my low. No. He could go fuck himself.

"Yeah," I said snottily. "You and my mom are having a baby. I won't be part of your family. I got it, okay?!"

"Are you smarting off to me?" he yelled as we zoomed down a side street. I grabbed the door handle nervously, unsure of whether he was seeking attention or trying to intimidate me.

A few minutes later, we arrived at the ball field. Ron parked in the small gravel lot where his Nissan 300ZX had been broken into a few years before. I wasn't even sure why he was parking when he usually dropped me at the curb. He wasn't friends with any of my teammates' parents. He'd barely spoken to Kelly's father all the years we'd been friends. Ron was as uninvolved as Mom in anything involving me.

Ignoring Ron altogether, I ran over to where Kelly and a couple other girls from school were standing by the batter's bench.

"Hi, Dana!" a few of the girls greeted, in the midst of gossiping about boys and summer vacations.

We were all wearing our red team jerseys with white lettering, matching hats, and gray capri-length ball player pants. I wore my brown leather mitt on my right hand, but I didn't have cleats on my shoes like the other girls. Mom and Ron hadn't deemed it a necessary expense when I would probably never play softball again—not after this summer, anyway.

"Hey," I responded, averting my eyes to prevent anyone from noticing any rogue tears that might have escaped my eyes in the car.

"What'd Ron do now?" Kelly asked with a tilted head and jutted hip.

Of course she saw through me.

Looking over my shoulder to make sure Ron wasn't within earshot, I saw him standing by Kelly's dad, chuckling at something he'd just said. Kelly's dad wasn't laughing, though. I hoped Ron hadn't made another bald joke. Kelly said her dad had been offended at Ron making fun of her dad's bald spot when he'd picked me up once before.

I turned back to Kelly and lowered my head. "Apparently, I'm not part of '*his*' family once the baby comes." I wiped the tears suddenly welling in my eyes. Saying things out loud seemed to make them more real.

"What a jerk!" she said.

"It's fine," I said, shrugging and shaking my head, just like Mom had when Ron had gone golfing with another woman. "I never wanted to be his daughter in the first place, so I sure as hell don't want to be part of '*his*' family." I used my fingers to make air quotes.

"I'd go straight to your mom with that crap," Kelly advised.

"I've tried, but she says that's just how Ron is, like I'm supposed to just be okay with that," I told her, checking to make sure Ron was still with Kelly's dad.

"Well, you need to *keep* telling her, then," Kelly said. "Because once that baby comes, she's going to have even less time and tolerance for everyone *but* the baby." Kelly would know. She was the oldest of four sisters, the youngest having been born recently. We'd thought it gross that our parents were still having sex at their age.

"Mom pisses me off too, though," I said. "Sometimes she confronts Ron, but then he denies whatever I've said, so then Mom accuses me of lying to get attention or to try to break them up or something. I can never win!"

"Ready to play some ball?" Kelly's dad called out with a clap of his hands.

Kelly looked at me with closed-mouth sympathy before grabbing her mitt off the bench. Then we ran over to her dad for our pre-game huddle. On the way, I saw Ron walk back to his car. *Good riddance*, I thought. As much as I wished for parents like all the others who set up lawn chairs and brought coolers full of Capri Suns and snacks, mine would have only brought me criticism for my athletic failures.

As chance would have it, I was standing out in center field, as usual, that night, when a fly ball came careening towards me. I crossed my arms over my head as I cringed back, expecting it to hit me in the face. Instead, it fell directly into my mitt. I hadn't even realized I'd caught the ball that won the out that won us the game, until my teammates ran at me, cheering and squealing. They threw themselves onto me, and we fell to the ground together, hugging and laughing.

Despite it being a total fluke, I was hailed a hero. And for that one glorious moment, I felt like I'd finally done something significant. Kelly's dad even let me keep the game-winning ball and took us all out for ice cream afterward. I couldn't wait to tell Mom.

"Changes"

My replacement was born on August 29, 1989, just in time for my first day of high school.

"It's a boy!" Great-Gram told me with her toothless smile. She'd come into her bedroom to ensure I was awake, though the shrill ring of the kitchen telephone had abruptly done the job for her.

"Oh," I said with indifference as I rubbed the crusties out of my eyes.

It's not that I didn't care. I was just more nervous about my first day of high school and the added stress of not being home to get ready.

"Your mother and the baby are doing good, so Ron is on his way to get you."

"All right," I said, sitting up.

"Quiéres café?" she asked.

"Please!" I begged. "Thanks, Great-Gram."

I'd been dropped off at Sonia's apartment in Chicago, where Great-Gram lived now, when Mom went to the hospital to have labor induced three days before. Although my "big brother" cousin Aaron wasn't there, having joined the Navy after high school, I'd been fine with the arrangement since it gave me time with Great-Gram. However, I'd expected to be home well before the morning of my first day.

Aside from the typical worries about remembering the combination for my locker, finding my classes, and having enough time to get from one end of the building to the other in the time allotted, I had anxiety about being late. Punctuality was not Mom and Ron's strong suit. So, as a result, I was often late to dance classes, orchestra rehearsals, viola lessons, parties, and events. Today, of all days, though, I didn't want to deal with the embarrassing stares.

My unpreparedness was testing my nerves too. When we'd left the house, I'd thrown some random comfy clothes, panties, and my toothbrush in the bag, thinking I'd be back by nightfall or maybe the next day at the latest. If I'd have known that I'd be going straight from Great-Gram's to school, I'd have at least packed my makeup and something to do my hair with, as well as an actual outfit. I'd have also consulted with Kelly, to find out what she was planning to wear to compare.

Looking at myself in the mirror, I was displeased with the plain face, solid-pink T-shirt, and elastic-waist gray shorts which conspired to make me look like I was lounging at home for the day. This was fine for hanging out with Great-Gram, but this was not the impression I wanted to make on all the new kids I'd encounter. It was my fault, though. If I hadn't fought Mom about going to the prestigious private high school she'd wanted me to attend instead of the public one the grade school fed into, I would've been provided with a uniform, thereby saving me from sticking out like a sore thumb. Ron had refused to pay for me to go there, though, and I'd refused to be separated from my friends just because Mom didn't trust me to say no to drugs. She insisted that the public school ran rampant with them, as if the rich kids where she wanted me to go didn't dabble in worse things.

With no other option but to wear one of Great-Gram's floral muumuus, I went to the kitchen in my frumpy outfit. The familiar aroma of Great-Gram's dark roast coffee instantly soothed me. Having been made in a coffee press, lightened with lots of creamer and sweetened with too much sugar, I was eager to gulp down the steaming cup of joe she set in front of me.

"Thanks, Great-Gram," I said as I sat, noticing the late August sunshine coming in through the small window above the sink. It just barely reflected off the white ceramic and appliances, keeping the room shaded and cool.

Great-Gram smiled before asking, "Did you sleep well?"

"Yeah," I replied with a yawn. I watched her stir what I suspected was Cream of Wheat, her forever go-to for breakfast. She sweetened and solidified it to perfection before adding a thin layer of milk to the surface. I liked that layer of milk but always stirred it into the cereal anyway.

After taking a long sip of coffee, savoring every drop of it, I confessed,

"Okay, I didn't. I'm actually really nervous."

"About the new baby?"

"No," I said before taking another sip of coffee. I was more worried about the homely first impression I'd make on the one day I should have been putting my best foot forward. "Just first-day jitters, I guess."

She set the bowl of creamy cereal in front of me, careful not to slosh and spill the milk. I looked up at her with a grateful smile. The comfort that she and these familiar reminders of my humble roots provided was exactly what I needed to ground me right now.

"If someone doesn't like the way you look or the way you talk . . ." she said then pursed her lips and attempted a raspberry. It came out wrong since she didn't have her teeth in.

I cracked up at Great-Gram's version of a pep talk.

"I know, but it's not that easy to ignore how people look at me with judgment or the way they talk down to me like I'm a piece of worthless crap," I said, recalling how hard it had been for me to fit in with the kids at school when Mom had moved us to the suburbs with Ron.

Great-Gram sat down across from me. With one bulky, wrinkly arm on the table, she said, "It sounds like you're talking about someone in particular."

I lowered my eyes and pushed my hot cereal around. "Yeah, I guess I am."

"Your mother's husband?" she asked. I looked up and saw her sparse gray brows prodding me into admission. So, I nodded. Ron was, in fact, the primary bully in my life.

"Your mother made her choice," Great-Gram said, repeating what she'd told me too many times before, "so we all need to respect it."

"How do I respect it when it affects me the way it does?" I said loud enough to be considered disrespectful in itself. Then I consciously calmed. "I'm sorry, Great-Gram. I can only take so much, though. The things he says to me, the things he does . . . it's not right to treat a kid that way. Especially when I have to go to school and deal with more of it there!"

Great-Gram put her finger up to her lips and shook her head before reprimanding, "Don't say that, Dana."

"But it's true! And Mom does nothing to stop him. She goes along with it like—"

"You need to learn to stay quiet about these things," Great-Gram said as she rose from her seat. "Your mother doesn't need your permission to do anything. And you don't need to give life to the things that bring negativity to you."

I shook my head in disagreement. "So, you're saying it's okay for Mom to turn her head to what's going on in our house, instead of protecting me like she should?"

"No. I'm saying you can't control what others say and do."

"But what about *me*? Am I just supposed to let people treat me however they want to?"

"You," Great-Gram said, raising her brows for emphasis, "just worry about you. Because, Dana, no one else will. And the sooner you learn to stop depending on other people to be what you want and do what you think they should do, the sooner you'll learn that you can only control how you show up in this world."

I stared at Great-Gram and sighed. Like Master Yoda of the *Star Wars* series, she always had profound advice encrypted in nonsensical conversations. Before I could respond, though, a car horn disrupted our morning mentoring. We looked at each other with widened eyes.

After shoveling most of the cereal in my mouth and swigging half the cup of coffee, I grabbed my bag and said, "Love you, Great-Gram!"

"God bless," Great-Gram said, crossing me and then placing her hand on my cheek. I smiled at the loving gesture then rushed out the back door from the kitchen before Ron could honk again. Great-Gram watched from the doorway, to make sure I got to the car safely, then waved goodbye to me before Ron sped off.

After a few minutes of silent tension, I looked over at Ron, who'd had yet to greet me or say one word at all. I'd expected him to be in a good mood, elated that his "own child" had finally come to grace us with his presence. His pursed lips and tight grip on the steering wheel conveyed a seriousness I didn't understand.

"How's Mom? And the baby?" I asked, wondering if something had happened between the call to Great-Gram and now.

"Fine," Ron snipped.

"Good," I responded warily. Then I turned my attention ahead, deducing that the inconvenience of having to take me to school was probably the reason for his hostility. So, I remained quiet thereafter, almost appreciating the way he drove through city traffic like a maniac.

As we approached the main building of the high school, the crowded and chaotic scene turned my nerves into straight up panic. There were cars and kids everywhere. It was way too much for my analytical brain to process the way I usually did, first surveying a situation and then scanning it for potential threats to my safety and security. I felt the same overwhelm as having been thrown into the deep end of the pool without knowing how to swim, when Mom had forced me to take classes at the YMCA when I was younger. I'd been so traumatized by the harsh lesson that I never did learn how to swim after that. In fact, I'd avoided deep water since. So, my faith in today going any better was pretty much nil.

As Ron turned into the drop-off area, we passed the parking lot for students. It was congested with cars pulling into the short supply of empty spaces too fast. One car accelerated towards a couple kids walking towards the school and then swerved at the last second. The two kids walking laughed, even though an accident could have left them injured. I wondered if I could ever be so carefree about something so serious. I wondered if I could ever be carefree at all, honestly.

Other cars weaved between the long yellow buses to fight for curb space, then all emptied of nerdy kids fully equipped with backpacks and lunch bags, eager to fulfill their parents' expectations of grades good enough to get into medical or law school. Cool kids didn't take the bus. You could tell who they were too, because they were either walking from the parking lot, having caught a ride with a friend or sibling, or they were walking from whatever random direction they lived to avoid the stigma of having to take the bus at all. None of the cool kids carried anything either. They walked hand-in-hand with a boyfriend or girlfriend who was equally attractive or popular, or in a group of other handsome people. Only the stoners walked alone, taking a last drag before entering supervised territory.

Propelled backward when Ron hit the gas, I instinctively grabbed the door handle. There was an opening right in front of the entrance where someone had just pulled away. I braced myself as Ron came to a screeching halt. There had been no need for the fifty-foot show of speed and agility, so everyone looked to see where the loud engine noise had come from.

Of course, the bright red Corvette stuck out among the other parents' silver sedans and the older students' beaters, which was exactly what Ron had intended.

I, on the other hand, didn't want to be noticed. But now everyone was staring or glancing over their shoulder. I wanted to die.

Ron looked over at me too, expecting I'd jump out of the car like I usually did. Instead, I lingered. I felt safer in the Corvette with Ron, from whom I had come to expect rejection and insult, than I did risking the same with the thousands of kids piling into the school.

"What are you waiting for?" he snipped.

I wished I could tell him how nervous I was. I wished I could tell him I was afraid no one would like me, and that I wouldn't fit in here any more than I ever had anywhere else. I wished Ron was the kind of father who would console and encourage me. But he wasn't. He was the reason I just assumed no one liked me, and why I didn't see any point in trying to make new friends. So, I kept my feelings to myself, since they didn't matter.

I could barely breathe anyway, never mind speak. My heart was racing. I was starting to sweat, though the hot, humid weather was partially to blame. I worried I'd start smelling too, like I sometimes did when my anxiety spiked. All I needed was to be dubbed the "smelly kid" on my first day of high school. I'd never live it down, no matter how fragrant I'd be tomorrow. I'd literally be Pig-Pen.

Feeling the intensity of Ron's stare, I knew I had to say something. "I . . ." I started.

"You what? I don't have time for this, Dana," Ron said with inconsiderate impatience.

"I . . ." I tried again. I wished he could sense how scared I was. He wouldn't care, though, so there was no point in saying anything at all.

It was better for me to just get out of the car and march into the school with whatever fake confidence I could muster. But I was afraid to get out of the expensive sports car now, since everyone probably expected some fancy-dressed, perfectly coiffed popular girl with blonde hair and blue eyes to emerge. Unless they made a homely brunette called "Hot Mess Barbie," I wasn't that girl.

Ron cussed under his breath then reached across me to open the passenger door himself. "Go," he said as he shoved my shoulder.

I looked at him with teary eyes, hoping that maybe he had an ounce of decency in him to empathize with how I was feeling. His clenched teeth reminded me he was incapable of that. So, with tear-filled eyes and a fear-filled heart, I got out of the car and closed the car door.

Ron pulled away, turning onto the street sharply enough to make his tires squeal. I shook my head, annoyed that everyone once again gave him the attention he sought. But then I was glad they weren't staring at me. I was self-conscious enough as I turned and looked at the massive three-story brick compound.

The next four years of my life would hinge on the reputation I'd earn today and in the days to come. How I acted, what I said, how I looked— everything would be scrutinized. Presumptions would be made about who I was, which was unfair when I didn't even know. Mom had taught me to conform to fit in, though, instead of encouraging me to be whoever I truly was like Great-Gram had attempted in the short time I'd spent with her that morning. So, I was whoever I *had* to be, depending on what was expected of me in a given situation. Right now, I was expected to go into this building and report to homeroom.

So, I exhaled long and hard, then put one foot in front of the other, up the stairs to the entrance. Hoping for the best but expecting the worst, I felt just the same as when Mom had married Ron. And we all know how well that turned out.

"I Cross My Heart"

High school was exactly what I expected—like the movie *The Breakfast Club*. I wasn't the pretty-in-pink princess Claire, who Molly Ringwald played, though; it was the darker Allison, played to perfection by Ally Sheedy, that I related to. We even had a similar haircut, except that my dark hair was curly.

So, I wasn't sure where I fit in. I wasn't an athlete. I didn't want to be a stuck-up cheerleader, no matter how popular some of those girls were. Despite having been in the "gifted" program in junior high, I wasn't a nerd either. I wasn't a stoner. I couldn't even be around people who smoked without coughing up a lung. I wasn't part of any ethnic club or debate team. I was just me, which meant I was nothing and no one, just like Ron always said.

I guess I should have been glad to be invisible, though. It saved me from unwanted attention and the insult I just assumed would follow. I had enough on my mind anyway, wondering how our family dynamic would change once my new baby brother came home.

With a nearly fourteen-year age gap, I'd be more of a built-in babysitter than a sibling to this kid. Because of mom and Ron's failures as parents to me, however, I felt a certain duty to protect this baby. I also prayed he didn't turn out to be like our parents, out of fear that he would hate me too.

As I was begrudgingly doing homework some teacher had had the nerve to give on the third day of school, a piercing cry interrupted the quiet of the house. My baby brother! I hadn't met him yet. Ron had been going between work and the hospital since the baby was born but hadn't thought to take me. So, I abandoned the boredom of my bedroom and crept down the stairs to spy on this curious new human whom Mom had struggled to bring into this world for her selfish and egotistical husband.

From where I stood at the bottom step, I watched Ron scamper around Mom, frantically trying to help her yet doing nothing much of anything really. It was humorous and strange to see him fawning over Mom as if she were carrying some priceless fragile relic. I honestly hadn't thought him capable of caring about anything or anyone but himself.

Hoping to catch a glimpse of the baby's face, I moved from the entryway to the kitchen, where Mom sat slumped in a kitchen chair. She hadn't bothered to take off her coat, which was as baggy as her gray sweatpants. She looked tired and stressed, with her creased forehead and thin-lipped grimace. I wondered if the baby's ceaseless cries were giving her a headache too. When I saw Ron scrambling to unpack the bag he'd carried in, as if looking for something, I realized Mom's impatience might be with him and not the baby. Apparently, the little thing was hungry.

Ron produced a bottle of white fluid, which I presumed to be formula, and handed it to Mom like a hot potato. She stuck it in the baby's mouth, and the baby started suckling, rewarding us all with much-preferred murmurs now that his urgent need had been met.

At first, I was surprised she wasn't breastfeeding like Kelly's mom did with their new baby, but then I recalled Mom once telling me I was formula-fed. I guessed that made sense since I'd been cared for by Great-Gram when I was born and not Mom. But Mom was taking care of this baby, so how come she wasn't trying to breastfeed *him*?

More curious to see my new baby brother up close, I stepped nearer to Mom to peek at the swaddled bundle. Wrapped in a white cloth with thick pink-and-blue stripes, the baby's fat face and chubby cheeks were the only part of him exposed. His skin was reddened, and his eyes were shut. With tiny lips, he gripped the nipple of the bottle tightly, making it bob slightly with each suck.

Since neither Mom nor Ron offered a proper introduction, I asked, "What did you decide to name him?"

"Jonathan," Ron said from behind me, where he was busy unpacking all the baby supplies they'd brought from the hospital.

"Hi, Jonathan," I whispered. Then I asked Mom, "Why is his head shaped like a cone?" Even with the pink-and-blue-striped beanie cap, I could see how its egg shape came up to a peak. The large proportion of his head to his body made him look like renderings of aliens I'd seen on TV. I tried not to laugh at the thought.

Mom slowly raised her head to look at me. "They had to suck him out of me," she said. I crinkled my brows, having never heard of such a thing. "The doctor uses suction, like a vacuum, when a baby won't come out on its own."

"Oh," I said, thinking that they should have waited for the baby to come naturally, then, instead of making him come out on their preferred timing. I wondered if his brain was misshapen now too.

Mom bent her neck back then.

"You okay?" Ron asked. He was still unpacking her bag and putting things away.

"Yeah," she said, even though she clearly wasn't. She looked exhausted, which seemed reasonable after having been in labor for so long. I'd expected her to show some sign of happiness, however, to finally have this baby after trying for so many years. But she didn't. Her eyes were actually dimmer than usual, like she was dead inside.

The possibility that she had regrets about this wasn't too far off base. I mean, it's not like it had been her idea. She'd had her tubes tied immediately after I was born, which told me she probably hadn't wanted *any* kids. It had been a fact I'd held on to all these years, in my attempt to not take her emotional detachment from me personally. But now Mom had two kids she potentially hadn't wanted. So, all we could do now was hope *this* one was enough for Ron.

I looked over at Ron then, who glared at me with his beady eyes. It's like he was warning me to stay away from his new family.

"Well, congratulations, Mom," I whispered as I stepped away from her and the baby. I didn't want to provoke an argument. Not in front of the baby. My baby brother hadn't asked to be brought into this hostile family dynamic, nor did he deserve to be thrown into it so quickly. "I'm going to go back upstairs, unless you need anything."

"No, we're fine," Mom said in a glum tone. That's what I always said too, except I think Mom forced herself to believe it.

Back in my bedroom, I was starting to realize I couldn't save Mom, because I couldn't help someone who didn't think they needed saving. I had my own mixed feelings about all this, anyway, which I needed to focus on more if there was any hope of saving myself.

That evening, after Ron had gone to lift weights at the gym, I heard Mom in the baby's room across the hall from mine. What used to be the den, where I'd been sat down on the Berber sofa to be told about a separation that never occurred, was now occupied with a dark wooden crib against one wood-paneled wall and a changing table against the other. The one small window at the top corner of the opposite wall barely shed light into this dreary space unfit for a new life.

"What's up, Dane?" Mom asked with the same haste as usual.

"Nothing," I said. I'd just wanted to see my little brother again without Ron breathing down my neck.

The baby was lying on the changing table, completely oblivious to the world around him. I wondered if he could even see or hear. I could certainly smell him regardless! "Oh, my—" I couldn't even finish my sentence. I pulled my T-shirt over my mouth and groaned.

"You don't have to be so dramatic," Mom said as she pulled wipe after wipe to clean up the pea-green shit literally oozing from the baby's butt. "It's not that bad."

I begged to differ. I turned away and gagged. Then I stepped out of the room to replace the air in my nostrils.

When I turned back, Mom was stretching across the room. She had one hand on Jonathan, to prevent him from rolling off the changing table, but couldn't quite reach the diaper bag hanging off the crib. I rushed to get it for her.

"Thanks," she said.

"Of course," I responded, retreating to the doorway, where the air smelled much better.

Focused on the task of putting the new diaper on Jonathan and then redressing him in a onesie, Mom was quiet. She didn't talk sweet to the baby as I'd seen Kelly's mother do when changing the new addition to their family. Kelly's mother cooed and smiled and let the baby reach up for her lips and nose. None of that was going on here, though.

"I joined cross country," I said in an attempt to remind Mom I'd started high school in her absence. I thought she might want to ask me how that was going so far.

"Cross what?"

"Cross country," I repeated. "It's a sport? Running?" I couldn't help my smart-ass tone. It annoyed me that she never paid attention to anything I said or did.

"What?" she asked with even more exasperation at my nuisance.

"Never mind," I said, then mumbled, "I was just excited to tell you the coach came to *me* because another coach saw me running during gym and told me I had a lot of potential."

"What, Dane?" Mom said.

I should've known she was too busy to listen to anything I had to share. It wasn't as important as the baby, anyway. So, I replied, "Nothing, Ma," and went back to my room.

That night, while we were all asleep, a shrill scream woke me. I assumed either Mom or Ron would tend to the baby, but after cringing at the sounds and hearing no attempts to resolve it, I got up to tend to the baby myself.

On my way, I looked towards Mom and Ron's bedroom. Although it was dark, my eyes had adjusted enough for me to see two long lumps in the bed. Neither moved nor flinched. There was no way they couldn't hear the baby, though. Were they ignoring him on purpose? I mean, it's not like they took sleeping pills or drank alcohol, to explain being oblivious to the noise.

I shook my head and huffed at their inconsideration of me and *my* need to sleep as I proceeded into the baby's room. I closed the door behind me, afraid they'd catch me in here. I still wasn't sure if I was allowed around the baby. Then I went to the crib to soothe Jonathan. I never wanted him to feel like no one heard him, like I'd felt my whole fucking life.

I didn't have much experience with babies, so I was careful when picking him up. I remembered how Kelly's mom had shown me to put one hand behind the head and the other underneath the body, because a baby couldn't hold its head up itself. I held him close to my chest as I reached back into his crib for his pacifier, then settled into the blue-cushioned rocking chair under the tiny window in the corner. Once I plugged the pacifier into his mouth and rocked, Jonathan stopped crying.

I grinned at my natural ability to affect the baby this way. Then again, I had always found soothing in the way Great-Gram had held me in her lap and rocked me. So, maybe that's something Jonathan and I had in common, aside from our mother.

The light of the moon cast a grayish glow on Jonathan's round face. I stared at him, noticing how peaceful he seemed curled up against my chest. His slits for eyes were closed, and he made the sweetest suckling sounds, which came and went with the in-and-out movement of the pacifier. His button nose was hard to resist pressing on and making some silly noise. I wouldn't do that now, though. I needed him to sleep so the rest of us could, though it should have been Mom or Ron ensuring that, not the other way around. They still hadn't come to check on him.

"Don't worry, baby brother. Sis is here," I said, as if my thoughts had been a conversation we were having. "Sissy's always going to be here. No matter what. I promise."

Smiling down at this innocent baby, who hadn't asked to be brought into such a complicated family, I silently made the million other promises I owed him. He wasn't mine, but I loved him like he was.

As such, I would ensure that Jonathan had a better life than I did. He deserved that. We both did. No one had saved me from the unhealed trauma Mom and Ron carried in their hearts, so I would save Jonathan. I would give him everything Mom and Ron hadn't given me—love, security, protection, connection. I never wanted him to feel an ounce of the pain I felt in my heart, or the sting of a harsh hand on his body. If anyone ever tried to hurt my baby brother, they'd have to get through me first. At least until he could defend himself.

"Long Way Home"

Sleepless nights of Jonathan screaming throughout were taking a toll on me and Mom. It was becoming increasingly difficult day after day to go to school, viola lessons, dance classes, and now cross country practices, when I could barely keep my eyes open at all.

Mom trudged around just the same, though at least she was lucky enough to work from home now. Ron had set up a desk for her in the corner of the basement, out of the way of the new leather sofas and ginormous TV whose rare use merely served as a display of Ron's perceived wealth and status.

Ron wasn't around much anymore. He went to work, lifted weights with other self-absorbed, steroid-using men whose muscles looked like that of the cartoon character Popeye. Then he came home sometime between dinner and bedtime, to eat and then watch TV until he fell asleep.

On the one hand, his absence was nice. It was much less tense without him around. On the other hand, I felt bad watching Mom try to do everything herself while Ron's life went on as if nothing had changed. He didn't even try to help her with the baby or their business duties, and God forbid he lifted a finger around the house.

Mom never said anything, though. She struggled to fulfill the demands of her daily duties to their business, with the constant interruption of the baby crying for food, nap, or a diaper change. She tidied and cleaned and washed dishes instead of napping with the baby. She still ironed Ron's jeans and shirts as he expected her to, though she let mine and hers go due to lack of time.

What I didn't see her do was smile. She had everything she wanted—a husband, financial stability, a house in the suburbs, nice cars, brand-name clothes. She just hadn't realized that the price for her dream come true was to be stuck with two kids she'd have never chosen to have otherwise, and a business Ron basically left her to run herself. He did go to work every day but spent most of his time working to restore another Corvette he'd purchased, then taking a few hours for "lunch." Where he really went was a wonder to everyone.

The only upside to our new dynamic was that Mom started cooking dinner. I suspected it was to lure Ron home from the gym earlier. Because it's not like she needed something else to do. Nor did she partake in these meals herself. I didn't see her consume much of anything other than Cokes and coffee. Unfortunately, her meals often ended up in Tupperware in the refrigerator, since Ron and I weren't always around when dinner was done, let alone at the same time.

Then again, there was no regularity around when Mom cooked. Sometimes, dinner was ready at five o'clock; other times, it was at eight. So, as much as I appreciated Mom's efforts, we just weren't the type of family who sat down to a meal together, and it was a shame.

I looked forward to whatever she made nonetheless, because it saved me some of the fifty dollars a week she gave me for food now. It was sufficient for lunches, but I preferred a home-cooked meal for dinner over whatever snack I could get out of a vending machine to suffice after cross country practice.

"Oh my god, does that smell good!" I said when I got home one late afternoon. I peeked over Mom's shoulder to see what she had on the stove.

"It's just spaghetti sauce, Dane."

"Are you making it with those multicolored rotini noodles?" I asked.

"Yeah," she replied.

I smiled. "Let me know when it's all done, then. I'm starving!" I said as I took a can of pop from the refrigerator and went up to my room to do my homework. I'd noticed the baby monitor on the kitchen counter and Jonathan's bedroom door closed upstairs. So, I closed my bedroom door too, guessing he was napping.

When I came out of my room a while later, Jonathan's door was open.

"The pasta is ready, so help yourself," Mom called out from within.

"Okay, thanks!" I said then went down to eat. My cross country coach did say carbohydrates were good for runners, which was my justification for the second helping I was spooning into my bowl as Ron walked in.

"Don't eat too much of that," he said as he slapped the mail down onto the counter.

"There's plenty for everyone," I defended.

"All that pasta will make you fat," he said, nodding to reference the amount in my bowl. Then he reached into the cupboard for his own.

Holding the spoon in the pot, I stopped and looked at my gluttony. As much as I hated Ron's constant criticism about what I ate, he was right. I didn't need to eat this much pasta. If I ever wanted a boyfriend, like a lot of other girls my age had, I had to stay skinny. No one would want me if I gained too much weight.

Suddenly desperate to burn off the carbohydrate energy of my first bowlful, I put my untouched second helping on the counter and set out on a walk. I had no particular destination or direction in mind. I just needed to exert my caloric overconsumption.

Pumping my arms like the old ladies who walked in the mall, I got them going, hard and high. I looked down at my belly after a minute, picking up the pace as I noticed how blatantly my little pooch protruded from the front of my black spandex biker shorts. I wished I'd thought to put a T-shirt on before I left. I felt fat and overexposed wearing just a sports bra on top.

Who I am is not determined by the size of my belly, I told myself. But that was bullshit. The only compliment I ever received from anyone was that I was pretty. That's what Ron had always said about Mom, before she got pregnant at least. So, how could I not see my appearance as the entirety of my worth?

As much as I hated Ron's ability to affect the way I saw myself, I hated myself more. Most people didn't consider a hundred and ten pounds overweight for an almost fourteen-year-old girl. My thirty-year-old mother hadn't weighed much more before Jonathan. Yet, I was letting a short, stocky middle-aged man with a Fred Flintstone build and receding hairline make me believe *my* body was subpar?

Apparently so. Because as soon as my full stomach would allow me to run without aching, I did. Whether Ron was right or wrong about the pasta making me fat, I didn't want to be fat. I saw how the heavier girls at school struggled to breathe during gym class. None could run the full mile our physical education teacher timed us on once a year. They could barely move or stretch without some sort of difficulty. I never wanted my body to hinder me. My health and physical ability were about all I could control in my life anymore, anyway. As such, I purposely headed down the frontage road behind our neighborhood towards the overpass for the expressway. Uphill runs built more muscle and burned more calories than walking on level ground, and a toned and slender body was my ultimate goal.

When my rubbery legs felt like they would give out over the other side of the bridge, I slowed and started in the direction of my high school. After a crippling cross country practice and now this run, I didn't think I'd make it up and over that bridge again, whereas the school was straight down this one street. There was one last bus that left the school around 6:30 p.m., for any kids who'd had a late practice, game, or rehearsal of some sort. Tonight, it would be my saving grace, if I could catch it. By the look of the darkening sky, it would be close.

Unfortunately, the buses had already pulled out into the main street as I approached. I kept moving, though, knowing the front entrance would still be unlocked for anyone who was waiting for a ride. Once in, I used a pay phone to call Mom to come pick me up. I'd learned in grade school to always keep a quarter in my shoe just in case.

"I didn't even know you left, but no, I can't, Dane. I have the baby," she said, clearly annoyed that I'd even asked.

"What about Ron?" My legs hurt so bad I'd have gladly endured an awful car ride with him if it meant not walking or running anymore.

Mom huffed. "He's watching TV in the basement. I'm not going to ask him after the long day he's had," she said.

I wanted to argue about this long day he'd supposedly endured, living his life like a leisurely millionaire, but I was too tired to fight.

"You're just going to have to find your own way back. I gotta go," Mom said. I heard Jonathan fussing as she hung up.

This wasn't the first time I'd been in the position of having to find my own way. I often had to ask for rides to and from practices or lessons when

Ron couldn't drive me, or just walk or ride my bicycle to wherever to avoid Ron altogether. I'd even called Kelly's dad to drive me to school once when Mom and Ron had refused because I'd run late that morning and they'd wanted to teach me a lesson.

However, after being forced to run multiple miles at cross country practice, at speeds that pushed the bounds of possibility, I had just hoped that tonight Mom might make the five-minute drive for me. But it was my fault for having left. So, I blew out a long breath then headed back home.

I couldn't help but feel somewhat resentful, though, that something or someone always came before me. Whether she was working, doing dishes, folding laundry, Mom was always too busy for me. Now that she had the baby to take care of, it'd be a wonder if she bothered with me at all.

My irritation wasn't with Jonathan, though. It was in *always* being the low man on the totem pole. The most unimportant. The least of any priorities, though I'd argue I wasn't a priority at all. Being made to feel so insignificant had worn on my self-esteem until none remained. Confidence escaped me too. But then, how *could* I feel good about myself when no one else saw anything valuable in me?

As the blue sky turned black above me, I realized how symbolic it was of the way one phase of my life had just ended. I wasn't in grade school anymore. I wasn't an only child anymore either. I was a teenager, which meant I was almost an adult. I had to start thinking like one and preparing for the life I would lead on my own, for I was intent on leaving home as soon as I turned eighteen and relieving us all of the burden I imposed on our lives. That way, Mom and Ron could have their perfect little family with Jonathan, and I could go out into the world and seek the happiness I lacked in the life I was stuck in now.

Forcing my feet towards a house that was never meant to be my home felt wrong, just the same as how running cross country for a coach I wasn't fast enough for didn't increase my sense of self-worth like sport was supposed to. The way I felt now, I wasn't sure I could ever even walk again, never mind run.

So, I wouldn't keep seeking approval from people who refused to give it. That meant no more cross country—hyperventilating and muscle pain sucked anyway—and no more trying to be who Mom and Ron decided I should be. Great-Gram, my uncles, my friends, and their parents thought I was perfectly fine as I was. It was about time I started thinking the same way and doing what I felt was right for me. And right now, I wanted a date for the Homecoming Dance, because music and dancing made me happier than anything else. And I deserved to be happy.

"Just A Friend"

*T*he whole school had been buzzing about Homecoming. There would be a parade, a pep rally, a spirit day, then a big football game before the formal dance. It sounded epic.

Girls in my classes bragged about who they were going with, what they were wearing, how they'd have their hair done . . . So, of course, I wanted to go too. I wanted to wear a pretty dress and have my hair all done up. The only problem was I didn't have a date.

Kelly didn't have a date either. We thought we could go as friends. However, the school only allowed tickets to be purchased for traditional boy-girl pairs. I was bummed, but Kelly didn't care. She wasn't into any of the boys we knew, and she didn't see any need to be at the dance for social notice either. I wished I had her confidence because I felt like I'd be hailed the school loser if I didn't attend the one big event that anyone who was anyone would be at.

Even Miranda, whose family couldn't afford to buy her a nice dress, never mind the tickets themselves, had gotten a date for the dance. She tended towards guys in their twenties for some reason—usually sleezy rock-and-roll types with mullets that had gone out of style—but a date was a date and something I didn't have.

Desperate to find *someone* to ask me to this dance, I considered whether I had to. Times had changed. It was 1989. Maybe I didn't have to wait for a boy to ask me. Maybe I could be a modern woman who asked a young man instead.

Who could I ask, though? Who would even say yes? I didn't want to risk the rejection of asking a stranger. That's when I thought of Kevin, the Czech boy who'd been my boyfriend in seventh grade. We'd gotten along grandly until I'd cut my hair short. My hair had grown out into a bob since then, so I thought he might reconsider dating me now that I looked like a girl again. He didn't seem to be involved with anyone else, anyway.

So, one day at lunch, I saw Kevin sitting at a table with some friends. I didn't dare approach him to ask him to the dance in front of them. It was embarrassing enough to have to beg for a date, anyway. I mean, if Kevin had wanted to take me, he'd have asked me himself!

As I sat there stewing about how to go about this, one of Kevin's friends got up and went to a vending machine. I knew the kid from junior high. He was really nice. So, I thought he might be the key to Kevin.

"Hey!" I said as I walked up from behind.

"Oh, hi, Dana!" Kevin's friend said, glancing at me and then back at the machine. He looked misplaced, being a foot shorter than everyone including me. His thick glasses magnified his crossed eyes, almost distracting from his oddly egg-shaped head.

"How's everything been going?" I asked, pretending to decide on a snack too.

"Good," the friend said as he deposited coins into the machine and made a selection.

"Kevin doing good too?" I asked.

"Yeah!" he said as he pushed his glasses back upon his flat nose. "He's on the gymnastics team, though, so we don't hang out as much as we used to."

"That sucks," I said, scrunching my nose. "I feel like a lot of us have lost touch since starting high school."

"I know. I barely see anyone anymore," the friend said with a mouth full of his Snickers bar. It looked really good. I had to remember not to eat candy, though; Ron said too much sugar would make me fat.

"Can I ask you a favor?" I asked, refocusing on what I'd approached him about.

"Sure. Whaddya need?" he said before gnawing another bite of chocolate nougat.

"Will you ask Kevin if he still likes me?" I cringed. "I was kind of hoping he'd be my date to the Homecoming Dance."

The boy looked at me with a raised brow. I knew it wasn't right for a girl to be so forward. I didn't know what else to do, though. So, I was relieved when he shrugged and said, "Okay." Then he walked over to the table where Kevin was while I awaited his return.

I remained at the vending machine, pretending to be making a decision about what to get. I glanced over my shoulder once to make sure the friend was doing as I asked. I didn't want to look stupid standing there that long.

Perhaps it was my hormones or my obsession with finding a date, but I couldn't help but notice how much more of a man Kevin had become in the short time since we'd gone together. He'd always been gorgeous with that bright blond hair that he wore just a bit too long. The style was reminiscent of the "bowl" cut the straight-haired kids had when we were younger. He had a million-dollar smile too, to match the upbeat personality that drew people to him.

Where he'd been pudgy before, however, muscles had taken shape. His face was more defined too, from his European cheekbones to the point of his chin. He was a total babe now. I bet his ass was tight too, from all the clenching those gymnasts had to do to maintain balance. Embarrassed at my own thoughts, I turned away to avoid him noticing my stare.

Just then, Kevin's friend reappeared at my side. "He said he likes you as a friend, but that's it," he reported. "And he wants to keep his options open now that we're in high school."

"Oh," I said, dropping my head. "Well, thanks for asking at least." Then, just as his friend turned to walk away, I threw out, "Tell him to call me if he changes his mind, though." The boy nodded in acknowledgment. But the call never came, and time was running out. So, I decided to call Kevin myself.

"Hello?" his mother answered.

I cringed, having hoped for Kevin to answer. It was embarrassing to have to talk to the parent of someone of the opposite sex. It's like they knew what you were calling about, and it felt wrong. But it would be more humiliating to hang up. "Hi! Can I talk to Kevin, please?" I asked in a high pitch that overcompensated for the politeness I strove for.

"Can I tell him who's calling?" she asked, sounding like his professional assistant.

"Um. It's Dana," I said in a tone that expressed my disappointment in myself for what I was doing.

"Oh. Hi, Dana," she said. "Hold on." Then I heard her call out for him.

I tapped my foot nervously, twisting the curly phone cord around my fingers while I waited for him to pick up.

"Got it, Mom!" he hollered before saying, "Hello?"

I waited for the click of his mother hanging up. Then I said, "Hey," hoping my upbeat tone disguised my insecurity.

"Oh, hi!" he said cheerily. "What's up?"

After having his friend ask him about going to the dance with me, he had to know that had something to do with this random call. So, I didn't beat around the bush. "Well, um, I was just wondering if . . . I don't know . . . if maybe you changed your mind about going to the Homecoming Dance? With me?"

Kevin was quiet for a moment. That wasn't good. "I don't know," he said with a reluctance that told the truth. It wasn't an outright rejection, though. So, there was the possibility of swaying him.

"I know you said you want to keep your options open and all. And I get it. I really do," I said. "But we can either sit at home the night of the dance or go with an old friend. And I don't know about you, but it sounds like it would be more fun to just go to the dance. Together."

Kevin sighed. "Yeah, but—"

"People go to dances as friends all the time," I argued.

"That's true, but—"

I wasn't taking no for an answer, especially when he hadn't said no yet. "But what? You do want to go to the dance, don't you?"

"Well, yeah, but—" He stopped himself. Then he said, "It's just . . . okay, listen. Back in junior high, you'd once asked me if I liked you enough to marry you."

Did I? I wondered, cringing at how desperate that must have sounded. I could *see* myself wanting to latch on to someone who would love me like Mom and Ron didn't. I just didn't remember *saying* that. Now I wished *he* hadn't either!

"Oh, yeah," I said, giggling to pass off the immaturity. "I was just . . . well . . ." I didn't know how to explain myself. The truth was no better than any lie I could come up with on the spot.

"The thing is, Dana, it kind of freaked me out," he admitted.

"I'm sorry," I said, having no excuse. It wasn't his fault I got attached to people too quickly.

"Don't get me wrong. I like you. I always have. But just as a friend. I don't want to get serious with someone who's, well, clingy."

I shuddered at the way he stigmatized me with that word. But I couldn't refute it because it was true. "I don't mean to be, though. It's just—"

"Your parents. I know," he said with the same sincerity I'd been initially attracted to in him.

Despite everything I'd shared with him in the past, he'd never judged me or made me feel strange for having feelings about a home life that made me different from everyone else. I'd never had to explain why I felt a certain way because he already knew. He knew me, and he liked me; he accepted me for who I was, which seemed to be a rarity in life.

So, in this silence, my desperation for a date—to be part of a paramount high school tradition—had just instantly shifted into renewed captivation for Kevin. I wanted to be his girlfriend again.

"Let's just start with the dance," I suggested, to avoid coming off as pushy. "Okay? No strings attached. No pressure. Just two friends going somewhere together."

There was another long pause before he asked, "Are you sure you can handle that?"

Honestly, I wasn't. I longed to belong to someone, not in a submissive or possessive way, but in the sense that I wanted to be someone's "somebody." I didn't think there was anything wrong with that either. Isn't that what everyone wanted?

"Yes, Kevin. I think I can handle going to a dance with you without a commitment," I lied. "So, are you going to be a gentleman and buy the tickets at school tomorrow, or should I?" I asked, borrowing from an assumptive closing technique I'd been taught when I'd had to go hocking Girl Scout cookies for my troop.

Kevin laughed. Then, to my surprise, he surrendered. "I'm the gentleman, so I'll get 'em."

I smiled. Not only was I going to the dance, but I was going with a hot guy who actually had a heart and who I trusted with mine. I couldn't have been happier. Nor could I wait to go shopping for a dress.

When I heard dishes clinking in the kitchen later that evening, I went downstairs, excited to tell Mom the news. Jonathan was in his bouncy seat nearby, staring at the brightly colored shapes dangling from the bar above him.

"Guess what, Mom?"

"What, Dane?" she said as emotionlessly as ever.

"I'm going to the Homecoming Dance!" I said, unable to contain my excitement. I shook one of the dangling shapes for Jonathan and watched him stare at it in awe.

"Oh, yeah?" she said, lacking my enthusiasm.

"Yeah! So can we go shopping for a dress?"

Mom shook her head. "I don't have time to go shopping! Between work and the baby . . ."

"Okay," I said, having expected the response. "I just thought . . . never mind."

I shook another one of the bobbles for Jonathan and then went back to my room to call Kelly. She was more than happy to hit the mall with me that weekend. We had the best time trying on different dresses together at different stores. Then, of course, we got some Mrs. Field's cookies. The white chocolate macadamia nut were my absolute favorite, so I couldn't pass them up.

When I returned home, I was eager to tell Mom about the dress I'd fallen in love with.

"You have to see it, Mom! It's black velvet and flares out. But the top of it is satin and wraps around off the shoulder," I shared.

"How much is it?"

"I don't know," I said with a shrug. "I didn't look at the tag. I just thought you would want to take me back to the store so I could try it on for you." I'd heard girls at school talk about how their mothers took them dress shopping and then to lunch. I longed for a mother-daughter date like that.

"I told you before, Dane. I don't have time—"

"Please, Mom! Just this once. I want to show it to you so you can see how perfect it is," I begged. "Please?"

With a long exhale intended to make me feel like the bother I already knew myself to be, Mom said, "Fine. But just that one store. I can't leave the baby with Ron that long, and I don't want to take him with."

I was beyond thrilled for her agreement. So, when Ron got home the next afternoon, a little earlier than he normally did, Mom took me to Lord & Taylor. She'd even put on jeans and fixed her hair, looking more like the mother I'd known before the baby had come along. She didn't sing in the car with me, though, which meant she wasn't in a good mood.

I led her to the second floor of the department store anyway and showed her the dress. She spied the price before even taking it off the rack. "Dane!" she said with widened eyes.

"Just let me try it on for you. Please?" I begged, having no clue how much it obviously cost.

Mom sighed. "I guess. But I don't know how you think we can just—"

I rushed to the dressing room before she finished her complaint. When I emerged, I stepped onto a short pedestal surrounded by mirrors angled in every possible direction. Then I looked over my shoulder at Mom, expecting to be met with "oohs" and "aahs."

Instead, she shrugged. "It's nice."

Disappointed that she hadn't specifically complimented how the dress looked on me, I looked down, doubting whether it did. Although I still wasn't sure, I did really like it. "So, can I get it?" I asked, turning my head to the side to avoid the expected rejection.

"If that's the dress you want . . .?"

"Yeah," I said weakly. *I also wanted a mother who gave a shit, though.*

"All right, then. Get changed so we can get back home," she said, standing from the chair she'd been waiting in.

"So, you're getting it for me?"

"I guess," she said with another quick shrug.

"Oh my god! Thank you, Mom!" I said, wanting to hug her for the favor. I clasped my hands under my chin instead and smiled widely.

"Just don't tell Ron I spent this much on it. Okay?"

"Of course not!" I said, shaking my head.

Conspiring against Ron, having this secret between us, made me feel more bonded to Mom than I had since she'd let me play viola in fifth grade.

So, I rushed up to my bedroom with the dress when we returned home, before Ron could even see it.

Then, when I left the house wearing the expensive frock the following Saturday, Ron didn't ask where it had come from. I'd already planned to say I'd borrowed it from a friend, so I wouldn't get Mom in trouble.

It made me even happier that Mom left the baby with Ron again to drive me and Kevin to the dance herself. So, maybe she did care about me a little bit. I was grateful for being spared a drive with Ron regardless.

When Kevin first saw me, I'd hoped to stun him with my curly bob, elegant dress, and muted red lips. Instead, he regarded me like an old friend, simply saying, "Hey." I was disappointed that he didn't see me as being as pretty as I felt, but I wasn't offended. I was fully aware that I wasn't anything extraordinary to look at.

Kevin's mom, who was standing at the open front door, prodded, "Kevin?"

"Oh, yeah," he mumbled. "My mom got this for you to wear."

He handed me a clear plastic container with a rose wristlet inside. By then, my mother had gotten out of the car to take pictures of Kevin following his mother's instruction to put it on me. He looked so handsome in his black suit, but I definitely felt like I was feeling more chemistry with him than he was with me. Then again, he'd only agreed to go to the dance with me as friends.

We had a good time too. We reunited with classmates from junior high. Our picture was taken by the professional photographer who'd instructed Kevin to hold me from behind. It felt good to snuggle up against him. We drank the legendary punch, which wasn't spiked with alcohol as we'd heard it would be. We slow-danced to "Right Here Waiting" by Richard Marx, and then Kevin sang "When I See You Smile" to me as I held on to him with my hands around his neck, barely swaying to the melody. I was on top of the world and pretty much head over heels for Kevin by the time we left the dance. So much so that I didn't even care that Ron had been charged with taking us to the local Blockbuster to rent a movie to watch back at Kevin's house. He left us on the curb as usual, telling me he'd be back for me in two hours.

Kevin lived in a modest ranch home on a very quiet street in the next town over. It was a stark contrast from the spinning lights and deafening music we'd left in the school gym. It was nice to get out of my high heels, though, and cuddle comfortably on the love seat in their den.

"I'll be in the living room if you two need anything," Kevin's mother said as she handed us a bowl of popcorn that she'd made for us to share while we watched the movie.

"Thanks, Mom," Kevin told her before she disappeared to the other end of the house. Then he powered up the VCR, inserted the tape, and pressed play. Then he flipped the lights off and settled in next to me.

The blue light emitting from the nineteen-inch screen allowed me to inspect Kevin's profile without his notice. He was a perfect specimen. He could have any girl he wanted. So, I was intent on making sure that girl was me. The arm he had around my bare shoulders was a good indication he might be open to the same. When I saw him glance at the open door of the den and then turn to me and smile, I was sure of it.

He leaned into me with a tilted head, so I met him halfway. I'd been dying to kiss him all night. So, when our lips touched, my whole body tingled; and when he put his tongue into my mouth, it was like electricity shocking me. His lips moved to my bare shoulders after that, then down into the front of my dress. I was on fire with a lust I thought I was too young to know.

Having had no idea how good it would feel to have his hands touch me in places nobody had ever touched before, I didn't stop him. I touched him too, wanting to return the favor of those titillating sensations between my legs. I wanted him to feel the overwhelming desire for me that I felt for him. I could tell that he did by how much harder he . . . kissed me.

We groped and licked, and I straddled his lap. I couldn't help myself. Neither could he. The chemistry between us was undeniable. I'd never thought I'd have this effect on a boy. I'd never thought I'd be ready for sex either, until I was here with him, struggling to deny us what we both obviously wanted. We had to, though. His mother was in the living room. I'd literally drop dead if an adult ever caught me in that act, especially the first time!

"Kevin," I whispered breathlessly between long intertwines of our tongues.

"Huh?" he asked as I reluctantly leaned away.

"Not with your mom in the house," I said quietly, though the blaring TV disguised all the salacious sounds we'd already created together.

Kevin blew a long exhale out of his mouth and slumped back into the couch. "You're right," he said, throwing his head and arms back too.

"I know," I said.

"I want to, though."

"I know," I said, smirking this time. "Me too."

Then I climbed off him and straightened myself up as he adjusted the large bulge in the crotch of his pants.

"What movie is this again?" I asked.

"*The Abyss*," he replied, returning his arm to where it had been around my shoulders.

"I'll show you my abyss," I flirted with a smirk. Kevin laughed. But I hadn't been joking.

"I Want You to Want Me"

$\mathcal{I}$n the weeks to follow, Kevin and I were definitely more than just friends. He'd sneak me into his house whenever he could but only when his mother wasn't home. So, I guessed he wasn't as noble as he came off. He was just as susceptible to sexual desire as any other teenage boy, though we never did more than mess around.

Perhaps I should have been bothered by him only changing his mind about our relationship when he saw what I was willing to give. Sadly, I wasn't. All high school boys wanted sexual favors, I'd heard. So, I thought that by doing those things with Kevin, he would love me in return.

Anyway, I couldn't deny how good it felt to be wanted, even if it was just physically; though I'd argue that we knew and liked each other well enough to make what we were doing okay. So, I continued telling Mom that I was going to a female friend's house and go to Kevin's house instead. She didn't seem to question it, and I never asked her for a ride. She seemed to be feeling better, anyway, and had even started going back to the office a few days a week, leaving Jonathan with our grandma.

On my late December birthday, Kevin and I were making out on his bed with a Def Leppard tape playing in the background. After a few minutes, he removed his shirt, then mine. Then he unbuttoned his pants to release what they could no longer contain. He pressed it into me before undressing me completely. Then he lay on my naked body.

I knew what was about to happen, and I felt completely comfortable proceeding. I'd always wanted my first time to be with someone I knew well and who cared about me—someone like Kevin. So, when Kevin looked into my eyes, conveying adoration and promise, I maintained his gaze with an intensity that expressed the same. With that quiet consent, Kevin used his knees to spread my legs and attempted to penetrate me. Unfortunately, my body wasn't as prepared as my heart was to let him in.

"I'm sorry," I said, embarrassed that my private part wouldn't cooperate. "Just keep trying."

He did, but the invisible chastity belt apparently had a lock neither of us had the key to. So, he eventually gave up.

"It's okay," he said as he climbed off of me.

"No. I want to," I argued. I really did! I didn't understand why my hoo-ha wouldn't let us!

"Don't worry about it, Dana. Really," he said, as he picked up our clothes off the floor. He seemed sincere. Still, I felt deficient, like I'd let us both down.

"We can try again another time," I offered, eager to maintain his interest. His closed-mouth smile appeased me.

Propping myself up on my elbow and watching him dress, I realized how much he looked like the actor and singer, Patrick Swayze. If his hair were a little longer and styled differently . . . how could my body reject this gorgeous hunk?

"Come on. Get dressed," he said, tossing my clothes at me playfully. "I'll take you somewhere for a birthday lunch."

Grateful that he wasn't treating me any differently after what had just happened, I got up and dressed. Then we went to a nearby hot dog stand for some Chicago dogs and fries.

Although we still labeled ourselves a couple, Kevin never invited me over to his house after that. We still hung out in friend groups at school and at the ice-skating rink we all frequented. He still called to talk sometimes, or to have me listen to his garage band over the phone after they'd perfected a popular song. But eventually, the calls lessened, and we were reduced to polite greetings as we passed in school corridors.

So, when he called my private phone line in the early spring of 1990, I was hopeful of resolving the strange dynamic between us and returning to what we'd started back up.

"Hey!" I said, as I turned down the new Mötley Crüe tape playing on my stereo. "What're you up to?"

"Nothing," Kevin said with unusual glum. He was rarely fazed by anything, so I knew something had to be weighing on his mind.

"What's wrong, then?" I asked.

A long pause followed. He finally said, "I have to talk to you about something, Dana."

Those words never ended well for me. So, I sat on the edge of my bed to receive whatever unpleasant news would follow. "Okay . . ." I prompted.

"I don't think we should be boyfriend and girlfriend anymore," he muttered.

I'd been right. I didn't want to hear this. I guessed I'd already known by the way he'd detached from me, though, that this was coming. Still, I wasn't prepared for the rejection.

"But why?" I begged. If it was something I could fix, like my hair, which had been an issue with him before, I would.

"I like you, Dana. I really do," he said.

He sounded sincere, but I was obviously lacking in some way. "What's the problem, then?"

Kevin sighed then said, "I just think maybe we should go our separate ways for now."

My panicked heart picked up its pace. I think it was finally realizing that this was really happening. "For now or forever?" I asked, hoping to hold on to whatever thin thread of hope I could, that there wasn't something so innately wrong with me that no one could ever love me.

"Please, Dana. Don't make this any harder than it has to be."

"You can't expect me to just say 'okay' and let you go!" I argued. I wouldn't let him just throw away the last few months. Not after what I'd almost given him.

"We'll always be friends, Dana. Always," he promised. "I just . . . I just think we should keep our options open. That's all."

I didn't want to keep my options open. I wanted to be enough for Kevin, so that he didn't need other options either. I wanted to be somebody's number one, the first person they called when something good happened, the person they turned to for comfort when life didn't go the way they wanted. I just wanted that best friend who I also kissed and grew into adulthood with, that person who wanted to make my dreams come true and vice versa. And I thought Kevin was that person. So, how come he didn't think the same of me?

"Dana?" Kevin asked to confirm I was still on the line.

"What?" I whimpered.

"Say something. Please."

I closed my eyes and shook my head. What was there to say?

"I hope you find what you're looking for," I said, though I hoped he'd realize sooner than later that it had always been me.

"Thanks," Kevin said. "You too."

Then he hung up, and I curled into fetal position on my bed and cried.

"Dane?" Mom asked. I looked up from where I'd hidden my face in my hands to see her standing in my doorway. "What's going on?"

"Nothing," I said, disinviting a conversation I didn't want to have with her.

"It's obviously not nothing," she snarked with an insensitivity that demonstrated why I didn't want to tell her anything.

I wanted soothing more than to be left alone, though. So, I gave her an answer, hoping she might be the mom I needed, even if for just a minute. "Kevin just broke up with me! Okay?"

Mom huffed out of her mouth. "You're only fourteen, Dane. It's not like it's the end of the world," she said as she turned to leave me.

But it was. I was apparently a pathetic virgin who had to beg boys for dates because nobody wanted me otherwise—including my mother.

"Poor, Poor Pitiful Me"

*T*owards the end of the school year, I overheard a girl in my Spanish class telling another girl that she'd invited Kevin to the upcoming concert the classic rock band Chicago was putting on. I quietly fumed as she gloated about how excited she was that he'd accepted the invitation.

Even though Kevin and I weren't a couple, and the rational part of my brain knew he had every right to go wherever with whomever, I felt betrayed all over again. I naively thought that lying my naked body underneath him warranted some respect or claim on him that precluded the idea of another girl having the same opportunity.

So, I marched straight to his locker immediately after class to confront him about it.

"Going to the Chicago concert, huh?" I asked with major attitude.

Kevin took a step back when he saw my scowl. "You know?"

"Yeah, I fucking know! Jesus Christ! I almost—" I stopped before I said it out loud. Then I looked around to make sure no one overheard my near slip. "All that bullshit about 'keeping our options open' . . . God, I feel stupid!"

"I'm sorry, Dana. I really am," he said with genuine sincerity. That didn't make me any less angry, though. I was fully aware of my raging jealousy, which was a better reaction to the feeling of deficiency I really felt than whatever other self-sabotaging behaviors I could have enacted instead.

"I'm sure you are, Kevin. But I'll make sure she's sorry too," I threatened, as if it might make him feel a tinge of the pain I did. Then I walked away, holding my fists tightly at my side.

I'd save my physical aggression for that girl. I'd show Kevin to what lengths I'd go to literally fight for him. It would feel good to pull some of her hair out and prove to Kevin I was willing to do anything to be his. Then I dropped my head shamefully, regretting the uncharacteristic anger I knew I wouldn't follow through with.

"Can I talk to you for a second, Dana?"

I turned around and immediately corrected my expression when I saw my chemistry teacher, Mr. Fogel.

"Yeah," I said, faking a pleasant demeanor.

"Come on into the room over here?" he said, nodding his head toward an empty classroom. I followed him in, wondering if I'd gotten a bad grade or something. He pushed his thick-lensed glasses back upon his nose and said, "I overheard what you just said to that boy out there."

"Oh," I mumbled, averting my eyes.

"Look, it's not my place to get involved in your personal life, but I felt like I had to say something before you went and did something silly like that."

Shit. Was I going to get detention for threatening to hurt that girl? I'd never had to serve a detention before. How would I explain it to Mom?

"I didn't mean anything by it. Really!" I scrambled to defend myself. "I just . . ." How would I explain my thoughts? My life? My temporary lunacy?

"I know," Mr. Fogel said, nodding. How could he, though? He didn't know me. He was as new to me as he was to teaching. Plus, he was an adult. What did he know about anything? He must have sensed my cynicism, because he said, "You probably think I just stand up there and lecture about science. But I notice you all. I see your different personalities, and I can see when there's something 'off' with one of you."

My brows scrunched at him. I'd been called a lot of things, including a "dog" by some strange boy who'd spat on me between classes recently, but I'd never been referred to as "off."

"I don't mean that in a bad way," he explained. "You just seem really aware of people, like you're more affected by others and the things they say and do. And lately, you've seemed more tense than usual."

"My mom says I'm sensitive too," I muttered before dropping my head again.

"Being sensitive isn't a bad thing." I looked up at him, confused. "I just don't want you to get so upset that you do something that'll get you hurt."

"You mean the threat I made against the girl who asked my ex-boyfriend out to a concert?"

"Yeah," he said. "I know the girl. She's in one of my classes, and I overheard her talking about him and the concert. But she's a gymnast, Dana. She's much stronger than you are. So, what do you think you can really do to her?" He smirked as if he was trying not to laugh at me. I wanted to be mad about his underestimation, but then I cracked up too.

"I know," I said. "I just want her to hurt like I'm hurting."

Mr. Fogel looked me right in the eyes. He was exactly my height, though his curly black hair made him seem an inch taller. "Look, I understand you might feel slighted, but there's nothing you can do to stop people from doing what they're going to do. It'll just make you look like a bad person, and we all know you're not. So, just go home. Relax. And if you ever want to talk about anything, you know where to find me." He offered a kind, closed-mouth smile of reassurance as he nodded to attain my compliance.

"Okay," I said. But I wasn't sure how I was supposed to just go home and relax. Mom was always stressed out because of the crying baby; or she demanded total quiet for the sleeping baby, which would stress *me* out. Ron would eventually come home and add a whole level of fuckery to the chaos. But yeah, I'd go home and relax.

As I walked out to the line of buses waiting at the front of the school, I was glad that my new teacher had taken the time to ground me like a father would a daughter, instead of using his authority to reprimand me. I wasn't used to that. So, maybe I *would* take his advice and at least *try* to relax when I got home. This thing with Kevin wasn't worth getting worked up over anyway.

"Hey, TF Queen!" a couple boys in the far back of the bus called out as soon as I stepped aboard. Then they laughed. I recognized them from a class. I didn't know what they were talking about, though. So, I ignored their taunts and settled into an empty seat towards the front.

"Ignoring us, TF Queen?" the boys repeated, laughing louder. Then one of them walked up the aisle and said it to my face.

Completely confused about why these two boys were calling me that, I stood up and turned to them and asked. That just made them laugh harder.

"You don't know what that means?" one asked.

The bus was filling quickly, so I didn't want to admit that I didn't and seem uncool. So, I just stood there, dumbfounded.

"Seriously?" the other boy asked. "TF?" He enunciated each letter as if it would suddenly resonate, but it didn't.

I huffed out my nose and sat back down, running through every "T" and "F" word in my vocabulary. All I could come up with was "two feet," but that didn't seem that funny.

A nerdy boy with thick, messy hair and glasses leaned over from the seat across from me then, as if wanting to tell me something.

"Tight . . ." he whispered with high brows. Then he nodded.

Fuck.

I shrunk in my seat then, wanting to just die.

"Goody Two-Shoes"

I sat against my bed, sobbing in a fetal position that night. I wasn't sure if Kevin's rejection of me hurt more than his presumed betrayal, but being made fun of for the one thing I couldn't do with him was an embarrassment my low self-esteem couldn't survive.

I also felt duped. I'd never thought that Kevin would share something so private. He'd always been respectful, not just to me but to everyone! Maybe he'd confided in his close friend, and someone overheard; or maybe he'd trusted the wrong person. I didn't know. I couldn't make sense of anything right now. All I knew was I couldn't possibly show my face in that school ever again.

I wished I could talk to Mom about all this. She'd often spoken of how awful it had been to be ridiculed by her classmates for becoming pregnant with me. So, she was the one person who'd understand the humiliation I felt. How could I tell her what happened, though, without also admitting I'd tried to have sex with Kevin? She'd have killed me if she knew that! Still, I needed consolation. I needed *someone* to tell me everything would be okay.

As if answering my prayer, Mom opened my bedroom door and peeked in. I thought I'd locked it like I always did. Perhaps I subconsciously forgot on purpose this time.

"Mom?" I pleaded with teary eyes. My heart was practically bleeding on the floor, begging for a reason not to wish myself dead.

Looking down at me with reproach, she said, "Could you keep it down, Dane? I'm trying to get Jonathan to sleep."

If it wasn't Jonathan, it would have been something else. Work, the dishes . . . when would *I* matter? When would *I* rate at some higher level of importance to her?

"Mom!" I said louder, slightly scolding.

"We can all hear you out here," she said with an accusatory tone that made me feel worse.

"Mom, I'm . . . I'm so . . ." I attempted to verbalize my feelings in a way that might appeal to her.

Ron came from Jonathan's room across the hall then, looking at me crossly. I immediately tensed. "What's going on?" he demanded to know.

"She's being overly sensitive again," Mom responded. I could almost hear her eyes roll.

"About what?"

"I don't know," Mom said dismissively.

"I'm right here!" I cried out, annoyed that they were speaking about me in third person.

"Don't you raise your voice to us!" Ron scolded as he moved towards me, waving that pointy finger in my face. I cowered, expecting a more vicious assault.

"Just stop, Dane. You're getting everyone upset now," Mom pleaded.

"*I'm* getting everyone upset?" I yelled. Ron stepped back as I sat up. "Crap, Mom! I'm in here crying, and you just barged in to tell me I'm bothering you. Do you not see me hurting? Do you not care?"

"I'm not dealing with this shit," Ron said to Mom as he started walking out.

I climbed onto my bed and lay with my back to the door, where Mom still stood. "Just go! I'm sorry I bothered you! Okay? It won't happen again!" I screamed, though the sound was muffled in the pillow I buried my face in.

"Are you on drugs or something?" Mom accused. "Ron, I think she's on drugs. Do you think we should have her tested?"

I sat up and faced Mom. "Jesus Christ, Mom! I'm not on fucking drugs!" I screamed, pounding my bed with clenched fists.

"I think we should take her to the hospital to be tested," Mom told Ron when he reappeared in my doorway. She was so eerily calm, it made me feel like I was batshit crazy.

"If that's what you want to do, I'll stay here with Jonathan," he offered, speaking to Mom with the same tranquil tone.

"I'M NOT ON FUCKING DRUGS!" I screamed so loud my throat hurt. I just wanted someone to hear me!

Ron rushed at me, seething, and grabbed my wrists so tightly I thought he'd break them. "How many times do I have to tell you to stop using that language?"

"STOP!" I screamed, trying to pull my wrists out of his grip. I couldn't, though. Then I couldn't breathe. My entire body tensed to the point where I thought I might just implode from the unhinged rage inside me. "You're hurting me! Mom! Help!"

Mom walked over. "Just stop it, Dane!" she weakly scolded, as if I were a five-year-old having a tantrum over a toy. I couldn't understand why she wasn't reacting to the violent struggle escalating right in front of her!

"Mom!" I cried out again, begging for her defense. I was fighting Ron so hard I was sweating, but he held his grip on me. So, I kicked him in the leg, but then Mom grabbed my ankles. Why was she helping him? Why was she on his side? "Mom! Stop!"

She held on, even though I kicked and struggled. Then she said to Ron, "She's definitely on drugs. I'm taking her in."

"No!" I screamed, shocked at her participation. "NO!"

Mom pulled on my legs then, dragging me down to the floor. I wriggled and writhed, fighting to get loose. But Mom gripped my lower legs tightly, unconcerned about my head hitting the parquet floor after bouncing off the transition from the carpet. The scrapy feel on my back as she continued to pull me into the hall and past Jonathan's door distracted me from my fear. Only Ron had been physically aggressive with me before. Not my own mother!

"Let go!" I screamed, pleading for her to release me.

"Not until you calm down, Dane," Mom said with the emotionless tone of a zombie.

Ron looked down at me with reproachful condescension as he stepped past my head and went into Jonathan's room. Feeling Mom's grip loosen, I yanked my legs out of her hold, then I crab-walked backwards until I was out of her reach. With my back against the wall, I stood and stared at Mom, like I was seeing her for who she really was for the first time. She wasn't Mom at all, I realized. She was Ron's wife.

After all the years of denying and negating to delude herself and attempting to do the same with me, it was a relief to see her finally embrace exactly who she was too. She'd never shown this side of herself to anyone before. But I was very clear about who this woman was, glaring hatefully back at me.

At a standstill in the hallway, I waited for her to make the next move, intending to go to any lengths necessary to demonstrate the strong will I'd had to develop in this world where no one could be trusted. She averted her eyes, proving herself weaker. Then she went downstairs, abruptly ending something that certainly wasn't over.

I followed behind her, eager to escape to the main floor anyway. I'd seen enough scary movies to know it was best not to corner myself, especially in my second-floor corner bedroom, outside of which Ron awaited.

Mom wasn't in the house, though, and the front door was open. So, I followed the natural inclination to slip my feet into my white Keds and go out to find Mom. She was already in her car with the engine and headlights on, so I jumped into the passenger seat, even though I had no idea where we were going. Anywhere was better than here.

"Where're we going?" I asked after she'd already started driving.

"The hospital," she said firmly. I didn't believe her. I figured she'd drive around for a few minutes to scare me and then go back home and give me the silent treatment for the next week. So, I strapped the seat belt across my chest and waist, and sat back, expecting to call her bluff.

Ten minutes later, we arrived at the emergency room of the local hospital. I looked at Mom as she turned off the ignition, sure that she was just taking her threat too far. But when she got out of the car, I guessed I had no choice but to continue this charade.

I knew I wasn't on drugs, anyway. I'd never even tried any. I'd never smoked anything either. I'd tried a sip of an alcoholic drink at a party once, but then I'd left because I wasn't interested in acting stupid like the other kids. If Mom had taken a minute to notice, she might have actually noticed what a good girl I was and been quite proud of the strong daughter she'd raised.

"Can I help you, ma'am?" the receptionist at the counter asked.

"Yes, I need my daughter tested for drugs," she said with her usual flat tone.

"On what basis, ma'am?" the receptionist asked, glancing at me for a quick assessment.

"She, uh . . . she's displaying erratic behavior," Mom answered.

The receptionist peered around Mom to observe me better. Having voluntarily walked in with Mom, I stood very still and quiet behind her. I offered a weak, closed-mouth smile to be polite, though I wanted to laugh at the ridiculousness of the situation.

"Hmm," the receptionist sounded. Then she looked at Mom again. With her frizzy black hair sticking up and out like she'd been electrically shocked, Mom could have passed for a tame version of the Bride of Frankenstein, without the benefit of makeup.

The receptionist registered me in the system anyway and then passed us off to a nurse carrying a metal clipboard and a pen. She verified my name, age, and basic information on the way to a white-curtained examination area. "And who is this who brought you in?" she asked me.

"That's Mom," I said, as opposed to simply referring to her as the woman who bore me, which was all I felt about her anymore.

"Can I ask you to please step into the waiting room, ma'am?" she told Mom.

Mom pursed her lips but complied anyway.

After closing the curtain for privacy, the nurse turned back to me. "Okay, Dana, I have orders to take a urine sample and blood test. We'll start with the urine sample, so I can withdraw the blood while we wait for the urine to be processed."

"All right," I said, taking the small plastic cup she handed me.

"But listen," she continued. "I know you probably don't want your mother to know this, but before I run the urine sample, I have to ask: Are you sexually active?"

"No!" I immediately responded, horrified that she'd asked such a personal question.

The nurse raised her brows and pressed her lips together. "I need you to be honest with me so there's no surprises after your mother rejoins us. I promise this won't go any further than me," she said, prodding me to make an admission I couldn't make.

I thought to inform her I was the "TF Queen" but opted for an insistent

"I swear" instead. "I use tampons, but I've never . . . you know."

"So, there's no chance you could be pregnant?"

I huffed out my mouth. "No!" I rebuked, shaking my head.

The nurse stared directly into my eyes, as if scrutinizing them. I stared back, wondering what she was looking for. Truth? Dilated pupils? Or was it an intimidation tactic to break me down into an admission of guilt? I was strangely calm, despite feeling slightly offended, standing firm in my truth in a stare-down that felt as captious as the one I'd had with Mom. Why was everyone trying to make me out to be some rebellious teenager I wasn't?

"Okay," she said then proceeded to review the instructions for properly collecting my urine in the cup and directed me to the bathroom.

When I returned, I was told to sit on the edge of the white-sheeted hospital bed, where the nurse went about taking my blood pressure and temperature and asking a few basic questions about my health. I complied but opted not to tell her I had a stomachache. It would raise questions about pregnancy again, which wasn't any more possible than the Immaculate Conception it would have to have been to be real.

Another gal came in after that to take the blood sample. I squeezed my eyes shut as the needle pierced my arm. I squeezed my fist tighter too, to avoid crying like a baby. I'd always hated having my blood drawn. I couldn't stand needles or knives or anything sharp, and I had no idea where the fear had come from. I just knew that the inherent fear alone would disprove my supposed drug use—not that Mom and Ron knew me well enough to know that, or anything else about me.

"All right, Dana," the original nurse said with a kind smile, "a doctor will be in shortly to talk to you, so just sit tight. Okay?"

Was she giving me an option? I thought but nodded and said, "Yep." Then I remained on the bed, fumbling my fingers as I waited.

A couple minutes later, a young male doctor with a stethoscope hanging around his neck came through the curtain. "Dana?"

"Yes?"

He introduced himself as doctor so-and-so, though the pin attached to his white lab coat said he was a psychiatrist. This evening was getting more interesting by the minute.

"So, do you want to tell me why you think you're here tonight?" he asked.

Living with Mom and Ron and all the lies they told made me hyperaware of verbiage and the intention behind them. So, I didn't like the doctor asking me why I "thought" I was there. I knew damn well why. I just had to be careful not to come off as angry or annoyed as I felt, because they might perceive that as what Mom had referred to as "erratic."

"I had a really bad day at school and was upset about it. So, Mom thinks I'm on drugs because she found me crying in my room," I said, remembering that less was more when being questioned—another lesson learned from living with people who were constantly accusing me of things I wasn't guilty of.

The doctor wrote something on his clipboard then looked back up at me with a smile that showed only in his bright-white teeth. "Do you cry often?"

Yeah, I thought. But who wouldn't if they lived my life? "No more than anyone else does," I said instead, failing to hide my snark.

"What do you mean by that?"

"I don't know," I answered with a shrug. "I don't really know how often one person cries versus another. I just assume people cry when they're sad or upset . . ."

He wrote something else on his board. "How often would you say you *feel* sad or upset?" he asked, using my own words against me. I recognized the tactic from articles I'd read in *Psychology Today* magazines at the library.

Every second my eyes are open, I wanted to tell him. That wouldn't get me anywhere except straight to the psych ward, though. Plus, it wasn't entirely true. I did experience joy in life, just not with Mom and Ron, and not at home.

"I really don't know how to answer that," I said. "I mean, if someone hurts my feelings, I might shed a tear or two. Doesn't everyone, though?" I wasn't trying to be a smart-ass. I was just calling it like I saw it; and I didn't think I was any different from any other person in the way I reacted to mistreatment.

"I see," the doctor said, taking more notes. "Was there something in particular that caused you to feel overemotional tonight?" Mom was the only person who accused me of being "sensitive," as if it were a bad thing. So, I wondered if this guy had talked to Mom before coming in to interrogate me.

I wanted so badly to tell this doctor everything that had happened. However, telling him I was a jealous ex-girlfriend of a boy who couldn't stick it to me even though I'd wanted him to, thereby earning me the title of "TF Queen," which depressed me to the point that Mom and Ron and I had brawled in front of the baby, sounded really bad for all of us. So, I stuck to the short version. "I'm just having a tough time fitting in at school, I guess."

"What grade are you in again?" he asked.

"I'm a freshman," I told him for the first time in our conversation. Notably.

"Oh, okay," he said, nodding. Then he flipped the papers on the clipboard and reviewed whatever was on them. "You're fourteen, so I presume you're menstruating?"

"Yes," I said, remembering when I'd gotten my first period in seventh grade. I'd been so embarrassed to stand up when the bell rang to see red stains where I'd sat. The blood had permeated my blue jeans. I'd wanted to crawl in a hole and die when the kids around me pointed and laughed.

"Can I ask when your last period was?"

"I just got done with it," I responded, holding back on an offer to look at the pantiliner I was wearing to collect the last bit of spotting, as proof that I wasn't pregnant.

"Okay!" he said cheerily, as he wrote the last of his notes. Then he looked up and smiled at me. "I think we're done here. I'll let the nurse know you're ready for her again."

"All right," I said, unenthusiastic about another potential invasion into my privacy.

The doctor stared at me with a closed-mouth smile, as if he wanted to say more. His eyes matched his mouth this time, appearing genuinely sympathetic. "Hey," he said in a lower, more casual tone, "it'll get better. High school's tough for a lot of kids."

"Thanks," I said. Then he disappeared through the curtain, leaving me resentful towards Mom for humiliating me for my feelings instead of offering the same simple empathetic words at home.

The original nurse returned shortly after, with my irk-faced mother behind her. She wouldn't look at me, though I maintained my focus on her, failing to make her acknowledge me and what she had put me through tonight.

"Thank you both for waiting so patiently," the nurse said, distracting my attention to her. "So, we ran the urine and blood samples. Both came back negative for recreational drug use as well as pregnancy." I wanted to say, *I told you so*, but I refrained. "We had our staff psychiatrist perform an evaluation as well, and he didn't detect any reason for concern. So, we'll get you checked out and have you on your way home shortly!" I lacked the same enthusiasm her smile conveyed when delivering the news. I'd have almost *rather* gone to the psych ward than go home.

"What about the marks on her body?" Mom threw in, sounding desperate to pin me with something for her trouble.

"Um," the nurse said, perplexed about what to do with this new information. "Let me get the doctor for you, ma'am."

In the midst of everything that had happened tonight, I hadn't even thought about the aches and burns I felt. I couldn't inspect myself now, though. Not in front of them. So, I sat still and quiet, trying to act unfazed despite the panic I was trying to subdue.

Doctor Psycho came through the curtain seconds after, looking as confused as the nurse had been. "Was there something else I could do for you?" he asked, looking back and forth between me and Mom.

"Yes," Mom responded. "I just wonder what you make of the scratches and bruises on her arms. Did she say where they came from?"

"I did see some light scratches on her arms," the doctor confirmed as he came over and delicately raised one of my arms in his hands. Craning my head to look at the back of my bicep, where he was inspecting what could have passed for a rash, I saw the rug burn that had been caused by being dragged. He examined a light bruise on my forearm next while I attempted to appear unbothered by the inspection. "They don't look like the self-inflicted wounds we typically see with extreme cases of anxiety," he thought out loud.

"I would never hurt myself," I asserted, leaving out the fact that I sometimes wished I could, so I could put an end to *all* of our misery. Then I offered an explanation I'd just made up. "I just got a little banged up playing floor hockey in gym class."

"Kids!" the doctor shrugged dismissively. Then he gently laid my arm down.

"Are you sure?" Mom asked. "We've had trouble with Dana lying about things. You know, to get attention."

Was she trying to get the doctor to declare me a "cutter" so she could have me committed?

"I don't see any reason for alarm, ma'am," the doctor said. "Dana does show indications of circumstantial depression, maybe some anxiety, but considering what she's going through—transitioning into high school and all—it's completely understandable."

Having some backing straightened me up from my slump. Mom looked displeased, though, as if scanning her mind for some other deficiency to pin on me so she wouldn't have to go home to Ron and tell him she'd been wrong.

"She doesn't need anything for depression or anxiety, then?" Mom pressed in a last-ditch effort to stigmatize me with a diagnosis she could use against me.

"No. Everyone gets sad now and then. Right, Dana?" he said, turning to me. I nodded. Then he turned back to Mom. "She'll be back to her normal self once she settles into high school a little better. Aside from that, you have yourself a good girl here!"

He smiled and patted Mom's shoulder as he exited for the second time. Mom just stood there with slumped shoulders and a resentful pout of defeat, still refusing to look at me. Then the nurse came back with my discharge papers, indicating I was clean as a whistle, and sent us home.

Not a word was said in the car ride back. My head was pounding, my stomach ached, and I was emotionally and physically exhausted. So, I went straight to my bedroom when we got back, locked the door, and curled up in bed to sleep.

Jonathan must have sensed I needed a break from his crying and graced me with it that night. I slept really well and even woke up later than usual the next morning. It was a Saturday, though, so it didn't matter because I didn't have to be at dance class for another hour.

On my way to the bathroom to brush my teeth and pee, I stopped when I overheard Mom on the phone with someone downstairs. It was probably my grandma or Sonia, because those were the only two people she seemed to talk with anymore.

"She was out of control! She kicked Ron. She was calling us all kinds of names—I don't know where she learned to talk like that . . . yeah . . . and then she came after me! She kicked, punched, screamed . . . I have bruises all over my body from where she kicked me!"

Was she fucking kidding me? That's not at all what happened! But then Ron came up the stairs and saw me standing outside the bathroom, spying. He glared at me, immediately scaring me into closing the door and locking myself inside. I waited and listened, to make sure he wouldn't force his way in.

After taking a deep breath to calm down, I wondered what else Mom had told our family about me. What else did they believe about me because of whatever lies she'd told before? I could only imagine, after what I'd just heard. Why would Mom do that to me, though? Why was she constantly throwing me under the bus to make me look like the bad guy? Did she not want our own family to love me either? Or was this her way of justifying her inability to love her own daughter?

I dropped to the floor and buried my face in my knees. I was careful not to cry, though. I gulped and breathed and fought back the tears instead. I needed to learn to stifle my emotions better because I didn't need a repeat of the night before. Not now, not ever. Or at least not until I could legally leave *here*.

"Why Not Me"

The summer of 1990, I'd had to tag along on an appointment Mom made for Jonathan to meet with a children's talent agent. She and Ron were so convinced that Jonathan was the cutest and most entertaining one-year-old that ever was that they wanted to see if they could get him on TV or in commercials.

The appointment was at a hotel just outside of Chicago. There were dozens of parents hauling their small children in and out of the place, so the receptionist knew exactly where to direct us when we walked in with Jonathan on Mom's hip. Having barely made it on time, we were called into a large conference room right away.

The room was quite plain in every way. The walls were tan and bare. The long wood-laminate table extended most of the length of the space, with high-backed black office chairs pushed into every side of it. The dark-green carpet was the only pizazz this room bore. There wasn't a picture or a plant to give it any oomph otherwise.

"Have a seat!" one of the two ladies at one end of the table said. I presumed they were agents or executives of whatever agency they represented.

Without offering a greeting or a polite thank-you, Mom settled into one of the chairs nearest the door and plopped Jonathan onto her lap. I sat next to her, smiling meekly at the talent reps, who sat at the far opposite end, since Mom had failed to do so herself. She always wore a grimace, as if unfairly burdened with all the toil of the world. Our grubby jeans and jackets conveyed the same angst, appearing almost poverty-stricken compared to the blouses and suit jackets worn by our well-dressed hosts.

"What's *your* name, sweetheart?" one of the women asked me. Her blonde hair, enviably done in a French twist, contrasted her navy jacket and gold jewelry perfectly.

"Dana," I said shyly, feeling severely underdressed and unworthy of being in the presence of these beautiful women.

"This appointment is for my son, Jonathan," Mom immediately corrected. I glanced over at her, wondering why she couldn't allow this woman to simply say hello to me without making me feel like I hadn't deserved the courtesy of acknowledgment.

"Yes, of course," the woman said, smiling at Mom with fake politeness. Then she looked down at some papers in front of her, whispered something to the other woman, then they both looked up. "Are Jonathan and Dana both your children?"

"Yes," Mom said, "but we just made the appointment for Jonathan."

"Well, he *is* adorable," the woman said, barely glancing at him as he fussed with the zipper on Mom's long, baggy jacket. "However, we might be more interested in Dana. How old are you, dear?" she asked me.

"Fourteen," I mumbled, as if I'd done something wrong by inadvertently hijacking Jonathan's shot at stardom. I dropped my head slightly too, to simultaneously avoid any more unwarranted attention and the glare my mother was likely shooting me.

Nervous about the tense silence, I peeked up at the women and witnessed them exchange a knowing look. "That's a little older than our normal clientele. We typically represent babies and toddlers in print and film. Like the Gerber baby! Surely you've seen that face on jars and advertisements everywhere," one said. "However, we do work with companies that want older kids for television shows and commercials. Would you be interested in doing something like that, Dana?"

I'd never thought about it, really. Then again, I never considered it a *real* possibility—at least for me. Aside from my phenomenal performance in the lead role of *Rumpelstiltskin* in the fourth grade, wherein I wowed the school by cartwheeling across the stage, I'd only achieved background chorus status in junior high and high school theater. But if these women saw a starlet in me, then maybe it was worth a shot! Because, seriously, who *didn't* want to be on TV?!

So, with bright eyes and raised brows, I nodded eagerly. Then I instinctively looked at Mom to share the excitement. Her pursed lips reminded me she wasn't the type of mom who'd ever encourage my talent or ambition, causing my short-lived zeal to dissipate into the complacence I'd learned to live with.

"My husband and I thought you might be more interested in Jonathan," Mom said to distract their attention back to him. She sufficiently put me back in my place as number two in the process. I felt that in every sense.

"We will certainly consider him with all the other children we meet today. However, we'd really be interested in pursuing representation of your daughter if you're willing," the woman insisted.

Mom considered it for a moment. Or maybe she was thinking about how to decline the invitation. I couldn't tell. I was hanging on the edge of my seat, waiting for her to respond.

"I'll have to think about that," she finally said. She wasn't going to think about anything, though, unless it was for Jonathan's benefit.

"Of course," the woman said. Then she offered her card and a packet of information about what would be required if she chose to proceed. I looked through it on the way home.

"They need a headshot taken by a professional photographer . . ." I began reading in the car.

"Do you know how expensive that is, Dane?" Mom snarked.

"No, but—" I started, thinking about the professional photos they'd just had done of Jonathan. Mom had even had three of them blown up into sixteen-by-twenty portraits that had cost a couple hundred dollars each. Then she'd had them professionally framed at an art gallery!

"A lot," she said, cutting me off. "So don't even think Ron is going to go for that."

"But—"

"No, Dana!" Mom said, cutting me off again. "If they really wanted to represent you, they'd pay for your headshot themselves."

"But Mom—" I tried again.

"No," she said louder, shutting down the conversation altogether.

I sat back with a pout and crossed my arms, feeling like Mom intentionally inhibited any possibility of my success or achievement. Then as soon as we got home, I called one of my friends to vent.

"Man, that would be so *cool* if you had an agent and got on TV!" my friend, Patty, agreed.

"I know! If they'd been interested in Jonathan, Mom would've signed him up in a heartbeat! But it's me, so . . ."

"Maybe she'll come around," Patty suggested.

"I highly doubt it," I said. "I mean, this isn't the first time someone has told her I should get an agent. When I was little, people would stop us on the street and tell her I looked like a young Brooke Shields. Remember her? The girl in *Blue Lagoon*."

"Yeah!"

"Well, people would say I should be a model or a movie actress too."

"What did your mom say when people said that?"

"Nothing, really," I tried to recall. "She just dismissed them, like they were silly to think such a thing."

"That's weird," Patty said. "You'd think anyone would be excited to have a kid who might become famous."

"Yeah. You'd think," I said with a huff.

"I'm sorry," Patty said.

"It's not *your* fault," I responded. "I just wish I *was* pretty enough or talented enough or enough of anything for her to acknowledge some pride in me."

"I'm sure she's proud of you, Dana," Patty insisted. "You get good grades, you're first chair in orchestra, you taught yourself to play piano, you don't get into trouble . . ."

"Yet she's never once told me she's proud of me."

"Not once?" Patty asked in disbelief.

"Not once. Literally," I affirmed. Neither had Ron, but that was a given.

"Maybe your mom is jealous of you, then?"

"I don't know why she would be!" I responded, disagreeing completely. "I mean, I know she's having issues with losing the weight she gained in her pregnancy with Jonathan, but I'm her daughter! Plus, she loves when we go into the 7-Eleven and the owner tells her we look like sisters."

"Maybe she's jealous of your talent, then? Between dance and orchestra and theater . . . you're always on a stage performing something!" Patty chuckled, making me do so too.

"Maybe," I said, but I didn't buy it. "Anyway, I'll figure it out. If I have to pick up some extra babysitting jobs or something, I'll find the money somewhere. I mean, this modeling and acting thing might be my way out of here."

"I can't even imagine how much money you could make doing stuff like that. Maybe you could even afford that emancipation thing you talked about before," she said, referring to an article I'd told her I'd read, about a kid my age who'd gotten a lawyer to declare him free of his parents' guardianship.

"I'd have to make a hell of a lot of money to do that, though!" I said.

When we ended the call, I went down to the kitchen and sat at the table. Mom was preparing something for Jonathan to eat while he impatiently pounded on the tray of his high chair. I immediately joined in, except I pounded twice and clapped once, like in Queen's song "We Will Rock You." Jonathan thought it was funny.

"What's up, Dane?" Mom asked above the clatter.

"Nothing," I said then immediately backpedaled. "I just wanted to talk to you more about the modeling thing."

Mom sighed. "I already told you no. We're not spending the money on photos for you. It would be like throwing money out the window."

Ouch! I mean, I knew I wasn't that attractive and probably not even that talented compared to other kids, but I'd hoped my own mother would believe in me a little more than that!

"I really want to do this, though!" I pleaded. "I promise to pay you back for the photos. Just please let me do this! Or at least think about it. For real."

The look of scorn Mom shot me before turning her attention back to the food she was cooking for her precious son gave me the same two-letter answer she'd been using as a mantra to torment me for years. So, I gave up. I could only take so much rejection. I stood up from the wooden chair abruptly and noisily, huffed at Mom with pursed lips, then pounded my feet up the stairs to my bedroom like a pouty toddler. I was as tired of being the low man on the totem pole as I was suppressing my feelings all the time.

The next Saturday, Mom and I were sitting in her office. She was working at her desk, and I was sitting on the floor with my back against the wall, repeatedly throwing a rubber ball against the opposite wall while I waited for her to be finished.

"Have you thought any more about that modeling agency, Mom?" I asked out of nowhere. I figured it was worth a shot, since Mom was usually in a better disposition when we were away from Ron and Jonathan.

"I did talk to Ron about it," Mom said without removing her eyes from her work.

"Yeah?" I asked with surprise. "And?"

"Like I told you, it's a lot of money."

"I know," I said, not even trying to hide my usual disappointment in her for dismissing anything I showed interest in.

"But maybe we can work something out."

I whipped my head towards her and let my rubber ball bounce to a slow roll back to me. "Does that mean . . .?"

"I didn't say yes, Dane," Mom warned. "And for the record, neither of us support this. We think—"

"But you might be willing to let me get my headshot done?" I asked, focusing on the positive.

"We'll see," Mom said. "I need to call the photographer they recommended first, to see if we can swing it."

"Then I can do it?"

"We'll see," Mom repeated with more emphasis.

A week later, she was carting me off to a photographer for my photoshoot. I didn't know how she'd convinced Ron to let her spend the money on me, but I was on top of the world for the rare favor. I didn't know what to do with my hair, though. Nor did I have Mom's help with it or my makeup or to choose the three outfits the photographer said to bring.

I did the best I could on my own and had a headshot that sufficed. Mom even had it blown up into a sixteen-by-twenty photograph that hung on the wall by the three of Jonathan, except mine was put into a cheap gold frame she'd bought at Venture. It was okay, though. I'd gotten what I wanted, plus the bonus compliment of being put on the wall.

I even got a call for an audition right away, for a Sunbeam electric blanket commercial. Mom took me to an office in a neighboring town, where I was asked to lie down and snuggle with the blanket while they filmed me. It felt awkward and weird to pretend to enjoy just lying there getting my skin fried, but I did the best I could.

Unfortunately, the company chose a younger, much cuter blonde girl with Cindy Brady pigtails to star in the commercial instead. I couldn't compete with that, just like I couldn't compete with Jonathan. Nor was I trying to. I just knew I'd never measure up to his fine pedigree; if *he'd* been allowed the audition, he'd have probably gotten the gig.

"Someone to Love"

By the start of the new school year that fall, I'd been called for a few more auditions. Mom said she couldn't leave work to take me to them. So, aside from a movie audition I'd been able to walk to myself (and didn't get a call-back on), I gave up on the idea of modeling and acting just like Mom had before even giving me a chance. The agency stopped calling too, seeing that Mom obviously didn't want to put any effort into the cause.

Despite my disappointment, I was distracted by the new buffet of boys I was coming across in all my new classes. Several caught my eye, and some were checking me out too! I hadn't thought I'd changed, except that my hair had grown into a shoulder-length mess of curls, and I never left the house without dark eyeliner above my lids. My wardrobe was better too, since Mom let me shop at Contempo Casuals now. I just wasn't the Gap girl she wanted me to be.

So, I made out with a Mike, who I met through cooperative band and orchestra performances. He was so nice he bored me. Plus, I might as well have been kissing our old bulldog, Bogie, the way he slopped his tongue all over my face. I ended up getting into some heavier petting with another Mike, who looked like a real-life Ken doll. He was just looking for sex, though, and I was looking for more. So, when I refused to give him what he wanted, he moved on. Then there was an Arie, who was tall, dark, and handsome, not to mention funny, romantic, well-dressed, and well-versed. I *really* liked him. He drove a Corvette and took me on fancy dates in downtown Chicago. His parents were a lot more lenient than mine, though, and allowed him to stay out well past my early curfew, which impeded us from going out at all. So, I moved on to Dino, who was sweet, caring, and gentle, despite being a six-foot-four, two-hundred-and-twenty-pound football player. Some of our classmates called us the "Green Giant" and "Sprout," after the characters on the brand's green bean commercial. Between football, hunting, and family, however, he didn't have much time for me. It was a shame too; I could've seen us being in it for the long haul.

A boy who sat by me in earth science class attracted my attention next. He had curly brown hair, bright-blue eyes, and a baby face with chubby cheeks like Jonathan's. He had a pudgier body too but wasn't overweight. I could tell by his simple jeans-and-T-shirt style that he wasn't concerned about being cool or keeping up with anybody, and I liked that.

This boy seemed different than others. He kept to himself but not in a weird way. His quietude was alluring and sweet, like the cute smirk and dimples that showed whenever classmates made sarcastic comments that even the teacher couldn't resist laughing at.

Unfortunately, those classmates were the boys who called me the "TF Queen." They sat at the same table as my quiet crush, occasionally reviving my terrible nickname, which had otherwise worn off. The boy I liked didn't express amusement at the awful teasing I endured, making me wonder if he'd been the target of the same before.

An exotic-looking European girl, who sat next to my crush and the troublesome twosome, flirtatiously laughed every time I was teased, flipping her curly reddish hair over her shoulders. The boys' eyes would bulge at the sight of her swelling bosom then, watching carefully as her breasts jiggled while she giggled.

Seeing how much attention she received compelled me to wear more provocative clothing to achieve the same notice. I had the body of a twelve-year-old boy except for some fuller curves in the hips, but the fitting off-the-shoulder tops and tight jeans earned me a few extra looks I hadn't received before—including a double take from my earth science crush. Unfortunately, Ron noticed too, and he didn't hesitate to share his negative opinions about my new style. He'd called me a "whore" so often, however, that the insult had lost its effect.

One afternoon, the earth science teacher assigned a project we had to do in teams of two. The class immediately livened, with kids calling across the room to friends or nodding to the person next to them in cooperative agreement.

"Does everyone have a partner?" the teacher asked, raising his voice above the chitchat. I looked around, desperate to find another odd man out like me. "If you don't have a partner yet, raise your hand."

That would be like publicly admitting I was a loser! But then I saw my crush raise his hand, so I threw mine up too.

The teacher surveyed the room then pointed at me and my crush, who were the only ones with our hands up. "Okay, you two. Looks like you're a team now."

The boy and I made eye contact, so I offered a closed-mouth smile and nod. He averted his eyes downward. I could still see his smirk.

As soon as class was dismissed, I went over to him. "Hi, I'm Dana," I said.

He was attempting to stuff our oversized science book into his backpack but glanced up and said, "I know." Then he zippered his bag, threw it over his shoulder, and said, "I'm Liam."

"I know," I said, smiling so he'd know my mock was meant to be clever. His crystal-blue eyes met my amber browns then. Mesmerized by the color of his gaze, I held it too long before realizing how creepy I must seem. "I guess we should exchange phone numbers?" I asked, fumbling to tear off part of a page of the notebook in my arms.

"Oh, yeah," he said then removed a pen from the outside pocket of his backpack. "For the project!"

"Yeah, for the project," I said with a smile. Then we scribbled our numbers down and tore the paper down the middle.

"That's my private line," he said. I supposed he thought it would impress me, though I was more impressed by the way he kept his head slightly bowed and his shoulders slumped forward. It showed humility, and I respected that.

"The number I gave you is my private line too," I said. I wanted Liam to know he wouldn't have to worry about the embarrassment of talking to a parent to have access to me.

"Okay, cool," Liam said, nodding and smiling. "I'll talk to you later, then."

I smiled back. I couldn't wait.

The next afternoon, Liam and I were laying stomach-down on his bedroom floor with our science books and notebooks laid out before us.

"Your mom is so pretty," I commented while we wrote down some points from our textbook. She'd greeted us with a suspicious smile when we'd come into his house together after school. I'd seen where Liam got his good looks and dimples but suspected it was a big deal for him to have a girl over. That was a good sign, though, that he wasn't a player.

"I guess Jim thought so too," he said with a resentful tone.

"Who's Jim?"

"My stepdad," he said with a bitterness I understood too well. He stopped writing and met my stare. "What?"

Embarrassed I'd examined his face too long again, I returned my focus to my notebook. "Nothing!" I lied. Then I immediately retracted, "I just didn't know you had a stepdad, and . . . well . . . let's just say I can relate to your obvious feelings about him."

"What do you mean?"

I put my pen down and said, "I have a stepfather too."

"So, you get it."

I laughed. "Uh, yeah."

"How long ago did your parents get divorced?"

"Oh! My mom and dad were never married," I said. "Mom just decided to marry someone who wanted me less than she did. But I still get how you feel stuck here with him because of your mom, because I'm in the same boat."

"Yeah," Liam said, dropping his head before continuing, "I love my mom. I just wish I could be with my dad instead."

"Where is your dad, anyway? Does he live nearby?"

Liam rolled off his stomach to sit up and face me. I did the same.

"After my mom and dad got divorced, he went to California. Mom got with Jim, sold our house, and we ended up here," he summed up.

"We?"

"Me and my brother," Liam clarified. "He's a couple years older. His bedroom is upstairs, so you'll never see him because he's always hiding in it. Even when he does come out, he doesn't really talk to anyone." I could relate.

"Sounds like you got lucky, then, getting the private bedroom and bathroom in the lower level, away from everyone else," I said.

"I guess," Liam responded.

"So, how do you feel about your mom having your stepdad's baby, then?" I asked, referring to her noticeable pregnancy. Just her stomach bulged, though; the rest of her body remained slender.

"I don't know," Liam said with a creased brow and shrug. "No one's ever asked me that, and I honestly haven't thought about it."

"And here I am, asking you the question of all questions," I stated, smiling at my own sarcasm. Liam chuckled.

Then he gave the honest answer he hadn't thought about. "The thing is, Jim is a politician. He wants to be governor someday. So, we're just supposed to smile like he does for the photo ops and let him put out the idea that he's this great family guy who's raising his new wife's sons and has his own kid on the way. Looks good for voters."

"But . . .?"

"But it seems insincere. Because it's all for show."

I nodded and smirked. "Is he a Democrat or Republican?"

Liam creased his brow. "Democrat. Why?"

"So I know which party to side against when I'm old enough to vote," I joked. Liam laughed with me.

"You have any brothers or sisters?" Liam asked, shifting the focus away from his life.

"Funny you should ask," I said. "Mom and her husband just had their 'own' child together, so my stepfather could have his 'own' family, which apparently doesn't include me." I used air quotes and rolled my eyes for effect.

Liam nodded. "So you really do get it."

"Short, stocky dick of a man marrying a young hot chick who's way out of his league and then marking his territory with a baby that makes her undesirable to other men who threaten his position, all the while putting on a facade of a happy family with her kids who he hates and who hate him? Yeah, I get it," I said.

Liam shook his head and laughed, confirming we were two peas in a pod. We returned to our project then and were pretty much inseparable after that.

"Private Eyes"

We "studied" in Liam's bedroom quite often, learning nothing except how good it felt for our emotional connection to transfer into what felt like a spiritual connection when we kissed. Ron would tell me I "smelled like a whore" whenever Mom sent him to pick me up at Liam's on the way home from the gym where he worked out. I didn't know what the hell he thought he smelled, but I didn't even care.

Since neither of us had a vehicle, we had to rely on rides from unwilling stepdads or sustain the cold by putting boots to pavement to get to each other over the winter. I hated being cold almost as much as I hated being wet, though, and since I didn't want to submit Liam to the tension in my house, I spent many snowy evenings talking to him on the phone in my bedroom instead.

One early January evening in 1991, I'd gone down to the kitchen for some hot cocoa to warm up. The house was always cold because Ron was too cheap to run the heat at a temperature that was higher than necessary to keep the pipes from freezing, so it was likely fifty degrees inside the house. Mom was in the kitchen thawing some meat to make Ron for dinner.

"Hey, Dane," she said as I squeezed past her to get to the pantry.

"Hey," I responded.

"I'm glad I caught you," she said. "I wanted to talk to you about something."

"What's up?" I asked as I flapped the packet of Nestlé hot cocoa (with marshmallows, of course) before tearing it open and emptying it into a mug.

"I hired a private investigator," she said. This was more interesting than I'd expected, so I stopped and turned towards her to give her my full attention. The cocoa could wait. "You've been asking about your real dad for a long time, and . . . well, I thought it was time to find him."

I was shocked. Mom had always preferred to pretend he didn't exist and clammed up at any mention of him. Plus, I'd always assumed she knew where he was, since his mother had called mine at her office that one day several years back. I hadn't even asked about him since then, figuring Mom just wouldn't budge on her stance about me knowing him. So, I wondered what had changed. Why, all of a sudden, had she decided to find him? I also wondered if Ron knew about this.

On the other hand, maybe this had been his idea. Maybe this was Ron's way of pawning me off. Maybe he hoped my real dad would want to take me to live with him, so they didn't have to bother with me at all anymore. Assuming my real dad was *willing* to take me, I'd go with him in a heartbeat.

"So, did you?" I asked anxiously. "Did you find him?"

Mom bowed her head and closed her eyes for a moment. My heart fell, thinking he had passed away and I'd never know him or where I came from. But then she looked back up at me and said, "Yes."

A wave of adrenaline rushed through me like an instant high. I was bursting at the seams inside. It didn't seem appropriate to let on, though, considering Mom's mournful demeanor. She'd have probably preferred him to be dead.

"So, where does he live?" I asked, eager to know everything she did.

"Here," Mom responded. She sounded annoyed, like he had some nerve living wherever "here" was.

"Where is 'here' exactly?" I asked, trying not to sound sarcastic. It was a valid question, though.

"Three miles away," Mom said.

That meant he lived in the same town or the next town over. We had probably crossed paths at the 7-Eleven or somewhere else, without even recognizing each other. This was unbelievable!

"Do you have an address?" I asked. "I'd like to visit him or write him a letter, if that's okay."

"I already called him," Mom said, still speaking in a grim tone.

"Well, what did he say?" I asked anxiously.

Mom glared at me with accusing eyes, as if I'd betrayed her somehow. Then she looked down at the meat as she cut it and muttered, "You don't understand, Dana. You'll never understand."

I didn't know what she was talking about, but I was tired of her always giving me the runaround. "I don't think *you* understand, Mom. You'll never understand what it's like to not know where I came from," I pled.

"You know where you came from," Mom scolded, negating my feelings as usual.

"No, Mom, I don't!" I argued. "I mean, I know I came out of you, but I'm not *like* you. I obviously don't fit in here. Sometimes I don't even think I fit into this *world!* Then I've got Ron constantly telling me I was never meant to exist, so—"

"Because he understands the circumstances of your birth!" Mom lashed back, cutting me off. The scorn in her piercing eyes stupefied me. "You think you know everything, Dana, but you don't! You don't know what I went through back then, or what your biological father put me through. So, it's a little insulting that you're so insistent on meeting him."

"You're right! I don't know what you went through. But it's not my fault! *I* didn't ask to be born! I sure as shit didn't ask you to *keep* me either! But *goddamn* if you don't make me pay for whatever he supposedly did to you every frickin' day of my *life!*"

Mom glared at me again. I hadn't meant to hurt her, nor to be so harsh. Yet, I wasn't sorry for speaking my truth. Someone had to say what it was for once.

"You know, Dane, you think you have it so bad. You don't know what bad is, though. Ron never put you in the bathtub and held a gun to your head like my father did with me and my brothers."

I'd heard the shocking instance of what her father had done before. I felt bad that Mom and my uncles had had to endure that. No child deserved such horrific treatment. It was hard to feel sympathy for her, however, when she was using it to minimize my feelings about what her husband was doing to me.

"I never said he did, Mom. But that doesn't excuse the way he talks to me and treats me," I asserted. "Anyway, what does any of this have to do with my real dad?"

"Well, Dane, I just think you don't appreciate Ron like you should. He has given you this nice house to live in, a bed to sleep in, food to eat . . . It just seems like you have this fantasy in your head about who your biological father is, and I think you'll be disappointed when you find out the truth."

Mom's vague references to whatever the terrible truth was about my father had failed to convince me that he was any worse than anyone else, namely Ron. So, I didn't appreciate Mom pushing Ron's supposed generosity on me, as if it justified any ill feelings and bad behavior he enacted towards me. I mean, he'd known what he was getting into when he married a younger woman with a kid. So, I didn't owe him anything, never mind undying loyalty for mind fucking and beating an innocent and defenseless little girl, thereby robbing her of a normal childhood.

"You can praise Ron all you want for the house and the car and the clothes and all the other *crap* you enjoy in your life. But I'd trade all of it in a second to have a parent who actually loves me," I said.

"You think Ron and I don't love you? After everything we've done for you?" Mom huffed loudly and shook her head.

"No, I don't," I boldly asserted, making my way out of the kitchen without the cocoa I'd come down for.

"So, what, you think your biological father is going to love you better?" she called out after me.

"Maybe!" I retorted. Then I pounded up the stairs to my bedroom and locked the door, wondering how the earth-shattering news about my dad living nearby had turned into a rally for Ron.

I wasn't swayed into settling for scraps, though. If Ron wanted sole credit for my paternity, then he should have raised me like a father should. But he chose to disparage me instead. So, there was no way I'd let Mom convince me to side against my dad. The devil himself could have been my biological father, and I'd choose him as the lesser of two evils over Ron any day, hands down. I'd choose him over Mom too. But Mom couldn't handle the truth. She preferred to live her lie.

"I Just Want to Be Your Everything"

The idea that my real dad was so close but still so far from reach gnawed at me. I wanted to know where he lived, so I could go there and spy on him. Just a glimpse would suffice. I just needed to see that he was real, that he existed at all. Then maybe I'd approach him if he looked like he was normal and receptive.

I didn't know how to broach the subject with Mom again, though. After giving me the impression that he was a worthless drunk and drug addict, it was doubtful she wanted me to engage with him at all. I didn't blame her, assuming her assessment of him was correct. But considering all the lies she'd told and then convinced herself were truth, I couldn't trust that she was. Anyway, he couldn't be as bad a person as she claimed if she'd gone through the trouble of seeking him out.

A couple nights later, I was home alone when the house phone rang. I went to the master bedroom to answer it, thinking it was Mom checking in. She was getting to be almost as controlling with me as Ron was with her, having to know exactly what I was doing every second of every day.

"Hello?" I said, sitting on Mom's side of the unmade bed.

"Dana?" the man on the other end asked.

"Yeah?" I asked, having no idea who he was or how he knew me.

"This is Dan. Your dad."

My heart stopped. My jaw dropped. I'm pretty sure the entire universe came to a screeching halt. I'd waited literally my whole life to hear this voice and these words. But as much as I'd fantasized about this moment, I had never thought about what I would say. So, I said nothing.

"Are you there?" he asked with a slight chuckle.

"Uh, yeah," I stuttered. "I . . ." I had nothing.

"I know. This is crazy, huh?" he said with the accent and nonchalance of an Italian mobster who'd just happened upon the next person he'd been assigned to execute.

"Yeah," I said with a nervous chuckle.

"So, how are you? What're ya, fifteen now?"

He knew my age? "Yeah! I just turned fifteen! And good! I mean, *I'm* good," I said, stumbling over my words. I was still processing the deep tone of his voice and trying to imagine if he still bore any resemblance to the skinny, long-haired boy he'd been in the picture Mom had given me.

"Good!" he tittered, seeming to have my same nervous reaction. "Yeah, so this guy's been following me around and parking outside my place, like he doesn't know I see what he's doing. Then one day he knocks on my door. Of course, I'm suspicious. So, I grab my gun—I do security and stuff—and I open the door with one finger on the trigger 'cause I don't know what this guy's deal is! Then he asks who I am. I don't tell him because I still don't know who *he* is. So, I ask him, and he says your mom hired him to find me. I let him say his piece, but, man, I'm glad I didn't shoot him!"

"Me too!" I responded, giggling at how he really did sound like a mobster telling me about his latest run-in with the law. "I'd hate to have to meet you in person for the first time when I bailed you out of jail! How awkward would that be?"

We both laughed again, then he continued to explain, "So, yeah, next thing I know, your mom calls me. Tells me you've been asking about me and said I should give you a call sometime. So, here we are!"

Although I was thrilled to finally have my dad on the phone, I was still uncertain and unnerved about my mother's claim that I'd been asking about him when I hadn't recently. I didn't want to waste our time together talking about her, though.

"I just always wondered about you is all," I told him, intentionally leaving out that it was primarily because of how displaced I felt with Mom and Ron. I thought knowing where I came from would help me understand who I was and why I was here.

"Well, I've been wondering about you for a long time too, Dana," he said with such genuine certainty that I immediately disbelieved my mother's claim that he had essentially abandoned us long ago.

Now that my guard was down, my dad and I talked for what seemed like forever. He asked if I had a boyfriend. I told him about Liam. Then I asked if he was married. He said he wasn't, nor did he have any other kids—at least none that he knew of other than me, he joked. I told him about my musical talent and my love of dance. He told me he talked in tongues when he slept. I didn't believe him, but it made me laugh nonetheless.

Aside from being so easy to talk to and so personable, I was amazed at how alike we were. We had a similarly sarcastic sense of humor. Our political and religious beliefs aligned. We shared tendencies like reheating our coffee over and over in the morning to maintain its heat. It might have seemed silly to someone who'd grown up with both biological parents, but knowing I had so much in common with my dad gave me a certain sense of peace I hadn't had before. It made sense of my being here, since Mom and I were so different on so many levels.

So, when my dad asked if I'd want to meet in person, I felt completely comfortable saying yes. I'd literally waited my whole life for the chance! I told him I was off from school the next Monday for some dead president's birthday, so we planned to go to lunch. Neither Mom nor Ron would be home then to make things weird. So, I gave my dad our address and ended the call. Then I remained on the bed, holding the phone to my heart, thanking whatever powers that be for this dream come true.

Back in my room, I thought about how my dad seemed nothing like Mom had described. He sounded too coherent and sensible to be a drunk, aside from the possibility he had been drunk when he thought he spoke in tongues. He didn't seem like a drug addict either. As a matter of fact, he sounded like he was very responsible and had his crap together like a grown man should. He even took care of his elderly mother, which I thought was a tremendous act of selflessness for a bachelor his age.

Anyway, if he had experimented with drugs or alcohol before, I wouldn't hold that against him. It wasn't fair to hold anyone accountable for their poor choices made at fifteen. People grew up. People changed. All I could judge him on was who he was now, to me, which was a totally different dynamic than the one Mom had had with him sixteen years before. I would decide for myself, after meeting him in person, who and how he was and proceed accordingly.

The next Monday, I paced between the foyer and kitchen, awaiting my dad's arrival. I peeked out the window through the ruffled sheer curtains every time I passed through, seeing nothing but the clouds in the overcast sky. He wasn't late or anything; I was just worried he'd change his mind. I recalled Mom telling me once that he was supposed to come see me and hadn't shown. She claimed she'd never heard from him again.

In my last look out, I saw a strange car pull up and a tall man emerge. That had to be him! I couldn't stop staring as he walked towards the door. I didn't even care if he noticed. I just wanted to take in every detail of him.

Ding-dong! The doorbell chimed, sending my heart into a crazed panic. I questioned my appearance, worrying if I looked okay in the black-and-white Steelers jersey I'd borrowed from Liam. With my black leggings and red lipstick, maybe it was too gothic-looking like Mom always criticized. I should have chosen something brighter and prettier, like one of the yellow polo shirts she'd bought me from the Gap, even though I still hated that happy-ass color more than all others.

A couple knocks in quick succession told me I didn't have time to change. So, I checked myself in the mirrored closet doors once more, telling myself to ignore the rude remarks Ron's nephews had recently made about me always wearing black like Wednesday from *The Addams Family*. Then I answered the door.

Standing in the doorway, taking up the entire space of it, was a husky Italian with thinning brown hair and Ray Liotta eyes. His wide grin told me he liked what he saw just fine.

"Hi, Dana!" he said with the same enthusiasm I felt in my heart.

"Hi," I said breathlessly. I was in awe. It wasn't even his appearance that struck me; it was his mere presence. He'd been an idea for so long, a blur in my mind. I'd never believed he would ever be here, standing in front of me.

"You ready to go?" he asked.

"Uh, yeah!" I said, returning to reality. I grabbed my purse and shut the door behind me, suddenly nervous about Mom making one of her surprise pop-ins to see what I was doing at home alone. I hadn't told her I was meeting my dad. I didn't remember what I'd told her now that I thought about it. That's why I wasn't good at lying!

"So, where do you wanna go for lunch? You got a favorite spot?" Dad asked after starting up his Coupe.

"Is IHOP okay?" I was obsessed with their bacon cheeseburgers.

"Yeah, sure!" he said. "It's hard to believe we've lived so close to each other for so long, isn't it? I bet we passed each other at some point and didn't even know it!"

"I thought the same thing!" I told him, pleased to know our minds worked the same way. "My mom's office is just a few blocks from where you said you live, actually."

"I know," he said, smirking at me like he was sly. "I looked her up after that PI said she hired him. Just scoping things out to see what her deal was. Know what I mean?"

"Sure," I said with a shrug. I couldn't dispute his concern. "Can I ask you something?"

"You just did," he said, looking over to see if I was grinning with him.

"Ha, ha," I said, shaking my head at his joke. "No, really. I was just wondering—and I'm not passing judgment—but did you ever think about trying to find me? Before now?"

My dad's chest rose and fell. His face got serious too. I hoped I hadn't upset him by asking something too personal. I wanted to know, though.

"A lot happened back then, Dana. I came around to see you after you were born, but your mom didn't like that much. And I didn't want to upset her any more than I already had by bothering her about it. Anyway, I had a lot of my own stuff going on."

That was more consideration than Mom had ever had for him, which said a lot about his character. It also explained why he'd stopped coming around, like Great-Gram had told me.

"Mom had me believing you took off because you were scared when you found out she was pregnant with me. For the record, I never held that against you. I mean, you *were* fifteen! I'd have taken off too!"

"It wasn't like that, though," my dad said, shaking his head. "Your mom and I just wanted different things, you know? She wanted to get married and have a house and all that. And I needed the military to straighten me out." A smirk came over his lips for a moment. "When I got back, I asked around. You know, 'cause you're my kid. I needed to know you were okay."

I thought to ask him if his mother denied my biological relation to them, like Mom had told me, but opted not to. The fact that he was with me now, and that he was open to a relationship with me, was answer enough.

"So, that's when you found out where we were?"

"Yeah. I heard your mom had moved out of the city with some guy—your stepdad, I guess. Heard she'd made a nice life for the two of you. So, I left well enough alone, thinking you were good. And here you are! You look good too!" He glanced at me and smiled.

"Thanks," I said, relieved that he approved.

"And I was glad to know your mom found someone," my dad added. "Every kid needs a dad. So, I'm grateful your stepdad could be there when I couldn't."

"Hmm," I sounded, curling in my lips.

"What?" my dad asked, glancing over and grinning at my obvious sarcasm.

I sighed before saying, "Well, about my stepdad . . . He's kind of a dick."

My dad burst out laughing. "Dana!"

"Well, he is!" I insisted, unable to contain my giggles. "I didn't know how to bring this up to you, but it hasn't been easy with him. It's been pretty rough, actually."

"A lot of kids don't get along with stepparents. It's very common."

"This is more than not getting along," I hinted.

My dad scrunched his brows, suddenly concerned, and asked, "He hasn't touched you sexually or anything, has he?"

"Oh, God no!" I instantly responded. My dad sighed in relief. "He has been *physically* rough with me, though. And *verbally*."

"You sure you're not mistaking what he says to you or—"

"No," I said, cutting him off. "There's no mistaking when someone repeatedly tells you your own mother doesn't love you and that no one ever wanted you to be born and stuff like that."

My dad shook his head. "And he hits you too? Is that what you're saying?"

"Yeah," I said, hoping my dad would tell me right then and there he was taking custody of me.

"He hit your mom too?"

"Honestly? I don't know. But you're not the first person to ask me that," I said as my dad pulled into the IHOP parking lot.

"Man," my dad said, shaking his head again. "I don't know what to say."

"It's okay. There's nothing *to* say."

"I just thought your mom and you were living in a nice house in the suburbs, and she had a business with this guy, and everything seemed to be okay for you . . ."

"Things aren't what they seem," I said. I didn't want to waste any more of this precious time talking about my piece of shit stepfather, though, so I reached for the lever to open the door and said, "Forget about it for now. Let's go grab some grub."

After being seated in a booth with our menus, my dad opened his and asked, "So, what do you normally get here?"

"Bacon cheeseburger and fries," I immediately answered. "My viola instructor bought me one at orchestra camp last summer. I've been hooked ever since!"

Dad snickered. "You're really into that orchestra stuff, huh?"

"Yeah. I love music in general, but I especially love orchestra because of the way all of our sounds meld together to create magnificence!" I said the last word with silly emphasis to make Dad laugh. Then I threw in, "Plus, I like the travelling."

"You get to go places with the orchestra?" Dad asked.

"Oh, yeah! We went to Colorado last fall. The train ride there was so cool. My friends and I sat in one car that had floor-to-ceiling windows where we could see the mountains and sunsets. Orchestra camp was in far north Wisconsin, though. Not as exciting."

"That's cool that you get to get out and see the world like that," he commented as he closed his menu and set it down.

"I do like going on trips. Gets me out of the house and away from Mom and Ron," I remarked snidely, "unless they're the ones I'm going on vacation *with*." I dropped my head slightly, thinking of how vacations with Mom and Ron were never an escape from the demeaning insults I experienced at home. Then I suddenly recalled that I'd brought my dad a gift. "Oh, I have something for you!"

I pulled a mini photo album out of my purse and set it on the table in front of my dad. "What's this?" he asked with a wide smile.

"Since you didn't get to see me growing up, I put together a couple dozen pictures of me for you to have. They're mostly from vacations since that's the only time my picture gets taken, really."

Dad maintained his toothy grin as he flipped through the album. He stopped on one photo and laughed. "Where was this?" He turned the photo album to show a picture of me with an orange slice in my mouth, peel side out.

I snort-laughed. "That was in Cancun, Mexico, a few years ago. Mom ordered a piña colada, so I got one too, only mine wasn't supposed to have alcohol in it. The waitress mixed them up!"

"So, you got the one with the alcohol?" Dad asked with raised brows.

"Yep! Mom said, 'Mine doesn't taste right.' Then she tasted mine and realized they'd messed up. I'd already sucked half of mine down, though! That's when I stuck the orange in my mouth!"

Dad and I laughed together as he perused the rest of the photos. "Looks like you've had a pretty good life so far!"

"I guess," I said dismally. Then I bowed my head, wishing I saw it that way.

I mean, on the one hand, I did enjoy perks other kids didn't have. I had Cavaricci pants in every color, which, at eighty dollars each, friends like Kelly and Miranda couldn't even think about asking their parents for. Mom and Ron took me on vacation every December during winter break. Ron even hired a limousine service to drive us to and from the airport sometimes!

On the other hand, I couldn't get an ounce of affection from Mom and Ron. Mom loved me with material things, and then Ron would complain about the money spent on a child that wasn't his. So, as much as I liked having "things," I would have traded them all for a humble life with Great-Gram or for a shot at a life with my dad who actually liked me, regardless of what material benefit he could offer.

"What's your favorite trip so far?" my dad asked, wanting to perk me back up.

I raised my head with brightened eyes and affirmed, "Puerto Rico. But not the trip I just took there with Mom, Ron, and Jonathan. The trip I took with Great-Gram and Uncle Juni a few years ago. We spent a good part of the summer there, and it was the best!"

The waitress brought our food then. So, I told my dad all about that glorious trip over lunch. Then we shared stories about school, haunts we'd experienced in places we'd lived, dreams we'd dreamt, and things we wanted to do in the future.

I loved how I could talk to my dad about anything and nothing without the worry of criticism or judgment. I could say what I thought and how I felt without being told I was dumb or wrong, or have my truth negated altogether. He didn't ridicule me about how I *should* feel or what I *should* have said or how I *should* be acting, nor did I have to put on some pretense to get him to like me. He liked me just fine. He accepted me as I was. And I was so much more relaxed being free to be me.

But after chowing down our burgers and fries, my dad dropped me back home, back to the reality of having to strategize and plan just to survive.

Fortunately, Mom never suspected I'd met him. Neither did Ron. I didn't feel any obligation to tell them, letting them believe I'd been home the whole day doing nothing. They'd decided I was a liar long ago, anyway. I wasn't really lying, however; I was just withholding the truth—something Mom would know a little about.

"Sympathy for the Devil"

My dad called almost every evening to talk on the phone. Since Mom had given him our phone number to begin with, I took that as permission to engage in these calls, whether she was home or not. She'd even answered the phone to him sometimes, but aside from a straight-lipped expression when she brought the cordless phone to my room, she never asked about my dad or the relationship I was developing with him.

Every time I talked to him, I hung up with a happy heart. I finally had a parent who liked me, thought I was funny, was proud of my achievements no matter how small, and who, most importantly, validated my existence. He encouraged me and reminded me of my worthiness in this world. He was more of a parent to me in the short time I'd known him than Mom and Ron had ever been to me. I couldn't dismiss the fact that it was because of the desire; Mom and Ron didn't want to be my parents, but my dad did, and it showed.

After a few weeks, however, Mom got quiet with me, communicating only if absolutely necessary, and Ron shot me hateful glares instead of words.

When I told Liam about their behavior, he suggested, "They probably don't like seeing you so happy, especially since it's obviously associated with your dad coming into your life."

I hadn't realized I was any different than I'd always been. Then again, I suddenly had a parent who found me innately perfect, as opposed to the two who were only attuned to all that was wrong.

"Is it that obvious?" I asked him.

"Yeah, you've been smiling more and just in a better mood overall."

I guess I was. I also guessed that was a direct result of my dad bringing out the best in me. *What a terrible man!* I mocked Mom in my mind.

Then, one evening, I went down to the kitchen to get something to eat and drink before Ron came home to comment on my consumption. It was about the only subject he'd break his silence on.

"Hey, Mom," I said. She was wiping the counters.

"Hey," she murmured, barely loud enough for me to hear.

I put my hand on my hip and jutted it. "Ron's been giving me the silent treatment too. So, what's up?"

"Nothing."

"Nothing means something," I said, expressing the little patience I had to play these games. "So, what is it? My dad, I assume?"

"Ron is your father," she corrected with a side-eye.

"No, he's not, Mom. You may have put his name on my birth certificate, which I'll never understand the legality of, but he's never acted like one to me," I told her.

"Oh, but *Dan* has?" There it was.

"If you mean my *real* dad, then yes. He has been everything a father should be to a daughter," I said. "I'm sorry if that's not what you want to hear, but it's what I feel!"

Mom pressed her lips together and continued her task in silence. I stared at her, willing her to look at me, even with one of those hateful glares she'd learned from Ron. She refused to acknowledge me, though, just like she refused to acknowledge my feelings about anything, ever.

After a long couple of minutes of watching her ignore my existence, I asked, "Why do you hate him so much, anyway, Mom? What did he ever do to you that was so bad that you just refuse to give him a break?"

She whipped her head towards me and narrowed her eyes.

"I know," I answered for her. "He got to finish high school and go live his life while you got shafted with a kid you didn't want." I rolled my eyes at the constant whine about how she hadn't gotten her way.

Mom's jaw tightened. I could see her gritting her teeth. She was holding back whatever it was she wanted to say to me. I wished she would just say it, because I felt like she'd been wanting to say it forever.

Impatience emboldened me to continue to say what I felt, regardless of the repercussions. "I don't get you, Mom. I've spent my whole life wondering who I was and where I came from because I never fit in anywhere. So, you do this huge thing for me! You find my dad. You get us in touch. And now you're punishing me for it!"

"Well, I thought you'd stop being so curious about him once you saw what kind of a person he really is!"

"That's the thing, Mom. He's *not* this terrible person you've made him out to be!"

"I've never spoken an unkind word about him. Or anyone," she said with a haughty conviction that proved the disturbing level of delusion by which she lived.

"Oh, really? You have *never* spoken badly about *anyone?*" I asked with a raised brow. All the woman *did* was gossip about people to the few she talked with.

"I see he's got you convinced that I'm the bad guy," Mom accused.

"He doesn't talk about you at all, actually. He's only said you two wanted different things and that he appreciated Ron for being my father figure. So, yeah, he's so awful," I mocked with an exaggerated roll of my eyes.

Mom glared at me again. "You just don't know the *real* him."

"Or maybe I do, and you just refuse to accept that he's not who you've made him out to be," I told her. She responded with another glare. "You know, I finally have peace with things, but it's like you just don't want to let go of the idea that he's a better person than Ron will ever be! I mean, Jesus Christ, it's not like he raped you."

I casually opened the refrigerator and took out a can of pop, feeling very comfortable in my truth and equally relieved that I'd spoken it. When I turned back to the counter, I noticed Mom hadn't moved or stopped glaring at me. It's like she was trying to communicate something to me without saying it, doubly stunned at my directness.

"What?" I begged. Then I recalled my last flippant remark. "Are you trying to imply that he—?" I shook my head at the thought. Then Mom stormed out.

There was no way that was true. But the zombie woman rarely exhibited strong emotions as much as she had tonight. So, I followed her out to the foyer, determined to pin her down for the truth.

The door to the basement had just firmly shut. I thought to chase her down, but she obviously wanted to be alone, or at least nowhere near *me*. So, I went back to the kitchen and gulped my soda. Then I started to wonder if that horrific thing I'd said was, in fact, truth.

I thought about everything she'd ever said about him, as well as everything she hadn't. She'd said they were at a party together the night I was conceived. She claimed he took drugs and had been drinking too. A lot of people used recreational drugs in the seventies, though. I wasn't condoning it. I just didn't think it precluded a problem, nor could I conclude that she hadn't done any either.

She'd said they were dating. That didn't mean consensual sex had taken place. I'd give her that. However, she hadn't ever mentioned taking issue with him until he'd refused to marry her. Mom was admittedly resentful about that, saying that her father had tried to pressure his mother into forcing my dad to make the commitment to Mom anyway. When my dad and his mom refused, mom said they'd disclaimed me being his altogether and made her out to be a whore who slept around.

Was it a terrible ordeal? Yes. Did that make my dad a rapist, though? No. Maybe a scared fifteen-year-old with a mother who strove to vindicate him, as many mothers would, but that didn't make them bad people.

Anyway, if he had taken advantage of Mom and denied me, how come his mother hadn't denied me when she'd called Mom at her office a handful of years before? How come my dad didn't deny me now? I hated to believe someone I'd just met over the woman who'd bore me, but Mom had told too many lies for me to trust her at all.

Even my grandma and Great-Gram had told me about how my dad had come around to see me after I was born. If Mom had been raped, there's no way they'd have allowed him anywhere near me nor their home. My uncles wouldn't have maintained a friendly acquaintance with him, like they'd said they had. I'm guessing Mom wouldn't have hired a PI to locate her rapist and then call him. And I sure as shit didn't believe for one second that someone would give their rapist their home phone number to start a relationship with their kid!

There were too many "ifs" that didn't add up, including my name. Mom had admitted she'd named me after my dad. If he'd really raped her, why would she name me after him? Why would she have even kept me?

It's not that I didn't want to believe I was a product of a criminal sexual offense, but nothing Mom had said supported the accusation. Plus, she'd neither confirmed nor denied it. She'd just *implied* it. Mom suggested a lot of things when trying to present circumstances in a way that prevented her from having to take accountability. Just like pretending Ron was my biological father, that we were as Caucasian as the neighbors, and a normal fucking family living a boring fucking life, this was just another story created by Mom to distort the past to her advantage and remain the forever victim of everything.

"I Can't Go for That (No Can Do)"

After a couple more days of getting the silent treatment from Mom and Ron, I overheard them arguing in their bedroom. I turned down my radio to hear their hushed voices better.

"If that's how he's going to talk to you, then I don't want that man calling my house ever again!" Ron declared.

I guessed "he" was my dad, though I couldn't imagine what he could have said to offend them, when he only ever called to talk to *me*.

"I would have never given him our number if I thought he would say something like that to me," Mom groveled. "I guess I'd hoped he'd changed, or grown up, by now."

"Well, you better put an end to this shit," Ron warned. "Otherwise, I will."

"But what do I tell Dana?"

"I don't care what you tell her! But *no* more phone calls! Not as long as she lives under *my* roof!"

"Okay," Mom said.

I froze at the instantaneous devastation that her one-word response presumed. It's like they had to take away anything that brought me joy, including a dad I'd just met. Knowing there was nothing I could do about it sent my heart racing in a panic.

"I mean it," Ron responded in a threatening tone. Then I heard his loud footsteps pound down the stairs and out the front door.

A knock on my bedroom door immediately followed. "I need to talk to you, Dane," Mom said in a tone both serious and sorry at the same time. She confused me more than she ever made sense.

"I heard through the wall, Ma," I responded to bypass the bullshit. Mom looked dumbfounded. "I just wanna know why, though. I mean, *you're* the one who found him. *You* gave him our phone number. We get along *really* well. So, why? Why are you trying to take him away from me? Do you not want me to be happy?"

Mom huffed in annoyance. "You know, Dane," she said, crossing her arms and jutting a hip. "You think you know everything, but you don't. You don't *know* your biological father—not like I do."

"Oh, really? What don't I know, then?"

Mom pressed her lips together. "I never wanted to give you any kind of negative impression about him," she said, lowering her head humbly. I immediately recounted all the snide remarks she'd made about him and expected I'd hear some more now. "But I will tell you what happened, so you understand how Ron and I feel about you suddenly having a relationship with him."

"Okay . . ." I said, despite having no interest in whatever twisted story she'd concocted.

"Last night when your—*Dan*—called here to talk to you . . ." She stalled then looked down for dramatic effect. I waited while she tried to summon up tears. She looked back up at me with a sorrowful expression instead and continued, "I answered. When he heard my voice, he asked if I looked like I used to when we were teenagers."

"So?" I asked.

"He was *hitting* on me, Dana," she clarified.

"Hitting on you?" I repeated. I didn't believe it for a second. I mean, first she tells me he'd refused to marry her, now she claims he's interested in her again. So, which was it?

"Yes," she said, dropping her head again, "and it made me feel . . . cheap." She looked into my eyes for effect then.

I shook my head. I was pretty sure this was another one of Mom's self-centered twists of someone's words, like the time she'd misinterpreted a customer telling her she should work for J.D. Powers and Associates, a customer review company. The customer had been complimenting her professional demeanor on the phone. She, however, went around telling everyone the guy thought she should go to John Robert Powers (a modeling school with a similar name) to pursue a career in modeling. I'd tried to correct her error, but she'd dismissed it in favor of her much more envious version of events.

When she saw that I wasn't reacting with the horror that she wanted me to, she pressed, "It's disrespectful to my marriage to Ron for Dan to try to get with me after all these years."

"You think he's trying to 'get with' you?" I chuckled with an inappropriate smirk. I couldn't take her seriously. If she had such an innate need to feel attractive, maybe she should keep doing her Jane Fonda videos until Ron liked how she looked again.

"Yes," she said shamefully. "I really wish you didn't have to know this side of him, Dane. Really."

Bullshit, I thought. But I said, "Well, I'm sorry for whatever you *think* happened. But I'm not going to stop talking to my dad. I'll just try to talk to him when you're not home, I guess. But he works too, so it's hard to avoid." I went to close my bedroom door then, to end this conversation. Mom took the hint and went back to her room.

The house phone rang shortly after, bringing Mom back to my door. "It's for you, Dane," she said. "It's—"

"Got it," I said, snatching the phone from her hand. "Hello?" I said into the phone, noticing how Mom widened my door all the way open.

"Hi, Dana!" my dad responded.

"Hey," I said, lacking my usual enthusiasm to hear his voice.

"What's going on today? Anything new?"

"No," I said glumly. "Everything's *exactly* the same as always."

"Is it Ron? Is he bothering you?" my dad asked. His anxiousness to know made me feel cared for and protected in a way I'd never felt from my own mother, who lingered in Jonathan's room across the hall.

"No, it's the other one tonight," I said, referencing Mom.

"Well, whatever it is, just give her a break. She's got a lot going on with taking care of your little brother and running their business." It pissed me off that he was defending a woman who blasphemed him at every opportunity.

I didn't want to instigate any trouble between them, though, so I said, "I know."

"You don't sound convinced," my dad replied with a snicker.

I couldn't help but smirk at how he saw through me. "No, not really," I chuckled.

"What's going on, then? You wanna talk about it?" he asked. I appreciated that he didn't pressure or talk in code like Mom. He was respectful of my comfort and gave me the space to feel and think and process at my own pace. *What a monster!*

Sighing as I debated how to broach the issue with Dad, I noticed Mom walk down the hall with Jonathan on her hip. Then I heard the familiar creek of the wood under the carpeted stairs. Thinking it was safe to speak freely now that Mom was out of earshot, I whispered, "Apparently, you hit on her?"

"I what?" my dad asked.

"She said you asked her if she looked like she used to or something?" I whispered a little louder. "That you were hitting on her or trying to get with her or whatever?"

"Geez!" my dad said, sounding as surprised as I'd expected. "We talked for like a minute last night, but I was just making conversation! You know, telling her how it's been a long time, and I couldn't believe we had a fifteen-year-old. I said something about how you were just as pretty as she was back then and that I wondered if she'd aged as well as I had. It was a joke, though. You've obviously seen me."

I cracked up. He looked nothing like the picture Mom had given me from 1975. He was still tall, but he was otherwise the Stay-Puft Marshmallow Man version of the lean and lanky hippie he'd been.

"That sounds about right," I said, nodding. "Mom's perception has always been a little skewed."

"Yeah, she was always a little different," he said.

"She still is. Trust me."

My dad chuckled at my snide remark. Then sadness overcame me. My relationship with my dad was so easy, whereas the relationship with Mom was so strained. She'd never let me have this, though. Not after what Ron had demanded. That meant this beautiful father-daughter relationship I'd developed was better ended now, on my terms, as opposed to whatever abrupt ending Mom and Ron would affect later.

"Well, hey, I hate to do this, but I should probably let you go."

"Oh! You got somewhere to go?"

"No," I admitted, "but Mom brought all that crap up about you hitting on her right before you called, so it might make my life a little easier if I cut our call short tonight."

"Okay. Yeah. I don't want to cause any trouble for you, Dana."

"I know you don't. I cause enough trouble all on my own around here," I muttered.

"Don't say that. Your mother loves you." He sounded like he really believed that. Too bad I didn't.

"Well, thanks for being so cool about everything."

"Yeah! We'll talk another time," he said.

"Okay, Dad," I said, unsure whether we would. "I love you."

"Love you too, Dana," he said. Then we ended the call, and I hung on to his words like a precious memory.

Every time the phone rang every evening after, Ron would pierce me with his evil eye. Mom's worried face would impress the disapproval. Still, she'd hand me the phone, thereby handing off accountability for my dad calling at all.

I didn't care so much about Ron and the perceived offense to his ego. I did still care about Mom, though, whether she deserved my love or not. Knowing she'd told Ron she'd put an end to my dad's calls, I was afraid about how he would avenge his pride. Although I still wasn't sure whether he had ever hit Mom, I couldn't consciously be the reason why he started.

So, for both my sake and Mom's, I cut the calls with Dad shorter and shorter. I'd tell my dad I couldn't talk for this reason or that, until he finally stopped calling altogether.

I hated that I had to push him away. I didn't want my dad to think I didn't want a relationship with him. I didn't want him to think there was anything wrong with him either. As much as I didn't want Ron to manipulate me into cutting contact, though, it was the only way to avoid the physical and emotional power struggles Mom and I would be subjected to if I didn't.

I just hoped my dad would use his keen sense of what was what—something he'd likely developed in the Marines—to infer the position I was in. Because dealing with Ron was like warfare: anything was fair game, outside influencers were the enemy, and both sides had to strategize based on our predictions of what the opponent would do next.

Unfortunately for Ron, I was becoming better at this game every day. Perhaps I'd inherited that trait from my dad. Regardless, I'd learned it was every man for himself in this house, because I couldn't even count on my mother not to side with the enemy.

"I Want Love"

At the end of February 1991, I asked Liam to accompany me to our school's Turnabout Dance—in which girls asked boys to be their dates instead of the traditional practice of boys asking girls. I was thrilled he'd said yes, though I thought his mom was even more excited to see her son go to his first dance with a girl.

"Oh my gosh, look at the two of you!" she gushed as she took pictures of us in her living room. Mom had driven me there to pick up Liam but remained at the front door with a polite smile while Liam's mom rambled on, wearing a wide grin. "You look so classy and elegant, Dana. I just—" Her mouth dropped open, and a heavy sigh came out instead of words. Liam squeezed my hand and smiled while his mother posed us in every potential position she could think to capture.

His blue eyes sparkled more than usual, so I hoped that meant he liked how I looked. I'd worn a black velvet cocktail dress, strapless and fitted at the crystal-lined top, with a skirt that flared in alternating folds of black velvet and satin. I'd added black satin gloves that went up to my elbows, like a glamorous Hollywood starlet of old, and simple black satin heels. The red lipstick was a little much, but completely appropriate for the occasion, and complimented my dark dress and pale skin brilliantly.

"You do look really nice," Liam confirmed as we held hands on the way to my mom's car.

"Thanks," I said, hiding my smile at the flattery. "You clean up pretty good too," I returned, referring to the white dress shirt and black pants and tie, which was a startling difference from the usual jeans and rock band

T-shirt. Not that it mattered; I was totally smitten regardless.

Our school gymnasium had been transformed into a magical place where girls twirled on the dance floor with their well-dressed dates under the dazzling reflections of the disco ball, which made the place look like stars shining in the night sky.

We waited in line to have our picture taken by the professional photographer who promised two five-by-seven photos within weeks. Liam saw some friends from his grade school sitting at a corner table then and led me over to introduce me. I noticed their high-browed looks as we approached.

"Hey, guys," Liam greeted the group of dark-haired Jewish girls I'd seen hanging out together in school before.

"Hi, Liam," a thicker girl with a nasally voice responded while looking me up and down. She was wearing a dark floral dress that I'd have worn to church, so I felt some judgment for my strapless and much more formal choice. I really wanted to impress Liam's friends, though, so I pretended I hadn't noticed. "Who's this?" she asked snottily.

"Dana," he said. "My date." He glanced at me and smiled.

"I've seen you around," I reminded the ignorant girl. Just then, the exotic girl from our earth science class walked up, looking as perfectly perfect as always in a fitted red gown out of which her bouncy bosom blatantly overflowed.

"Yeah, well . . . This is my *other* best friend, Julie," she said.

"Hi, Julie," I said with a little wave, despite feeling defeminized in her presence. "We had earth science together. Remember?"

"Oh, yeah! Hi!" Julie said with genuine kindness. Then she struck up a conversation with a skinny pointy-chinned girl who was sitting at their table.

"Liam and Julie and I have known each other since grade school," the snooty girl declared. "Liam and I *still* talk almost every night."

Sensing she was asserting her position in Liam's life, as if I were infringing on it, I politely nodded and said, "Oh, that's super cool."

Liam shifted nervously in his stance, and I noticed his eyes darting everywhere else but where we were. "Well, we're going to walk around and probably dance or something," he said, smiling at me again.

"I did ask you to a dance to dance!" I joked. Liam chuckled. His bitchy friend did not.

"*I've* never known you to dance, Liam," she said.

"Well, I can't disappoint my gorgeous date, can I?" he snarked back with a smile. Then he led me away, straight to the dance floor.

Liam's lame attempts to move his body like a gangster when C+C Music Factory's "Gonna Make You Sweat" came on cracked me up, but I appreciated his efforts. It's not like I looked any better, anyway. Not that I cared. I loved music. I loved moving my body to it. And I loved it more when the Damn Yankees' ballad "High Enough" played, giving me the opportunity to put my arms around Liam's neck and feel his body close to mine as we slowly swayed. At one point, Liam leaned down and kissed me ever so softly. The slip of the tongue took away the innocence of it, but it was the perfect ending to what we called "our song" after that.

After what had seemed like the most amazing night of my life, which put me on a high I could never imagine coming down from, Liam walked me out at the time my mother had designated, to wait with me for my ride home. The sight of Ron's Corvette immediately deflated my mood.

At first, he was quiet when I got in his car. So, I ignored his scowl and sat back, recalling my glorious night, when out of nowhere he growled, "You look like a . . ."

I looked at Ron, waiting for him to finish his insult. When he didn't, I said, "I don't give a rat's ass what you think."

"Don't you mouth off to me," he warned with narrowed eyes.

"I'm not mouthing off to you," I said with an inflected tone of arrogance, knowing damn well I was mouthing off. I wouldn't let him ruin the night with his degrading bullshit, though. Not this night.

Forced against the seat by the gravity of Ron's powerful acceleration, I turned and looked out the window, thankful it was only a five-minute drive home to hell.

I complained to my mom about Ron after he left the next morning.

"You know, he wouldn't be so extreme with you if he didn't care about you so much," she said.

"So, you're trying to tell me he's an ass to me because he loves me?" I clarified. "I mean, if you want to tell yourself that load of crap, fine. But I don't buy it."

"I don't know why you use that language when there are so many other words you can use," she scolded, turning back to the sink.

"Well, listen to yourself, Mom! You're basically saying his abuse is coming from a place of love, and that's total bullshit!"

"Stop with the language!" Mom ordered, averting her eyes towards Jonathan as a hint to her reason for the demand. "And stop calling Ron abusive! Your life isn't that bad. You have a house, nice clothes, I give you money for food every week . . . What more could you want?"

"Love, Mom! I want my frickin' mother and maybe even my stepfather to love me! Maybe even give me a damn hug once in a while! Is that too much to ask?" I yelled, as if my volume would make it resonate more this time, as opposed to all the other times we'd had the same argument before.

"It's okay, Jonathan. I'll never understand why your sissy has so much anger inside of her," Mom soothed Jonathan, as if I'd upset him. He was completely oblivious to the high emotions and tension, focused more on grasping the Cheerios on his tray with his grubby and chubby little hands.

"Now I'm angry?" I asked. "Maybe it's because I'm tired of begging my mother for love!"

Mom's long exhale made me feel like I was exhausting her with the inconvenience of my unmet needs. "You get so emotional over things that aren't a big deal," she dismissed.

"Asking you to love me isn't a big deal?" I repeated.

"It's your hormones," she said. "You *are* at that age, which reminds me—I should take you to my gynecologist. You should be having yearly exams now that you're menstruating."

"So now we're having a sex talk?" I screeched, frustrated at how she so skillfully ignored my feelings. Then I rushed out of the kitchen and up to my bedroom, trying to decipher how Ron being an asshole had turned into me needing a gynecological exam. I swear the woman was trying to make me crazy.

It didn't take me long to realize, however, that I was "at that age" that Mom had gotten pregnant with me. I had a boyfriend now too. But I wasn't like Mom. I wouldn't just go to a party and drink and have sex with my boyfriend like it was just another Tuesday. I'd be choosier and more careful when I decided to give myself to someone that way. And I wouldn't get pregnant either. Thanks to her, I was so scared of my innate ineptitude to be a good parent that I didn't want kids anyway.

"What a Fool Believes"

On the way back from my appointment with Mom's gynecologist, Mom's silence added to the discomfort I already felt about the wrinkly old man touching my boobs and sticking his fingers and sharp metal instruments where I'd only ever allowed entry to a Playtex tampon. I felt violated and gross, like the old geezer was more interested in getting his jollies off of me than in really examining me at all. I wanted to talk to Mom about it, but I knew she wouldn't understand. She seemed to be punishing me with silence anyway, though I didn't know why.

"Did I do something?" I finally asked, looking at Mom's perturbed expression.

"I don't know. Did you?" The snootiness in her tone confused me. It was like she was asking me a trick question.

"What do you mean?" I asked. "You're obviously not happy with me, but I don't know what I did to upset you, so . . ." I lingered on my last word.

"I'm upset because you're never honest with me," she responded.

"What is it that you think I'm lying about *now*? Can you just tell me what's going on?"

After a long pause, Mom cryptically confessed, "I know what you did."

"Can you please just tell me, then? Because I *don't* know!"

She paused again for dramatic effect, which successfully achieved the nervous anticipation I felt. Then, with a sullen tone that sounded like the end of the world had come, she finally divulged, "The gynecologist told me you're not a virgin anymore."

I creased my brows at her. Aside from *trying* to have sex with Kevin,

I'd never even been naked with another boy. "But I am," I said.

"That's not what my doctor told me," she arrogantly affirmed.

"Well, I'm sorry to break it to you, but he's wrong," I insisted. "I don't know how he could even determine something like that, but I swear to God on Jonathan's life *and* mine that I have never *had* sex." I realized too late that adding my life for emphasis would have no effect.

"So, you think my doctor is lying to me?" Mom said, huffing at the assumed audacity.

"Yes!" I defended.

"He's just making this up, then? He's a liar just like you have been saying Ron is for so many years?"

"I don't know, Mom. All I know is the truth; and the truth is I've never had sex! Whether or not you believe me is up to you," I said, shaking my head. She only believed what she wanted to believe, which was whatever suited her delusions. In any case, she never believed *me*.

While some cheery oldie played on the radio, I slumped into my seat, wondering why that doctor would tell Mom I wasn't a virgin, anyway. As paranoid as it sounded, it felt like he was in cahoots with Mom, like she was trying to prove that I was the whore Ron always said I was.

Then it finally came to me. I looked up at Mom and said, "While the doctor was . . . you know," I said, referring to the examination of my private parts, "he *asked* if I'd had sex before. I told him I hadn't but that I used tampons. So . . ."

I waited for Mom to consider what I'd said, but she kept her eyes fixed on the road, as if I wasn't even there.

"I swear I've never had sex, Mom," I pleaded. I hoped for any acknowledgment, even more of a fight. She remained unresponsive for the remaining hour drive home.

Disappointed that Mom was more concerned about my virginity than with counseling me through my feelings about my first gynecological exam, I suddenly missed my dad. It would have been embarrassing to talk to him about my female parts, but I was sure he would have found a way to validate and reassure me, regardless of how awkward it might have been.

Instead, I was stuck with Mom, who refused to believe anything that didn't conform to the little she and Ron had decided to reduce me to.

"Don't Let the Sun Go Down on Me"

*T*he next thing I knew, I was sitting on a small red-upholstered sofa, waiting for another adult to find something wrong with me. According to what mom told me on the drive over, she and Ron had decided I should see a psychologist because they didn't know "what else to do with me."

The low-lit room featured brass fixtures and heavy burgundy drapes that reminded me of Hugh Hefner's legendary red house coat. I imagined Mr. Hefner sitting in a fancy high-backed chair in front of a glowing fireplace in the darkened room, with a cloud of smoke from a Cuban cigar floating in front of him. Really, I was facing a short and rotund dark-haired lady who'd introduced herself as Dr. Lehrfield. Her poofy hairdo and pearl necklace gave away the age of a grandma, as did the hefty ankles settled onto thick-heeled pumps.

"I'd like to start by having you draw me a picture of your family—as *you* see it," she said, wearing a closed-mouth smile reminiscent of creepy killers in movies as she set a piece of paper and a box of crayons on the coffee table in front of me. Then she returned to her seat and stared at me with that creepy smile again, causing me to question whether the roles should be reversed.

"Okay . . .?" I responded warily, thinking she was accustomed to working with five-year-olds instead of teenagers. I'd expected to be presented with black splotches on paper and asked to tell her what I saw in them. But if she wanted to treat me like a kindergartener, I'd draw her the damn picture.

The scrutinous pressure of her staring at me while I drew made me even more self-conscious than I already was. Perhaps I should have shared with her that delving into my issues with my self-image would be more productive. I didn't want to admit to having any issues nor be there any longer than I had to, though. So, I drew as fast as I could so I could go back home to my room where no one would bother me with childish bullshit.

"I'm done," I said, looking up at the doctor.

She extended her hand, so I took the hint and brought her the drawing. Then I slumped back into the loveseat with my arms crossed, awaiting her professional assessment.

"Hmm," she sounded, making me wonder what was so thought-provoking about a few stick figures. "I'm wondering why you drew a man, a boy, and a curly-haired woman holding hands, and then another female with wavy hair on the opposite side, alone."

"Well," I mocked to be a smart ass, "Ron and Mom have their son, Jonathan, now, and the three of them are a family. I am just . . . there."

"So, you feel like they are their own family? A family you're not part of?" Dr. Lehrfield asked.

"It's not what I *feel*. Ron *told* me I wasn't part of 'his' family, before my brother was even born," I corrected.

"Hmm," she responded, pressing her lips together. She set the drawing on the round table beside her chair. "What exactly did your dad say to you that you *perceived* that way?"

"Please don't refer to Ron as my dad. I barely want him referred to as my stepfather," I said before telling her what he'd told me on the way to that softball game a couple summers before.

"Are you sure you didn't misconstrue something, or take it out of context?"

"I'm sure," I said. Then I tilted my head to the side to stretch my tense neck and shoulder muscles. I heard a crack.

"You seem upset," she commented.

"Well, yeah. I *feel* like sitting here with you is a waste of time, because no amount of talking about my feelings is going to change the fact that Mom never wanted me and that Ron is a jerk."

"Sometimes talking about things can help you see situations and people from a different perspective," she suggested.

"But I'm the only one who does see anything for what it really is!" I asserted.

"Tell me about that, then—about whatever it is that makes you feel like you're alone and not part of your family."

I sighed then explained, "I *feel* like Mom does nothing to protect me from Ron or defend me when there's a conflict between us, because she doesn't *believe* me when I tell her about anything that's happened. But even when she witnesses things, I *feel* like she deludes herself into believing some altered version of events so she doesn't have any bad feelings towards Ron. Because if she has bad feelings towards Ron, she might consider leaving him. But for some frickin' reason, she actually loves him, or loves the life and things she's able to have with him, which seems to trump everything, including me!" My elevated tone and volume at the end expressed an anger I usually subdued for the sake of peace. It felt good to release it, though.

"You have some very strong feelings about your parents, don't you?" Dr. Lehrfield asked, nodding her head. I recognized what she was doing as a way to manipulate me into thinking she understood me and was on my side, which just made me distrust her more. Because if I trusted her, I'd have confided in her about the dreams I'd had in which I murdered my parents, ridding myself of them and all the emotions I felt about them altogether.

"Obviously," I snarked.

"I noticed you didn't mention your brother, though. How do you feel about him, seeing as you were an only child for so long before he was born."

"He has nothing to do with any of this."

"But if you think your brother is the reason you were removed from the family, surely you'd have feelings about that. Perhaps jealousy?" Dr. Lehrfield presumed.

"Jonathan is innocent in all this. He didn't ask to be born into this dysfunction," I told her. Anyway, I loved my little brother. Yes, I envied the doting and attention I was deprived of, but I wasn't jealous.

"Can you give me an example of a time when you experienced this 'dysfunction'?" she asked.

"Yeah," I said before proceeding to tell her all the diminishing comments Ron had used to destroy my self-esteem and sense of self. "It's not right, you know, to mess with a kid's head that way," I asserted. Then my eyes moistened. I dropped my head to prevent her from seeing them.

After allowing me a respectful pause, I looked back up at Dr. Lehrfield to signal my readiness to proceed. I felt the sympathy in her upturned brows and tilted head; I hoped it was sincere and not some ploy to get me to trust her enough to confide whatever she expected me to.

"When you say 'mess with a kid's head that way,' I wonder what you mean by that," she prodded.

"Well, I don't think it's right for someone to say those things to a kid. Do you?" I responded with more belligerence than intended.

"Of course not," Dr. Lehrfield responded, though I couldn't be sure if she meant that, or if she was tricking me into believing we were in agreement.

"So, if you agree it's not right, and I'm telling you Ron said those things to me, then wouldn't you agree he should be sitting here instead of me?" I asked, feeling confident in the impressive way I used her own psychology against her.

Silence. I thought so.

Dr. Lehrfield reached over and picked up the drawing. After a serious examination of it, she set it down and looked at me again. I hated it when people stared at me. I felt scrutinized. "Tell me, Dana, why did you draw a bright yellow sun all the way on the left side of the paper where your mom, brother and dad are standing holding hands?"

"I didn't realize the position of the sun mattered, but now that I think about it, maybe the sun is shining down on the three of them because they're all so frickin' happy now that they have the biological family Ron wanted," I said, frustrated that we were discussing color choices instead of the verbal and emotional abuse I'd endured.

"So, you're not happy?"

"Not at home!" I lashed back. "I'm happy when I'm not there, though. Most of the time," I added as a correction.

"What does make you happy, Dana?"

I sighed. Answering all these useless questions was becoming increasingly annoying. "Dancing. And singing, though no one would ever want to hear me sing. I love music and song lyrics, playing piano and viola, hanging out with my couple of friends, and my boyfriend . . ."

Dr. Lehrfield tilted her head and smiled, as if it were cute that I had a boyfriend. "Is he your first boyfriend?" she asked, nodding.

"Kind of," I said, pointedly avoiding any mention of Kevin and the nickname I'd earned after trying to have sex with him. "He's the first one I *love*, at least," I mumbled, presuming every adult deemed teenagers incapable of anything more than sexual relationships.

"Your voice softened just then," Dr. Lehrfield observed. "It's different than when you speak about your mom and dad."

I thought I was pretty self-aware for my age, but I hadn't made that association before. After considering the observation, I realized the doctor was right. "Well, it's probably because I actually like Liam, his mother, my friends . . . They're all easy to get along with," I said.

"How so?"

"They don't judge me. They don't make me feel bad about myself. They're just cool, I guess." *Like my dad*, I wanted to say, but I didn't dare bring him up. She'd have a field day trying to make sense of that whole situation.

"And your mother isn't any of those things?"

"Not even close! She makes me feel like the same worthless piece of stupid crap Ron does," I said, thinking she became more like Ron with every day that passed.

"Those are strong words," Dr. Lehrfield said.

"Well, they're *strong* feelings!" I snapped. "Don't you think I want a good relationship with my mom? Doesn't every daughter?"

"I don't know. Do you?" she asked with her high, penciled brows. "Because based on how strongly you feel about your mother and Ron, I'm not sure."

I threw my arms to the side, frustrated that I had to explain my psyche to a professional whose job it was to make sense of it for all of us. "Well, of course I want a good relationship with Mom!" I said with a raised voice. "But she didn't want me in the first place, and she still doesn't want me now!" Maybe if I repeated those facts enough, someone would fucking believe me!

Dr. Lehrfield pressed her lips together and exhaled out of her nose. "I would like to think there's a big misconception here, and that maybe, with some good communication and understanding, you and your mother will discover that you want the same thing."

I huffed. "I'm sorry, but I totally disagree. Mom and Ron won't be happy until I'm out of the picture. And if everything goes as I'd like it to, it won't be much longer."

"What do you mean by that?" Dr. Lehrfield asked with the creased brow of concern. I realized she might have taken my comment to mean I was going to take my own life.

"I *mean* I'll be leaving their house the second I turn eighteen and can legally be on my own," I clarified, "though I've read I can get emancipated before that. I just don't have enough money saved up from babysitting yet to be able to afford an attorney to do that for me." Not that I knew what that amount was.

"So, you're planning to leave your parents' home at eighteen? What about college?"

"I have no plans to go to college," I said. "I want to go to beauty school."

Dr. Lehrfield squirmed in her seat and looked at her wristwatch with scrunched brows. "Hmm," she stalled. Then she sighed. We were obviously out of time. "I hope we can talk about this a little more next time," she said as she stood.

Next time? I thought as I exhaled. I didn't even want to be here *this* time! But like a good girl, I followed her cue to escape this place for now.

Mom and Ron were waiting in the small room just outside the doctor's confines. I immediately dropped my head, wondering how much they'd been able to hear through the door.

"Would you wait out here for a couple minutes, Dana, while I talk to your parents?" Dr. Lehrfield directed.

I nodded, presuming I had no choice but to allow them their private huddle about what a nut job I was. Then Mom and Ron eagerly brushed past me, and the three closed themselves into the doctor's office. Maybe the doctor would have them draw pictures for her too.

After several minutes of staring at the scenic portrait on the wall of the tiny waiting room, the door reopened. Ron glared at me as he moved to the exit, and Mom gave me a tight-lipped look of disapproval. I glanced at the doctor for some indication of what I had said to piss them off now. She just stood there with that creepy smile, looking as trustworthy as the evil clown from Stephen King's *It*.

"Don't Be Cruel"

Ron didn't speak to me for a couple weeks after that. That awful, hateful squinty-eyed expression of disapproval was more of a favor than a punishment, anyway. Mom's standoffishness, however, was more offensive to me. Because assuming they were upset about whatever Dr. Lehrfield told them about me, their united front was perpetuating the feelings of exclusion that stemmed from such behavior in the first place!

So, I stayed out of the house as much as I could to avoid them, using viola lessons, orchestra, and dance classes as my usual excuses. I spent whatever free time remained at Liam's house, regardless of whether he was home. His mom let me hang out with her or amuse myself in Liam's bedroom until Liam returned from wherever.

I'd become such a fixture at Liam's house that his mother started setting a place for me at their dinner table. Maybe I'd watched too many TV sitcoms, but I'd longed to be part of a family that sat together every evening and shared the happenings of their day. That all happened at Liam's house, at promptly six o'clock. They talked about good news and bad, laughed at funny stories, supported and encouraged—it felt like I was finally part of a real family.

One night, Liam and I were laughing at something the "Fresh Prince" said on his TV show of the same name while his brother started serving himself the potatoes that had already been placed on the table. Liam's mom and stepfather were at the kitchen counter tending to the steak they'd grilled.

Even from behind, they looked like an odd couple. The top of Jim's head was bald but surrounded by a fringe of dark hair around the side.

Aside from the bald spot, Jim looked like Ernie from *Sesame Street*, just like Liam had once joked. I tried not to smirk at the recollection. Jim was dressed much more seriously than the children's show character, though, wearing black dress pants and a long-sleeved white button-up shirt, rolled up at the cuffs. He definitely looked mismatched with Liam's mom, who was tall and toned with beautiful light-brown hair, every curl of which hung perfectly to her waistline. Surely her stomach would be just as slender as soon as their baby was born.

"Can you cut a few of those in half?" I overheard Liam's mom ask "Ernie."

He took a knife but griped, "I shouldn't have to make four steaks feed five people."

"Stop," Liam's mom scolded in a whisper. "She's right there at the table!"

Suddenly feeling like the same burden to this family as I was in my own home, I dropped my head to hide my shame.

"You okay?" Liam asked, noticing my sudden change in demeanor.

I fake-smiled and nodded. "Yeah!" I appreciated how attentive he was to me, but I didn't want to make an issue of anything in front of anyone. I was trouble enough already, apparently.

"Cut one more in half, would you?" I overheard Liam's mom tell Jim.

"This is ridiculous," he remarked. "She's not even my kid. I shouldn't have to feed her every single night."

At that, tears welled in my eyes. I wanted to run away and never show my face there again. Remaining was the lesser embarrassment of the two options I had, though. So, I stifled my tears and kept my head down to avoid notice.

Liam was laughing at the Fresh Prince's latest sarcastic remark when he glanced over to see if I'd found it just as funny. I offered a weak smile, unable to muster much more. Liam squinted, as if psychically asking what was wrong, then took the hint of my quick head shake to leave well enough alone. His mom and Jim were sitting down just then anyway.

"Here you go, Dana," his mom said as she moved the first piece of meat towards my plate.

"Oh, no thanks," I said, waving my hand.

Liam looked at me suspiciously as his mother asked, "Are you sure?"

I didn't need another man to have to pay for a child who wasn't his.

"Yeah. I'll have some potatoes, but I think my mom is saving me a plate of dinner tonight, so I'll eat when I go home in a bit."

Liam looked at me again, having heard me complain about how hungry I was not long before, but I didn't make eye contact.

"Okay!" she said as she continued to serve Jim and the boys before herself.

I ate the small heap of mashed potatoes I'd taken then watched quietly as everyone chowed down on their meat and discussed the events of their days. My stomach grumbled in envy. I thought to take more potatoes, since there were plenty, but I'd heard Ron say that carbohydrates from potatoes make you fat. So, I opted not to.

Then, as soon as everyone was finished eating and I'd helped clear the table, I excused myself to call home for a ride.

"You sure you're okay?" Liam asked as he walked me out to wait for Ron to come get me.

"Yeah!" I lied in an overly cheery tone.

"It's me, Dana," he said, looking into my eyes with high brows. "I know you, and you were unusually quiet at dinner. So, what's up?"

I wanted to tell him how his stepdad had made me feel just like Ron did with his comment. But then Liam would say something to his mom, she'd confront Jim, and then I'd feel weird coming over—if I'd ever come over at all after that. "I just hate going home. You know?" I offered instead.

"I know," he said. Then he stood there, holding my hand quietly, until Ron pulled up.

"I'm tired of picking you up here and having to smell that boy on you," Ron ridiculed as soon as I got into his sportscar.

"I know," I said in a monotone, leaning my head back against the headrest and looking out the passenger window into the starry night sky. "I'm a whore."

"Outsider"

⁓

*T*hick fingers gripped my ankles. Was I having a nightmare? Or was I awake?

Stomach-down on the full-size bed in my room, the bright Saturday morning sun assaulted my eyes. I clutched the fitted pink sheet to prevent my slide backward, desperate to save myself from whatever demon had been hiding under my bed, awaiting the opportunity to pull me to the depths of hell with it.

Just before my torso was about to fall off the foot of the bed, I realized I was awake. This was really happening. I felt my heart pounding, racing to escape, when I thought to clench the sides of the mattress. Then I glanced over my shoulder to assess my adversary. Having expected the evil clown from *Poltergeist*, my eyes widened when they met Ron's.

I grabbed at the sides of the mattress, grunting as I tried to pull the lower half of my body back up onto the bed. "Stop!" I screamed. "Mom! Help!"

"You're mother's not here!" Ron seethed as he yanked at my ankles.

Unable to compete with his bodybuilder strength, I lost my grip. I instinctively closed my eyes as my body flew into midair and then flung to the floor. Despite the soft landing the pink carpet offered for my hands and chin, my torso hit harder with a thud. The screech of my skin being forced across the bit of parquet flooring could be heard before the burn of it could be felt. Then the scrape of the hallway carpet picked up where the floor left off.

"Stop!" I cried. "I was sleeping! I didn't do anything!"

Ron continued to drag me backwards, down the carpeted hallway. When I felt myself being pulled into the stairway, I used my hands and forearms to prevent my face from hitting them on the way down.

"I told you to pick up your shoes!" Ron shouted when he halted at the landing.

His hold on my ankles loosened, so I scrambled on all fours to move my feet out of his reach. A half dozen stairs up, I turned around to see him scowling and waving his finger from the landing.

"If you don't pick up your shoes from the front door right now," he began to threaten.

With my skinned arms folded close to my chest, I held them tighter and gulped. Then I inhaled sharply to calm the quick shallow breaths competing with the pace of my heart.

"Get down there! Right now!" Ron demanded, pointing down the remainder of the stairs from the landing. I was stunned still. I didn't know what to do, but I knew I didn't want to pass him. So, I remained where I'd frozen. "I'm not going to ask you again!" he warned.

After I strained for another deep inhale, I used one hand for leverage to stand. I didn't remove my stare from Ron as I proceeded one cautious step at a time, down the far-right side of the stairway. Ron maintained his position, intimidating me with his narrowed eyes as I slithered past, still facing him, then clutched the wall again as I continued down.

Down in the foyer, I saw a pile of my shoes where Mom preferred to have them lined nicely against the wall. I took as many pairs of mine as I could hold in my arms while Ron watched with furrowed brows and pursed lips. Then I went back up to my bedroom and locked the door. Although I hadn't heard Ron stomp back up behind me, I moved one of my stereo speakers in front of my door, just in case.

I hid in my room until I heard Mom and Jonathan in the kitchen later. I didn't tell her what had happened, nor did she notice my withdrawn demeanor. She didn't notice the rug burn on my chin and forearms either. She was busy, like she always was, with her son, the dishes, and whatever else was more important than me.

By the time of my appointment with Dr. Lehrfield the next Monday evening, I had resolved myself to our household dynamic. I finally understood that I only got Mom to myself whenever we were in the car without Ron.

So, I turned up the radio and sang along to "Angel Eyes" on the oldies station, bopping around and expecting Mom to join me. When she didn't join in, I looked over at her. Then my solo serenade died down when I saw her melancholy stare through the windshield.

Mom seemed to be a shadow of who she used to be when we'd lived in Chicago and interacted with family daily. I supposed I was different too. I wasn't as fazed by Ron's insults or Mom's lack of presence. These sessions with Dr. Lehrfield didn't bother me anymore either, though I still didn't think I was the one who needed therapy. I had nothing to lose by laying it all out there, anyway, on the off chance that the two-faced doctor could transform our talks into better circumstances. She had yet to prove she could, though.

"Well, hello!" Dr. Lehrfield said when I casually entered her confines. She was sitting in her high-backed Hefner chair, wearing an unflattering solid-navy dress that stopped under her chubby knees.

"Hi!" I returned, closing the door behind me and settling into the short love seat across from her.

She set down the appointment book she was writing in and gave me her full attention. "How have things been this week?" she asked with a genuine smile.

"Good, I guess," I replied with a shrug, thinking there was nothing different or significant to report.

"Well, how about we start with where we left off last time?" she suggested.

"Okay," I replied.

"We were discussing how you don't feel like you fit in anywhere?"

I sighed, recalling the conversation. Then I nodded. Not belonging seemed to be the theme of my sorry life.

"You've made it clear that you don't feel like you fit in at home. I'm trying to get a clearer picture of your social life, though, since you say you don't feel like you fit in at school either. Yet, you have a boyfriend. And I'm assuming you have some friends too?"

"Yeah," I said, shrugging again.

"So, what do you find in those relationships, with your boyfriend and your friends, that you are lacking elsewhere?" Her creased forehead begged to understand.

I thought about it for a second. I didn't have to think long, though. "Safety," I stated. "My boyfriend, Liam, wouldn't let anyone harm a hair on my head. And I know that with every fiber of my being. So, I trust him, like I trust my couple of friends, Kelly and Miranda."

"Do these friends, Kelly and Miranda, make you feel 'safe,' as you say, too?"

"I never thought about it much," I said as I thought about it now. "I wouldn't say they make me feel *protected* like Liam makes me feel, but they make me feel safe in more of an *emotional* way. Like I can just be me without the criticism or judgment." *The same way my dad made me feel*, I thought.

"So, you feel physically safe with Liam and emotionally safe with your couple of friends?" Dr. Lehrfield clarified.

"I guess so," I said, nodding in agreement.

"And if I'm interpreting what you're saying correctly, that's what differentiates your relationships with them from your relationship with your parents?"

"Well, yeah! Every time I turn around, Ron is coming at me with some insult or comment about my deficiency in something, and then using physical force to exert his authority," I blurted, immediately wishing I hadn't. I'd made a point of avoiding any mention of physical abuse, since I knew she reported our conversations to Mom and Ron.

"Exactly how does he 'exert his authority'?" Dr. Lehrfield followed with the slightest crease of concern visible in her forehead.

I thought about telling her how he'd dragged me out of a deep sleep because of a few measly pairs of shoes, and the time he'd beat me with the telephone, and when he'd banged my head against the wall. But I didn't trust *anyone* anymore. And I didn't trust Mom and Ron not to punish me with consequences for exposing them for who they really were.

So, I opted to share some instances of when Ron had gripped me by a limb too tightly and left it at that.

Dr. Lehrfield met my eyes with a stern gaze, as if deciding whether to believe me. "What do you do when these things happen? Do you tell your mother? Or any other adults?"

"I *used* to tell my mom," I said, nodding.

"And what did she say?"

"Nothing!" I said with obvious resentment. "She defended him, told me I was lying to get attention, that I shouldn't provoke him . . . That's why I don't tell her *anything* anymore."

"Hmm," Dr. Lehrfield sounded.

"My favorite is that he wouldn't treat me so badly if he didn't care about me so much. I mean, my friends' parents don't say and do the terrible things Ron does, and I assume they love *their* kids," I argued.

"So, you see the differences in your friends' family dynamics versus yours?" she asked.

"Yeah, which is why I try to avoid being home at *all* if I don't have to be."

"I see," she said. "Where do you go, then?"

"I stay pretty busy with viola and dance. I'll hang at my boyfriend's house. Or I just go for walks to get out. Any place is better than being home. Except for school," I muttered.

"What is it about school that makes you feel that way?"

I flung my hands up and said, "I don't know! I just don't fit in there either, I guess."

"You're in orchestra, though, right? First chair?"

"Yeah, but most of those kids are Korean. I don't mean that in a racist way. It's just that, in our school, there's Korean Club, Filipino Club . . . They speak their different languages and keep to their own, just like the nerds and the athletes. There's a separation and distinction, like how I was different from all the other kids when Mom and I first moved in with Ron."

"Could you and your friends start a club of some sort?" she suggested.

I shook my head. "No. Kelly and I are in dance classes together on Saturdays. Otherwise, she plays softball and is busy with her sisters and family," I said, intentionally leaving out Kelly's penchant for pot now. "Miranda is heavily involved with the yearbook committee, which she's asked me to participate in, but it's not my thing."

"Do you spend time with Miranda outside of school?"

"Sometimes, but she works most evenings and weekends. So, aside from an occasional sleepover, not really."

"Are there any extracurricular activities you *do* have interest in? Where you might find a proper place?"

"Pom tryouts are coming up," I said, instantly brightening at the thought. I hadn't made the squad the year before, though, so I didn't want to get my hopes up too high about making it this year.

"Pom?" the doctor asked with a raised brow.

"Pompon," I clarified with a giggle. "They're the ones who wear uniforms like the cheerleaders, except the pommers dance."

"Oh!" Dr. Lehrfield said with a raised-brow emotion she rarely displayed. "I recall you saying you love to dance. So, that would be a wonderful opportunity for you to share that passion with other girls your age."

"I would do *anything* to be on poms!" I admitted. "They perform hip-hop routines that get the crowds pumped at basketball games. They perform with the marching band during halftime at football games. They're the pep rally entertainment throughout the school year. They even travel across the country to compete with other squads and perform in parades! Everybody wants to be a pommer!"

Dr. Lehrfield smiled. "I don't think I've ever seen you so excited about something, Dana! This must be very important to you!"

I sighed. "You have no idea."

"And when are these tryouts?"

"Soon," I said. "It's a week-long thing. The current squad teaches the tryout routine and then coaches us while we practice with them until the formal tryouts are held on the last day of that week."

"That sounds very intense!"

"Eh, not for me. I do an hour-long workout every morning, walk to and from school, walk or ride bikes to my friends' houses if weather allows . . ." I said to demonstrate the ease with which I would acclimate to the physical demands of poms too.

"I didn't know you were so active," she commented as she took her appointment book from her side table.

"Yeah, well . . ." I shrugged, thankful she was too focused on figuring out the next time she could fit me into her schedule to delve into my excessive obsession with working off the calories I consumed. That was a secret my friends and Liam weren't even privy to.

After handing me an appointment card to give to Mom, I handed Doc the check my mom had sent with me to pay for my session. "Well, I hope you make it onto the squad! I think it'll be good for you," she said as she walked me out to her empty waiting room.

"Me too," I said. "See ya!"

Standing outside, waiting for my ride home in the light rain, I recalled all the times I'd waited for Mom to show up for me: at school, at sports games, music concerts and plays. . . I had been waiting my whole life, essentially, for Mom to notice me. Yet, all she ever saw in me was a hindrance, and a distorted reflection of that part of her that she didn't want revealed. Seemed to me that she should be the one seeing Dr. Lehrfield. But what did I know? I was just a kid.

"Tiny Dancer"

Before I knew it, the day of pom tryouts had arrived. Liam and I stood just outside one of the large rooms within the much larger school gymnasium with dozens of other girls, stretching and mimicking the movements of the tryout routine, while we waited to be called in for our auditions.

"You're going to do great, Dana. I know it!" Liam encouraged, holding both of my hands in his.

Kelly and I had practiced the routine together to the point of exhaustion. I was pretty sure I could do it in my sleep. We'd felt pretty good about our chances of making it onto the squad, considering the many years of dance classes we'd taken together. Still, I was jittery and nervous seeing how much better some of the more professionally trained dancers there were.

"I don't know, Liam. I can barely breathe," I said as I inhaled deeply to calm myself. The harshness of the caged fluorescent lights above, combined with the multiple boom boxes playing Journey's "Any Way You Want It" at different intervals, inhibited my ability to center myself. The swish of pom-poms being thrust into the air to varying footwork and jumps just added to the chaos in the hall and nearby stairway.

"Here," he said, putting one of my hands on his chest. "Do you feel my heartbeat?"

"Yeah?"

"Just feel the beat," he said, staring into my eyes very intently, "and breathe in sync with it. Calm and steady."

I closed my eyes, attempting to shut out the ruckus around me. I focused on the pulse of his heart, which was much slower than mine. My shoulders relaxed as my heartbeat slowed to match his.

"There you go," he said. I opened my eyes and smiled at this sweet boy who knew me too well. His dimples showed when he grinned back.

The clunk of the metal push bar hitting the steel door to the room distracted everyone's attention that way.

"Dana, Kelly, Lisa! You're up!" the pom coach called out with impatient urgency.

"Oh God," I worried out loud. "Liam?" I didn't even know what I was asking of him.

"You're gonna do it this time, babe," he said, nodding and smiling simultaneously. "I'll be right here waiting. Okay?"

I took one last deep breath and nodded. "Okay," I said, though I was nowhere near. Then I went into the room, glancing back at Liam to see his double thumbs-up before the heavy door closed firmly behind me.

When I busted out of the room a short time later, I jumped into Liam's waiting arms excitedly. He lifted me off the ground and spun me around. I squealed in delight.

"Did you make it?" he asked anxiously as he set me down.

"I don't know, but I *killed* that audition!"

"When will you find out?"

"Tonight," I said. Then I leaned into him and whispered, "They say they will post it on the gym bulletin board tomorrow, but there's a rumor that they kidnap you or something the night of the audition if you made it."

"You want me to walk you home, then?"

"Yeah. If you don't mind," I said.

It was already after dinnertime and dark out when I walked into my house.

"Hey, Dane," Mom called out from the kitchen.

"Hi, Mom," I said, tickling Jonathan's toes as I passed his highchair. I ignored Ron on my way to the refrigerator. I didn't see any leftovers, though, so I moved to the pantry to see if I could scrounge up something to eat from a box or a can. A handful of fudge-striped cookies seemed to be the most convenient option.

I leaned against the wooden pantry door at the back of the galley kitchen, chomping on a cookie while I waited for Mom to ask me how the tryouts went. Even Liam's mom had wished me good luck the day before, offering me the encouragement Mom hadn't remembered to give.

Mom was focused on her "Golden Child," though. So was Ron, who bounced in his seat to the rhythm of his chuckles. I wished for just a fraction of the positive regard that kid got from them, to disprove that their starkly conflicting treatment of us really was a choice.

I'd even brought it up to Dr. Lehrfield once. She wouldn't subscribe to the idea that Jonathan and I were being raised differently by the same two parents. However, she'd been impressed that I'd made the observation on my own. It hadn't been hard, though; psychoanalysis came easily to me because I lived in a house full of psychotic people whose next moves had to be gauged to predict and protect my emotional and physical welfare.

I watched the psycho circus now, like someone snacking on popcorn while watching the plot of a movie unfold. After being ignored for a couple more minutes, though, I couldn't take another second of these two loving their other child while I stood there, unseen. So, I decided to take a shower and await the possibility of my kidnapping upstairs.

On my way out of the kitchen, Ron criticized, "Cookies for dinner?"

"Yep," I said with indignance. Then I stared straight into his eyes as I shoved the last cookie in my mouth and left.

In the darkness of my bedroom, I laid in bed, trying to summon up the energy to wash up. I was so tired that I dozed off instead, waking a while later to the ring of my phone.

"Hello?" I answered.

"Dana?" a female voice asked.

"Yes?" I said, sitting up in bed expectantly.

"YOU MADE THE POM SQUAD!" the female squealed. Then she hung up!

I sat there with the phone in my hand, confused about why she hadn't given me a chance to respond, when I heard someone run up the stairs. A second later, the co-captain of the pom squad burst into my bedroom. "What are you doing in bed, Dana? Come on!" she exclaimed as she tore my covers off of me.

Dumbfounded and shocked, I remained frozen on my bed, processing the fact that this petite Filipino girl had tricked me by calling my personal phone line from the house line in the kitchen below. The dark-haired girl smiled as she took the phone from my hand and put it onto the base before pulling me by my arm and leading me out. I was being "kidnapped"!

I'd heard rumors about senior members of the squad hazing new members by snatching them from their houses and driving them somewhere. So, I was excited that this meant I really had made poms. Except that I didn't like surprises.

"Where are we going?" I worried. "Can I at least change?" I was still wearing the spandex leggings and T-shirt I'd sweat through during the tryout.

"No!" the girl said as we passed Mom in the foyer. "We don't have time for that! The other girls are waiting!"

I slipped on my white Keds without bothering to tie them. Then I glanced back at Mom as I exited the house. She looked just as confused as I felt but said nothing to stop us.

A small four-door sedan had been left running behind Ron's car in the driveway. One of the back doors had been left open, so I could see the back seat full of blindfolded girls with the overhead light. They were giggling and gossiping over the pop song blaring on the car radio.

The co-captain who'd retrieved me from my bed reached into her pocket for a black cloth. "Turn around, Dana!" she ordered before throwing it over my eyes and tying it around my head.

I did as I was told, cooperating with my initiation into the exclusive group. Then I let the girl cram me into the back seat with the others, where I squealed and laughed and belted out songs with them to celebrate. To say I was elated to officially be a "pommer" would have been an understatement. I felt as whole as I had when I'd met my dad, to finally belong to this group.

The car stopped and turned off a little while later. We were taken out of the car, and our blindfolds were removed. Two dozen of us were standing in a restaurant parking lot together, looking around at each other in wonderment. I was disappointed not to see Kelly, though, since she probably deserved to be there more than I did.

"Congratulations! You are the 1991-1992 pom squad!" The pom captain announced from atop the trunk of her car.

I stood there for a moment, debating with myself whether it was okay for me to be happy about accomplishing something my closest friend hadn't. It was hard not to participate with all the girls screaming and bouncing around me. Plus, Kelly wasn't the jealous kind. She knew I'd been desperate to be part of this sisterhood that I didn't have elsewhere, anyway. So, I gave myself permission to join in, somehow finding the energy to jump up and down and cheer and whoop and holler with all the other girls.

Despite the differences in age, grade, ethnicity, and social class, all of us girls, most strangers to each other before, hugged and embraced under the streetlights glowing in the otherwise dark, cool night. Together, we were one—one squad, one sisterhood, inherently conjoined by our talent and passion. I finally belonged.

Together, we went into the restaurant, where the former squad captains introduced the new ones, and we all shared table-size ice cream sundaes with every topping imaginable and lit sparklers on top.

Although I could hear Ron in the back of my head telling me how fat the dessert would make me, I overindulged until I had a stomachache. Even then, I kept shoveling spoonfuls of ice cream and hot fudge and nuts and whipped cream and bananas into my mouth, as if I'd never be allowed such tasty treats again. All the pom practices I would have now justified the celebratory indulgence, anyway.

When I was dropped back home late that night, I was disappointed to see that the house was dark. No one had waited up for me, not that I'd expected anyone to. I'd just hoped to tell Mom about the glorious night. We didn't have that kind of relationship, though, and it was too late to wake her or call anyone else. So, I trudged up the stairs and tried to sleep, despite all the sugar and adrenaline fueling me.

The next morning, Mom woke me before she left, since I hadn't gotten up on my own. She didn't ask me where I'd gone the night before. She didn't congratulate me on making the squad. She didn't act any different than she did any other day. Because nothing that happened to me mattered. Because I didn't matter. At least not to her.

"More Than Words"

*L*iam was waiting for me at my school locker the next morning. The exterior of it had been decorated with streamers and balloons and a sign indicating my highly coveted position on the pom squad, so he already knew the obvious good news.

"Congratulations!" he said, smiling as he threw his arms around me. "I knew you would make it!"

Then he held his head a little higher as he walked me to homeroom, holding my hand. He bragged to his friends and classmates throughout the day about my achievement. It felt so good to have someone exhibit pride for me, for once.

He even made Jim drive him to my house that night to bring me a gift. I hurried to tear the pretty pink paper from the rectangular package. Inside, I found a pale pink wooden jewelry box with a ballerina that spun to a sweet melody when I opened the top. It was the most thoughtful gift anyone could have ever given me, and I cherished it as such.

Unfortunately, pom practice took over my life after that. Practice was held every single weekday after school, and Saturday mornings too. So, I had to quit dance classes and orchestra, leaving little time for my private viola lessons and the practice sessions for two solo performances my instructor had arranged at local festivals that summer. Since I wasn't home much to bother Mom and Ron, they quit making me see Dr. Lehrfield too. Sundays seemed to be my only free day, which I still spent at Great-Gram's in Chicago, visiting with her.

All of this left little time for Liam. He didn't let anything get in the way of being with me, though. He would often wait in the school cafeteria for me to finish pom practice, just to be able to kiss me goodnight when we boarded the last buses home. Then we'd talk on the phone every single night, fantasizing about what our life together would look like when we were out of school and old enough to have our own apartment together. We talked about moving to California, the different jobs we could get to support ourselves, the places we'd go, and the things we'd do. We wanted to get married—on the beach, of course—and grow old together as best friends and lovers.

On our last day of our sophomore year, we were released from school early. I didn't have to be anywhere until later that day, so I went home with Liam to pass the free time with him.

We were sitting on the floor of his bedroom, talking and joking, when we saw his mother outside the window strolling the baby away for a walk. Liam and I whipped our heads towards each other and smirked.

Within seconds, I was on his lap, my legs wrapped around his torso. Like magnets unable to resist the strong attraction, our lips and tongues enmeshed with hungry passion. His kisses held the intensity of our emotional connection, which our physical bodies could no longer resist. So, when Liam put his hand up my shirt, I let him unsnap my bra. We made out feverishly, like we just couldn't get enough of each other.

With one hand behind my head, Liam laid me down on the carpet ever so gently. Then our mouths met again, expressing their longing for the other. We removed our bottom garments next and giggled at the way we tossed them aside. Then Liam kissed my neck and breasts while rubbing parts of my body that begged for his touch. I smiled and threw my head back, relishing the physical expression of our young love.

Then, all of a sudden, Liam was inside me.

In that instant, we both froze. We gaped at each other, expressing the same surprise at our unintended act. Yes, we were naked and all, but we hadn't planned to go all the way!

"Are you okay?" he asked, unmoving. The sincerity in his tone, and his concern for me in this particular moment, proved he loved me as much as he said he did. And I loved him too. So . . .

"Yeah," I said, unconcerned about any consequence. Mom had already assumed I wasn't a virgin, and Ron thought I was a whore anyway. So, what would it matter?

"I'm glad you're my first, Baby Blue," I whispered, calling him by the nickname I'd given him after the song by Badfinger.

Then I ran my fingers through his curly hair and pulled his head back down for more kisses. Considering my mind and body were in alignment with giving Liam what I couldn't give Kevin, I put my other hand on Liam's butt to invite him to continue. It was as perfect as anyone could ever imagine their first time being.

At pom camp the following month, I was lying in the bed of the college dorm that was hosting us for the week, my hand on my sickened stomach. We'd just finished our training for the day and only had an hour to shower and dress in the coordinating team outfits we'd been assigned to wear to dinner.

"I don't know if I can even move, let alone take a shower!" I complained to the fellow pommer I was rooming with.

"I know," she said. "Dancing and jumping and learning routines outside in this heat . . ." She groaned, expressing the exhaustion we both felt.

"Maybe that's why I feel so dizzy and nauseous," I thought out loud.

"Yeah, it's probably heatstroke," she agreed. "Just drink as much water as you can."

"I hate water," I said with a sigh, "but I can't get enough of it lately."

"Me neither," she said, gulping more of it out of the multi-gallon jug beside her bed.

"I'm just glad I haven't gotten my period yet," I told her. "I was supposed to get it this week, but I can't imagine exerting myself to this extent with cramps and a headache and bleeding too."

"You're late?" the girl asked with raised brows.

"Not necessarily *late*," I said, unwilling to acknowledge the fact. "Just not exactly on time."

"Dana . . .?" she prodded with a smile, turning onto her side as if awaiting some juicy gossip.

"Don't turn this into something it's not," I warned with an inappropriate smirk that didn't deny the sexual activity I'd been engaging in since that first time with Liam. "Athletes and dancers miss periods all the time."

"Yeah, you're right," she said, "but—"

"But nothing, 'nosy Rosy.' I'll probably get my period as soon as we get back from camp. In the meantime, I'm going to take a shower while you lie here thinking your dirty thoughts."

We both giggled as I went into the bathroom. But I couldn't help but worry a little bit, since my period *had* always come like clockwork. I didn't want to worry too much, though, because I'd heard that stress can delay menstruation too.

I didn't think there was any way I could have kept up with the demanding physical requirements of poms if I were pregnant, anyway. Plus, I was losing weight because of the strenuous daily activity. So, I had no reason to believe my missed periods were anything other than the result of extreme physical exertion.

Anyway, I was relishing how well things were going for once. I'd made new friends on poms. I'd slayed the solo viola performance I'd given on the big stage at a local cultural festival in mid-August, which Liam's mother had attended, standing front row and center with her newborn. I'd started my junior year of high school with much more confidence and self-esteem than I'd ever felt before. And I was finally happy. Nothing could bring me down from this high, aside from the constant queasiness I'd developed that was making me vomit too often.

"Two Sparrows in a Hurricane"

"Liam?" I said, holding both of his hands in mine. I'd skipped going to Great-Gram's with my mom this particular September Sunday so I could tell Liam what was going on.

"What did you want to talk to me about?" he asked, looking at me with concern as we sat on his bed to talk. The overcast sky outside seemed to darken his unlit room, as if matching the foreboding topic I was about to broach.

I exhaled, nervous to share my worry. I hadn't shared my concern with anyone yet, nor had I thought I would ever have to.

"I think I might be pregnant," I said, facing the issue head-on.

"What?" Liam asked, staring at me with bulging eyes that didn't believe what his ears had just heard.

"Yeah," I responded, dropping my head shamefully. "I've missed three periods. And I've been throwing up a lot lately."

"Three? Why didn't you tell me?" he accused. "We've been having sex all summer! And we haven't been using—"

"Protection, I know."

We hadn't thought we needed to, since neither of us had ever had sex to have any kind of sexually transmitted disease to pass on to the other. I hadn't even considered the possibility of pregnancy. That seemed like something that happened to other people. Plus, I hadn't thought history would be so cruel as to repeat itself with me.

Liam shook his head. "Three months, though? That's a long time," he said with a cringe.

"I know," I jumped in, eager to justify myself. "I honestly thought I was just missing my period because of all the physical exertion of poms. I figured I'd eventually get it, and this would all have been a silly scare."

"I had no idea, though. You never let on that anything was wrong," he said, still shaking his head. His creased brow begged to understand the reality of the situation. It had taken me a while to let the idea sink in too.

"I didn't want to worry you needlessly," I said. "Or lose you altogether."

"You wouldn't have lost me," Liam reassured.

"How would I know that, though? My mom said my dad walked away when she got pregnant with me. So, why would I think you'd do any different?"

"Because I love you," Liam said. "You know that, right?"

"Yeah, but I'm really scared. Because *I'm* the one who might have our baby inside of me. So, I'm the one who is stuck having to deal with the brunt of this," I said, suddenly feeling like Mom must have felt back then.

Liam looked into my eyes. "You're not going to go through this alone, no matter what. Okay?"

I stared into those baby blues, looking for reasons to believe him. Although we were only fifteen—the same age as my dad when I'd been conceived—I knew Liam would stand by me just like he'd said he would. Regardless of the outcome, he'd never leave me to deal with the consequences myself.

"So, what should we do? I mean, do I wait and see if I get my period *next* month? Or—"

"No, I think you should take a pregnancy test," Liam said, shaking his head. "I can't believe I'm even saying that out loud."

"I know," I said, rubbing my thumb along his hand. "But what if—"

"Then we deal with it together," he interrupted. A sigh of relief escaped my lips. "But let's just take this one step at a time for now and not worry about something we're not sure of yet. Okay?"

"Okay," I said, even though I was already pretty sure.

"Do you want me to get it?" Liam offered.

"The test? Oh God, no!" I said with widened eyes. "I'll just go somewhere no one knows me and get one. I can say it's for my mom or something."

"Okay," Liam said.

"I'm a good girl, so no one would ever think it's for me anyway," I threw in, as if needing to convince myself.

Liam looked up at me with a raised brow and smirked. "You're a good girl?"

I smiled and snort-laughed, realizing how dumb that sounded after the conversation we'd just had. Then I affirmed, "Yes, actually. I still am a good girl. Just because—"

Liam interrupted me with a soft kiss. "I love you," he said as he pulled away.

"I love you too. I just hope—"

"I know," he said. "But it's going to be okay. I promise."

"All By Myself"

om and Ron took Jonathan apple picking the next Saturday afternoon. I'd been waiting for an opportunity to be alone in the house to take the pregnancy test I'd been hiding between my mattress and box spring. So, I watched their car pull out of the driveway from the second-floor bathroom window then anxiously waited a half hour to make sure they were already far enough away that they wouldn't return for something they might have forgotten. When I couldn't wait any longer, I pulled out the box, ripped it open, read the instructions twice, then removed the plastic stick that would determine doom or delight.

My hand shook nervously as I put the fortune-telling wand between my thighs. I couldn't gauge exactly where to hold the damn thing but took my best guess. After peeing all over my hand, the stick, and part of the toilet seat too, I set the wand on the sink and waited, hoping I'd hit it with enough urine to give me an accurate result.

The instructions said it would provide an answer in about ten minutes. I wasn't sure I could wait that long. I'd needed to know two months ago, when I'd first missed my period. I'd just been so afraid to face the possibility that I'd ignored it and hoped a randomly late menstruation would just make it all go away. It never did. So, now I feared the worst.

As I wiped the toilet seat clean to pass part of the time, I thought of how I'd never been one of those little girls who'd wanted to have lots of babies. I had actually decided by about junior high that I didn't want kids at all. It's not that I didn't like kids. I was just terrified that I'd treat my children like Mom and Ron treated me. I couldn't live with myself if I ever inflicted that kind of pain on another human. However, I didn't trust myself to know any way to avoid it.

Then again, if I was pregnant, I wanted the baby. Despite my age, I knew Liam and I would love our child just as much as we loved each other. Plus, Great-Gram had given me the foundation of knowing what motherly love was and what it felt like. So, maybe I was better equipped to handle raising a child than I thought.

My only hindrance would be whatever consequences Mom and Ron would inflict on me. Ironically, that scared me more than the idea of being pregnant!

Suddenly feeling clammy and dizzy, I knelt at the base of the porcelain potty, just in time to puke. After wiping my mouth, my sweaty forehead, and the toilet clean again, I moved to the sink to splash cold water on my face. From the corner of my eye, I could see color filling the empty space on the test I'd left lying on the side. I leaned in closer to confirm, blinking to see clearly. Did that mean . . .? I panicked as I scurried around the bathroom and then my bedroom, looking for the instructions.

Two stripes meant the test was positive. I read it again then looked at the test again to make sure I'd *seen* two stripes. There was no mistaking the little daggers, though. They were bright pink, clear as day, and would have made someone else very happy.

Numbed with shock, I felt nothing at first. Then I realized I wasn't breathing and strained to inhale air into my lungs. It wasn't enough, so I inhaled again, exhaling just as deeply to calm myself. I lifted my tense shoulders and heard a crack. Then I breathed again. I couldn't believe I was pregnant.

I wanted to be happy. I wanted every child to be born into this world with the same excitement Mom and Ron had exhibited when sharing the news that their pregnancy with Jonathan was viable. I never wanted any child to be born into a situation where they weren't wanted or wouldn't be loved, like I'd been. Which was why I *couldn't* be happy.

I loved Liam. I loved the idea that a part of him was growing inside of me, that we'd made something unique and beautiful together. Since I was a minor, though, this baby and I would be under the legal guardianship and control of the two people in this world I trusted least. They wouldn't want this baby any more than they'd ever wanted me, so I'd have hell to pay for what should have been a blessing.

I began to think of where Liam and I could run away to before Mom and Ron could come anywhere near this precious angel. We had to make a plan fast, too, before anyone knew. The urgency in my mind permeated my body with a racing heartbeat and swirling thoughts. I had to talk to Liam. Or get out of this house. Something needed to happen. Now!

With every unanswered ring of Liam's phone, I panicked more. Worry that Liam wouldn't stay with me, or that he'd already abandoned me to fight for our baby's life on my own, taunted me. I told myself that was Ron hijacking my self-talk, though. Liam would never do that to me. He promised he wouldn't.

But where was he? He knew I'd planned to take the test today! I guessed he was with his best friend and younger cousin, who he'd been spending more time with lately since I was always busy. But I wasn't used to being less than his top priority. I'd expected him to be waiting by his phone for my call.

Liam's answering machine picked up, but I opted not to leave a message. What I had to say warranted a conversation, and I didn't want my words recorded. I assumed Liam would call me later to check in, anyway. He would tell me then that it would all work out. Because it would. It had to.

Still, I couldn't help but think of how history was repeating Mom's circumstances with me. Was this my punishment for invalidating her experiences? I didn't want to believe God would punish me for my failure to see Mom's pain for what it was by making me experience the same. My God was a forgiving one. Wasn't He?

Knowing my God saw me and my situation for what it really was, I had to believe that the outcome would be different from Mom's with me. *My* boyfriend and I were in love. *My* boyfriend and I talked about getting married and living our lives far away from here. *My* boyfriend wouldn't abandon me to the ridicule and shame of being a pregnant teenager, like Mom claimed my dad had. Liam and I were in this together. He'd go to any lengths to protect me.

Despite strengthening myself against self-doubt, my physical body was weak. I curled up in bed to subdue the nausea and doubly await Liam's

264

return call. I closed my eyes, envisioning Liam and I with our curly-haired baby boy or girl, frolicking in the waters of the same California beach where we'd marry, until I dozed off.

The shrill ring of the telephone startled me awake a little later.

"Hello?" I answered, blinking my eyes as they adjusted to the afternoon sun coming through my bedroom window.

"Hey," Liam said. "So . . . did you take it?"

"Yeah," I replied, sure that the downturn of my voice gave away the answer.

"And . . ."

He hadn't gotten the hint. I was afraid to say it out loud, but my thoughts left my lips. "I don't know how to tell you . . ."

"Tell me what?" Liam asked. Then it clicked. "Oh! You're . . ."

"Yeah."

There was a long pause. Too long. I worried about what he was thinking. I panicked that he'd changed his mind and was figuring out how to tell me we were done. Then he said, "Okay, we'll figure this out."

I didn't know how we would, though. We didn't have any income or anywhere to go without money. We were too young to live on our own, anyway. So, really, what options did we have?

"I'm really scared, Liam," I confided with a quivering voice.

"I know," he said glumly.

"If my parents find out . . . I can't stay here."

"I know," he repeated, obviously *not* having any ideas that were plausible under these circumstances.

"So, we need to 'figure this out' soon. I can only wear loose clothing for so long."

I was so tiny that my little bulging belly was starting to become noticeable but still passable as bloat. The way Mom and Ron assumed the worst about me, though, it was only a matter of time before they'd come to a conclusion that would actually prove correct for once.

"Let's just sleep on it for now. We'll think of something," Liam said.

I wished I could believe him. I didn't see any options for us, though. At least none that boded well for me.

"You promise?" I asked.

"Yeah. It's going to be okay. I promise."

"Okay," I said, even though nothing was. "I love you."

"I love you too," he responded. His dim tone worried me, though.

"You sure?" I asked.

"Yes, I'm sure," he said, obliging my constant need for reassurance. "I'll talk to you tomorrow, though. Okay?"

"Okay," I said again before hanging up. But I wasn't okay. If Mom and Ron found out about this, nothing would ever be okay again.

"Live and Let Die"

L iam and I didn't have many options. We could either take off together and hope we weren't found, give the baby up for adoption, or abort the pregnancy altogether. I couldn't imagine enduring a pregnancy in this hell house, nor ending the life growing inside me. So, my decision was clear.

How would we go about disappearing together, though? At our age, and with limited resources, where would we go? How would we survive? Could we make it on our own? Where could I even safely birth a baby without medical insurance or the ability to afford the doctor and hospital bills? Perhaps I was overanalyzing everything, like I usually did, but I needed answers, and I needed them now. The life of my baby literally depended on it.

I skipped going to Great-Gram's on Sunday again, to pin Liam down to a decision. I didn't know how to act around everyone, and I worried that my awkwardness would make someone suspicious. Plus, Ron was going with Mom this time, giving me a half day of privacy I desperately needed to figure things out without interruption.

So, as soon as they left the house, I called Liam. I expressed to him how anxious I was to determine a plan of action. He wasn't home alone, though, so he asked me to meet him at a midpoint between our houses, where we could discuss the situation privately and freely.

The midpoint was a neighborhood not far from our school. Well-maintained brick bungalows, mostly light tan in color, lined the street with the same consistency as the perfectly round trees in front of them. It was another beautiful September afternoon. The sun was shining. It was pleasant enough outside to not have to wear a jacket over my simple black A-line dress. Liam had always liked it on me. I'd worn it partially because of that and also because the short, flared style hid my little belly. My closet didn't offer many comfortable options for a skinny size small with a protruding belly.

I smiled when I saw Liam walking towards me in his light denim blue jeans and black Metallica T-shirt. He had a certain swag when he walked, in the way his hips moved too casually but cool enough to be sexy.

"Hey," I said when we were finally face to face. I got up on my tiptoes to give him a quick peck.

"Hey back," he said with a smirk. Then he stepped back and checked me out. "I haven't seen you wear that dress in a while. You look—"

"Don't say pregnant!" I warned with a smile.

"I was going to say great, but—"

"Too soon?"

"Yeah, a little," he said as he dropped his head. He was chuckling, though. I always could make him laugh, just like I could always finish his sentences.

"Shall we?" I asked, motioning ahead.

"We shall," he said, taking my hand.

I immediately went into a monologue about our three options, sharing the pros and cons I'd determined about each.

"Giving the baby up for adoption is out, then," he said.

"I agree," I said. "I don't see giving up the baby, when the pregnancy alone will bring on whatever punishment my mother and Ron see fit. I mean, I don't expect them to be happy but . . ."

"But what happens after the baby is born then? Would they have control over it like they do over you?"

"That's the part that scares me," I said. "Because I honestly don't know what the legalities are, with me and the baby both being minors. But I'll be damned if I'll ever let them treat my baby like they've treated me or have any say about him or her at all!"

Liam shook his head and sighed. "I know you said abortion is out too, but . . .?" he asked with a cringe. I looked at him with open-mouthed horror that he would even say that. He immediately retracted. "I'm not saying that's what we should do. I'm just wondering whether it might be our best option."

A deep inhale and longer exhale gave me time to reconsider his opinion. As much as I hated to admit Liam was right, I couldn't dispute that it was the best solution overall. It's not what I wanted, though, and I shouldn't have to do something I didn't want to do just because my parents couldn't control their hatred of me. But what else was there to do?

"Not being pregnant would definitely make things easier," I said with a drooped head. I kicked a random rock that had gotten in the way of my foot shuffling.

"I'm not going to lie. It would be easier for *all* of us if you weren't pregnant. I mean, my stepfather is a politician who wants to be governor. Having a teenage stepson with a pregnant girlfriend doesn't exactly fit into his campaigning. If he got wind of this—"

"I'm sorry, but I don't give a rat's ass about Jim and his bullshit facade any more than I care about Ron's," I said, aware of the insensitivity and potential selfishness. "It's bad enough that they're the reason our baby's life is on the line."

Liam sighed.

"I know," I said. "I feel the same way."

"So, if we can't keep it, and we can't adopt it out . . ." Liam deduced.

"Then I can't be pregnant," I summed up. Tears welled in my eyes at the thought of terminating this pregnancy. "There's got to be another option, Liam."

He dropped his head and sighed again. "I don't think there is."

My bottom lip began to tremble as we came to a stop. I looked up into Liam's sorrowful eyes as we both prematurely mourned a death neither of us really wanted to be party to.

"I'm scared," I said, maintaining my stare.

"I know, babe. I don't know any other way around this, though."

"Please, Liam," I said, shaking my head. "Please. Anything but that."

He pressed his lips together in a slight frown. This was the one thing he couldn't make better. He just didn't want to break my heart by stating the obvious.

"Please, Liam," I urged, desperate to think of a solution we hadn't already considered. "We can both get jobs somewhere. We'll find a cheap apartment. It won't be anything fancy, but—"

"Dana," he said firmly enough to stop my nervous rambling. "Maybe in the future, maybe with another baby. But not with this one. Not now."

I dropped my face into my hands and cried. Liam held me while I did.

Why couldn't we be happy? I thought. Why did everything good in my life have to be taken away from me, as if to punish me for not being good enough or old enough or whatever I wasn't "enough" of? And why did I have to end one life to save both of ours?

It wasn't fair to this innocent unborn child, just like it hadn't been fair to me to be dealt the consequences of everyone's attempt to portray themselves in a certain way. I mean, regardless of the fact that I hadn't been planned, my mother had had to be incredibly strong to endure the difficulties of being a teenage mother. So, why wasn't she proud of that? Why hadn't she turned her experience into a testament of what a warrior she was to have risen from a modest life in the city to a middle-class business owner with a beautifully furnished home, a husband who drove a Corvette, and a talented daughter who wanted nothing but her love? If she was that person, that warrior, then there would be a safe space for me to raise my daughter just the same. But life wasn't always what we wanted it to be, was it?

When I pulled back from Liam, he held my hands again. "Just make the appointment. Okay? I'll get the money somehow, and we'll go together. You and me. I won't leave you to do this alone."

Despite my inability to resolve myself to a horrific plan I couldn't fathom executing, I nodded. I still had time to figure a different way out of this, and I was sure of Liam's unwavering support if I did. So, I hugged Liam a little tighter and held him a little longer before parting just in case I decided to disappear without him. Then I walked home alone, crying about how helpless I felt to enact the future I preferred, simply because of the offensive reaction our parents would have to it.

Since no one was home when I returned, I took advantage of the opportunity to look up the number for the nearest abortion clinic in the Yellow Pages. Then I stopped at the 7-Eleven convenient store on the way home from school the next day to use the pay phone to call.

Too nervous to remember what the woman said her name was when she answered, never mind the name of the clinic itself, I stuttered, "Yeah, uh, hi. I, uh . . . I . . . I guess I need to make an appointment?"

"All right, sweetie," the woman responded kindly. "Am I to assume you are wanting to terminate a pregnancy?"

The harshness of the words pained my unwilling heart so much that I had to close my eyes and catch my breath. I reminded myself I could always cancel the appointment if I discovered an alternative option. So, I whispered, "Yes," though I'd argue the point of wanting.

"And how many weeks along are you?" she asked.

I hadn't even thought about that. I mean, we'd first had sex in early June. I missed my period in July. This was September. So, I guessed I was . . . I did the math in my head real quick.

Before I could answer, the woman said, "We have to know because abortions aren't legal after twenty weeks."

"Oh!" I hadn't known that either.

"It's okay, though. Just give me an estimate. We'll do an ultrasound to confirm when you come in for the procedure."

Calling the end of my baby's life a "procedure" sounded so cold. She hadn't meant it, I know. She was just doing her job. But still, this was a baby. *My* baby. And it deserved some respect, particularly given the short life it would have in me.

"I guess I'm about three months along?" I said, hoping whatever date they had available wouldn't be cutting it too close. Then I wondered what would happen if I was beyond the cut-off.

"All right," the woman said. "And is this your first time?"

"First time?" I asked, confused as to why my sex life was her concern.

"Having this procedure," she clarified.

"Oh, um, yeah," I said, feeling stupid. Then again, it was still a stupid question. I couldn't imagine anyone making a habit of this.

The woman proceeded to tell me how much money to bring to the appointment in a couple weeks, adding that options for local or regional anesthesia would cost more. She also advised that someone should drive me because I would be weak after the procedure, regardless of whether I opted for anesthetics. Then she took my name and basic information before ending the call.

"I made the appointment," I told Liam over the phone when I got home that night.

"Okay. Did they say how much we needed to bring?"

"Yeah. Four hundred dollars," I responded, intentionally leaving out that there was an extra cost for pain medications. I didn't think we could even afford the base amount, which only allowed for a local anesthetic to numb my private part. So, asking for Liam to come up with more money to make the procedure less painful just seemed selfish. I assumed the physical pain was a deserving punishment I should be expected to endure.

"Well, I only have two hundred, but I'll get the other two from my mom. I'll just tell her I need to borrow it for a stereo speaker or something," he decided.

I didn't care what he told her. I was completely zoned out, numb to what we were planning, so I didn't have to feel the anguish already engulfing my heart.

"The only thing we need now is a ride," he said, oblivious to my conscious detachment from my emotions and this situation.

"I'll see what I can do," I said before quickly ended the call. I couldn't take much more of this scheming. Aside from the dishonesty of it all, it was dishonest to myself to participate in something I felt so strongly against. I mean, how was I supposed to abort a baby I wanted when Mom had had me instead of aborting her *unwanted* pregnancy with me?

Thinking about who I could trust to keep this very delicate information a secret, I called Kelly. She had just turned sixteen and gotten her driver's license, and her parents let her borrow their old station wagon whenever she asked.

"Hey, what're you doing?" she said when she got on the phone.

"Nothing much," I said, as if toning down the major life decision I'd been struggling with would lessen the weight of it. "I actually called to ask a big favor."

"Yeah, name it!" she said.

"I need a ride somewhere next Saturday. Do you think you could help me out?"

"I'm sorry, but no. I have to work," she said. "Do you want me to ask my dad if he can take you wherever you need to go?" He was always willing to help me with a ride when he could.

"Oh God, no!" I said a little too defensively.

"That was quick and dramatic," she said. "So, what're you doing that you don't want the 'rents to know about?"

I chuckled at her correct assessment. "Um . . . I really didn't want to tell anyone. It's not anything I want out there. Know what I mean?"

"Which means it's something big," Kelly responded. "Is everything okay?"

I was silent for a moment. I had planned to just tell her everything was fine. But it wasn't. And I really needed a friend right now.

"You know you can tell me anything," she prodded when I still didn't give in.

She was right. Since second grade, Kelly had been the one person I could count on and turn to no matter what was going on, and she'd never returned with judgment. She was more of a sister to me than a friend.

"I'm pregnant, Kelly," I blurted.

"Oh my god!" she gasped.

"I know," I whimpered.

"What are you going to do? And what does Saturday have to do with it?"

"You know how my life is. You know there's no way I could even let on to Mom and Ron that I'm—you know," I hinted to avoid saying it out loud a second time. "So, there's only one thing to do."

"Are you getting an abortion?" she asked in a whisper. I sensed the shock in her tone. Of course she was surprised. She'd known me nearly ten years and knew I'd never do that willingly, especially considering how sensitive I was to the insinuations Mom had expressed about having wanted to abort me. Plus, we were Catholic. We were supposed to be pro-life no matter what.

"I don't know what else to do!" I said with trembling lips and moistening eyes.

"I don't know what to say, Dana. I'm so sorry," Kelly said in a dim tone, as if already mourning my loss with me.

"There's nothing to say, Kelly," I told her, sniffling. "I just have to get this over with so I don't have to think about it anymore."

"Now I feel worse that I can't help you with a ride," she said.

"It's okay. It's almost better if no one else is party to this. It's bad enough I have to be."

"But how are you going to get there?" Kelly asked.

"I'll have to call for a cab," I said. "It's not close enough for us to walk."

There was silence then. And in that quiet moment, I felt less alone knowing someone else—particularly someone who shared my faith—understood the gravity of my terrible plight. My pitiful soul needed all the prayers it could get right now, while I prayed for that of my unborn baby.

"Tears in Heaven"

That Saturday, Liam and I met at the 7-Eleven near my house and called a cab to pick us up. We sat in the back seat, holding hands in silence during the twenty-minute drive. Just like with Kelly, there was nothing to say. I'd worked so hard to numb myself to my inequitable feelings about it all, anyway. There was no other way to cope with what I was about to do.

My anxiety amped up as soon as we pulled up to the clinic. Dozens of people littered the steps, holding homemade signs that read "Abortion is Murder" and "Killers Go to Hell." I'd seen scenes like this on the news but never realized how terrifying they really were for the people they were intended to persuade. I'd never thought I'd be one of those people either.

I watched in horror as the protesters flocked towards a middle-aged woman attempting to pass through them to enter the building. They ganged up on her, blocking her path as they screamed in her face at close range. She put her head down and pushed through, like a football player with a helmet, using it to make way. Eventually, the woman forced her way inside. The protestors banged on the glass as the door closed behind her, though, in their last-ditch efforts to change her mind.

"Liam?" I said, reaching for his hand without removing my stare from the angry mob.

He squeezed it and said, "It's okay, Dana," before exiting and paying the driver. Then he came around to my side and opened the door.

I shook my head and refused to take his extended hand.

"C'mon," he urged. "I promise I won't let anything happen to you."

I trusted Liam, but I didn't trust in his sole ability to protect me against the militant aggression of the group now watching him try to get me out of the car. Then again, I almost hoped they would harm me. I didn't deserve to live after what I was about to do. Nor did I want to live with the regret of having done it. So, I took his hand and emerged, to face whatever fate suited my crime.

"Just put your head down," Liam instructed as he put his arm around me. I did as he said, catching a glimpse of the oncoming onslaught as he led me towards the steps to the door.

"Baby killer!" a woman screamed in my ear as we pushed through the swarm of protestors around us.

"Thou shalt not kill," another began to preach, citing books from the Bible as he used God's judgment to sway me.

I squeezed my eyes closed as tugs and elbows and hands tried to pull me out of Liam's protective hold. Liam held on to me tightly, though, thinking he was protecting me from harm, but their words were affecting me more than any physical offense ever could.

"Murderer!" I heard over and over.

I bowed my head in shame, fighting tears of guilt and fear.

"Get off of her!" Liam growled as one protestor latched on to me.

I looked over my shoulder to where the woman was hanging on to me and pleading, "You don't have to do this. Don't do this to your baby. Your baby deserves to live. This isn't the way!"

My eyes met hers and maintained the stare. I'd needed someone to say those words to me. My mom. Someone else's mother. A teacher. A friend. Anyone. But it was a total stranger instead. I wanted to succumb to her pleas. I was entranced by the idea that I could. If she would just take me away and shelter and feed me until this baby was born . . .

Liam used his free hand to shove her off me angrily. I looked to where she'd stumbled into another woman's arms and then stood back up, staring at me. She knew she'd made an impression upon me. It was just too bad it was too late.

The stark quiet of the lobby area just inside the doors was almost as assaulting as the chaos we'd encountered outside. The walls were a calming white. The place was clean. It looked like any other medical office, really, with rows of light-gray-upholstered chairs, intermittently broken up by white-laminate side tables. Random magazines with cheery-faced celebrities and fruit pies on the covers conveyed a very normal tone to what otherwise occurred in this place.

I noticed a couple women waiting, with their heads down like mine. They were both older, maybe in their thirties or forties, and apparently alone. I wondered if they were ending unwanted pregnancies from one-night stands, or if they had had to make the same difficult decision we'd been forced to for reasons we were still trying to justify to ourselves.

We checked in at the reception desk. Then Liam pulled a wad of bills out of his jeans pocket to pay. As soon as we sat to wait, a blonde nurse came through a door with a clipboard.

"Dana?" she called out.

I looked at Liam nervously. I hadn't expected to be called in so quickly, especially when there were the two women here before me.

"Can he come with me?" I asked, referring to Liam, whose hand I refused to release.

"I'm sorry, but only patients are allowed back," the nurse said. I looked back to Liam, scared to proceed without him.

With a squeeze of my hand, he promised, "I'm not going anywhere. I'll be right here when you come back out." Then he nodded towards the nurse.

I nodded too, knowing what needed to be done. Then I averted my eyes and proceeded to follow the nurse to eternal damnation.

Before approving the procedure, I was required to have an ultrasound. I lay on the cold table while the nurse squeezed cold gel onto my little belly. Then, within the black void of the screen, there were whites and grays in which I could make out a fully formed head and tiny little hands. I gaped at the pulsing image in awe, amazed at the ability to see the baby's heart pumping and its little fingers and toes. Seeing an actual baby took the abstract idea of it and made it that much more real. And the reality of a life that would never be overcame me just then, diminishing a delight I should have never allowed myself to feel. I burst into tears.

"Is this your first time, honey?" the nurse asked in a soothing voice.

I nodded as I sniffled to compose myself, despite my stunned surprise at being asked this once again. "There'll never be a next time," I asserted, wiping away my pointless tears. "I don't even want *this* time to be happening."

"I'm sorry, sweetie," she said. Then she put her hand on mine. "Are you sure you want to do this, then?"

I looked at the screen again. Although I couldn't tell from the black and white image, I had a feeling it was a girl. Like me, she was innocent. She relied on me for her every breath. She trusted me to be the kind of mother who would protect her with my life. More importantly, she deserved to have a mother who would. We both did. So, we were both being blind-sided by my cooperation with this callous act.

"Yeah," I whispered. Then I wiped my tears, subduing the guttural screams inside begging me to turn around as I let the nurse lead me into the room where it would all end.

The white-walled room was empty except for a stainless-steel table in the center. Smears of blood, probably belonging to the woman who'd been there before me, were streaked across the surface. A masked and gloved man wearing a blue surgical covering gave no indication of remorse or regret as he sprayed and wiped the evidence off the table. I watched with open-mouthed shock as I bore witness to the robotic workings of this cold and sterile place, laying one woman down after another and extracting the life force from within each.

The nurse extended her arm towards the sterilized table, inviting me to willingly subject myself to the horror which so many before me had endured. It felt like it wasn't just the baby they were killing; it was a part of me, a part of Liam, and a part of my soul I'd never get back.

Despite everything in me still telling me to run, I let the nurse assist me in lying on the cold metal. I stared straight into the fluorescent lights on the ceiling as she gently placed my socked feet into stirrups. Then I looked back down to see her nod to a blue-clad male who'd been silently standing by, preparing some instrument that looked too much like a drill or hand mixer. I imagined what that thing would do to my baby, once placed inside of me. I didn't like my premonition. Nor did I like the fact that no one spoke a word. The dead quiet was like a silent vigil for the death looming ahead, though I couldn't decide whether it was for my baby or for me.

"We're going to start now. Okay?" the nurse said from where she stood next to me.

No, it wasn't okay. None of this was okay. Nothing would ever be okay after this either. I'd damned Mom, and now I was about to damn myself. I exhaled and nodded to the nurse with slothful slowness.

"It'll be about seven minutes. Just stay still, and remember to breathe," she said with a touch of her gloved hand on the shoulder of my hospital gown.

I felt the sharp pinch of a needle in my private area then and decided to look at the huge white-faced clock on the wall to the right. As the initial piercing of the needle faded into slight numbness, a high-pitched whir indicated that these would be the last moments of my baby's life. I gulped and closed my eyes, wishing I'd reopen them to the relief that this had all been a bad dream. Unfortunately, the pressure of something entering me reminded me of reality. I opened my eyes to the clock then, noting the time so I could be cognizant of the exact moment at which my angel went to heaven. It was 12:07 in the afternoon. I was born on the twenty-seventh of December. I didn't think that similarity a coincidence.

I continued to stare at the small red needle on the clock, making its way around the large black numbers and the dashes in between. I watched every second tick by, every agonizing minute, as I felt the most torturous pain I'd ever felt in my life. It would never be as painful as the sadness I'd carry in my heart for the death of my baby, though. I prayed she would forgive me.

After exactly seven minutes, the nurse touched my shoulder again. "It's over," she said. What sounded like a drill slowed to a stop.

I lifted my head to see the doctor carrying away a black plastic bag.

Oh my god! Was that . . .? What did I do? The tears dripping down my face and onto the metal table below gave me my answers.

"Come on, honey," the nurse said, putting her arms around my shoulders as she helped me off the table. Blood smeared on the table under me then fell upon the floor. "We'll get you cleaned up and out of here, so you can go home and rest."

She had no idea that home was hell. And that I was already there.

When I returned to where Liam was in the waiting room, I stood there with slumped shoulders and a blank face, unmoving and unemotional. My stomach hurt worse than any menstrual cramp I'd ever had, and I was practically hemorrhaging. Yet, I barely felt any of it. I didn't feel anything, really. It was like I'd died inside the moment my baby had.

Liam jumped out of his chair, eager to tend to me. I'd forced myself into a state of unemotional dullness, or maybe shock. I didn't know because I didn't care. Nothing mattered anymore.

"Are you okay, Dana?" Liam asked before pulling me into a tight embrace. He held me so close, as if he would never let me go. I recognized his attempt to show me the love and protection I normally needed. In this instance, however, it was a protection that came too late.

I didn't feel deserving of love, anyway, after doing the most heinous thing a person could do. I didn't deserve protection, either, since I hadn't protected my child like I should have. As far as I was concerned, I was no better than Mom now.

The only difference between us was that I'd spared my daughter what Mom had done to me. She'd had me because she'd needed me, to project the shame and blame of having had me so young onto me. She'd made me absorb all of her unhealed trauma, because she was unwilling to take accountability for it herself. Ironically, her failure as a mother essentially made her responsible for why I was here now, in this situation, which just made me resent the bitch even more. I'd never forgive her for what I'd just had to do.

Liam called a cab to take us back and gave the driver my home address to drop me off first. I'd used taxi services before when my parents couldn't drive me somewhere. So, no one would suspect that I'd been up to no good.

"You okay?" he whispered as the cab pulled away.

Without removing my stare from the vacant steps outside the building, wondering why those protestors hadn't fought harder, I responded with an emotionless, "No."

With a squeeze of my hand, Liam left me to my silent sorrow for the duration of the ride back. I went straight to bed when I got home. When Mom came home and found me in bed, I told her I was really sick with the flu. So, she left me alone to deal with the consequence of the truth.

Whether my eyes were open or closed, the haunting memory of my sweet angel, curled in fetal position while she innocently sucked her little thumb in the warmth of my womb, was all I could see. I held onto that vision, though. It was all I had left of my baby girl.

As sick as it sounded, I just hoped she understood the sacrifice I'd made had been done out of my love for her. I could never be the mother she deserved, anyway. I was ill-equipped after having been raised by a monster.

"Close My Eyes Forever"

Mom and Ron took Jonathan to visit the grandmas and Juni the next day. Since I looked like the agony I felt, Mom didn't bat an eye at my continued claim to illness. She'd even pulled my baby pink comforter over me and felt my forehead before they left. I wished I felt the loving gesture for what it was, but it would have been a betrayal to my own daughter if I had.

Aside from calling Liam to check in that afternoon, I only trudged out of bed every couple of hours to change the enormous maxi pads I had to wear in lieu of tampons. I was told I'd experience heavy bleeding for a few days. This was more like a hemorrhage, though, at the rate it was gushing out of me. It was a wonder I had any blood left, or a uterus at all.

Between the drowsiness of the painkiller, the unbearable abdominal pain, and perhaps the emotional turmoil too, I realized the suffering Mom must have felt during all those years of reversing her tubal ligation. I'd never understood it until now, when it took everything in me just to get through school on Monday.

Liam was very attentive, meeting me at my locker between every single class.

"You holding up okay?" he asked.

I tilted my head at him but didn't have the energy to snark back with some sarcastic comment about how haggard I must have looked. "I can barely keep my eyes open," I told him instead. My body was begging for bed. "And I can't stop crying." Fortunately, classmates and teachers assumed allergies were the cause of my teary eyes and sniffling, sparing me the agony of embarrassment and the effort of an excuse.

"Why don't you just go home? I'll walk you if you want," he offered.

"As much as I would love to, I can't risk my goody two-shoes record by skipping classes for the first time in my academic career. If they call my mom and ask where I am . . ."

"Go down to the nurse, then. Tell her you don't feel good, so she'll send you home. You do look—"

"Thanks," I said before he could finish. I knew what I looked like. I was wearing black leggings and an oversized shirt, which was quite different from the skirts and sparkly dangling earrings I usually donned. I hadn't even tried to do my hair or makeup either. With my slumped shoulders and bags under my eyes, I looked like a recovering addict at best. "I don't want to call any more attention to myself than necessary. Plus, I have pom practice after school."

"You can barely move, babe! You can't go to practice!"

"But if I miss two practices the whole year, I'm off the squad. I won't risk that," I said.

So, I got through the day. I attended pom practice afterward, attempting to participate with the least exertion possible while Liam watched from the sidelines.

The pom coach pulled me aside during a water break. I knew why before she even spoke. It's not like I hadn't noticed some of the girls on the squad looking at me like I wasn't putting the same physical effort into perfecting the moves as they were.

"Is everything all right?" she asked in a hushed tone.

"I just don't feel good," I said. Feeling like I had to give more of a reason than that, I explained, "Female issues."

"Oh," she said as if that were explanation enough. "Do you have any Midol or ibuprofen you can take?"

"The doctor actually put me on a prescription. That's why I'm so drowsy," I half lied. "I didn't want to miss practice, though." We were learning the routines for the Homecoming pep rally and football game.

Pressing her lips together, the short curly-haired coach nodded as if she understood my dilemma. "Okay, well, your commitment is commendable. Just let me know if you get to the point where you can't do it anymore. I don't want you hurting yourself."

We were well beyond that point. But with the strict attendance requirements and zero-tolerance policy, I had no choice but to push through.

With just an hour to spare between pom practice and our rehearsal of the halftime performance with the marching band that night, I went home for the respite I desperately needed. I bypassed Mom in favor of a nap, stopping in the kitchen to eat just ten minutes before I had to be on my way back to school.

Mom was completely silent while I heated some leftover white rice I'd found in a half-empty Chinese takeout container in the refrigerator. I didn't say anything, figuring she was just in a bad mood. I didn't have the energy to deal with her on top of everything else, anyway.

Despite the uncomfortable tension, I took the opportunity to sit at the table to eat before having to exert myself walking around the football field for the next couple of hours. Ron and Jonathan weren't home yet, so it was a rare opportunity to partake in peace.

"Do you even know who the father is?" Mom asked out of nowhere.

With a spoonful of rice lifted halfway to my mouth, I froze. I didn't even breathe. I could hear my heart pounding, though, like a low drum warning of impending doom.

How did she even know? And what exactly *did* she know?

The only person I'd told was Kelly. She wouldn't have dared tell her parents such a thing, though Mom and Ron didn't talk to Kelly's parents anyway, unless to say a quick hello or goodbye when picking up or dropping me off somewhere.

But then I recalled the numerous times I'd discovered my room scavenged recently. My closet had been rifled through one day. I'd asked Mom if she'd been in there, and she'd said she'd been looking to borrow a hat from me. Another day I'd found one of my dresser drawers messed up. She'd said she'd been looking to borrow a barrette or headband because her hair was especially frizzy. My mattress had been moved slightly off the box spring another time. I hadn't bothered asking her about that, though I'd stopped hiding things under there afterward.

She'd never gone through my room in the past. So, she'd apparently been looking for *something* to condemn me for. Drugs, I assumed. That was her go-to allegation for any wrongful behavior she judged anyone for, particularly my real dad, and now me as his byproduct. You couldn't convince Mom against anything she believed either. If I had feelings, I was on drugs. If I had emotions, I was hormonal. If I had a boyfriend, I must be having sex. I had my own room, so I was obviously hiding something in there.

Oh, shit—the pregnancy test. In the panic of trying to determine whether the two lines indicated a positive result, I'd thrown the test and its packaging in the bathroom garbage without thinking. How stupid was I? I'd put it underneath all the other garbage, but if Mom was determined to find something to incriminate me, I wouldn't put it past her to have dug through the garbage! So, she really *did* know! Except that she'd asked if I knew who the father *is*. She thought I was still pregnant.

"I know you heard me, Dana," Mom prodded to try to provoke me into an admission I wasn't prepared to give.

I took a deep breath. I didn't want to lie, but anything I said about being pregnant would result in World War III. If Ron happened to come home in the midst of that, it would be like the atomic bomb that obliterated Hiroshima. I'd be toast.

As I racked my brain, I considered the possibility of telling her the truth, which was that I wasn't pregnant. Not anymore, at least—but she didn't have to know that part. Because, even if she had found that positive test in the garbage, she had no way to know it was accurate. Store-bought tests could give false positives. Yet, if she tested me now, I would, in fact, be without child.

That would be opening a really big can of worms, though. So, in a sneaky move, I decided to address the insult instead. "That's an ignorant thing to ask when you know I'm with Liam," I said with haughtiness too bold for the situation I was in. Anyway, I really was surprised that she would hurt me with the same offense she'd been traumatized by when in the same situation.

"I know he's your *boyfriend*, but I don't know who you're running around *sleeping* with," Mom snarked back.

I glared at Mom. Ron called me a whore enough. I wouldn't tolerate it from her now too!

"I can't believe you did this to me! After everything I went through," she complained.

Tears began to well in my eyes. It was always about her. She was always more concerned about how anything I said or did reflected on *her*. But what about *me*? When would *my* feelings ever matter?

I couldn't expect a woman who'd never wanted to be my mother to suddenly act like one in my time of need, though. So, I'd do us both a favor and remove myself from the situation altogether.

"I have practice," I said and got up to leave.

"Don't you go anywhere!" Mom raised her voice from behind me.

"I have to leave!" I raised my voice back while I put my shoes on by the front door.

"Listen to me," she said with a pointed sternness I rarely heard from her. Then she came to where I was in the foyer. "Ron and I discussed this already. We're going to send you to a boarding school in Europe. Once the baby is born, we'll bring it back here and tell everyone we adopted it from an orphanage abroad and raise it as our own."

"What?" I cried out, horrified at the thought.

"We'll pay for you to stay in Europe," she said matter-of-factly. "You'll get a good education there. We'll make sure you have everything you need if you want to live the rest of your life there. And you won't have to worry about having to deal with the baby."

"Deal with" my baby? A baby I'd *wanted* but opted to deprive of life because of the woman facing me now? And did she really think a life in Europe and promise of relief would lure me into cooperating with their plan, which had really been concocted as a way to prevent my mother from further shame? How vile of a human being did she think I was? Better yet, how vile was *she*?

"I can't even talk to you right now," I said with a level of disgust I'd never imagined feeling towards another person, never mind my own mother.

"Well, we're going to have to talk about this at some point," she said, crossing her arms.

"No. We don't," I retorted before walking out and slamming the door behind me. Then I ran. I ran as fast as I could down the street and between the two houses that took me the shortest way to the main street, until severe cramps in my abdomen reminded me that I wasn't supposed to exert myself.

I slowed to a walk, then I stopped to catch my breath. With my hands on my knees, I sobbed. I couldn't believe they'd planned to get rid of me and then tear my baby away from me as if exchanging me for another little girl who might submit to their control more easily! They would have had to literally take her over my dead body, though. Unlike Mom, I loved my daughter. If I'd been able to have her, I'd have loved her no matter what. It would have been harder to love her if she turned out to be like Mom and Ron, as a result of whatever influence they would have had on her. So, maybe I'd been right to do what I'd done. Maybe my angel was better off in heaven. Maybe we both were. Because I didn't want to be here without her. The way things were going, I didn't want to be here at all.

"Papa Don't Preach"

fter a few more days of pushing myself to the max at school and enduring the silent treatment at home, I couldn't do it anymore. I was halfway through the school day, still struggling to stay awake while stifling the pain and the annoyance of the persistent bleeding. I'd been told to go to the emergency room if the bleeding was excessive or hadn't slowed to a stop within the week. That wasn't an option for me, though. There was no way I'd endure the wrath I'd face if Mom and Ron found out what I'd done. So, I had to suck it up and deal, like I always had.

I left school in the middle of the afternoon, ditching classes for the first time ever. It was a slow, torturous walk home, wherein I held my stomach as if my baby were still inside. It hurt so bad that I just wanted to take my prescription and sleep the pain away. I'd worry about my mom or detention or whatever consequence I'd face later.

The house was quiet when I entered, just as I'd expected. Mom and Ron usually didn't return from work until dinnertime, so I figured I had at least a few hours to rest before the pitter-patter of Jonathan's quick little feet woke me up.

I set my purse on the arm of the living room sectional then reached into the lining at the bottom where I'd hidden the orange bottle of pills. The bottle wasn't there. I rummaged through my purse some more, assuming it had escaped its confines to intermingle with lipsticks and keys and candies, but it was nowhere to be found. Thinking it might have fallen out of my purse by accident, I looked at the floor around my feet. Like a drug addict desperate for her fix, I panicked as I searched and rechecked everywhere I could think of.

Mom came in the front door then and stopped dead in her tracks when she saw me.

"Oh, hi," I said with the full-bodied shake of a startle. I was surprised and annoyed that she'd come home so early, today of all days. Unless, of course, the school had called her.

"You looking for something?" Mom asked with the plain face she wore when something was brewing but she didn't want to let on.

"No," I said, playing off whatever she might have seen. "I was just trying to find some ibuprofen I thought I had in my purse because my head is pounding. That's actually why I came home. Just couldn't make it through the whole day with this pain." I put my hand on my forehead and winced.

"Ibuprofen, huh?"

"Yeah," I said, acting cool, "but I guess I was wrong. I'll just grab some out of the medicine cabinet upstairs and go lay down."

"You sure?" Mom asked.

"Sure about what?" I responded as I closed my purse and grabbed the handle to take it upstairs with me.

"You sure you don't want these?"

I turned around and saw Mom holding the prescription bottle I'd been looking for. I had no idea when she'd gone through my purse to take it away, but I was in no mood to deal with her bullshit. With clenched teeth to hold my sharp tongue, I grabbed for the medicine. She pulled it out of my reach before I could snatch it from her hand.

"I need that, Mom," I said firmly, holding out my hand in demand.

Without a word, she went into the kitchen.

"I'm not messing around, Mom. Give me the fucking bottle."

"When were you going to tell me?" she asked.

"About what?" I asked, unsure of what she even knew.

"The abortion."

The words were like a doomsday siren alerting everyone to take shelter. I stood there, stunned, silent, and still for a moment, trying to decipher if she'd actually even said them, or if my mind was playing paranoid tricks on me.

I didn't breathe. I think my heart even slowed to fall under the radar of detection, though I'd have thought it would stop altogether at the realization that my greatest regret in life had been enacted for nothing now.

"How did you know?" I finally muttered, staring at her with narrowed eyes.

"I called the number on the prescription bottle and pretended to be you," Mom responded with an arrogant tone that gave away how clever she thought she was.

"Well, good for you," I said sarcastically. "Now give me back my prescription. I need it." I put my hand out again and waited.

She ignored me and looked through the mail instead.

"Are you kidding me, Mom?" I asked with a raised voice. "The doctor prescribed me that medicine because I need it! So, hand it over! Unless you *want* me to suffer."

"No," she said like a defiant toddler.

I didn't have it in me to stand there and argue with her. So, I huffed and went upstairs to get ibuprofen from the medicine cabinet. Then I replaced the heavily soaked maternity pad, which felt more like a diaper that didn't fit inside my size small panties, before laying down for a nap. As riled up as I was, I instantly fell asleep.

My bedroom was dark when I awoke later. I could see the stars shining brightly in the night sky outside the long, narrow window. I thought of my baby girl up in heaven and wondered if she was one of those shining stars.

I rolled over onto my side and reached for my phone, which I'd silenced when I'd gotten in bed. Liam was the only one I could talk to about the gloom and guilt in my heart. He probably wondered where I'd disappeared to before the end of the school day, anyway, since I'd left the school without telling anybody.

When I put the receiver to my ear, however, I heard Ron's voice instead of a dial tone. "Do you know what your son did to my daughter?" My jaw dropped. "He got her pregnant!" Ron blurted without waiting for a response.

"How do you even know it *was* my stepson? *We* don't know who else your daughter's been sleeping with!" a familiar voice responded. Stepson, daughter . . . Oh my god, it was Jim!

"Well, who *else* could it be?" Ron retorted, shocking me with the defense my own mother hadn't provided me. "They've been running around together for a while now, mostly to *your* house. *You're* the one who leaves them alone, unsupervised apparently. So, *you're* responsible for this!"

"How dare you ..." Liam's stepfather started, but I replaced the receiver lightly before I could hear them hurl any more accusations at each other. Although phone lines sometimes crossed, I hadn't been prepared to overhear our stepfathers placing blame for the creation of an innocent baby they were never supposed to know about anyway.

Sickened by the additional insult of their lack of concern for my physical and mental well-being, and since it was obviously not a good time to try to reach Liam, I cried into my pillow. It was bad enough I'd lost my baby and my hope that my mother could ever be understanding or supportive. Ron's call with Jim meant Liam's mother would be collateral damage as well, since she'd trusted me and Liam alone in their house, and we'd let her down in the most prolific way.

What pissed me off the most, however, was that all these adults, who were charged with our welfare, hadn't stopped thinking about themselves long enough to ask how I might be doing. Did it even occur to them that I might be dealing with suicidal ideation for what I'd done? Did they even bother to think about how all of this had affected Liam? I knew for certain none of them knew I'd missed my follow-up exam because I hadn't had a way to get there. But did my pain or possibility of potentially never being able to have children even cross any of their egocentric minds? No! And their failure as our parents was, to me, the biggest tragedy of all.

"Tainted Love"

Grateful to have been left to myself the night before, with no indication that Mom or Ron knew what I'd overheard, I woke up the next morning, eager to know what the fallout of the call had been at Liam's house. So, I skipped my usual coffee and Malt-O-Meal and set out on my walk to school. I was hungry and craved the normalcy of my regular routine, but I think normal had flown out the window the second I'd gotten pregnant.

It was a quarter to seven in the morning, so only nerds dotted the floors and lounges this early, studying to ensure they aced whatever assignment or test. Since Liam and I always met at my locker before seven-thirty homeroom, I sat on the floor there, flipping through the chapter of a book I was supposed to have read for English. Before long, Liam made his way up the hall. Wearing worn jeans and a black Metallica T-shirt, he picked up his pace when he saw me.

"Are you okay?" he asked as I stood to hug him. I laid my head on his broad chest and closed my eyes, feeling safer in his tight embrace.

When I finally pulled away, I said, "Yeah. I just stayed in my bedroom all night and avoided my parents altogether. What about you?"

"I tried to do the same," he said, rubbing his forehead, "but Jim was yelling at me all night about how I might have cost him his re-election. And my mom was upset that we didn't come to her . . ."

I shook my head and huffed, disgusted that Jim's political position was more important than us and our baby. He was no better than Mom and Ron.

Feeling like this was going to turn into a Romeo and Juliet situation, wherein our parents would try to tear us apart, I asked, "What're we gonna do?"

"I don't know, babe," he said, pulling me back into him. I knew it was a loaded question that didn't have a realistic answer; I just wished someone could tell me that my fairy godmother would come and wave a magic wand over me, and I'd wake up somewhere else, like Dorothy did in *The Wizard of Oz*, and that everything would be okay.

Instead, the days that followed were like the apocalypse of my life.

Since I couldn't physically keep up with pom practices but didn't want to lose my spot on the team, I confessed to the squad about why I couldn't participate in the exhaustive practices and drills. I thought I could trust my sisterhood with the truth, to protect me and my secret. Instead, one or all betrayed me, spreading word of my abortion throughout the school. I was called a whore in the halls. Girls whispered about me behind my back. Liam got into a fight with a kid who was writing something about me being "easy" in the boy's bathroom. A boy even asked me to Homecoming because I was a "sure thing," and then his gangbanger girlfriend chased me to the bus after school with a knife.

Home wasn't any better. I was still getting the silent treatment from Mom and Ron. They cancelled my private viola lessons, claiming they wouldn't pay for something I couldn't responsibly focus on. The decision cost me a solo performance in the upcoming Symphonic Orchestra concert. I'd been in a prime position to get it, since it was the same musical piece I'd performed at the cultural festival over the summer.

Feeling like everything I'd worked hard for was falling apart, I wanted to escape to Liam's. But I couldn't do that anymore either. Aside from being embarrassed to show my face there, Liam said Jim had told him I wasn't welcome there anymore.

By Thursday of that week, I was so depressed that I decided there was no point in living anymore. I couldn't tell anyone, though, because they'd think I was nuts. So, I tried to think of ways I could die that wouldn't hurt as much as slitting my wrists. Overdosing on drugs seemed like a viable option, except that we didn't have any in our house because Mom and Ron were such straight fricking arrows with no medical problems. Plus, I didn't want Jonathan to find me. I just wanted Mom to, so she might possibly feel some guilt for what she had ultimately influenced by neglecting me.

When it really came down to it, though, I couldn't work up the nerve to get to the point of even planning to take my own life. It's like I had been given a life sentence for taking my daughter's, except that the punishment was to live—with the guilt, the pain, the suffering, and the memory of her black-and-white image on that medical monitor. So, I just wanted to sleep, only I couldn't even do that because I was so distraught.

I needed someone to talk to. Kelly and Miranda couldn't know what it was like to end a life, though. Mr. Fogel couldn't help me process my feelings about having killed a child whose every breath hinged on mine. I couldn't talk to Dr. Lehrfield either, because Mom and Ron had stopped taking me to her. It's like they'd given up on trying to fix me or given up on me altogether, which was just another reason to support my cause.

Despite the tension between us, I just wanted my mom, like any girl would. She knew what it was like to be a pregnant teenager. She knew what it was like to struggle through a pregnancy and deal with the judgment and shame in the aftermath. Mom probably wouldn't understand about me wanting to die, but maybe if I explained it right, she'd give me that crumb of affection or reassurance I so desperately needed right now. Even if she really didn't love me, on a human level, she'd have to uplift me. Wouldn't she?

So, I went out to the dark hallway and stood in the doorway of the master bedroom. The bluish-white glare of the TV reflected off Mom, who was lying in bed and staring at it like a zombie.

"Mom?" I whimpered.

She didn't flinch. She didn't avert her eyes either. I could clearly see they were open, though, just like I could see Ron sitting up next to her, wearing a smug look of satisfaction that she was ignoring me.

"Mom," I said a little louder. I worried about waking Jonathan, who was sleeping behind his closed bedroom door across the hall.

She remained unmoved.

"Mom!" I yelled.

She didn't even flinch.

My frustration at her intentional cruelty angered me with every second that passed. My breaths became heavier, then they became faster, until I finally screamed, "Why the fuck don't you care about me?"

At that, she jumped out of bed and came at me. I cowered first then rushed back to my bedroom and slammed the door shut. With the entire weight of my body against the back of the door, I pressed the button on the doorknob to lock Mom out. She turned the knob from the other side at the same exact time, though, so the lock didn't engage. She tried to push the door open, but I pushed back. Then she muscled her way in with so much force that I was thrown back against the wall when the door swung all the way open.

Flashes of light from the TV in her adjacent bedroom cast intermittent glimpses of Mom piercing me with narrowed eyes. My glare expressed the same hatred towards her. Then, without warning, she slapped my face. Stunned by her assault, I put my hand on my cheek. It stung like tiny little pins stabbing me all at once. So, I slapped her right back. I guessed I was like her after all, wanting her to feel the same pain as me.

Her mouth fell open in shock. I was shocked too but glad I'd had the braveness to return her favor.

All of a sudden, bright light from the hallway distracted us both from our standoff. I squinted as my eyes adjusted enough to catch Jonathan walking from his room to the master bedroom with a giddy smile on his face. It seemed so out of place given the situation, but I was glad he was oblivious to what was really going on.

Ron followed behind Jonathan, glaring at me with blame for waking my little brother. Instead of going into the master bedroom with Jonathan, though, Ron came to where we were, just inside my bedroom doorway.

"This shit is going to stop right now!" Ron scolded, waving that finger in my face. I hadn't seen my nemesis in a while and had thought it had finally stuck itself up Ron's ass where it belonged.

I crossed my arms and turned away, shaking my head in disbelief that these two adults, who were supposed to guard and protect me as their daughter, had been my first two bullies instead.

"Look at me when I'm talking to you!" Ron shouted.

Like the possessed girl in the movie *The Exorcist*, I wore a smug expression as I slowly twisted my neck to face him.

"You think this is funny?" he screamed, trying to impress his authority on me.

"Not at all," I said calmly, shaking my head.

In a sudden rage, Mom grabbed my arm and yanked me out of my room and into the hallway. I wrestled to get away, but then Ron got involved in the scuffle, wrangling me down to the carpeted floor of the hall. Mom straddled me to prevent escape while Ron pinned my wrists next to my head. Then she slapped me across the face on the same cheek that still stung from before. With a loud grunt, she slapped me again but harder.

With no way to defend myself, I zoned out like I'd done during the dilation and curettage that had killed my baby, so I didn't have to feel the emotional turbulence of Mom condemning me with her hands. It was too late, anyway. I'd already condemned myself for what I'd done, though I'd have done it again to spare my daughter the agony of the slow death she'd endure if she had still been with me tonight. My womb was empty, though, and despite the intense pain of Mom sitting on it, I didn't even cry.

When my maternal assailant paused to catch her breath, I turned my head towards the master bedroom and stared numbly at my little brother. It seemed surreal to see him jumping up and down on his parents' bed, giggling as he held my gaze. He had no clue of the horror I was enduring right before his twinkling eyes.

Perhaps it was my focus on Jonathan that reminded Mom he was there, or perhaps she and Ron felt like they'd made their point, but Mom stood then. Ron released me too and went to their bedroom to round up his son. Mom remained, glaring at me in a way I couldn't gauge. So, without removing my eyes from hers, I stood too and backed away slowly.

"I fucking hate you," I said with pointed loathe.

At that, Mom lunged at me. My eyes bulged in shock as she wrapped her hands around my neck and squeezed as hard as she could. I saw determination in hers, though. I opened my mouth and strained for air, like I was trying to catch as much of it as I could before no more could pass through. The constriction on my throat disallowed me from inhaling, making me gasp even harder. The walls began to spin around me. I couldn't catch my breath, and Mom didn't want me to; she wanted to kill me. And honestly, a part of me didn't even care.

But then I remembered that this was the woman who'd taken away any possibility of me ever having anything I wanted. She wouldn't be my mother. She'd taken me away from Great-Gram, who was as much a mother to me as I could have ever wished for. Mom was the sole reason I couldn't be a mother. The injustice of what I'd had to do to protect my baby girl raged inside of me, telling me to fight for what was right. So, for me and my daughter, I fought to live.

I grabbed at Mom's fingers, trying to peel them off, but I was too weak. They didn't budge. I grabbed at her wrists next, desperate to pull them away, but I could see in her clenched teeth that she had no intention of releasing the full force with which she held my scrawny neck. I gasped for air again, but only crackling sounds came out. Then my vision blurred, and everything went dim. Despite my best efforts, this was it. Mom was finally getting what she wanted and giving Ron his greatest wish.

Just before everything went black, I thought of how Mom and Ron would probably go on to tell everyone I attacked her and that she'd had to kill me in self-defense. They'd use my counseling sessions with Dr. Lehrfield as proof that I'd been mentally unstable, and they'd get away with murder.

Family and neighbors would pity them for having such a difficult daughter. They might even be glorified for their supposed efforts to save me. They would soak it all up, play their roles as grieving, helpless parents, and then appear strong as they moved on with their young son. Collecting the money from the life insurance policy they took out on me when I was twelve would be the icing on the cake. That had probably been the plan all along—to create the narrative that I was crazy, somehow ensure I died, then take the money as reward for all the trouble I'd been to them. The whole thing made me sick and motivated me to take another shot at life.

My legs were free, so I kicked Mom as hard as I could in the stomach. Her hands released my neck as she fell backwards into the door of the linen closet. Because of the push and pull with which I'd been strangled, I was propelled backwards as well, and fell down six stairs to the landing. I lay crumpled up against the wall and the railing, looking up at Mom, who stood at the top of the stairs in shock.

Ron came to see what had become of me then glared at me for being alive. Before he could finish what they'd started, I ran down to the basement and curled up in fetal position in the corner of the storage closet under the stairs. The pound of my fast heartbeat was so deafening, I was sure it would give away my hiding spot.

In the still, quiet place, I waited for any indication of movement upstairs. I heard nothing but my quick breaths reminding me to inhale now that I could. The strain of gasping so desperately during our fight made the slightest breath feel like needles poking and scraping my throat. Still, air never tasted so sweet. It almost distracted me from the other pains in and on my body.

A few minutes later, I heard Ron's feet pounding down the stairs from the second floor. I immediately tensed and instinctively held my breath. I was terrified of what he'd do if he found me.

I heard his footsteps walk around the main floor above me. Then the basement door opened, and I heard the click of the stairway light being switched on. After another moment, I heard the click again. Then the basement door shut, and Ron's feet stomped back up to the second floor.

After a few minutes of dead quiet, I crept up the stairs in the dark, going undetected by avoiding the stairs that creaked. Just past the landing to the second floor, I could see the glow of Mom and Ron's TV. There was no way to my room without passing their open doorway, so I took a deep breath and moved swiftly.

Intending to get in and out, I grabbed my backpack, threw a few things in it, then ran back down the stairs and out the front door before either of them could come after me. I stopped at the end of the street and looked back at the house to see if they had. But no one was in the doorway. No lights had been flipped on. The house remained dark and still.

I hid behind a tree to avoid being seen, conflicted with feelings of gladness and resentment. I didn't want to be dragged back there, but it would have been nice to know Mom didn't want me on the streets overnight either. I guess I shouldn't have expected her to suddenly care about a daughter she'd just tried to kill.

Intending to get far away from Mom, Ron, and that house, to free myself from the bounds of its misery, I ran several blocks at full speed. I didn't know where I was running to, just what I was running from. Then I realized I couldn't escape my life no matter how much distance I put between me and everything that comprised it, because I had no money, no support, and nowhere to go.

Feeling defeated, I slowed to a stop and sobbed. It was cold. I was alone. I didn't know where I'd sleep or if I'd sleep at all. And despite what had happened, I was scared and wanted Mom.

A car pulled up then, making me anxious about what sort of trouble I'd meet now and whether it would be worse than if I'd just stayed home. I stood and watched the window roll down, relieved to see a familiar face.

"Dana?" the pom captain asked.

"Oh, hi," I said. I instinctively pushed my hair out of my face, as if the last-second primping would make me appear normal. But it was late, and I was out on a random side street on a weeknight, so nothing about this would be perceived as normal at all.

The girl's eyes widened when she saw my face. I imagined my eye makeup was smeared from the scuffle and the tears. "Are you okay?" she asked as she jumped out of the front passenger seat of the car. The overhead light showed a boy driving, who I assumed to be her boyfriend.

Overwhelmed by the loaded question, I put my face in my hands and cried. It still stung to the touch, but I endured it to avoid embarrassment. The pom captain put her arm around my shoulder and led me to the car. Then she opened the door to the back seat, and I got in.

"I don't know if you've ever met my boyfriend . . ." she said, as she slid in next to me.

Her boyfriend turned back and waved, "Hi."

"Hi," I responded politely, keeping my head down to avoid eye contact.

"What are you doing out here so late? Can we give you a ride somewhere?" she asked.

"I don't know," I whimpered. "Maybe *my* boyfriend's house?" I knew Liam had said Jim didn't want me there, but I didn't know where else I could go without answering questions I'd rather not have to.

"Yeah, no problem. What's the address?"

I told her, and her boyfriend started driving. She kept her arm around my shoulders the entirety of the short drive and even walked me up to Liam's front door.

When Liam's mom answered, the girl said, "We found her crying on a side street not far from here. Hopefully you can help?"

"Oh! Of course!" Liam's mom said, ushering me into the house. I was surprised at her willingness to allow me in but didn't question her kindheartedness. Still, I kept my head down to avoid the shame of facing her directly. "Thank you for making sure she got somewhere safe," she told my pom captain before closing the door behind me.

"What's going on?" Liam's mom asked. "Is everything okay?" I sensed the concern in her tone but peered up at her warily, since I wasn't sure where I stood with her. Plus, Jim had just come half down the stairs wearing a thin white undershirt, which exposed the fatness of his belly overhanging the waist of his dark suit pants.

"Dana?" Liam said, coming up from his room. He rushed over and ran his thumb gently across the one cheek that had gotten the brunt of Mom's anger. His mom winced for me, so I could only imagine what I looked like.

Just then, the baby's cry rang through the house. Jim grumbled as he turned to go back upstairs, making me feel worse for being at fault.

"Come on up with me," Liam's mom told us.

With Liam's arm around my hunched shoulders, I kept my head down as we followed his mom upstairs. Once in the baby's nursery, we sat on the twin bed beside the crib. Liam kept his arm around me, holding me close, while his mother changed the baby's diaper on the table against the opposite wall.

"What's going on?" Jim snipped from where he leaned in at the doorway. "Why is *she* here?"

I didn't appreciate being spoken about in the third person. It was bad enough that I felt so unwelcome in a place I used to feel safe. I couldn't handle any more emotions, though, so I kept my head down and focused on my fidgety fingers.

When no one answered Jim, Liam leaned his forehead on my shoulder and whispered, "What's going on, babe? Did something happen at home?"

I nodded and sniffled, then a few quick breaths snuck in. Liam squeezed me, knowing I needed the comfort.

"We need to know what happened, so we know how we can help you, Dana," Liam's mom said. I wanted to tell her everything, just not in front of Jim. He stood in the doorway, wearing a scowl and tapping his foot impatiently.

"Dana?" Liam prodded.

I turned and looked into those blue eyes. They'd always shown a sincerity I could trust. So, I ignored the tension emanating from Jim and relayed the events of the night. As I got towards the end of the retelling, Liam's mom handed their baby girl to Jim and came over to me. Her sympathetic smile and sorrowful eyes offered the comfort and understanding I desperately sought. Before she could say anything, though, Jim intervened.

"I want her out. She can't be here."

Liam's mom shot him a dirty look as she squatted in front of me.

"I mean it," he demanded. "If they call her into the police as a runaway or missing person, I don't want them finding her here. She needs to go!" Liam's mom stood then, with slumped shoulders of defeat.

I'd have argued that neither Mom nor Ron were concerned about my whereabouts. If they were, they'd have come running after me or called around to find out where I'd ended up. Seeing as my arrival to Liam's was a surprise, it was safe to assume everyone at my house was sleeping peacefully, unconcerned about me at all. Ron had probably even said a prayer for me to get kidnapped or run over so I wouldn't return, on the off chance there was something to religion.

"I have nowhere to go," I whimpered.

"Mom, please just let her stay here tonight," Liam begged.

"Absolutely not!" Jim asserted.

"Liam . . ." his mom drew out, asking him to relent without saying no.

"Mom, please," Liam said, attempting to appeal to her motherly nature.

She looked over at Jim with pleading eyes, as if asking him to put his humanity before his political aspirations.

"No! She's gotta go!" he said before turning to take the baby back to the master bedroom with him.

"I'm sorry, Dana. I really am. But after everything that's happened . . ." Liam's mom said, shaking her head as she offered her hand to me. "Let's go down to the kitchen. I'll make you some cocoa or something, and you can use the phone to call whomever you need to find a place to stay tonight."

I begrudgingly went with her, feeling even more unwanted by the way I was being passed off to burden someone else with my existence. The only person I thought to bother at this late hour was Kelly. Fortunately, her parents agreed to let me stay there without asking any questions.

Jim ungraciously delivered me to her house in his fancy green Jaguar. He didn't even wait for me to walk up to the side door of Kelly's dark house before pulling away, which just went further to prove what an insensitive asshole he was.

Fortunately, Kelly was waiting just inside the door to take me down to her room in the basement. She smiled, but we didn't speak. Her house was completely dark, and I didn't want to ruin my welcome by waking her parents or sisters, who'd apparently gone back to bed between my call and arrival.

"Thank you," I said as Kelly tucked me in the blankets of her queen-size bed beside her.

"No need," Kelly said. "This is what friends are for."

She was right. And I was safe now. So, I closed my eyes to a long-awaited sleep.

The next morning, while I was getting ready in the bathroom, I noticed how reddened one side of my face was. Mom had wailed on me but just slapped. So, I was able to cover it up with foundation, to ensure no one would notice. I checked my neck next. There were purplish marks all over it. Having learned the trick of concealer, I used some of Kelly's that I'd found in her medicine cabinet to cover up the evidence of my strangling. Then I put on the mock turtleneck pom uniform sweater, thankful we'd been assigned to wear it to school as advertisement for the home football game to be held that night. I had aches and pains elsewhere, but my black leggings covered all those.

On our way out to catch the bus, Kelly's mom handed us each a brown bag lunch.

"Thank you," I said with a bowed head, unsure of what she thought about the night before.

"It's just a peanut butter and jelly sandwich," she dismissed with a genuinely kind smile.

"Well, I appreciate it," I said, considering that measly sandwich was a show of more love and care than my own mother could ever extend.

"Well, you're welcome!" she said. "By the way, I called your parents this morning and let them know you stayed here last night. They were really worried about you."

"Oh!" I said, surprised she'd ratted me out. Then I threw in a "thanks" to be polite.

Although I was disappointed that she'd bought their bullshit act, I couldn't hold it against her. Everyone thought Mom and Ron were the fucking bee's knees. I was the only one who knew the truth about them.

"Renegade"

"The police are looking for you, Dana," Miranda whispered when she caught up with me after our first classes.

"What?!"

"Yeah! This tall, sandy-blond hunk in a uniform came to my last class asking if you were in there," Miranda informed me. "Sounded like he was going room to room. What did you *do?*"

"Nothing!" I said with widened eyes to emphasize my innocence. "Thanks for the heads up, though!"

Anxious and worried about what the police could possibly want with me, I headed in the direction of Liam's locker. I mean, I'd never been in *any* kind of trouble, aside from being sent to the principal's office during junior high for talking out of turn in class. On the way, I noticed a tall, blond policeman scanning the hundreds of teenagers buzzing around him. I dropped my head to avoid notice and turned to go the opposite direction.

"Dana?" I heard a female call out from just ahead. Like a moron, I instinctively looked up. I recognized the short, straight-haired blonde as my school advisor, who helped me select classes every semester. "Can you come to my office for a minute?" she asked with a kind smile.

I looked over my shoulder to see where the policeman was. His black uniform hat was easy to see above the crowd. Thankfully, he was looking the other way.

This wasn't a coincidence, though. Whatever the advisor wanted to talk about had something to do with whatever the police were there for, and I suspected it all had to do with last night. What I didn't know was what the police would do with me if they found me. Aside from perhaps being deemed a runaway, which didn't seem like it should apply when Kelly's mom had informed mine where I was, police involvement didn't make sense to the domestic occurrence.

I thought of going with the advisor and confiding everything that had happened, because I didn't want to seem uncooperative. Cooperation presumed innocence, and I *was* a good girl. I got good grades without effort. I followed the rules. I'd never smoked. I'd never used drugs. I'd never drank alcohol, except for the coquito my grandma made at Christmas time. I wasn't the kind of kid who should have cops looking for me. So, I was terrified.

On the other hand, the extent of my interactions with the advisor had been too superficial to make any determination about her trustworthiness. And I didn't trust anyone except for Liam, Kelly, and Miranda right now.

"Yeah," I said, stalling until I could plan my next move. "I just have to get something from my locker really quick."

"Okay, I'll be waiting," she said before going on her way.

I forced a smile despite the panic rising within me. Then I continued my search for Liam, though I couldn't deny thinking of making a break for it—just taking off and never looking back.

Just then, I heard a stern male voice behind me say, "Dana?"

I turned to see the policeman I'd avoided moments before. *Fuck was I dumb!*

Desperate to escape, my eyes darted around, looking for somewhere to duck out. My racing heart had already taken off without the rest of me.

"We can do this the easy way or the hard way," the officer warned.

Trapped like a wild animal, I knew better than to try to outrun the cop. It would just make me look guiltier of whatever I hadn't done. Being presumed a criminal, though, and enduring yet another punishment I wouldn't deserve, felt like I was being held down in the hallway at home again, unable to escape Mom's stranglehold on my throat. I touched my neck now as I strained to take in a deep breath. It was sore to the touch. No one could see the purple handprints I'd seen in my reflection that morning since my mock turtleneck covered them up. But maybe those handprints were all I needed to make the police believe me about what had happened. So, I decided to succumb. The police were supposed to protect the innocent, anyway, weren't they?

So, despite my worry about how quickly this situation had escalated to a seemingly criminal level I'd have never anticipated, I nodded to the officer to indicate my compliance. He put his hand on my shoulder to lead me away. I dropped my head to avoid notice, though no one was in the hallway to witness since the bell to indicate the start of the next class had just rung.

Everything was a blur after that. I remember the school advisor offering a diplomatic smile while she waited with me outside the dean's office, where the policeman huddled with school administrators in the privacy of the head honcho's closed quarters. I remember being signed out of school and taken to the squad car outside. Then I was in the back of a police car, looking as guilty as any other criminal who'd sat in that seat before me, terrified about what would become of me. Would I end up behind bars? Did they even put teenagers in jail? Would I ever see Liam again? I wished I had found him, at least to say goodbye.

As the car began to move, I looked out the rear window, thinking it might be the last time I laid eyes on my high school. It had been such an ominous and foreboding place when I'd first arrived as a freshman. Now, it was an auspicious place I was sad to leave.

A couple of kids, either on lunch break or ditching class, halted to stare with open-mouthed shock at the squad care taking me away. One was a girl from the pom squad. Our eyes met, but then I averted mine when I saw her gaping back at me. Surely she would tell the other girls on poms. Then, just like my abortion, the whole school would know I'd been detained.

I guess I should have been glad that word would get to Liam. Maybe he could do something to help me, though I'm not sure his politically driven stepfather would permit his involvement. It would attract negative attention to their seemingly perfect blended family and whatever bullshit campaign he promoted next.

Scared into total silence and submission, I remained shut down at the police station, where I was led into a tiny room with fluorescent lights that brightened the already white and bare walls. The sign on the door read "Interrogation Room." I guessed this was my opportunity to tell them what had happened, though I didn't plan to say much at all. I was starting to realize that truth had no place in the real world, and I wasn't interested in participating in more lies.

The officer who'd gotten me from school extended his hand to indicate I should sit. I chose the closest of the four chairs to the door and stared down at the white-laminate table to await what was next. The chair was noticeably hard and rigid, like the face of the officer, who whispered with another man outside the door. I presumed he was being apprised of the situation. I would have appreciated being given the same courtesy, since whatever they think they knew was probably some skewed version of the truth, having been concocted and relayed by Mom and Ron. It was certainly suited to protect their reputations, which didn't bode well for mine.

So, my body tensed when this other man came in and sat across from me. He was of medium build with a belly overhanging the waistline of his poop-colored pants, much like Jim's. He had a dark mustache and a sparse amount of hair outlining the bald spot on his head. I guessed he was in his forties. However, the arm hair coming out from the cuffs of his white button-up shirt was gray, so maybe he was older. Either way, I suspected he'd been a cop for some time.

The way he looked directly into my eyes, as if assessing me or intimidating me into telling the truth, or both, made me uncomfortable. So, I averted mine. I hoped he didn't think that was a sign of guilt. I was just nervous, which I hoped he considered reasonable considering the situation.

"So, Dana," he said as he quickly reviewed some papers from a file he held, "it seems there was an incident at your house last night?" He raised his brows when he looked to me for an answer.

I nodded.

"Do you want to tell me about it?" he asked.

I shook my head. Then I averted my eyes and gulped.

"Well, unfortunately, you're going to have to tell us something. Because we need to know what happened in order to figure this all out," he said, leaning back in his chair. My cynical mind saw his casual move as a way to trick me into relaxing too. I wouldn't fall for it, though. I remained quiet and kept my eyes down.

I wasn't trying to be difficult; I just didn't know what to say. Should I tell the truth? Would he believe me? I mean, I had the purple hand marks on my neck and multiple other bruises and scratches as evidence of the assault. However, Mom and Ron had told people that I'd self-inflicted wounds in the past, even though I'd never done such a thing. Unsure of whether they'd used that same excuse now, I hesitated to offer up what I'd previously thought would be evidence to support my case.

"Dana?" the man prodded.

I met his stare to acknowledge him. I still wasn't sure what to do, though. My only reference to police interrogations was whatever I'd seen on TV shows and in movies. In all those instances, the person being interrogated had had the right to an attorney. So, why hadn't I been given the right to an attorney? Was it because I was a minor? Were kids not allowed legal representation? I didn't know what my rights were because I'd never gotten into trouble with the law before. I wasn't even sure I *was* in trouble. If anything, Mom and Ron should be behind bars for everything they'd done to me over the years!

"You gotta help me out, kid," the man said with an impatient sigh.

My shoulders heaved as I took a deep breath. Then, with upturned brows pleading for patience, I whispered, "I'm not sure what you want to know."

He put his hands behind his head and leaned back further. "Let me help you out, then," he said. "Let's start with what you were doing before you attacked your parents last night."

"That's not at all what happened," I insisted in a knee-jerk reaction. "Because if that's what this is about, it's a lie!"

"Well, then, what *did* happen, Dana?" he asked, leaning forward on the table.

"Mom and her husband attacked *me!*" I asserted with furrowed brows. "I admit I used bad language with them, but *they* came after *me!* Not the other way around!" My eyes filled with tears as I told the man how I'd been pinned down and straddled and repeatedly slapped for simply asking Mom why she didn't care about me.

I couldn't tell if the man believed me because his face never changed. He just quietly wrote some notes on his papers. So, I stopped before telling him about the strangling, on the off chance I might inadvertently implicate myself instead of them.

The man put his pen into the pocket of his shirt and reclined again, this time laying his hands on his protruding gut. He twiddled his fingers, as if trying to determine what to do next. I could have heard a pin drop in the silent tension.

"You sure you're telling me everything?" the man finally said. "Telling me the truth?"

"Yes!" I said, a little too snarky.

"So, that's your story and you're sticking to it?" he asked. I couldn't tell whether he was being facetious or serious because his poker face never changed.

"It's not a story. It's the truth!"

"So, you didn't attack your parents while they slept last night?"

"What? No!" I shrieked. "They weren't even sleeping! They were watching TV like they do every night. It was Mom and Ron who came after me!"

"Hmm," the man sounded, sitting straight up. "Well, we've got two different versions of the same event. So, I guess we're going to have to wait and see what Child Services says before we can determine what *really* happened."

Child Services? I thought as my eyes widened. Then I realized their involvement was a good thing. Maybe they'd find reason to take me away, so I could finally be free of Mom and Ron once and for all!

Taking his file in his hand, the man stood to leave. "You want some water or a Coke or anything while we figure this all out?"

"A Coke," I muttered, dropping my head. I stared at my fumbling fingers while the door clicked closed and locked. This may not have been jail, but it sure felt like I'd been convicted of a crime I hadn't committed, left to await my unfair sentence.

After the Coke, a small snack, and a trip to the restroom where I'd had to endure the humiliation of an officer waiting outside the door for me, I was led to another interrogation room. Through the large window of it, I saw Mom and Ron sitting at the table inside.

Their sorrowful expressions reminded me of the characters Rooster and Lily in the movie *Annie*, when they'd posed themselves as Annie's distraught biological parents who were eager to reclaim their precious daughter. I tried not to roll my eyes at the farce of the facade.

My guard was up, anyway. With the officer who'd brought me to the station standing against the wall, and the half-bald man who'd questioned me sitting in a chair just inside the door, I felt like an inmate attending my sentencing.

"Have a seat," Baldie said, indicating the empty chair next to him. I did as I was told. I didn't want to be anywhere near Mom and Ron, anyway. I kept my head down to avoid eye contact with them altogether.

"Thank you so much for finding her," Ron said like a loving father would. "We've been so worried about her since she took off last night."

What a fucking liar!

"I'm sure," the officer responded, buying Ron's bullshit. "Unfortunately, we did have to involve the Department of Child and Family Services, since there was a claim of abuse in your home. They did an initial investigation, which involved speaking with some of your neighbors for character references. They spoke to a couple of your employees too."

"Oh!" Ron said, glancing at Mom. I was glad to see him sweat a little. She looked unfazed, though, staring down at her lap.

"Everyone seems to think very highly of you. Certainly incapable of what your daughter described," the man reported. "So, I'm not sure what went on in your house last night. There's obviously tension between you two and your daughter. But there doesn't appear to be reason to pursue this any further. She's been found. So, you can go home."

"I'm not going with them," I whispered to the mustached man, keeping my head down.

"What?" he asked, leaning towards me to hear better.

"I will *not* go back to that house," I repeated just a little louder.

The man met my stare then sighed as he looked back at Rooster and Lily. Being just a few feet away, they'd obviously heard me.

"It seems she doesn't want to go home with you," the bald man told them. "Is there any place you might allow her to stay until things cool off?"

There was a moment of silence as everyone thought about what to do with me. I kept my head down but averted my eyes between the cop, the man in the suit, and Mom and Ron, waiting for someone to decide a fate other than going home.

"Well, we've talked about it already," Ron started, looking at Mom for agreement, though it seemed to be more of a show than his really wanting her permission to proceed. "We are willing to place her in the care of my wife's uncle in Chicago."

I knew the uncle they spoke of. He was my grandma's youngest brother, who had five daughters of his own. The two oldest were my age, so I'd spent many nights over there as a kid. I'd have been fine there, except that I didn't trust that the family wouldn't be influenced to relinquish me back to Mom and Ron. Plus, my uncle lived on the south side of Chicago, and I wanted to remain close to Liam and my friends.

"I won't go there," I whispered to the man next to me.

"If you don't go there, Dana, and you won't go home either, then the only option is to send you to a juvenile facility. Is that what you want?" the man asked me.

I shook my head. Mom and Ron could just as easily send me to stay with my grandma and Great-Gram, or—dare I suggest—my dad. They just wouldn't, because they knew their control over me would be overridden.

"Considering Dana's erratic behavior," Ron intervened, "it's probably best if she stays somewhere that can provide her with the help she needs."

What the fuck was that supposed to mean? The only "help" I needed was to get the fuck out of their house! If he was referring to mental help, as I assumed, he should reconsider who actually needed the psychotherapy.

"The closest facility would be the one over by the hospital. They have a very good program there, and an entire floor and staff dedicated to teenagers with mental health issues. Perhaps check with your insurance first, and if they agree to cover her stay there, we'll transfer her."

I looked at the man in a panic. He was kidding, right? I wasn't crazy. I didn't have mental health issues. The only issue I had was being mind fucked and physically abused by the two people who were supposed to love and care for me. Now he was being tricked by them too, like they tricked everyone into believing they were these honest and perfect fucking people they weren't.

"We looked into that already, just in case it was necessary," Ron said, "and the insurance will cover it."

I shouldn't have been surprised that they'd already had a plan in place. I had to credit them for thinking of everything. I supposed I should have been grateful, too, that this option allowed me to stay nearby, whereas carting me off to a boarding school in Europe would have been much more traumatic given geography alone. Still, I resented the fact that their lies superseded the truth, and that they were essentially getting away with getting rid of me.

So, I stared at Mom very intently, willing her to face me with her farce. Her head remained in a mournful droop, though, evading accountability as usual, while Ron proceeded to make the arrangements. I held my stare, watching Mom put a tissue on her nose for effect. Then, without a word or a glance from either, Ron put his arm around Mom, pretending to console his grief-stricken wife as he led her out of the station. It was all very convincing, like they'd just been told I was dead.

"What Have I Done to Deserve This"

Expressing the anger and frustration I felt about the fate I'd been left to suffer would serve no purpose where I was, nor where I was going. So, I held it all inside as I was led out to a squad car with an officer on either side of me.

I looked up at the sky, noticing how brightly the stars glittered in the darkness. I'd made a point of taking in the sight of them whenever the pom squad marched onto the football field to perform our halftime routine with the band. The stars were clearly visible before the Friday night lights took over. I wondered if anyone would notice that I was missing from my rightful spot on that football field tonight.

I guessed that it was past dinnertime but not quite bedtime, based on the minimal traffic on the surrounding streets. I'd lost track of time in the station, which seemed odd considering how preoccupied I usually was with it, always having to get to a rehearsal or practice.

I'd miss talking to Liam before going to sleep tonight. He'd probably been calling my private phone line, wondering where I was and what was happening. I wished I could tell him all that had transpired. I'd tell him I loved him, that I was scared, and that I didn't know how long I'd be locked up or what would become of me after I got out. I needed to know he'd be waiting for me, too, so I had something to look forward to.

When the squad car pulled into the local hospital complex about ten minutes later, I was slightly soothed to see I wasn't too far from home. We were in the same town as my school, Liam, and some of my friends, though I didn't expect a place like this allow visitors, particularly those who were underage.

Too exhausted to think beyond the present anyway, I was just glad to be allowed to stay somewhere I could sleep without worry of Mom and Ron's retaliation for the embarrassment this scandal had likely caused them.

The two officers retrieved me from the back seat and walked on either side of me towards a four-story building. One placed his hand on my shoulder as a sort of leash until we were granted access through the securely locked main entrance door. One officer waited with me in the dimly lit lobby while the other spoke with the lady at the front desk. No one else seemed to be around except for the uniformed man standing at the elevator on the left.

I suspected he was a security guard by the way he was dressed. He didn't say a word when I was passed off to him. He simply put his hand on my shoulder like the officers had then swiped the ID card hanging from his neck over the metal panel near the elevator button. It beeped and a green light came on, then the doors opened for us to step inside. Once the doors closed us in, he swiped his card again and pressed a button for the third floor. Then he crossed his arms while the elevator went up. The serious expression he wore warned me not to speak even polite courtesies to him. So, I just watched the lighted numbers above the door until the elevator stopped at three.

When the doors reopened, I was met with two smiling aides wearing nurse scrubs who were obviously expecting me. Without a word, they took me by my elbows and gently led me past a reception desk and down a hallway to the left. I was scared at first, feeling like I was being treated like some insane person who needed to be put in a straitjacket before hurting myself or someone else. I looked over my shoulder to see where the security man was, in case I needed to call for help. I caught a slight glimpse of him, where he remained unmoved in the elevator, just before the doors closed.

In a small but well-lit room that seemed more like it should be a janitor's closet, one female aide took a small plastic bin from a metal shelving unit, which was the only item occupying the space.

"You can take off your clothing, as well as your socks and shoes and any jewelry or hair accessories you may be wearing, and put them in this bin," one aide ordered, pointing to the bin the other held out.

I did as I was told while they waited stone-faced and silent. Feeling overexposed in just my bra and panties, I folded my arms over my chest and lowered my head.

"You can leave your panties on," one aide said as she covered my front with an open hospital gown. I took the hint and removed my bra, careful to hide my bare breasts from view. She helped my arms through the holes then and tied the gown in the back.

"Thank you," I said, risking the basic communication. She nodded and then opened the door.

With an aide on each elbow again, I was led further down the hall. It was so quiet I could hear the buzz of the fluorescent lights caged in metal above us. They reflected off the white walls and gray doors, giving an impression of sterility. However, I presumed the plain color choices were meant to reduce or prevent stimulation of the deranged minds resting behind all these closed doors.

I wondered about the other teenagers here. Did they really have mental disabilities that disallowed them from participating in normal society? Or had they been cast away here like me because someone hadn't wanted to deal with their truth? Most of the doors had some sort of access panel to slide a card or enter a code, so I feared the high security was necessary for some seriously psychotic residents, which didn't help my nerves.

Almost at the end of the hallway, the aides unlocked a door, flipped the lights on, and led me in. The door automatically engaging its lock behind us reverberated more like the clink of a jail cell. I turned to see that there was an access panel on the inside of the door as well.

"Sorry to wake you, sweetie, but we've got to tuck in your new roommate," one aide announced. Movement in the messed bed against the opposite wall caught my attention.

An auburn-haired girl with a fair complexion like mine rubbed her eyes with her fists as she rolled over to face us. Her hair was curly too but short like a boy's. When she removed her fists from her eyes and leaned her head on her elbow to assess me, I realized she looked exactly like the character Blanche from the TV sitcom *The Golden Girls*, except much younger.

"So, what's *your* name?" she asked with a forwardness I hadn't expected.

"Dana," I said shyly, looking to the aide next to me as if seeking permission to speak. She didn't say anything. Neither did the other, who was pulling back the white sheets and thin blanket on the only other bed in the room.

"Well, nice to meet you, Dana," the girl said as I was guided into the twin bed. "I'm Rosa."

Her rolled "R" told me she was Hispanic too. I'd never seen her around, though, so I didn't think she attended my high school.

"Nice to meet you too, Rosa," I said as one of the aides pulled the sheet and blanket over me.

The other disappeared into the bathroom I'd seen when we'd entered the room. She emerged with a Dixie cup full of water, which she handed to me with a couple of pills.

I didn't like taking anything unless I knew exactly what it was. So, I looked at her with a raised brow.

"It's okay. It's just something to help you sleep," she said to doubly reassure and prod me.

I looked at her warily. I didn't think I needed anything to help me sleep. However, I worried that any resistance would be perceived as refusal to cooperate. Anyway, I couldn't imagine they'd give me anything that would harm me. Right? So, although I was hesitant, I took the two pills and swallowed them with water. I guess I needed to get a good night's sleep before facing the unknown of the next day, anyway.

"Good girl," the aide said. Then she turned to Rosa and warned, "Don't keep this one up. She needs to get some sleep before meeting with the doctor tomorrow."

"Yeah, yeah," Rosa responded. Then the lights went out, and the door clicked shut.

Although it was dark, I lied there with my eyes open. There was just a little bit of moonlight coming in through the window above Rosa's bed. I wished I had been given the bed by the window so I could look out at the stars. I'd always found comfort and perspective in how miniscule my problems really were in the scheme of the universe.

"So, what's your deal, Miss Dana?" Rosa asked. I cracked up at her bluntness and looked over at her shadowy figure.

"What do you want to know?" I asked.

"Start by giving me the lowdown on why you're here, girl!"

I liked her fun and outgoing personality. I could use a friend here, anyway. So, I told her what had happened the night before and then at the police station today.

"Damn," she responded when I was finished. "That's some crazy shit."

I chuckled at her directness again. I definitely liked this girl.

"Yeah. But what about you, Rosa? What did you do to get yourself locked up here?" I asked.

"Well, my friend pissed me off, so I stabbed her," Rosa said with a bluntness I took as joking.

She didn't laugh, though. "You're kidding, right?"

"Nope," Rosa said without hesitation. "I did what I did, Miss Dana. I don't regret it either."

I couldn't believe her. She was too nice to have done such a horrific thing. There had to be some reason why, like self-defense. "Come on, Rosa. For real."

"I'm telling you the truth," she asserted. "We were twelve. Hanging out like we usually did. And she crossed a line with me. So, I stabbed her."

The matter-of-fact tone she used to relay this horrible act mismatched the severity of it, so I was still having trouble believing her. More so, I worried about it being true. "What happened to your friend, then? I mean, was she taken to the hospital? Did her parents file charges against you?"

"She's dead," Rosa said with a nonchalance that disturbed me even more.

Unless she was a really convincing prankster, she seemed to be telling the truth.

"I'm a minor, though," Rosa continued while wild thoughts about her smothering me with a pillow as I slept raced through my worried mind. "So, instead of sending me to juvey, the attorney got me an insanity deal so I could be sent here instead. To rehabilitate or something."

My body stiffened. I could barely breathe, let alone respond. What was there to say, anyway? *Please don't kill me while I'm here?* How the hell would that sound to a killer? And the aides had just given me something to help me sleep! How was I supposed to sleep when I was locked in a room with a murderer?

"So, you've been here for how long?" I asked, treading lightly to determine where she was in the supposed rehabilitation process. I mean, if she was truly able to heal from whatever had pushed her to commit such a heinous act, then she deserved a second chance like anyone else. Right?

"It's been a couple years," she said nonchalantly.

A couple years? I couldn't stay here for two years! Could they even hold me that long, against my will? Even after I was legally an adult? If I weren't so drowsy, I would have felt every bit of the panic my mind was trying to negotiate!

"You're probably getting tired, huh?" Rosa asked.

"Yeah," I said regretfully.

"It's those pills they gave you. They give 'em to everyone on their first night," she told me.

"Really?"

"Yeah, so you don't freak out," she said.

"Oh." I guessed that was smart. I couldn't imagine anyone acclimating to a mental hospital right off the bat. Unless they really were crazy.

"You better get some sleep, anyway. Tomorrow's gonna be another long one for you. Takes everyone a couple days to get used to this place."

I didn't need the additional worries to ruminate about all night. Despite the pills I'd been made to take, I wasn't planning on sleeping. Not after she'd said she'd shanked her friend.

Then I wondered if this had been Mom and Ron's plan all along—get rid of me by locking me in this place, where there was the possibility that I'd be shanked by an inmate, just like in prison. It would be the perfect situation for them to kill me without getting their hands dirty.

That sounded paranoid, though, so I noted that I shouldn't mention that to anyone here. I didn't need to sound any crazier than I was already thought to be, especially when I needed to get out of here as soon as I could.

I rolled over on my side then, facing Rosa's bed to keep an eye on her. The feeling of my back against the wall was no more comfortable than lying flat on this cheap mattress. I suddenly missed my bed, with the plush pink comforter and fluffy pillows. I was missing the stuffed white cat Liam had given me too. I'd clutched it while I slept every night since, a reminder that he was always with me.

He wasn't here now, though, and I missed him terribly. I wished we had just run away together, somewhere far where no one would find us.

Then I wouldn't be here, in a room with a killer who actually seemed really nice, fighting the heaviness of my eyelids to avoid sleep.

Before I knew it, though, my eyes opened to sunlight.

"Crazy Train"

"**R**ise and shine, girls!" I heard a female voice say as she knocked on the door. Then I heard her repeat the same as she knocked on every door down the hallway. I guessed she was our alarm clock.

I squinted at the bright light coming in through the window. Then I looked around, confused at first, then remembering where I was.

"Morning, girl!" Rosa said, instantly perky as she sat up and stretched her arms over her head. "How'd you sleep?"

"I don't even remember falling asleep!" I said, rubbing my eyes.

"That's them drugs they give you. Knock you out!" she said with a nod and raised brows. It was almost disturbing that she knew that. I mean, I liked her, but after what she'd said she'd done, I didn't trust her. Not with my life, at least.

A female aide came in then. "You being nice to the new girl, Rosa?"

"Yes, ma'am," Rosa said with high-pitched innocence and a sarcastic smile that cracked me up.

"Why don't you go take a shower, then, while I get this one checked out," the aide told her, referring to me.

Rosa got up and grabbed some clothes from a drawer. I noticed she was wearing a T-shirt and fleece shorts, and I wondered if I would be allowed to wear something other than the hospital gown they'd provided.

"Have fun!" she said in a singsong voice, making a silly cross-eyed face at me as she passed behind the aide. I couldn't help but snicker.

"How are you feeling?" the aide asked as she took my blood pressure.

"Okay, I guess," I said with a shrug.

After she'd taken my temperature and listened to my heartbeat, she gave me a small bag.

"There's a toothbrush, toothpaste, soap . . . Think you'll need anything else?"

"Um, yeah," I said with a cringe. "Is there any way I could get some maxi pads?"

"Of course!" the aide responded. "Light? Heavy?"

"Heavy," I replied, though I hadn't bled through the one I'd put on at the police station the evening before. I figured it was better to have more protection as opposed to less, to avoid embarrassing myself in front of whomever I'd encounter here.

"Okay. Anything else?"

"Any chance I can make a quick phone call?"

The aide shook her head. "Sorry, but no. Only certain patients are allowed telephone rights. You'll have to talk to the doctor about that when you see him," she said.

"When will that be?" I asked, hoping to get a hold of Liam soon, even if just to tell him where I was.

She cringed. "I'm just in charge of getting you up and going. Someone will let you know after breakfast," she said. "I'll be right back with those pads for you. And then once Rosa is done, you can have your turn in the shower."

"Okay," I said as I sat slumped on the bed.

I looked out the high window above Rosa's bed, thinking how it was probably a cool October Saturday for most. If I weren't here, I'd be getting ready for pom practice. I might have been on the phone with Liam, too, making plans to go to a movie or something that night. I wondered what Liam was doing instead, and if he'd been up all night worrying about where I had disappeared to. Then I thought about how long I'd be here. Homecoming was at the end of the month, and I didn't want to miss going to the dance with my babe.

The aide returned with my feminine products just as Rosa came out of the bathroom.

"Your turn!" Rosa said as she threw her dirty clothes next to her bed. "I'll see you on the outside!" she said as she left.

"Rosa!" the aide admonished, scolding the reference to prison. She was right, though; this place was highly secure and highly regimented from what little I'd seen so far.

The aide held open the door to the bathroom for me then followed me in. I thought she was just there to show me whatever she thought I needed to know, but she stood against the wall instead.

"I've got to stay in here with you," she said, responding to my wide-eyed horror. "To supervise. That's the rule."

"Supervise what?" I wondered.

"It's my job to make sure you don't try to hurt yourself, or anyone else for that matter," she said. We were the only two there, though. Had she been referencing herself?

I sighed. I didn't want to seem difficult by protesting, but I didn't feel comfortable addressing my female issues with a witness. So, I just stood there, dumbfounded as to how to handle this.

"I'll turn away to give you a little bit of privacy," she offered. "But don't try any funny stuff, okay?"

"I won't," I said, shaking my head.

"All right," she said, eyeing me sternly before turning towards the wall.

I turned on the shower and removed the hospital gown then, thinking about what might have happened to have this rule in effect at all. I wasn't that girl, though. Hopefully, in time, my actions would prove that. Because honestly, I had a hard time pooping, and the last thing I needed was someone watching me while I struggled and strained for however long it took me to go!

After brushing my teeth and replacing the pad in my panties, the aide led me back out in the towel I'd wrapped around myself. She went into a drawer near Rosa's bed and pulled out a plain gray T-shirt and sweatpants.

"You'll have to wear these until your mother brings you some clothes from home," she said.

"Okay," I said, glad I didn't have to go through the day with the ass of my granny panties hanging out.

After that, I was ushered to a common area, where I scanned the place and people from the doorway.

The room was just as plain as any other area I'd already seen, except that it was much larger and had an entire wall of windows on one side.

The windows overlooked the parking lots between all the buildings in the medical complex. It wasn't much to look at, but I appreciated the way the natural sunlight brightened the room. I hated fluorescent lights and the way they caused color spots in my already questionable vision.

There was a long table against the wall to the left where random breakfast items were available to eat, from donuts to those mini cereal boxes I'd always begged Mom to buy. Corn Flakes seemed to taste better when provided in a personal container. There was water and orange juice too but no coffee that I could see from where I stood.

Further to the left, there was wooden entertainment center that looked like it had been donated from someone's 1980s living room. An older twenty-inch TV sat within the largest opening of it, with a VCR and some VHS tapes in their covers stacked above.

The room was otherwise open, with small tables for four taking up half the space. There were a dozen teenagers there, ranging from thirteen to seventeen. Most were girls and sat with a companion. The few boys there opted to go it alone, hunching over bowls of cereal at tables strewn with multiples of opened mini boxes.

One of the boys looked up just then. "Dana?"

Surprised that anyone here knew my name, I narrowed my eyes at him, trying to recall where I knew the vaguely familiar face from. Then it hit me. "Oh my god! Tristan?" I asked to confirm.

"Yeah," he nodded and smiled, as glad as I was to encounter a friendly classmate in the most unexpected of places.

I rushed over, smiling as he stood to greet me with a hug we'd have never exchanged anywhere else. We were in the same grade and knew some of the same people but had no connection otherwise.

"The whole school is talking about you! You just disappeared, like, what, a month ago?" I asked as we sat.

"Yeah," he said with a long sigh.

"Well, what happened? Have you been in *here* the whole time?"

"Sure have," he nodded. "My drunk-ass mother stuck me in here."

"For what?" From what little I knew of Tristan, he was a straight arrow—good student, athlete, never got in trouble. Like me.

"She was totally out of control drunk one night and threatening to harm herself. So, we got into it. Just yelling at first, but then it got physical, and she called the cops and told them I was assaulting her."

"But you weren't, were you?"

"No! I was trying to stop her from hurting *herself* and possibly me. Next thing I know, I'm locked up in here!"

"Geez," I said, wondering if this was how people with money reprimanded their children. Wouldn't it have been easier to just ground us for the weekend?

"What about you?" Tristan asked. "You're the last person I ever thought I'd see in a place like this."

I nodded, having been able to say the same. "Yeah, well, similar story. My parents aren't drunks, though. They're just assholes who beat me up and then lied to the cops."

"So, the cops didn't believe you either, huh?"

I shook my head and huffed. "Nope. They believed my parents, that I ran away and have mental problems. The cops were going to send me back home with them, but I refused, so now I'm stuck here too."

"That's whack!"

"You're telling me!" I affirmed. "But I gotta get outta here. I can't stay here."

"Good luck with *that*," Tristan said.

"Why?" I asked, almost afraid to know.

Tristan scanned the room. "If your parents have good insurance, you'll be staying here a *while*."

That's not what I wanted to hear.

"How long is 'a while'?" I asked, recalling Rosa's couple-year stint, which didn't seem to be coming to an end anytime soon.

"Depending on the doctor's assessment and diagnosis, about thirty days from what I've seen."

"I can't stay here thirty days!" I said, suddenly worried I would be. Then I reminded myself that Ron was too cheap to have insurance that good. Whether getting rid of me was worth the out-of-pocket expense, however, was an entirely different consideration I couldn't gauge.

Just then, a loud clang rang through the room. Everyone turned to see an overweight African-American girl holding a chair midair. *Did she just bang that chair against the window?* I wondered. She couldn't have. The window didn't show the slightest sign of having been affected.

As if answering my unvoiced thoughts, the girl clenched her teeth and used every bit of her strength to propel that chair into the window for what I assumed to be a second time. The thunderous sound of the metal chair hitting whatever material the unshattered window was made of made me put my hands over my ears. Still, I heard the girl grunt with every forceful thrust as she repeatedly attempted to shatter what looked like glass.

I cringed at the sounds. And at her failure too. Was this place that insufferable that she had been willing to jump from the third floor to the blacktop parking lot below? Or was she so mentally disturbed that this was a normal occurrence for her? Either way, I was overwhelmed with worry about what would become of *me* if I remained here too long.

Some men in scrubs rushed in and stuck a needle in her arm. The girl immediately calmed to the extent that it took multiple staff members to keep her steady. "No, no, no," she said over and over as they practically dragged her out. I covered my mouth with my hand, horrified at the scene.

"Listen to me," my classmate whispered, leaning in closer. I followed suit. "Your best bet is to just cooperate. Whatever they ask, you do. Whatever they say to you in your private counseling sessions—which they'll involve your parents in, by the way—just agree with. Tell everyone everything they want to hear, don't do anything that'll cause concern, and you'll get outta here sooner than if you don't. But for right now, go get a tray from the breakfast table. They're always watching and always taking notes, so you gotta act as normal as you can."

I did as he said. But it was hard to act "normal" when I was locked in a loony bin that was bound to drive me every bit of the crazy I'd been accused of.

"Don't Leave Me This Way"

A s Tristan had forewarned, I was retrieved by an aide immediately after breakfast to consult with the staff psychiatrist.

In his private office down the hall, which was equivalent in every way to the closet-sized room where I'd changed into the hospital gown the night before, I sat slumped in a metal chair, looking down at the floor. My mother was there, sitting against the adjacent wall, wearing her usual stone-cold expression. She looked blankly at the psychiatrist, a middle-aged man wearing a long white lab coat, who sat across from me, forming a perfect triangle between the three of us.

With a foot crossed onto his knee, he leaned back in his chair, twirling a pen in his fingers like a baton. "Thanks for joining us today, Dana," the psychiatrist said. He peered at me over the top of his gold-rimmed eyeglasses. I nodded once in response despite not having a choice.

Without removing his stare, he asked, "Do you know why you're here?"

I tried not to convey any attitude when I sighed, but this was sounding a lot like the start of the same conversation I'd had with the psychiatrist in the emergency room, when my mother had taken me to be tested for drugs. "Yes," I said, remembering to cooperate.

"Can you tell us, then? Just so we're all on the same page?"

I really didn't want to. I was afraid to say anything that would get me in any more trouble than I was already in. Recalling the character Carol Anne saying "less is more" in the movie *Poltergeist III*, I followed the advice (despite it being meant for makeup) for the sake of compliance. "Yeah. I'm here because I refused to go home from the police station last night."

"And you were at the police station because . . ."

I glanced at my mother, who averted her eyes. "Because I ran out of the house after a fight with my mother."

"That's a good start, Dana," the psychiatrist said, spinning his pen between both sets of fingers now. "So, our mission today is to assess whether you are cognizant of your behavior and to discuss your rehabilitation, with the end goal of you leaving here emotionally and physically able to lead a positive and productive life."

That sounded like a lot of doctor mumbo jumbo for him having to decide whether I was crazy. I'd do whatever was necessary, though, to get out of here as soon as possible, even if that meant going home with Mom. I looked over at Her Highness now. She remained as emotionally and physically unmoved as usual.

"Before I proceed, I want to make sure there was no way your husband could join us?" the doctor asked my mother.

"No," she said glumly, then she explained, "We run a small business, so one of us has to be there to oversee our employees."

In other words, Ron didn't give a flying fuck about me. Or he cared more about controlling others. Either way, he was a dick.

"Understandable," the doctor murmured. "This won't take long, anyway. You obviously know what's going on, Dana, so I'll take a safe guess that you're not delusional. Your mother says you're only on a painkiller right now, which I guess you haven't taken since being in police custody yesterday?" He looked at me with raised brows, wanting acknowledgment.

"That's correct," I said then glared at my mother with pressed lips. She just couldn't stop herself from trying to make me out to be a drug addict. Too bad I wasn't foaming at the mouth and seizing. If we weren't here, I might have, just as a sick joke. Remembering where I was, however, and who I was talking to, I defended, "They were prescribed to me by a doctor, after a medical procedure I had a couple weeks ago."

The psychiatrist wrote something on his paper, then asked, "What did you have done exactly?"

I hesitated. Then I gulped. "A D&C," I finally mumbled, shamefully bowing my head. D&Cs were performed for various gynecological issues, however, so he couldn't assume I'd had an abortion, nor would I volunteer that. I was surprised my mother didn't do it for me.

"Okay," he said without judgment, relieving me of the trauma of having to share any details about the abominable event. "Assuming you are otherwise as physically healthy as you seem to be, how would you describe your emotional health?"

"As far as what?" I asked for clarification.

"Well, what would you say your mood is for the most part? Do you feel happy more than sad? Sad more than happy? Angry at any time?"

Remaining calm, despite whatever my mother might have already suggested before I came in, I answered truthfully. "My mood depends on who I'm with and what's going on, just as it would with anyone." I shrugged.

"Can you be more specific?" the doctor asked.

"Well, when I'm with my friends, having fun, I am happy. If I'm at home with my mother, I am usually more tense. And—"

"Let's delve more into that, Dana," the doctor said, cutting me off. "Why do you feel tense around your mother?"

Thinking it was obvious by how silent and sullen she'd been, I said, "I don't know. We just don't see eye to eye on most things, I guess."

"Would you agree with that?" the psychiatrist asked my mother.

"Yes," she said shortly, offering nothing more.

"What about your relationship with your father?" he asked me next.

"Which one?" I blurted. "My stepfather, who we live with? Or my real dad?"

Raising his shoulders, he said, "Both, I suppose."

"Well, honestly, I don't care much for my stepfather. He's not very nice to me. I get along great with my real dad, though, except we don't talk anymore because my mother doesn't like him," I said frankly. My mother glared at me for my commentary.

"Do you have any input on that?" the psychiatrist asked my mother.

"No," she said. "Dana has always been opposed to my marriage, so it is true that she doesn't get along with my husband, even though he legally adopted her and provides for her in every way a father should." I didn't miss the side-eye she shot me for being ungrateful for Ron's supposed benefaction.

"Hmm," the doctor said, considering my mother's perspective. "Many children oppose whomever their parents choose to be with, if not the other biological parent. That certainly isn't a typical reason for any type of emotional or mental breakdown, however."

I appreciated his defense, though that had nothing to do with why I didn't like Ron. I didn't like Ron because he was an asshole.

"Of course," my mother said, as if pretending to agree would liken the doctor to favor her.

Putting his file on the desk, the doctor sighed and leaned forward onto his elbows.

"Here's what I think, Dana," he said matter-of-factly. "I think you are probably struggling like a lot of teenagers do, trying to figure out who you are and how you fit into this world, but I do not think you have any diagnosable mental disorders."

Although I could argue the point of a lazy and inadequate attempt to even make that determination, I perked up at the benefit of it being the first step towards my release.

"So," the doctor continued, directing his next comments to my mother, "I'm going to leave it up to you as far as how you want to proceed. I can release her now. You can take her home and work out whatever problems you have within your family dynamic. Or Dana can remain here, giving you all time to think about things without getting in each other's way, until you're ready to reintroduce her into the home."

I stared at my mother, hoping and praying she'd agree to take me. I mean, it had to be more embarrassing for them to tell people I was here as opposed to just letting me come home. I'd stay in my room. I wouldn't tell anyone what had really happened. No one would know except us. Unless Mom and Ron wanted people to think I was crazy, to perpetuate the narrative they'd already created about me.

The psychiatrist looked at Mom with the same raised brows I did, expectantly awaiting an answer that would determine my short-term fate.

"Um," my mother sounded. I sat upright and slid to the edge of my seat. *Please take me home! Please!* I willed her to say. "I think it's best if she remains here."

I couldn't believe my mother had betrayed me again. Had she not heard the doctor say there was nothing wrong with me? Or did she really not want me home to disrupt the new family she'd made with Ron and Jonathan?

"Very well," the psychiatrist said as he stood. My mother stood too, probably anxious to abandon me there. "I'll walk you out, then. And Dana, it was a pleasure. We'll reconvene another day."

He opened the door to escort my mother out. I looked up at him with worried eyes and an open mouth that hadn't yet had the chance to ask for those telephone rights I was told he determined.

"Dana?" the aide who'd brought me said from just outside the door. I looked up at her, dumbfounded as to what had just happened. "It's time to go back to your room."

I gulped, released the breath I'd been holding, then stood up and walked out, feeling like I'd lost . . . well, everything.

Back in the room, the aide pointed to a small bag on my bed. "Your mother dropped these off for you," she said cheerfully.

I looked at her, searching for something in her expression that felt some sense of the desperation and defeat I felt inside. She had no clue, though. Her fresh face and pulled-back hair made her look like someone who'd come from a supportive family who'd loved her as they should. Her dad probably opened doors for her mother and had taken her to daddy-daughter dances. He'd probably told her he was proud of her for how smart she was. Coming from that background, she seemed clueless to the fact that some of us hadn't had that same life experience.

"You okay?" she asked, distracting me out of my head.

"Yeah, I'm sorry," I said. "There's just a lot to take in here."

"It gets better," she said. "Just give it time."

That's exactly what I didn't want to do. She wasn't the one to argue with about that, though. So, I turned my attention to the bag.

I rummaged through, recognizing the plain-colored elastic-waist sweatpants and shorts and the few baggy T-shirts from pom camp. They weren't what I would have chosen from my closet, but I guessed I should have been glad that my mother hadn't sent preppy pastel polos from the Gap to wear with the straight-legged white jeans she was always trying to dress me in. I swore she wanted everyone to think we were country-club types who went sailing on the weekends.

Sensing my disappointment, the aide said, "I know it's not stylish stuff like what you're probably used to wearing, but we have some rules we have to abide by here."

"About clothes?"

"Yeah. We can't permit anything with any logos or printing on them. They might offend or trigger another patient. You're not allowed to wear anything with strings either, including shoes with shoelaces."

"That's weird," I commented.

The aide smirked. "Our job is to make sure everyone is safe here. So . . ."

Had someone tried to strangle themselves? Or someone else? I immediately thought of Rosa and realized it was a good rule to have, just in case.

After putting my clothes in an empty dresser drawer, I was led back to the community room, where everyone was free to do whatever they wished. Some read books, while others watched the fuzzy TV. Some played board games and one sat alone, rocking back and forth and moaning. The African-American girl had not rejoined the group, so I wondered what had become of her.

Regardless, I huddled with Tristan, telling him about my session. We talked about the rules, debating whether the jeans he wore should be allowed. He informed me of all the other restrictions too, like how we weren't allowed sharp objects, including pens or pencils. That disappointed me, since I'd hoped to ask for some paper and a pen to journal.

We spent the rest of that Saturday joking and talking and gossiping about kids we both knew from school. Tristan had gone to the same grade school as Liam and lived near to him too, so I told Tristan about how worried I was that Liam didn't know where I was.

"If I get outta here before you do, which I'm pretty sure I will, I promise I'll tell Liam you're here and that you're okay," Tristan said.

"Would you? I mean, I hope I'm not in here long, but . . ."

"I know," he said. Then we both dropped our heads, mourning our similar situations.

"Tell him I love him and miss him, okay?" I asked, despite it being weird. I had no other way to get the message to Liam, though.

"I will," Tristan nodded.

"Thank you," I said. Then I vowed the same to him, with regard to his friend group.

After an okay dinner of some mystery meat and mashed potatoes, the aides announced that we were having a movie night. I was excited for the treat until I saw Kristy McNichol on the nineteen-inch screen. I had nothing against the actress, but I'd seen *The Old Man* before. It had been the most boring and terrible entertainment nobody should ever have to suffer through once, and I suspected I was the only human on earth who'd now done it twice.

So, I was only too glad to go to bed afterward. I was exhausted from the nothing and everything that had occurred that day, anyway. The sleeping pills provided were a welcome wizard who sent me to Oz once again, making me forget about the possibility that Rosa might one night turn on me while in my vulnerable state.

The next morning, after repeating the shower routine with Rosa in our room, wherein I learned that I would be able to use the bathroom alone once I had been determined trustworthy, I returned to the community room for breakfast. Tristan wasn't there.

Presuming he'd been taken for some evaluation, or maybe even just sick, I went about the day, unconcerned. When he was still missing at dinnertime, however, I assumed he'd been released. I was glad for him but sad for me. Misery did selfishly love company, particularly in situations like this.

"Just Remember I Love You"

After eating breakfast with Rosa and another girl on Monday, I was led to the end of the long hallway to the "classroom." The aide who served as our teacher gave me a written assessment to complete, to determine what level of curriculum to assign me going forward. She was so impressed with my score that she asked me to help her with some of the other kids' lessons. I tried my best, but some were so drugged up they had no idea what was going on.

Rosa was receptive, though. She was so glad that I was able to help her understand some of her schoolwork better than the teacher had been able to that she bragged to everyone that her roommate was "the smart one."

"Yeah, that's *my* girl," she'd say, as if staking claim to me in some way. I was glad that she respected me. The praise built up my self-esteem in a way I'd rarely felt before.

In short time, my dutiful cooperation earned me a favorable reputation among the floor staff. They gave me a little more leniency, like being trusted in the bathroom alone and relieved of the obligation to take those sleeping pills at night. In fact, I wasn't even made to see the psychiatrist like all the other kids did, nor was I prescribed any medications to stabilize my mood like they all were.

So, one day, I decided I deserved a perk the doctor hadn't authorized. I boldly walked up to the reception desk where the same heavy-set lady sat day after day.

"What can I do for you, Dana?" she asked with a pink-lipped smile. Her thick golden locks curled under at her shoulders, matching the bangs that dangled above her thin brows.

"I'd like to make a phone call, please," I said, knowing full well that I wasn't permitted to make calls, not even to my mother.

"Of course, dear," the lady said with a smile. "Let me just make sure you're on today's list."

With a tilted head and a smile, I said, "I wouldn't have asked you if I wasn't, would I?"

She looked at me with discernment, making me nervous as to what the punishment would be if I were caught lying. I tried to act cool, though, politely smiling as I patiently awaited her determination.

"You're right, honey," she said, putting her paper down. "You go right ahead and make that call."

"Thank you!" I said cheerfully as I took the quarter she offered and went to the pay phone on the wall across from where she sat.

I felt bad for tricking her, but I was more anxious to call Liam since I'd been isolated in this place without warning. I was sure Liam was worried about me, especially if Tristan had indeed informed him where I was. Anyway, I wanted to hear his voice. We'd never gone a day without talking.

Liam's phone rang endlessly on the other end, dispiriting and disappointing my eager heart. I guessed I'd expected him to be sitting in his bedroom, pining for me or devising a plan to bust me out.

Eventually, his answering machine picked up. "It's Liam. You know what to do!" The sound of his recorded voice was a consolation prize I hadn't thought to appreciate until now.

At the sound of the beep, I spoke lowly and quickly to get everything in. "It's me, Baby Blue! The police took me from school, and then my parents ended up putting me in that mental health place by the hospital. I'm not allowed . . ." I stopped and glanced over my shoulder to make sure I hadn't just incriminated myself, then resumed, "I don't know when I'll be able to see you or talk to you again, but I wanted you to know where I was and that I miss you and I love you and that we probably won't be able to go to the Homecoming dance together, but I'll be dancing with you in my dreams. I think I might be here for, like, thirty days. I don't know. I'll do everything I can to get outta here as soon as I can, though. I love you so much. Don't forget me! Okay, bye!"

I hung up the phone then turned to the lady at the desk and smiled appreciatively. She returned the kindness. Having proven not to be a danger to myself or anyone else, I had been allowed the freedom of opting to be in mine and Rosa's room alone. So, I went there to lay in bed and think instead of returning to the community room.

Staring out the window over Rosa's bed at the poofy clouds in the blue sky, I thought about how I'd never be lying around like this at home. I was relaxed here. I was doing better than I could have ever expected actually, aside from the loneliness. It had been better when Tristan was here. I liked Rosa enough, but I missed poms and dancing to music videos with Kelly and visiting Great-Gram on Sunday afternoons. I missed my little brother too, and I wondered if he'd even noticed I wasn't there anymore. The only company I had here was that of whatever aides were on duty, whom I'd begun to confide in and chat with about everything from clothes to boys to TV shows to family—anything that reminded me of the normal life I'd taken for granted.

So, I was thrilled when I was told I had a visitor one afternoon. I hadn't thought I was allowed any, and I was curious to know who'd made the effort to get through the proverbial red tape to see me. I couldn't imagine they'd have allowed Liam, Kelly, or Miranda in, especially since they were minors. Maybe my Great-Gram or grandma insisted my mother bring them to see me. That would have been a treat, minus my mother.

When the aide who'd retrieved me opened the door to the private room where my visitor was waiting, I inhaled sharply. It's like I'd manifested my short, curly-haired chemistry teacher, from the tight black curls on top of his head to the thick-lensed glasses perched atop his big nose. He chuckled at my reaction. Then I ran the few feet into his embrace, practically plowing him over before squeezing him as if holding on to the only remnant of the life I'd known before.

"It's good to see you too!" Mr. Fogel said with another chuckle.

I stepped back and smiled as I looked him up and down. I needed to make sure he was real, that he was indeed standing before me and that I wasn't imagining he was there. From his usual athletic shorts, which revealed his hairy but muscular calves, to the heather-gray T-shirt that left one to guess whether his bulk was made of muscle or fat, my favorite Jewish scientist never looked better.

"I'm so glad to—" I started but got choked up. I gulped and exhaled to compose myself. "I'm just so happy to see . . . well, anyone! How did you even get in here?"

He sat in one of the metal chairs. I did the same. "I might have told them you had a mandatory science project that had to be completed to prevent you from failing the class," he said with a cringe.

"Do I?" I asked, suddenly concerned about my grade. I glanced at the small microscope he had set up on the metal desk.

"No. They'd only let me in under certain conditions, though. So, I brought this stuff to make it look like I was telling the truth. I don't want to get either of us in trouble," he admitted.

"Um, it might be a little too late for that," I joked, scrolling my eyes around the place to reference where I was.

Mr. Fogel dropped his head to laugh and then looked back up. "Really, though. How are you?"

I sighed and said, "I'm okay, I guess. I mean, I'm probably better off here than at home, though I'm not sure exactly how much you know about that."

"I heard you'd been taken by the police, and that Child Services came in to look at your records. The administration told us teachers you'd be indefinitely absent. But then I heard some kids talking about you being here—"

"Yeah!" I cut him off. "There was another kid from school here—Tristan. He promised he'd let Liam and a couple of my other friends know where I was if he got out before me."

"Well, he must have, though I didn't believe what I'd heard," Mr. Fogel said. "Not at first. Then when I was able to confirm it, I called and acted like it was urgent for you to complete this lab work for class. I'd have been here sooner, but I had to wait for the doctor to approve the visit."

"So, no one told you why I was taken by the police?" I asked.

"Something about you and your parents getting into a fight?" Mr. Fogel responded.

"Well, it's a little more complicated than that. But since you made the effort to come see me, I guess I owe you the truth about what happened," I said, though I worried of what he'd think of me after I told him about the abortion.

336

"I've got all the time in the world," Mr. Fogel said, slouching back in his chair with his hands behind his head. So, over the next forty-five minutes, I revealed everything.

Mr. Fogel listened to every word, nodding at times, cringing at others. He never interrupted. He didn't judge. He didn't lecture or advise. He didn't make me feel like there was something wrong with me or that I'd done anything wrong. That silent support made me feel heard and seen in a way I'd only felt with Great-Gram and my dad before. It also helped me accept the mistakes that I'd made without feeling ashamed for having made them.

Leaning forward with his elbows on his knees, Mr. Fogel shook his head. "I don't know what to say, Dana. You've been through so much."

"There's nothing to say. It is what it is."

"So, what happens after this? Are they sending you back home? Or . . ."

"That seems to be the plan," I said with disappointment. "I mean, where else would I go?"

"Well, what if . . ." Mr. Fogel started.

"What if what?" I asked eagerly, straightening up in my chair. If I had another option, I needed to know what it was!

"I don't want to cross a line or anything," he hesitated.

"Why? What are you thinking?"

"Well, I wonder if my wife and I can take you. Like maybe we can become your legal guardians, and you can come live with us until you're eighteen," he suggested. "Assuming you'd be comfortable with that."

I was astonished that he would even consider the thought when no one else had cared enough about my well-being to try to help me out of my situation. No one else seemed to even believe me. He did, though. Even after learning the truth about what I'd done, he didn't relinquish his support or treat me any differently than he had before. That meant I was safe with him, that I could trust him. So, yes, I would absolutely go with him and his wife, if he and his wife were willing and able.

"That would be awesome! But how would we go about that? Doesn't my mom need to legally sign me away or something?"

"I'm sure there are a lot of legal hoops to jump through to make that happen, especially since we're not related to you."

"Well, I would be grateful if you guys could try. I swear I wouldn't be a problem," I vowed. Then I promised myself not to get my hopes up. If my mother had to sign off on any part of that process, it was as good as null. She'd never allow an option that granted me better than what little she was willing to give.

"I know you wouldn't," Mr. Fogel said. "We wouldn't allow you to have boys over, anyway," he joked. I laughed too. It was a fair jab. "Now, let's get to this science project. I have to have something to show for my visit with you!"

Although science was one of my least favorite subjects, I'd never been so glad to look at whatever he'd put in that petri dish. When we were done, I helped Mr. Fogel pack up and thanked him for coming at all.

On the last Saturday of October, the aides treated us to cookies and cupcakes that were decorated with orange and green frosting for Halloween. I'd indulged since there wasn't anyone here to impress with my figure. Not that anyone could see my body underneath my baggy clothes. Anyway, I was still carrying some baby weight that passed as bloat, despite limiting my consumption of the potatoes and breads and other quick carbohydrates that seemed to be the center of every meal served here. So, I didn't think a few sugary treats would make any difference.

The aides had allowed Rosa and I to put Chicago's pop music station on the stereo. We danced and sang to every song. When I heard the introductory drum riff of Marky Mark and the Funky Bunch's "Good Vibrations," I squealed with excitement.

"This is the song the pom squad performed at the Homecoming pep rally!" I announced to whoever cared.

"Do it, Dana!" Rosa encouraged. So, I performed the routine as I recalled it. Rosa led the others to give me a standing ovation afterward. I curtsied to the maniacal monarchy in jest, having felt the most joy I'd felt since Fogel's visit.

The African-American girl, who'd been looking out the window, disrupted the good vibes by grunting and hitting it with her thick sausage of a finger.

"Oh no," Rosa groaned. The rest of us exchanged worried looks. Then Rosa went over to calm the girl before she had a breakdown that would end this little party for all of us. But then she waved us over, saying, "Someone's out in the parking lot looking up here, you guys!"

We all rushed over and looked out, except for the one boy who rocked in the corner all the time.

The bright lights inside prevented us from seeing much more than shadows outside. So, I had to squint to make out the outline of a van. There was something familiar about it that I couldn't match to a memory. A shadowy figure stood beside it, facing the building directly. The bend of elbows looked like this person had their hands in their pockets. I presumed it was a male because of the short haircut, which appeared curly on top. The broad shoulders, muscular biceps, and one jutted hip—the right hip, specifically—gave away his identity.

"Liam?" I whispered with hope and excitement. The butterflies I'd felt when he'd first kissed me fluttered in my heart.

"Is that the guy you're always talking about?" Rosa asked.

"Yeah," I said breathlessly, putting my hand on the window as if I could reach out and touch the shadow of him.

"Well, this is romantic as hell," Rosa remarked.

"Who is he?" another kid asked from behind us. I didn't answer, though. I was entranced by the boy who'd stolen my heart over a year before.

"All right, everyone," an aide said as she attempted to disband the group. "Break it up. There's nothing to see." Everyone returned to the stereo and snacks, but I remained at the window staring at Liam. "Dana," she nudged.

"But we would've been at the Homecoming dance together right now if I wasn't . . ."

"One minute," she said with sternness that didn't match her understanding eyes. She held her pointer finger up as a show to the other aides.

Without acknowledging her accommodation, I mouthed "I love you" through the glass. Then I put my hand on my heart, which was bursting and breaking all at once. Liam took his hand out of his pocket and put it on his heart too. I couldn't see his lips in the dark, but I was sure he'd mouthed "I love you" back. Then he put his hand on his mouth and extended it outward. I reached up to catch the kiss he just sent up to me before blowing one back. He waved once more before getting back in the van. Stray tears streamed down my cheek, simultaneously happy and sad, as the van drove away.

I'd been so worried that history had repeated itself with me, probably because my mother assumed it would and had almost convinced me of the same. Liam proved we were different, though, that the love between us was true and real. Whether pregnant or not, crazy or sane, locked up or free, he'd proved he'd never abandon me. He was with me, even if we weren't together, and he'd still be there when I got out, which I hoped would be soon.

"Mama, I'm Coming Home"

"**Y**ou're being released today, Dana!" an aide told me when I entered the common area for breakfast roughly a week later.

"I am?" I asked, unsure of how to feel. I'd gotten so used to this place, and so separated from the life I'd lived before it, that it hadn't even occurred to me that I'd ever be able to leave. Part of me wasn't even sure I wanted to.

Then I wondered how long I had been there. Had it been the thirty days Tristan had guessed? We had no calendars to refer to for any concept of time. I could pinpoint certain days based on whatever stood out about them, like the day Mr. Fogel had visited and the Saturday night Liam had come to see me. Aside from that, every day had just woven right into the next for what had seemed like forever.

"Yes!" she said excitedly. "The doctor signed your release papers! We're just waiting for your mother to come pick you up!"

"Oh," I smiled weakly, having hoped Mr. Fogel had been able to come through with his offer to stay with him and his wife instead. The disappointment I suddenly felt had been exactly the reason I hadn't wanted to get my hopes up about it.

Of course, I was thrilled that I'd finally be reunited with Liam. I longed to feel his arms around me, to feel safe and protected again. Yet, the whole reason for being in the mental health facility was to avoid having to go home to abusive parents. So, as far as I was concerned, I'd just wasted whatever time just to end up where I hadn't wanted to be in the first place.

The thought of facing my mother and Ron made me uneasy too. Aside from the one session I'd had with my mother that day after being admitted, I hadn't seen Ron since the police station. He'd probably enjoyed his vacation from me, but my return home would remind him of the embarrassment I'd caused them by having the police and DCFS investigate them for abuse. So, I expected consequences. I just hoped it would be a lesser sentence than what I'd served previously, since a second run-in with authorities wouldn't bode well for any of us.

Just after lunch, I was notified that my mother had arrived. Since she hadn't rushed to retrieve me earlier, I guessed she was about as thrilled to come get me as I was to go back home. So, I went to my room to collect my things with the same lack of urgency my mother had employed to make me feel like the usual inconvenience I was.

"I guess this is it, huh?" Rosa said glumly, as I packed the few pieces of clothing I'd been allowed to wear there.

I looked over at her, where she sat on her bed with slumped shoulders. I'd never seen her sad before. It made me wonder if she had remorse for what she'd done, because, really, she wasn't a bad person.

"I guess so," I muttered. "But hey, maybe your next roommate will be crazier, so you'll have better stories to tell the one after."

She barely laughed at my joke. But then she chided, "You really are boring, you know. I mean, pregnancy, abortion, and a brawl with your mother? That's nothing compared to—"

"You win!" I chuckled, cutting her off before she said anything to incriminate herself further. I didn't want to think of her that way, anyway. I couldn't defend what she'd done, but she didn't have to be defined by one terrible mistake, assuming she wouldn't do anything like that again.

"You're all right. You know that?" she said, looking up at me with a half-assed grin.

"You are too," I said, smiling back. I'd grown pretty fond of the stabbing senorita. So much so that I'd actually miss her. She'd made this place somewhat bearable. "Now, stay outta trouble, would ya?" I said as I picked up my bag to leave.

"You too, girl! Otherwise, you might end up right back here!" she joked. I shook my head and smiled at her once more before leaving our room. I knew I'd never see Rosa again. I just hoped she really was better than what she'd done.

The staff on duty, who'd come to know and like me during my time there, gathered in the hall as I made my way from my room to the elevator. They all smiled and wished me well. Some called out encouragements meant to cheer me, but none did. As much as I hadn't wanted to be there, it was hard to leave a place where I was liked by all, treated well, fed regularly, and made to feel good about myself. Most importantly, however, I'd felt safe. Beyond that elevator, there were no guarantees.

The lady at the reception desk was the last to say goodbye before sending me with the uniformed security person to the key-operated elevator. Once in, I turned around to see her and two other staff members smiling at me as the doors closed on that strangely memorable chapter of my life.

When the doors reopened on the main floor, I saw my mother. She stood with closed-mouth annoyance in the open area near the main entrance. I remained in the elevator, unwilling to step out to the unwelcome reception, until the security officer prodded me to step out.

As I walked towards my maker, I hoped she'd suddenly smile and throw her arms around me, relieved to be reunited with her firstborn. I wished for her to apologize for what had happened and to promise life would be better going forward. I don't know if I'd have forgiven her. However, any sign of wanting better for me and for all of us as a family was all I could ask.

Instead, my mother turned and walked to the exit without acknowledging me at all. She waited at the door silently while the security officer typed in a code to unlock it for us. Then she walked out to the car in the small parking lot, several feet ahead of me.

I stopped just outside the exit to breathe in the cool fall air. The last time I'd been outside was the night I'd been brought in. I closed my eyes as I lifted my chin to take in the little sunlight coming through the clouds. Then I inhaled deeply again, vowing to never take air for granted again. I thought for a moment about all the simple things people took for granted in life—like coffee and shoelaces, privacy and pencils—noting to myself to never go another day without appreciating all I had access to.

When I reopened my eyes, I saw my mother getting into the driver's seat of her silver sports car. I glanced back to see if the security officer just inside had witnessed the coldness with which my mother had received me.

He met my stare and then retreated, like every other person who'd recognized something concerning. I wondered how people could live with themselves, knowing another person was suffering but opting not to intervene.

I proceeded to the car, feeling much more like I was walking the doomed corridor of death row than I had when I'd arrived here. The grimace my mother gave me when I got into the passenger's seat made me want to bang on the doors of the loony bin and beg to be taken back in. I couldn't understand what it was about me that made me so reproachable when I tried so hard to be a daughter she could be proud of. She just refused to feel anything but apathy for me. So, as she pulled out of her parking spot and into the busy street that would take me back to the house where I'd never felt at home, I sat in the silent tension of her suffocating presence until I couldn't tolerate being ignored anymore.

"Instead of taking me home, could you just take me to school?" I said.

"School? After all *this*, you want to go to *school?*" my mother asked in disbelief.

Instead of arguing the point that I'd been through some crazy shit and that the last place I wanted to be was at the scene of the unspeakable crime of which I'd been the victim, I simply said, "Yes," followed by, "please." I'd learned how cooperation could get me much further than an attitude.

"Why? So you can go see that science teacher of yours?" she asked with pointed snark.

I hadn't even thought about the facility informing her about Mr. Fogel's visit. I didn't see why it was an issue to her, though. "He was just being nice, Mom. He wanted to make sure I did some required lab work for class," I said, offering the same story he'd said he'd used to see me.

Mom huffed and shook her head. "No. He's trying to have an inappropriate relationship with you. You're just so naive you don't see it," she accused. "If I find out he's talking to you outside of class, I'm going to report him to the school. He has no business using his position to—"

"He's not like that, Mom," I insisted, cutting her off.

"Do you realize that this whole incident is now part of your school record?" she said next, surprising me with the sudden change of subject.

I looked over at her warily. I wasn't sure how to respond because I wasn't sure what she was getting at by mentioning her obvious concern.

"So, when Jonathan starts school, his record will be tagged as a cautionary measure! Do you understand that? Do you understand what you've done?" she revealed and blamed all at once.

I folded in my lips and huffed out of my nose, refusing to take accountability for what she and Ron had done. They were responsible for whatever cautions the school took with me and Jonathan going forward, and rightfully so. Maybe then all of this trouble had been worth enduring after all, if it prevented further abuse and saved my little brother from the same.

There was nothing I could say to change my mother's delusions about her victimhood, though. So, I sat silent and still, eager to escape her and her car, temporarily and for good.

A few minutes later, I saw the familiar beige brick compound looming up ahead. She was taking me to school after all. I didn't understand the rare grace, but I didn't question it either.

I jumped out of the car the second she pulled up to the curb of the main entrance. "I'll catch a bus or walk home," I said. She pulled away without responding.

Turning to face the school, I was glad to be back. The parking lot to the right was full, but not a soul could be seen coming in or out of a car or building. So, I guessed classes were in session. It was probably better that way, making for a more peaceful transition back, like dipping my toes into the water before jumping in.

I went straight to the cafeteria upon entering, looking for any friend to share my liberation with but specifically wanting to find Liam. The mix of round and rectangular tables were sparsely filled with kids cramming for tests or hanging out with friends. Many of them looked up as I passed, staring as if seeing a ghost.

I ignored the looks and the whispers I could hear behind me. Rumors of what I'd done and where I'd been had probably been running rampant through the halls, becoming more exaggerated and wilder with each retelling but each version having some witness claiming it to be truth. I didn't owe anyone an explanation, though. It seemed more fun to let people believe what they would.

Assuming Liam was in class, I went to a common area near the main entrance to pass the time until the next bell. Miranda was there with another girl I'd seen her with before.

"Dana?" she asked with open-mouthed surprise.

I smiled and walked over to where she stood from her chair to greet me. I fell into her hug, relieved to have this long-awaited comfort.

"Where have you been?" she asked as she released me.

"Yeah, we heard the cops took you out of here in handcuffs and put you in jail!" the girl sitting with her said.

I shook my head and rolled my eyes. "It's a long story I'd rather not get into right now," I said with pleading eyes, "but I wasn't in jail."

"Where were you, then?" Miranda asked. "I tried calling your house, but your mom just said you were away. She wouldn't tell me where, though!"

The bell rang then, saving me from explanation. "I'll tell you all about it another time, okay? I wanna find Liam."

"He's probably with the potheads he's been hanging out with," she said as she gathered her books into her arms. "I have to get to class, anyway. But call me, okay?"

I nodded as she rushed off, thinking nothing of the remark she'd made. Liam did have a close friend with a shaggy mullet and penchant for weed, but we'd never partaken in that with him. Neither of us had ever smoked anything, for that matter, nor did we have any intention of doing so.

Standing on my tiptoes, I extended my neck, searching the hundreds of passersby for my love. Finding him in this corridor, of the dozens in the three levels and multiple sections of the building, was an ambitious feat. Plus, he had no way of knowing I'd been released, to know to come find me. So, when I spotted him coming up the hall towards me, I felt like the universe had conspired with whatever powers that be to reunite us.

When our eyes finally locked, I smiled. Liam's smile widened too, and he picked up his pace towards me. I expected him to start running with outstretched arms begging for me to run into them, like some slow-motion scene in a movie. Then, all of a sudden, he slowed to a cool strut and gave his friend a smug look over his shoulder. It was reminiscent of the scene in the movie *Grease* where Danny sees Sandy for the first time since their romantic summer fling but then treats her with dismissive indifference to prevent his friends from catching on to the connection they'd had. This wasn't a movie, though. It didn't resonate with the reality I'd known before either. This was starting to feel like a bad dream.

"Liam?" I asked when he eventually reached me, unfamiliar with this aloof persona he presented.

"That's me!" he said, looking side to side at his cousin and best friend who'd been walking about a foot behind him. They snickered.

"Why are you acting like this?" I begged, having expected eager affection for having missed me while I was away.

"Acting like what?" he said coolly, looking to his friend for a reaction again. His friend snort-laughed into his fist.

I was so hurt by this indifferent asshole that I started to panic that something had horribly changed. "Can we go talk somewhere? Just you and me?" I reached for his hand to remind him of my touch.

He shook it off and hollered, "Hey, does anyone see a *real* woman around here?" He looked all around, making an embarrassing spectacle of me. His cohorts laughed again.

I stared at Liam, wondering who he was and what he'd even meant by that. Because the Liam I knew—the boy who'd come to the parking lot of the mental facility that night of the Homecoming dance—wasn't the Liam standing before me.

The bell rang just then. "We gotta get to class," his friend said as he patted Liam's back. "We'll see you later."

Stunned by the shocking confusion of this whole scene, I remained silent while Liam watched his friends leisurely walk down the empty hallway, having no care about their lateness to their next class. Once they were out of sight, he threw his arms around me. He squeezed me tightly and buried his face in the crook of my neck.

Although I hadn't liked the show he'd put on for his friend and cousin, I returned the affection. I'd waited too long to feel his touch, his warmth, his strength, and his love to deny myself what I'd craved.

When he finally pulled back, he said, "I'm late for class, but wait for me? I'll meet up with you here afterward. Okay?"

"Of course," I said, nodding.

"Okay," he said. Then he kissed me on the forehead, looked me dead in the eyes, and said, "I love you."

"I love you too," I said, holding on to his hands too long. I didn't want to let them go, afraid he'd suddenly turn into that other version of himself if I did.

With a reassuring smile, he squeezed my hands once more before releasing them. I watched him walk down the hall, admiring how cute his bubble butt looked in his jeans. He glanced back and grinned. Embarrassed that he'd caught me, I averted my eyes shyly.

Still confused at that strange interaction, I turned back to the student lounge, hoping to find some quiet respite until Liam was out of class. A couple older girls from the pom squad were sitting nearby. "Hi," I said as I walked by.

"The same thing happened to me after I had *my* abortion," one told me.

I froze for a moment, stunned by her flippant confession. "*You* had an abortion?" I whispered back, clarifying what I'd heard.

"Yeah," she said, "and as soon as my guy told his friends and word got around, he became super cool for being the guy to get in my pants and get me pregnant. Like he was being exalted for his virility or something." She rolled her eyes at the other girl.

"I'm sorry you had to go through that," I said. "I don't think Liam would do that to me, though."

Or would he? I couldn't be so sure after how he'd just acted.

"Baby Blue"

L iam met back up with me after class that day. Under a big oak tree out on the huge front lawn of the school, he lifted my chin and kissed me like I'd thought he would when he first saw me. Then he held me like he'd never let me go. I never thought he would either, nor did I want him to.

Although I was sure I had pom practice, I hadn't officially reentered school. So, I gave myself a break, opting to walk home with Liam instead. Hand in hand, we smiled and joked, catching each other up but mostly talking about my experience in the cuckoo clink.

"Hello!" his mother called out in a cheery singsong after hearing the front door close behind us.

I halted in place, immediately nervous as to how she'd receive me. I'd been so caught up in my reunion with Liam that I hadn't considered how unwelcome I was there.

"It's okay, Dana," Liam assured, gently pulling on my hand. Then he responded, "It's me, Mom!"

"Not lifting weights today?" she asked as she emerged from the kitchen. I glanced at his biceps, wondering what she was talking about, but the way her smile dissipated at the sight of me was more noticeable. "Oh, I didn't know you were having company."

"She's been through a lot, Mom," Liam defended. I couldn't blame his mom for her reaction, though. It had been bold of us to even think she'd be okay with us coming into her house after everything that had happened.

With upturned brows pleading for the forgiveness my mouth was too scared to request itself, I stood there unmoved, waiting for permission to proceed.

After deep consideration, her eyes softened. "Keep the door open," she ordered, raising her brows for emphasis. Then she went back into the kitchen.

For the next couple of hours, we talked and listened to music. But I set out on the long walk home before Jim got there, to pointedly avoid him. It was hard to forget how eager he'd been to get rid of me in my most desperate hour of need.

As I turned onto my street, I saw the yellow glow of the kitchen light, which seemed brighter in the early dark of the fall evening. It's like life had gone on without me and was still going on as if I hadn't been released. I doubted that my mother had even wondered where I'd been since she'd dropped me at school, which made me even more sure that my so-called family wouldn't be any happier than I was about my return. So, I took a deep breath as I walked up the narrow concrete sidewalk to the door, hoping whatever awaited me inside was better than what I'd left the night I'd run away.

My mother and Ron were in the kitchen. I could hear Jonathan banging on his highchair tray and giggling. Although they momentarily paused their conversation when I closed the front door behind me, no one said hello or asked where I'd been, which meant they didn't care. So, I bypassed them and headed straight up to my room, thankful neither followed.

I hadn't been in my room since the night I'd been strangled, but it was clear *someone* had been. It looked like it had been ransacked. I suspected my mother to be the culprit. She was probably looking for more prescriptions drugs to pin on me or another justifiable reason to prevent my return.

My bedroom door had been removed too, so I couldn't close myself in for privacy. Annoyed at the offense, I picked up the phone to call Liam and complain, but there was no dial tone. I pushed the button on the base, thinking it might have gotten stuck. After multiple times, I realized there was no phone line at all anymore.

"That's right, Dana," I heard Ron say. I turned to see him standing outside my open doorway. "If you want to make a call, you can do it from our line." That meant using the phone in their bedroom or the kitchen.

I slumped down, feeling defeated, but then reminded myself this was nothing. After spending so much time without phone privileges and privacy already, these so-called punishments would be a cakewalk. So, I put the phone back on its receiver and yanked the cord from the wall. Then I spent the rest of the night cleaning up my room, reorganizing as I went. It was like giving myself a fresh start, a new beginning wherein I could put the past in the past, feeling stronger and more emboldened since I'd handled adversity like a champ.

I even moved my bed, positioning it, perpendicular to the door, providing a short wall I could hide behind to inhibit view from the hall. It was the only privacy I could ensure, as well as a way to prove to Ron that nothing he did would diminish my dignity. Then I kept to myself, waiting until everyone else had gone to bed to go down to the kitchen for food, just in case Ron decided to put some ridiculous restriction on my consumption too.

Back at school, I acclimated to classes as if I'd never been gone at all. Football season gave way to basketball season, so I was still very busy with pom practices and choreography sessions. It was my relationship with Liam that was hard to reconcile, which was strange since I thought it was the one thing I could rely on remaining exactly the same as it had always been.

And it was—sometimes. Liam was so tender and sweet and sensitive when we were alone. When he had an audience, however, he was aloof and cool, just like he'd been the day I was released. Either way, I didn't like the inconsistency. It precluded the safety I'd felt with him, which I hadn't experienced since my early years with Great-Gram. I stuck it out with him, though, because I loved him. I just wondered if he still loved me.

Liam was more concerned about lifting weights and hanging out with his friends than spending time with me at all anymore. Not to mention, he'd turned sixteen in mid-November and had a driver's license to go wherever he wanted now. It just seemed he went places he shouldn't, like a local bar that served alcohol to underage patrons. He never thought to invite me there with him. So, it was hard to hear him and his friends talk about the scantily dressed women and illegal drugs the members of the heavy metal bands who played there would do between sets. It didn't seem like Liam was thinking at all, really, which made me wonder what else he was doing that I didn't know about.

Despite the many ways Liam continued to show me where I rated in his life, I was excited when he agreed to a dinner date with me one night. I put on a simple flared black cotton dress he'd always liked on me, with black flats and a dressy leather coat. He picked me up in his mom's old beat-up van. It didn't matter what we drove in, though. Nor that he took me to IHOP. I was just glad to have him to myself for once.

Liam had been putting more effort into his appearance recently, wearing nicer jeans and more form-fitting T-shirts that exhibited his growing biceps. He had a different hairstyle now, more closely shaven at the sides, and he wore contact lenses now too. So, he was a sight for sore eyes while I rambled about teachers and classmates and whatever we were working on in poms.

He made no contribution to the conversation, though. I could sense his disinterest in the way he looked everywhere but at me, but I kept talking to prevent the awkward silence that would make me even more nervous about his strange behavior.

Before giving Liam the bill, the waitress asked, "Did you save room for dessert? We have apple pie," she enticed.

Since pom practices had toned me back up, I'd quickly responded, "Yes! Can I get it à la mode?"

"Sure thing!" she said. Then she turned to Liam and asked, "And you?"

"You don't need pie," Liam told me with a serious expression that indicated he wasn't joking.

Staring across the table, I fought the urge to cry as my sorrowful eyes begged to know why he would humiliate me like that when he knew how sensitive I was to Ron's comments about my body and consumption.

"Did you need a minute?" the waitress asked, not knowing what to do.

Neither did I. I loved Liam, but I loved pie too. Liam hadn't been making me very happy as of late, but that pie would make me feel better, even if just for now. So, although I didn't want to disappoint Liam with my decision or my body, I said, "No, but it looks like I'm the only one having pie."

Liam silently glowered while he watched me eat every delicious bit of it. But then he didn't hold my hand or the door on the way out.

"When Will I Be Loved"

The holidays weren't so bright that year. Liam was Jewish, so he celebrated Hannukah with his family, who excluded me despite having been happy to have me the year before. I was Catholic but had nothing to invite Liam to, since Mom had stopped taking me to church about the same time we'd stopped decorating our Christmas tree as a family, several years before.

I'd opted out of Ron's family Christmas too, claiming to be sick. I presumed Ron had told his family about my pregnancy and resulting stint in the loony bin, and I wasn't mentally strong enough to handle the jabs and pokes they liked to exchange at each other's expense. Mom didn't trust my excuse and fought me on it a bit but succumbed to leaving me home alone when I was still in my fuzzy pink robe and slippers when it was time for them to leave.

I spent the day in bed reading Charles Dickens' *A Tale of Two Cities* instead. My English literature professor had assigned us to read it over the holiday break. Although I had a hard time with Dickens' verbiage and style, I related to the injustice and glory of the same-aged character Lucie who discovered that her father had been unfairly imprisoned the entirety of her life. It made me miss my own dad. I wondered if he ever thought about me too.

Early that evening, my mother came through the front door with Jonathan. He toddled one direction while she set a small bag on the kitchen table, where I was eating a bowl of cereal for dinner.

"How was Christmas?" I asked her. She dreaded going to Ron's family events as much as I did, though you'd never know it by the way she tried so hard to fit in with them by dressing the way they did and using bigger words to try to sound college-educated like they were too.

Huffing before answering, she said, "It was awful. We had to rush Jonathan out."

"Why? Did something happen?" I asked, thinking something was wrong with my little brother.

My mother peeked around the corner to make sure Ron wasn't coming in the front door behind her before saying, "Well, Jonathan was jumping on their couch, when out of nowhere, we all heard Ron's brother-in-law scolding Jonathan—*harshly.*"

I raised my brows. "What did he say?"

"It's not so much what he said as much as what Ron's sister said when I went to grab Jonathan up." My mother's chest rose and fell as she inhaled through her nose. "She said, 'That kid needs a good beating with a hairbrush.'"

My mouth dropped open, recalling the many times Ron had hit *me* with a hairbrush when I was little. So, it wasn't the comment that bothered me so much as the appall my mother expressed that someone would even suggest doing the same to her precious son.

Ron walked in just then with an armful of brightly colored packaged toys and a scowl that silenced even our thoughts. As soon as he went back out, though, Mom picked right back up.

"Can you believe the nerve? I mean, Jonathan is only two! Yes, he has a lot of energy and gets a little wild. But for her to say he should be *beaten?*" Mom huffed and shook her head. "Not to mention the insinuation that I needed to be told how to parent my own child."

"Hmm," I sounded instead of pointing out how I wished she'd defended my honor when it had been me at the other end of an actual brush. Then again, this was the same woman who'd told me I didn't *deserve* a "Sweet Sixteen" party like all the other girls my age had had.

"Well, I guess it's a good thing you were there to protect Jonathan, then," I said with pointed snark intended to express my resentment towards her.

I supposed it was just as well that my brother had the "Hairbrush Hero" to save him from the inflictions I'd had to endure, because that relieved me of the duty and the guilt of leaving Jonathan when I left this house and this life in two years as planned.

Ron returned with another load of presents that had been bestowed on the chosen one, closing the door behind him this time. His angry face shut Mom up, and I shoveled a spoonful of cereal into my mouth, trying not to smirk at how happy everyone was with all the things they'd wished for.

"Don't Do Me Like That"

When classes resumed after the New Year of 1992, I found myself seeking Liam out every morning instead of finding him at my locker waiting for me. He was usually in the cafeteria, leaning back in a chair with one foot up on a table. His cousin and loser friend clung to every sarcastic remark or rude insult he hurled, encouraging him to be more of an ass every day. So, I guessed I should have been glad that he at least waited for me after pom practice once in a while for a quick romp in the back of his mom's van.

Thinking I could earn his heart back with a thoughtful gift, I presented Liam with two tickets to see the heavy metal band Skid Row, who were playing in Chicago on Valentine's Day. Like a puppy eager to receive affection that indicated it had pleased its owner, I waited for his reaction with high brows and a wide smile.

"Cool," he said. Then he handed one to his friend and said, "Wanna go?"

"Dude! Yes!" he said, clutching what was supposed to be my ticket into one of the fists he threw into the air like a champion. Unfortunately, that meant I was the loser now. Liam had no clue how heartbroken I had been then, nor on Valentine's night, which I spent crushed and alone, wondering where I'd gone wrong.

He'd attended a Guns N' Roses concert without me later that spring, knowing I'd wanted to go really bad too. Kelly and I ended up getting our own tickets, so we were there the same night. From where we sat in the nosebleed section, we saw Liam and his friends on the floor next to the stage, being showered by the sweat coming off Axel Rose as he thrashed his stringy blond hair towards them.

Then, by some miracle, we'd run into Liam and his friends during an intermission. But when I got on my tiptoes to give Liam a kiss, he leaned away from me to avoid the affection.

"You guys see anyone? Maybe a girl with bigger tits? A real woman who knows how to please a man?" he said, amusing his friends by craning his neck, pretending to search for someone other than me.

Instantly reduced to the same self-conscious doubt Ron had already instilled in me, I looked down at my fitted black top and noticed how deficient my B-cups were. Then I looked back up to Liam, who was chortling with his friends.

"Why are you doing this to me?" I asked, fully aware that this wasn't the time or place for this conversation. Still, I needed to know.

"Get outta here," he said, shoving my shoulder lightly with his hand before walking away. One of his friends glanced back and laughed as he elbowed Liam and nodded his head towards me. Liam looked back, and then he laughed at me too.

"Come on, Dana. Forget him," Kelly said. She'd had to grab my arm and pull me, though. If I didn't see the boy I loved walk away from me like this, I'd have never believed he would.

I tried to call him multiple times the next day, but I didn't want to talk to his answering machine. Still, I clung to the cordless receiver of the house phone, like I clung to the hope that all was not lost between me and my Baby Blue. When it rang, I scrambled to answer it.

"Hey," Liam said with an apathy I was becoming accustomed to.

"Hey! I was wondering what happened to you!" I overcompensated with too much enthusiasm, as if pretending would make things right between us. "Did you get caught up at work or something?"

"Not exactly," he replied. Then he went quiet.

After giving him ample time to elaborate, I trepidatiously asked, "What's going on?"

Still, he didn't say anything. Just as I was about to, he finally divulged, "Well, I ran into this girl from grade school. Remember that skinny one you met at the Turnabout dance?"

"Okay . . .?" I remembered her. She'd been in a few of my classes since.

"Yeah, so, she kinda came on to me," he said.

"What?" I was pissed. She knew damn well that Liam was with me.

"I think she's pretty ugly, and I don't like her or anything, but . . ."

"But what, Liam?" I asked, nervous about where this was going.

He sighed then said, "I was just curious to see how far I could get with her. So, we went back to her house and—"

"Oh my god," I gasped. "You didn't . . . did you?"

I gulped in the silence of his pause.

"No," he said.

"Oh, thank God," I said, releasing a long exhale.

"I mean, we were *about* to," he mumbled.

Instantaneously tense again, I felt like I couldn't breathe. So, I couldn't speak either.

"I just couldn't stand the smell," he snickered.

I don't know if the vulgarity of his comment repulsed me more than his betrayal, but I suddenly felt nauseated. It was like he'd stabbed me in the heart and then cut me in the gut just to make sure he'd finished me off.

"Why would you do that to me, Liam?" My voice quivered as I asked. I was on the verge of tears, though I wasn't sure he was worth shedding them for anymore.

"But I didn't!" he defended, as if he'd been unjustly deprived of some prize for his abstinence. "That's the thing! I love you. But I don't know if it's different with other girls if I don't try . . . you know?"

"No, Liam. I don't know," I asserted, "because *I* don't need to know what another boy feels like inside of me. I only want *you*. I only do that with *you!*"

"People change, I guess," Liam muttered. "Anyway, I just wanted to give you the respect of hearing it from me just in case it gets out. But I gotta go. I'll talk to you later."

"But—" I said before the dial tone cut me off.

Open-mouthed and alone, I sat there, stunned. I didn't understand who Liam had become in the short time I'd been away, nor why I wasn't enough for yet another person who'd said they loved me. All I knew for certain was that I couldn't trust Liam anymore—at least not around other girls.

So, when Liam got a summer job at the community pool, I was livid.

I never thought I'd be the jealous type. I hadn't had to be before. Yet, the thought of him gawking at girls in skimpy bikinis propelled my insecurities to straight-up outrage. So, I'd go to the pool to spy on him, to see who he was talking to and what he was doing when he didn't think I was around to witness. That would lead to endless arguments about his lack of respect and loyalty to me, which he'd proven not to have anymore. Apparently, I had no respect for myself either, because I knew I deserved better, but I was afraid to be alone.

Then, one early July afternoon, Liam called me at home.

"Hey!" I said, happy that he was initiating contact.

"What're you doing?" he asked in a glum tone.

"Nothing," I said. All my friends had jobs and driver's licenses, and cars to get to said jobs. My mother and Ron had told me I wasn't responsible enough to have a driver's license at sixteen. So, without a license or wheels, I had no job, nor much of a life. I spent most days in my room, bored out of my mind, unless I was at pom practice.

"Oh," Liam said.

"Why? You wanna do something?" I asked eagerly. "I can be ready in, like, fifteen minutes?"

"No, I have to work in a bit. I'm on the night swim shift," he said.

"That sucks," I replied, thinking I'd probably be stuck in my room again watching *Beetlejuice* for the millionth time. I practically played it on a loop.

"There's something I've been wanting to talk to you about for a while now, though," he said.

"What's that?" I asked.

A long exhale could be heard from the other end. Like he was preparing for something he didn't want to do. And that made me nervous.

"Liam?" I asked worriedly.

"I'm sorry," he said, making my heart race off the starting line without even knowing why.

"For what?" I asked, though I really didn't want to know.

"Neither of us has been happy in a really long time," he said dimly.

"No, Liam," I begged. "Please don't do this." I strained for a breath.

"I love you. I really do. But—"

"Don't, Liam!" I warned him again.

"I can't do this anymore, Dana," he finally revealed.

My lungs felt like they were closing up. I gulped and begged, "Please, Liam. We'll get back to where we were. I know—"

"I'm so sorry," he said, cutting me off. Then the dial tone told me that was it. I hadn't even had a chance to tell him I'd named our baby girl Faith.

I sat emotionless for a minute. I wanted to cry. I wanted to scream. I wanted to rage. I couldn't move, though. I was paralyzed, unable to move forward because I refused to forget the past.

Liam was my rock during rough times and my clown during the good. He always made me feel like everything was going to be okay, no matter what happened. I believed him because I could—at least before the baby. He'd followed through with every promise and never left my side when I'd needed him. So, what would I do now? What would I do without the one person who made me feel like I was worthy?

The phone rang just then. Thinking he'd realized his mistake, I answered right away.

"Liam?" I answered, anxious to renew the love we both knew we couldn't deny.

"No," the familiar voice said warily. It was one of Liam's friends, who we hung out with quite a bit.

"Oh, hi," I said, failing to disguise my disappointment.

"I'm sorry to bother you, but I, uh, heard, and . . . I just thought I should drop off some of the compact discs you let me borrow," he said.

"Oh," I said, sounding exactly as depressed as I felt.

"Yeah, so I'll drop them off on your doorstep sometime," he said. "And I guess I'll see you around?"

"Yeah, okay," I said, though I recognized those words as a soft landing for the hard reality of rejection.

Feeling like I'd just been abandoned in the middle of a dry, remote desert with no hope of survival, I broke down into mournful sobs. I thought Liam and I would be together forever. I thought nothing could tear us apart. I'd thought he was . . . someone it turned out he wasn't. Ironically, I didn't even know who I was anymore either, except alone and unwanted and apparently undeserving of anyone's love.

"Nothing Compares 2 U"

I stayed in my bedroom the rest of the summer, listening to love songs that made me wallow further into the depths of my despair. The only time I left was for pom camp. Although my heart wasn't in it, I was glad that Kelly had made the squad this year and was on the trip with me. Her outrageous sense of humor always cracked me up, but she was a good listener when I had a sudden longing for the boy who'd broken my heart.

On the second to last day of pom camp, the Universal Dance Association announced that they were having a nationwide contest to find the best dancers to perform in Paris, France, on New Year's Day. To be considered for this exciting opportunity, individuals would have to choreograph a dance to the song stipulated by the UDA and then perform their solos for the judges at the auditions, which were being held the next day.

"Oh my god! We have to audition, Kelly!" I told her on our walk back to the University of Wisconsin dorms which housed all of us "campers." I was already thinking up sequences of turns and kicks and pas de bourrées, obsessed more with the Eiffel Tower than with Liam now.

"I don't know," Kelly said. "I wouldn't want to miss Christmas with my family."

Kelly had a really nice family. I didn't have that problem, though. So, I stayed up later than usual that night, practicing different moves in the small floor space between the twin beds of our room while Kelly gave me suggestions and helpful critiques.

Then, the next afternoon, while I watched one girl after another perform the most perfect pirouettes and jumps and effect contortionist moves that made me feel like an amateur, I started to sweat. Like the clammy, panicky kind that makes you feel sticky and gross. I doubted my talent. I doubted whether I could even remember my routine at the level of anxiety I was feeling now. My tummy was aching too, like it always did when I was nervous. And then they called my name.

"Break a leg!" Kelly joked just before my squad cheered loudly for me. With reluctance and fear of such blatant exposition, I rose from the floor and climbed over multiple other squads until I was standing all by myself in the middle of a huge university gymnasium with thousands of eyes on me.

Judgment. Boredom. I couldn't overwhelm myself with trying to determine the energies coming off every onlooker. So, I closed my eyes, took a deep breath, and focused. When the music started, my body took over. Two minutes later, it was over.

"You did so good!" Kelly said in a hushed tone when I returned to my spot on the floor beside her.

"You think?" I asked.

"Yeah!" she said. Then we watched the other contestants perform while I caught my breath and relaxed my quick-paced heart.

Two hours later, I heard my name being called as one of the three girls on our squad who had been selected to represent America in the New Year's parade and performances in Paris.

I couldn't believe it! I wasn't nearly as good as half of the other dancers who'd competed. But someone had seen something in me, and that was all that mattered. So, I was going to Paris!

Wearing a wide grin, I went up to receive my ribbon, feeling a rare sense of pride and accomplishment. I wished I could call . . .

Liam had been my person for so long, it seemed strange not to share the news with him first. I called my mother instead, from a payphone at the entrance of the dormitory when we returned.

"A collect call from Dana . . ." the robotic voice told my mother.

When she accepted the call, she said, "What's up, Dane?"

"I won a contest at camp, Mom! I'm going to Paris to perform with a bunch of other girls from around the country in the 1993 New Year's Day parade there!" I said with an excitement I couldn't contain.

"Paris, France?" she asked to confirm.

"Yeah! Can you believe it?"

"How much is this going to cost?" she asked snidely.

Immediately deflated by her cynicism, I mumbled, "I don't know. I just thought—"

Another phone line started ringing at her office. "I gotta go, Dane. I'll see you when I pick you up at school tomorrow."

"Okay," I said as if I was. But the dial tone didn't let me finish.

Mom was in good spirits, smiling and taking my picture when I disembarked from the coach bus at the high school the next afternoon. Although I was glad to see her in good spirits, I was still a bit sour from how dismissive she'd been about my big news but waited until we got home to talk to her about it, thinking she might not have realized what a big deal it was. Jonathan was in the back seat, anyway, eager to tell me about the toy sword Mom had just bought him.

As soon as I walked into the kitchen, a piece of mail on top of the pile on the counter caught my eye. It was Jim's fat round face smiling on some patriotic-colored postcard. With his husky belly (full of food he didn't like to share) stuffed into a dark suit he apparently couldn't button the coat of, Jim held a baby that looked as dumbfounded as I looked now. Proclaiming Jim to be a "family man" who "loves children," the postcard pleaded for votes to make our town and our state "one people could be proud to raise their families in." I scoffed at the hypocrisy and tossed the propaganda away. Ron wouldn't miss it, anyway. He was a Republican.

"What was that?" my mother asked as she wrestled Jonathan into his highchair.

"Nothing," I said. "Can we talk about Paris?"

Ron walked in just then. "Hi, honey," he said to my mother. They exchanged a quick peck. I scrunched my nose, wondering when they'd started doing *that*.

"Dad!" Jonathan greeted with a high pitch, excitedly kicking the bottom of his chair with the heels of Nike high tops.

"Hey!" Ron said to Jonathan, throwing his hands up next to his exaggerated open-mouthed happy face. Then he went to the refrigerator instead of acknowledging me at all.

"So, Mom. About the Paris trip with the UDA . . ."

"Dana is talking about that trip she won," my mother told Ron as she quieted Jonathan with a snack.

"Your mother already told me they want us to pay for some part of that trip. So, it doesn't sound to me like you won anything," Ron said with arrogant gloat.

"But I did," I defended. "I had to choreograph and perform a solo routine in front of everyone!"

"And?" he asked.

"And I was picked to go to Paris," I said, missing what he wasn't understanding. "From what they said, we just have to pay a per-person fee to cover the hotel and airfare."

"Well, we're not paying for anything. So, I guess you're not going."

"Yes, I am!" I insisted like a five-year-old wanting her way. "Mom?"

"You heard him, Dane," she begged me to relent. "Don't start with us so soon. You just got back."

"I'm still going," I asserted.

"With what money?" Ron asked, passively reiterating that it wouldn't be with his.

"I have enough to not need yours!" I said, then I stomped up the stairs to my bedroom and—oh my god! I had a door again! So, I slammed it and pressed the lock button. Then I pulled open the top drawer of my dresser and pulled out the wad of cash I'd stuffed in an envelope underneath my bras and panties. I'd been saving for years. Whether from babysitting the neighbor kid to whatever Grandma put in a birthday card, I'd hoped to have enough to get me out of this hellhole when I turned eighteen. I was willing to use it for the Paris trip instead, though. I wouldn't miss the opportunity to go abroad. I needed something to look forward to, since there didn't seem to be anything left for me here.

"Hopelessly Devoted To You"

*T*he start of my last year of high school should have been a welcome distraction from the monotonous mayhem of home life, as well as the depression and self-loathing rounding out my existence. I had new classes to focus on, new teachers to brown-nose, and new responsibilities as a senior member and combined secretary and treasurer of the pom squad. I was almost too busy to notice Liam kissing that well-endowed exotic girl from science class in the hallways at school.

My good old friend Miranda suggested I get a job, arguing that it would get me out of the house when I would otherwise be bored and allow me to replenish the money I'd spent on the upcoming trip to Paris. It would also give me something to rely on to pay the bills when I moved out like I planned to in a year and a half, which was argument enough.

Since I still hadn't been allowed to get my driver's license, Miranda drove me to the mall where she had found work and helped me apply to nearly every place with a "Help Wanted" sign. The manager of the Sbarro pizza restaurant in the food court told me I could start right away. He was willing to work around my pom schedule, on whatever nights and weekends I was free. So, I agreed. I'd never had a job before, though, so I was really nervous to go in my first night.

My mother and Ron drove me, with Jonathan strapped in his car seat like we were going on a family road trip. They said they were doing some shopping in the mall, but then they showed up where I worked a little later. The manager didn't know they were my parents, though, and prodded me to serve them. I felt uneasy as I approached the two smiling at me from the other side of the counter, because I didn't trust them or their well-intentioned facade of support.

"How can I help you?" I said, robotically repeating what I'd been instructed to say.

"You're not going to say, 'hi'?" Ron reprehended. I was immediately embarrassed but felt better when I noticed my mother elbow him discreetly.

"We'll take two slices of sausage, Dane," she said. "And two Cokes."

"Make mine a diet," Ron threw in.

"Small, medium, or large?" I asked.

"Medium," my mother replied as she rummaged through her purse for cash. Ron stood next to her with the combined expression of amusement and condescension, apparently pleased that I was serving him. He was probably glad that I was doing something beneath my potential too.

Once their pizza was plated and their drinks set on their trays, I looked to my manager to cash them out. "No, you do it, Dana," he said, nodding toward the register. "This is a good opportunity for you to learn. While we're slow."

I looked at the cash register with foreboding. The manager had shown me how to use it, but I hadn't had to touch it yet, and I was afraid to look stupid in front of Ron. I looked back at the manager with pleading eyes, hoping he'd run the register for me. Instead, he nodded towards it again, prodding me to give it a shot.

"What, you don't know how to work the register?" Ron said with a chuckle, looking at my mother to laugh with him. I was glad she didn't. I could feel my cheeks becoming warm with the humiliation I was trying to stifle.

"Okay," I said to myself, sighing as I tried to recall what to do. I punched in their purchases, slowly and cautiously to avoid messing anything up. When it didn't total the bill like I thought it would, the manager had to come correct my error.

"She's like this at home too," Ron said to my manager, making me feel even less competent than I already did.

My manager did a quick double take. "Oh, you know her?" he asked Ron.

"Yeah, she's our daughter," Ron said, surprising me with the admission as my mother handed cash over the counter.

"Oh!" the manager said, smiling and nodding in his cultural form of respect. "Dana is doing very well, sir. We are happy to have her here."

Ron's "hmph" and side-eye as he walked away, leaving my mother to carry their tray of food and drinks, was the most efficient dismissal of multiple people accomplished with one simple act.

A week later, a new manager was assigned to our location. His name was Travis. He was of average height and weight, with blond hair that he wore in a 1970s feathered style. He had a thick mustache, reminiscent of Burt Reynolds' in *Smokey and the Bandit*. Travis's had overgrown his thin top lip, like the unmaintained shrubs of an abandoned old house. He was proud of it, though. He even referred to it as his "flavor saver," always following with some exaggerated story of sexual conquest. Then he'd smile widely to reveal a mouth of crooked and rotten teeth that hadn't been cared for in years.

He clearly thought he was God's gift to women, because he would stand behind the counter and catcall to female passersby with absolutely no respect or regard for whether they were with someone already. I watched him get phone numbers from some and then brag about what he was going to do to them when he got them alone. I was repulsed by his arrogance, which often showed in the way I'd scrunch my face.

"How old are *you*?" he asked me one weeknight. The mall was dead, so we were just standing there, watching no one go by.

"Sixteen," I said reluctantly, unsure of why he wanted to know.

"Mmm, jailbait," he said, licking his lips.

I groaned in disgust and shook my head. Then I looked away altogether.

"So, you've probably never . . ." He looked at the cook to laugh with him.

I glared at him and then rolled my eyes and huffed. I refused to respond to such tasteless comments, even to remind him that his conduct could be considered sexual harassment in the workplace.

"That's okay, Dana. I'll pop that cherry for ya."

He had no boundaries. I did, though, and I didn't feel comfortable with my boss speaking to me like that. "Please stop," I said.

"You won't ever say *that* to me," he responded with a snicker, "not after *I* break you in."

I looked away, wishing I could find another job. That's when I saw Liam.

Before I could think to duck, his eyes locked on to mine. I wanted to die. I looked so dopey in this green apron and red visor that I had to wear over an equally unflattering white button-up shirt and black twill pants. My eyes darted all around, desperate to find something to do so I could pretend I didn't see him or feel obligated to interact. I didn't want to look like any more of a weirdo than I already did, though, so I smiled nervously, offering a quick wave as he passed with his friend. Liam returned the courtesy.

"He knows a good piece of ass when he sees one, huh?" Travis said, intentionally loud enough for Liam to hear.

Liam turned back, seething with rage as he tightened his fists at his sides. Then he aggressed towards the counter, reached over the glass protecting the pizza pies, and grabbed Travis by the collar. My eyes widened with shock as he threatened, "Watch your fucking mouth around her. You understand me?"

I froze. On one hand, I was glad to know Liam still cared about me enough to defend my honor. Yet, this was my workplace, and Travis was my boss. As much as I hated working here now, I needed a good reference to get a job somewhere else, which I definitely planned to do after what had just happened.

As if completely oblivious to what was going on, Travis burst out laughing in Liam's face. His irreverence was like nothing I'd ever seen before.

"I'm not fucking joking!" Liam raged, shaking Travis's scrawny body back and forth with the enlarged biceps he'd gained from working out. I watched in open-mouthed horror as Travis laughed harder, despite his soft body being shaken like a rag doll.

"Gotcha, boss!" Travis said sarcastically, saluting him with one hand. Liam released him and shoved him backwards. Then he glared at Travis as he walked off, puffing out his chest to prove his strength and machismo.

I wanted to call out to Liam to come back, so I could tell him I still loved him too. Despite everything, I'd never stop. I wanted him to take me away from this place and away from Travis, who joked and laughed about the incident and at me the rest of the night and for days to come.

Most would just stop going to work. Unfortunately, Travis was the lesser of two evils between him and Ron. Plus, I really needed the money, which meant I needed the job, since I hadn't been able to find another that was as willing to provide such a flexible schedule.

As if the universe had heard my plea for help, the manager of a cosmetics company in the mall approached me while I was working that weekend. "What's a pretty girl like you doing here serving food?" she asked in a sexy Russian accent.

I shrugged. It was a better response than "nobody else wanted to hire me."

"Come talk to me when you have a few minutes, okay?" she said, smiling and winking as she walked away.

I nodded. Then I went to talk to her when I was on my break. She hired me immediately, as a sales consultant with her Merle Norman Cosmetics franchise location. I was really excited about the opportunity, since it was as close to working in the beauty industry as I could get at my age.

While closing the pizza place that evening, I approached Travis at his desk in the back office.

"Can I talk to you a second?" I asked, nervous about how to give the two-week's notice I'd been told was customary.

"Yeah, what's up?" Travis said without looking up.

I looked down at my fumbling fingers, unsure of what to say. "I kind of got offered another job. And I took it," I said. Then I cringed.

Travis looked at me then. "You're quitting?"

"Yes?" I said, cowering slightly.

He turned his chair to face me and leaned back with his hands behind his head. Apparently, I'd gotten his attention. "Where're you going?"

"The cosmetics place," I mumbled nervously.

"Oh! The one in this mall?"

"Yeah," I said. "I start there in two weeks."

"Okay," he said, nodding. Then he sat back up and returned to his work.

I stood there, stunned that Travis hadn't given me the hard time I'd expected. Then again, nothing about this interaction was typical of Travis, making me wonder which Travis was the real one—the womanizing jackass with the "flavor saver," or this serious and more normal personality?

"You need anything else?" Travis asked, looking up at me lingering.

"No. Sorry. I just . . ." I said, trailing off to avoid admitting I was psychoanalyzing him. I don't even know why I cared to understand his psyche. It was of no concern to me.

"Get outta here, then," he said. "Go home and enjoy whatever is left of the night."

"Okay," I said, though avoiding home was exactly why I was here.

Travis didn't know that, though. He didn't know how much I dreaded having to leave, that I waited outside the mall entrance in the dark night, never knowing whether it would be my mother or Ron picking me up.

The later it was, the greater the odds it was Ron, awaiting me like the Grim Reaper himself with his dark cloak and scythe to take me back to hell, where I suffered with the other whore who'd fallen from grace. Only now I didn't smell like a whore, like Ron had always accused. I smelled like pizza.

"Surrender"

I liked my new job selling cosmetics much more than working at the pizza place. Wearing dresses and nylons with heels made me feel better about myself. With my hair and makeup done, even I had to admit I looked okay. The only thing I missed was the free food—particularly the baked ziti and calzones, though pizza would always remain my favorite.

Travis passed by the cosmetics store too often to be coincidence. Sometimes, he'd just wave. Other times, he'd stop to say hello. Despite my initial repulsion, I entertained his visits because he didn't act like a pervert without an audience. So, when he asked me if I wanted to go to a movie with him, I agreed. It's not like I had any other suitors, anyway.

When he arrived at my house, I ran out before he could come to the door. I knew he'd just bought a new vehicle he was proud of—a base model Ford Taurus—but it wasn't the Jaguar Liam sometimes drove, nor the Corvette another boy had taken me out in. I wanted to spare Travis the insult of Ron's arrogant opinions about it and spare us both any interaction with Ron at all.

"Hey!" I said as I jumped into his passenger's seat.

"You don't want me to come in and meet your parents before we go?"

"Nope! Let's go!" I responded.

"Are you sure?" he asked, leaning forward as if prepared to get out of the car anyway. "Parents love me."

"I'm sure. But mine won't. They don't even love me. So, let's go. Seriously," I said, anxious to leave before Ron did come out to spy. Anyway, I was dying for a box of Raisinets.

Travis looked at me quizzically, attempting to process what I'd just flippantly shared.

"I mean it," I insisted. "Let's just go."

"Okay," he said with a singsong tone that told me he'd have preferred the opportunity to charm them. There was no time to catch him up on the complexity of my family dynamics. It would have been a waste of time, anyway, since I doubted he'd last long. I was just passing the time with him, though I wouldn't have minded if one of my friends leaked to Liam that I was dating an older man. This wasn't a date, though. Travis and I had established that when he'd asked me to the movie.

On the way to the theater, Travis mostly talked about his new vehicle. That led to talk about all of the vehicles Ron had owned, which segued into discussing our families and how we grew up.

I learned that Travis was twenty-one years old. He'd come from humble beginnings like I had. His family lived in a small town in Michigan, though he and his siblings had relocated to Illinois since. His mom had a daughter previous to her marriage to Travis's dad, but together they had Travis and his younger brother. Travis said he was close with his siblings and that his parents had just moved back from the Virgin Islands where they'd lived for the last handful of years. In fact, Travis's dad was living in his apartment with him and his roommate now while he looked for employment in Illinois so they could settle near their kids.

I liked that Travis was a normal guy who loved his family, and not the playboy he presented himself as at the pizza place. It reminded me of how Ron acted one way in public and differently at home, as well as how Liam had acted differently around his friends than he had when we were alone. I guessed all guys were like that, since I didn't know one who wasn't.

When we got to the theater, Travis got out of the car. I waited for him to come around and open my door. Date or not, I just presumed that's what men were supposed to do. When Travis didn't, I glanced back and saw him waiting for me at the back of the car. So, I got out myself, wondering if men from Michigan weren't taught proper manners, or if Travis thought he was excluded from the expectation of being a gentleman for some mysterious reason.

"One for *Honeymoon in Vegas*," Travis said to the kid behind the glass at the entrance.

"What about me?" I asked.

"This isn't a date," Travis responded.

"I know, but . . ." I started. Then I decided to save myself from further embarrassment. Regardless of whether Travis was pushing the point or really that uncouth, I didn't need the theater worker to witness me trying to convince Travis that I was worthy of the seven-dollar courtesy. So, I reached for a wad of bills out of my back pocket. "One for me as well, please."

Then we went inside where Travis ordered and paid for his own popcorn and drink, and I ordered and paid for my box of chocolate-covered raisins. We sat in our grimy seats just as the theater darkened and laughed at all the crazy situations Nicholas Cage's character negotiated, culminating with him jumping out of an airplane, impersonating the legendary "King."

On the drive home, we exchanged commentary about the movie, during which we discovered a shared love of Elvis Presley. Travis burst into an a capella rendition of "Hunk of Burning Love," which made me laugh and shake my shoulders to the imaginary beat. I was surprised to have had such a great time with Travis, even though he just dropped me off at the curb in front of my house afterward.

Despite my mixed feelings about Travis and his inconsistent behavior, I continued to spend my free time with him. He could say the crudest things, like "I've got over forty notches in my belt," but then he'd come to the Friday night football games at my high school to watch me perform with the pom squad at halftime. He'd drive us to his ex-girlfriend's house and leave me in the car while visiting her parents but then take me out to an expensive restaurant and actually pay for *both* of us. So, I wasn't sure if we really were just friends, or if he was interested in me romantically.

Then one afternoon, he walked into my history class at school, in the middle of the teacher's lecture. I was mortified to see him standing at the front of the room holding a life-size teddy bear. The humongous animal didn't distract from the large-brimmed ivory cowboy hat, nor the brown leather "shit-kickers," as he referred to his boots. Fortunately, no one knew who he was.

"Can I help you?" my nerdy Poindexter-like teacher asked, offended at the disruption.

"Yeah, I have a Sweetest Day delivery for Dana!" Travis said, staring me dead in the eyes. It was almost romantic, until his closed-mouth smile opened widely, showing his mouthful of rotten teeth. I sank a little lower in my seat, wanting to crawl into a hole and die.

"Dana?" the teacher said as if begging me to resolve this unexpected interruption.

"Um, I'm sorry," I stuttered as I rose from my chair. "I'll be right back."

Classmates giggled and chided, throwing out cowboy jokes in jest, as I rushed Travis out to the hallway before he could embarrass me further.

"What are you doing?" I asked.

"Hasn't anyone ever done anything romantic like this for you before?" he said.

"No!" I told him, snatching the big brown bear from him. "And no one ever needs to do anything like this again. Okay?"

"Yep!" Travis said with a proud smile and posture, as if he'd accomplished some double dog dare somebody had challenged him to do. I couldn't help but smile too then. What he'd done really was sweet, and I admired his bold confidence.

So, apparently Travis and I were a couple. As such, we expressed our affections in physical ways that crossed the barriers of friendship. He initiated kisses that grew from pecks to twisting tongues. He put his hands on parts of my body I'd have never allowed him before. Then, by Halloween, he wanted to have sex, even asking me to spend the night.

"I can't," I told him while we ate the Chinese takeout he'd picked up on the way to bring me to his empty apartment. "I'm only sixteen, remember? Anyway, my parents think I'm spending the night at Miranda's. They'd kill me if I spent the night here instead."

It was all true. But it was also all an excuse. I just didn't want to have sex with Travis. I liked him a lot, but I was just going with it, hoping Liam would come crawling back to me after he got his jollies with that redhead.

"They also think you're trick-or-treating with Miranda right now," Travis said with raised brows, as if questioning my adherence to whatever rules I was supposed to obey.

"True," I chuckled.

"So, can you just stay a little later than normal?" he asked.

"That I can do," I said, though I still had no intention of having sex. "Miranda did tell me we'd probably be staying at her other friend's house, anyway, and that they'd leave the basement door open for me to come in undetected whenever I got there."

"Oh, good," Travis said, sidling closer to me on the yellow-and-puke-green floral sofa he'd borrowed from the 1970s when he'd been there getting his hair cut.

He put his arms around my waist and pulled me into his scrawny body. Then he kissed me, softly at first before plunging his tongue down my throat. His grip on me was tighter too. It felt good to be wanted so badly, but I didn't have the emotional bond that inclined me to let him have what I'd only given to Liam before. We could get there. Maybe. For now, we'd just have a little fun.

We ended up horizontal, with Travis pulling me atop him. He pushed his pelvis into me repeatedly, making his desire for me obvious. Then one hand roamed to the front of my body and settled on my breast.

As we touched and groped and kissed, it was Liam who was on my mind. I almost felt bad, but I couldn't deny feelings I didn't have. I didn't like Travis's mustache. It was scratchy, and I couldn't help thinking of his constant reference to it as his "flavor saver." Nor could I stop thinking about his nasty teeth.

So, when Travis reached down to unbutton my jeans, I put my hand over his to stop him. "No," I whispered, taking a break from making out.

"My dad's at a movie, and my roommate is out of town," Travis said between kisses. Then he attempted to unbutton my jeans more forcefully. I tried to push his hand away again, but he wouldn't let go.

"Travis!" I said more firmly.

He sat up, so I thought he was respecting my wishes. My legs had naturally wrapped around his waist, and my arms were around his neck, so he put his mouth on mine again. Everything in my body tingled, so I went with it, thinking we would just continue to mess around. I didn't think anything of him taking me to his dark bedroom. It was probably better to screw around behind a closed door, anyway.

But when he laid me onto the bed and tugged at my pants buttons again, I panicked when they became undone.

"Travis, please," I said, though my insistence was so weak that even I wouldn't have taken me seriously.

"You don't want to?" he said as he put his fingers inside my panties and then inside me. His other hand pulled my jeans down and off my ankles. I didn't want this to be happening, but I didn't think I could stop it either.

"I'm scared, Travis. I've only been with one person," I said, hoping the lame excuse would fend him off. I made no other move to resist him or leave, though, so he proceeded to remove his jeans with only one hand, which was a level of skill that had come with some practice.

"I've been with enough women to know what you'll like." He was inside of me before he finished his sentence.

I really hadn't wanted to have sex with Travis. It was happening regardless. So, I laid there and let him do what he needed to do. I was almost indifferent to it, anyway. It was just an indulgent thrill contained to my body. I didn't have to process it at all in my mind if I didn't want to. So, I didn't.

When Travis was finished, I lay there for a moment, disappointed in myself for letting Travis have me in a way I hadn't been prepared to freely give. I felt like I'd betrayed Liam in some way too, even though we weren't together. A sudden unease overcame me, and I just wanted to leave.

So, I got off the bed and felt all around the floor until I found my clothes. "Can you take me back now? Miranda's probably wondering where I'm at," I said to avoid accountability for my rush to escape.

"Yeah," Travis said as he flipped on the light. Then his brows bounced about his forehead when he caught sight of me naked. I covered my breasts with my shirt while simultaneously looping my panties around my feet to pull them on.

As we were about to walk out of Travis's apartment, his dad was just coming in. I blinked at the bright fluorescent light flooding the dark apartment from the hallway.

"Blinded by the light?" his dad asked me.

"Good song," Travis commented as he ushered me out without an introduction.

I was shocked at the casualness of it all. It was like it was just another night for the two of them, which made me realize Travis probably hadn't been exaggerating about all the women he'd claimed to have sex with. It made me feel cheap and dirty. Like a whore.

We didn't talk much on the drive back. What was there to say, anyway? He'd wanted me. I'd let him have me. It was done. That was that.

I just sat in the passenger seat, listening to Travis belt out nearly every song on the country music station he listened to. He looked over at me and smiled once in a while, as if serenading me to reward my compliance.

At least one of us is feeling good about ourselves, I thought. But it sure as shit wasn't me.

"Don't Get Me Wrong"

I would have never been with Travis if Liam or any boy from school had any real interest in me instead. Then again, spending my free time with him and letting him have his way with me whenever he wanted seemed a small price to pay for the companionship and affection I would otherwise lack in my life. So, I continued to allow it.

Being with Travis wasn't so bad, anyway. He bought me dresses to wear to parties and outfitted me for the concerts he took me to. He got me into some of the bars he frequented, though his dad reamed him out for getting me drunk on Southern Comfort one night. I'd never had whiskey before, so forty-two proof hit me hard.

Travis's dad wouldn't let Travis take me home in that state. He'd made me nap, then made me coffee, then gave me a little lecture I probably deserved. The fatherly protection just made me miss my own dad, though. So much that I didn't even care how my mother and Ron would react if they ever discovered what I'd done. They already thought I was a drug-addicted delinquent and probably expected me to move on to alcohol next, like my real dad had supposedly done, according to Mom.

My multiple similarities to my dad made me wish I could call him. I needed a parent I felt comfortable confiding in about all these confusing feelings I had about Liam and Travis, never mind the decisions about what I wanted to do with the rest of my life, which needed to be tackled before graduation. Mom always negated my feelings and opposed any opinions I had. So, talking to her wouldn't be productive. But I couldn't talk to my dad either. It wouldn't be fair to drag him back into the mess of my mother's lies and the life of victimhood she perpetuated with them. So, Miranda became my confidante, whenever I could catch her between classes.

"Hey!" she said when I leaned against the locker beside hers.

"Can I talk to you a second?" I asked.

"Of course! What's up?" she said as she traded the books in her arms for a couple others.

Liam and that girl Julie walked by then. I couldn't help but gawk. Seeing him firmly grab one of her perfectly round butt cheeks and squeeze made me groan and look away.

Miranda glanced to where I was looking and said, "You miss him, don't you?"

"More than you can imagine," I said as I looked their way again. Liam was smiling at her the way he used to smile at me.

"Things are going good with you and Travis, though, right?" she asked.

"I don't know," I shrugged. "I just don't feel for him what I felt for Liam. You know?"

"Well, I didn't want to say anything before, but from what you've told me about how he dresses you and takes you places and brags about you being 'jailbait,' I feel like he treats you like a trophy wife, not a girlfriend," Miranda said as she closed her locker. We started walking down the hall.

"Really?"

"Yeah. That's not how you talk about someone you love. And I don't understand why you can't wear what you want to. It's like he's trying to control how people see you, or him, or—"

"I hadn't thought about it that way," I said as I considered all the evidence to support her view. If what she'd said was true, I almost didn't mind. I mean, I wanted more of an emotional connection, but I'd never been with anyone who thought I was pretty enough to show off. It was a flattery I kind of liked.

"There's nothing wrong with that, though," Miranda said, demonstrating how well she knew how my mind worked. "You're allowed to have some fun. Doesn't mean you have to marry the guy."

"Oh my god! I'd marry Liam right here, right now, but Travis? No. Never," I asserted.

Miranda chuckled at my reaction. "Well, then, do what you want to do with Travis. Maybe if Liam thinks you moved on and sees how happy you are without him, maybe he'll realize what he's lost," she suggested. She stopped at a classroom door then.

"I don't like playing games," I told her. I played enough of them at home.

"Well, he's not going to want to come back to a girl who mopes around all the time," she said with a shrug before going into class.

Miranda was much more knowledgeable about relationships and men. She'd had a few older boyfriends already. So, I thought to give her suggestion a shot.

I would brag to other girls in my classes about my escapades with Travis, making sure to mention he had his own apartment, a job, and a newer car, hoping the gossip would get back to Liam. I'd talk about all the places Travis took me, hoping Liam would be jealous that I was doing all these cool things and enact some desperate overture to win me back. Then we'd be together forever, high school sweethearts who would be inseparable until the day we died. Unfortunately, Liam was so into that exotic redhead that he failed to care about what or *who* I was doing at all.

So, Travis and I carried on as a couple, and at some point, I caught feelings. I don't know if it was when I started singing along to the radio with him in the car, or if it was when he started calling me every night when he got home from work. Even if just to say, "Goodnight" and "I love you," it was like the tuck into bed that made me feel safe. Just like Liam used to do.

But then one night, Travis didn't call.

A shift in someone's habits or behaviors indicated a change in their feelings for me. The rejection would follow, when the person felt guilty enough to end the farce for both of us, and I felt it now, like the foreplay to fallout.

I lay in bed, clutching the cordless phone from the kitchen, willing it ring to release me from the anxiety preventing sleep. Every second that passed, my breathing became shallower. Thoughts of Travis having wild sex with some random woman he'd catcalled in the mall haunted my mind. Then my heart picked up its pace until I felt a rush of anxious energy overpower logic and reasonable thought. Inclined to know the fate of our relationship right then, in that exact moment, made me jump out of bed and go down to the kitchen to call him. I refused to be made a fool of again.

A busy signal, sounding more like an alert to danger than an indication that someone else was using the phone, prevented me from peace. I paced the galley kitchen, dialing the number every time I couldn't wait a second longer to try again. The busy signal continued to mock me, making me that much more upset about the presumed ending of a relationship I hadn't even wanted in the first place.

Ron came down the stairs then, inviting trepidation to my pity party.

"What're you doing, Dana?" he asked as he sat at the table. He slumped back into the chair, squinting his tired eyes as they adjusted to the lights.

Despite our strained relationship, he was the only person I had at that moment. So, I said, "Travis always calls me when he gets home from work. Always! But he didn't call tonight. And his phone is busy. So, I don't know where he is or what's going on!" My bottom lip quivered as I shook my head frantically.

Ron rubbed his forehead and sighed. "He's twenty-one, Dana. There's only one thing a guy that age is thinking about late at night," he said, insensitive to my feelings.

That's exactly what I'd been afraid of, so the confirmation didn't help me feel any better about myself. Because if I were enough, Travis wouldn't need to be with someone else. Neither would Liam or Kevin.

"No!" I said, refuting Ron and my thoughts. "He wouldn't do that to me!"

Unfortunately, I knew he could. Of all the women he'd claimed to have been with, I couldn't possibly be the one who'd suddenly changed him into a monogamous and faithful man. So, why was I even with Travis? Other than the excitement of being much more reckless than was characteristic of me, I couldn't think of one good reason that had to do with him.

"He's a guy, Dana. He only wants one thing," Ron said. "You know that, right?"

Taking his insinuation that sex was all I was worth, I defended, "That's not true! He loves me!" Yet, even I knew "love" was a bit of an exaggeration. We did *care* for each other. What I felt for him, however, was nothing near as intense as what I'd felt for Liam.

"I don't think he does," Ron said, shaking his head. "But it's late, and standing in the kitchen worrying isn't going to change whatever he's doing, anyway. So, I'm going back to bed, and I suggest you do the same."

"I can't sleep. Not until I know what's going on," I maintained.

"Whatever," Ron said, rubbing his forehead again as he stood to leave me. "Just make sure you turn the lights off when you're done down here."

Once alone, I couldn't resist dialing Travis's number one last time, and once again I heard the warning sound telling me to get out while I could. But I couldn't. Even though I didn't love him, even though he wasn't the type of person I wanted to be with at all, I could not deny myself the love and affection he provided me. Morally, it wasn't right, just like it hadn't been right for my mother and Ron to refuse to give me the same. So, it was their fault I sought to have my basic needs met elsewhere. It was their fault I was with a guy like Travis instead of a nice, boring boy who opened doors and spoke to me with respect. It was . . . shit, everything was their fault, including these disordered thoughts making me lose sleep and feel crazy!

I went back to bed and tried anyway, remembering to turn the lights off behind me. Eventually, I nodded off. When I woke up the next morning, I immediately called Travis. He said his roommate had been on a long-distance call with his girlfriend all night, and that he'd conked out while waiting to use the phone.

It sounded reasonable. However, I couldn't dismiss the notion that he was lying or that he might cheat in the future. I mean, he told me he loved me, but so had the two boys I'd loved before him. And just like with them, I told him I loved him too. So, I guessed we were both living a lie, for whatever purpose it served.

"Kiss Me Deadly"

⁓

I was sitting in my boring math class one cold November day when I felt a lump on one side of my throat. My throat had been scratchy lately. I was unusually tired too but attributed that to my intense pom schedule and late nights on the phone with Travis. But when the lump got larger, I made my mother feel it. Mom was so worried, it worried me even more, because she usually didn't concern herself with much of anything regarding my well-being. So, I was relieved when the doctor diagnosed me with mononucleosis—the "kissing disease."

"You must have gotten it from Travis or whatever other boy you've been kissing," Mom reproached. I swear she'd have preferred that the lump had been a tumor like she'd suspected before the doctor told her otherwise, though I'm sure she would have still claimed it had been caused by some sexual looseness on my part.

The doctor advised that I rest, saying it might take up to a month to fully recover. So, Mom arranged to work from home. It had seemed like a loving gesture at first. She tucked me into her bed to rest, suggesting I'd be more comfortable in the darkness my brightly decorated room didn't otherwise offer. She set her TV to channel seven, so the trio of ABC soap operas I'd been watching since as far back as I can remember would keep me entertained while she went to the basement to work. I could barely get through an episode of *All My Children*, though. I had such a high fever. All I wanted to do was sleep.

Day in and day out, I slept in my mother's bed, only moving back to my bedroom when Ron and Jonathan came home. Ron didn't want me in his bed as much as Mom didn't want me home alone. I'd gathered by Mom's refusals to let Travis come and see me that her nursing me back to health was just a cover for making sure I didn't sneak in a quickie with Travis.

Regardless of the pretense, I liked having my mother care for me. Making me Malt-O-Meal, sweetened just right with a thin layer of milk floating on top, comforted me the same as Great-Gram's Cream of Wheat. Although meant for my body, the nourishment spread to my soul, like the chicken noodle soup and the peanut butter and jelly sandwich Mom would make me for lunch, knowing it had been my favorite hot lunch in grade school.

I relished in finally having my mother "mother" me, as well as the peace and quiet of the house during the day. It was such a stark difference from the usual hostility and tension. I couldn't help but think I really was the cause, like my mother and Ron accused, since being bed-bound and ill instantly brought it all to an end.

But then one early evening, the sound of the bedroom door bouncing off the doorstop behind it startled me awake. The hallway light went on, blinding me without notice. Then I heard the heavy stomp of Ron's feet getting louder as he approached.

I pulled the covers over my head, hoping he'd give me the mercy of letting me rest. The pitter-patter of Jonathan's feet closing in compelled me to uncover my face and muster a smile. Three-year-old Jonathan didn't deserve the unkindness I had no problem giving Ron.

Suddenly, a plastic dart from a Nerf gun pelted me in the face.

I winced at the assault, unsure whether more would come. Then I heard Jonathan giggle. He was standing bedside with a Nerf gun pointed directly in my face.

"Jonathan!" I scolded in a dry rasp. Then I heard Ron laughing from the hallway. Annoyed that he found Jonathan's inconsideration funny, I said, "Ron, can you please take him? I really don't feel good." I was sweating and shivering all at once. The shiver won, making me pull the heavy comforter back up to my chin.

Jonathan ran into the hallway. I'd assumed Ron was whispering to him to leave me alone, but then Jonathan turned around and giggled and shot me in the face a second time.

"Jonathan!" I scolded while I watched him and Ron laugh. "Ron, please!

This isn't funny!" I pleaded. "I need to sleep!"

Ron's face morphed into outright anger. My whole body tensed as he got up and came towards me. I cowered when I saw his finger wave.

"If you want to sleep, then get out of *my* bed and go to yours!" Ron hollered.

"Mom *said* I could lay in here!" I defended, wondering if she was within earshot.

"Why? So you can spread your herpes? You *want* Jonathan to get it next?"

Compelled out of my cower, I sat straight up. "What the hell are you talking about, herpes? I have *mono*," I corrected.

"Mono *is* a type of herpes, or don't they teach you that in sex ed?" Ron scolded before backing off. I'd taken the required class, and I didn't recall mono being mentioned as a sexually transmitted disease. So, I didn't appreciate the insinuation as he said, "That's what you get for whoring around," just as he picked up Jonathan.

I didn't have the energy to fight, but I wouldn't withstand his insults when I was already down and out either. So, I got out of *his* bed too fast, which made me pause until the dizziness passed. Then I grabbed my blanket and pillow and dragged them into my room.

After tucking myself into my much smaller bed with my back towards the open doorway, I lay in the dark, ruminating about why Ron would say I had herpes. The doctor had clearly said I had "mononucleosis," a glandular infection. Plus, I didn't have sores in places I shouldn't. I had swollen glands. So, even though both were transmitted through something infectious in saliva, mono and herpes were two different things. Weren't they?

Ron had spoken with such authority that I couldn't help but worry that maybe Travis had infected me with something he'd picked up from some mamacita at the mall. He certainly wasn't shy about his sexual prowess. However, I'd hoped he'd have been forthcoming about any diseases he had, like we'd been taught to do in sex ed if ever in that situation.

Wondering whether Ron was right or just wanted to make me question Travis's fidelity, he'd achieved his goal of making me doubt myself. He'd cast his web, and now I was stuck in the lair of his lies, trying to determine the truth. I hated that man, but I hated myself more for letting him get to me, especially when I needed my rest.

"Dancing Queen"

After finally recovering, I returned to school a month later to find out that another boy in my grade had been absent with mono at the same time I'd been. Of course, the rumor mill buzzed with gossip that me and that boy were having some secret affair, even though we'd never even met. I ignored it all, though, caring less about what people thought and concerning myself more with what I knew to be true.

Anyway, there was some excitement at pom practice that day. The alum who'd found me on the street that night that I'd run away after being strangled showed up at our pom practice with a special announcement.

"Hush, girls," the coach said to quiet us all down. We were sitting in the gym bleachers, waiting to hear what the gorgeous black-haired, blue-eyed former pom captain had to say.

"So, you all know I was the winner of the Miss Illinois Teen pageant last year," she said with her perfect white-toothed smile. "It was such an amazing experience that the director of the state pageant has asked me to come talk to you all about potentially competing in the pageant yourselves!"

Looking around at each other with high-browed anticipation, some of the girls murmured excitedly about the prospect. Then our former captain went on to share a well-rehearsed speech about everything she'd learned during her reign, and how glorious it was to represent the state of Illinois in the nationally televised Miss America's Teen pageant. Then she ended her presentation by asking, "Do any of you have any interest in following in my footsteps and representing our town in the state competition next summer?"

The buzz of chatter that followed echoed through the gymnasium like a swarm of flies swirling around me. Sure, it was an exciting opportunity for whoever wanted to undertake it. I knew it wouldn't be me, though. I wasn't very pretty. My belly and thighs were way too chunky for my hundred-and-ten-pound frame, but I'd be very happy and excited for whomever was selected, and eager to see if our school could produce two pageant queens in a row.

"What about you, Dana?" the former captain asked above the talk amongst the squad.

"Me?" I asked with high-browed surprise, pointing at my chest.

"Yeah, you," she chuckled. Then she turned to the coach, who sat beside her, and they nodded in agreement. Then some of the other girls on the squad turned to me and encouraged, "Yeah, Dana! You should do it!"

Stunned by the unexpected consensus that I should be the one to represent us, I sat in silence, looking around at everyone with open-mouthed confusion. I had no business glorifying myself in pursuit of some rhinestone tiara. It didn't match who I thought I was, anyway.

"It would look good on your college applications," the former captain coaxed. That might have worked on someone else, but I wasn't going to college. I wanted to go to beauty school.

With everyone's eyes on me now, I felt the pressure, and I never liked to disappoint. "Um," I stalled, worried more about getting myself out of this spotlight. "Okay. I guess I'll do it," I appeased.

After some claps and encouraging comments, the former captain said, "Great! I'll tell the pageant director to expect a nomination letter from the school, then!"

The coach followed with, "And I'll make sure the administration passes your information along to the pageant office to get in touch with you. Now, let's get warmed up, girls!" she ordered.

Despite the awkwardness of having been singled out, my ego felt a little boost it wasn't used to. I mean, to have all these girls decide that I was the one among them who was pretty enough to be in a pageant, and to have their support without the cattiness and jealousy I'd have expected, I started to wonder if I wasn't the overweight, dumb, insignificant, and sensitive girl my mother and Ron had made me believe I was. How could I be, when so many others saw me as so much more than that?

So, I kicked a little higher that day and carried myself with a more confident posture. Because even if I didn't have the backing of the people I should, I had my squad. And that was enough.

"Another Brick in the Wall"

"**I**'m dating a pageant queen?" Travis exclaimed when I told him the news over the phone that night.

"Let's not get ahead of ourselves now," I lightly warned. Instead of arguing all the points against the possibility of me winning the crown, however, I let Travis gloat about it. It made me feel special in a way I otherwise didn't, which was exactly why I hadn't told Mom about the nomination. She would've crushed me with counteractive comments about my appearance, and I didn't want to give up the little bit of self-esteem I was relishing. Mom and Ron were more concerned about the upcoming College Night the school was hosting, anyway, which I'd told them I had no intention to attend.

"But I want to go to beauty school," I whined amidst defending my decision.

"No daughter of mine is going to beauty school," Ron stated, suddenly claiming the familial relation because it conveniently served his authority over me. "That's not *real* school, anyway. You're going to college."

"But I don't want to go to college," I complained.

"Well, as long as you live under *my* roof, you're going to do what I say!" Ron declared.

I wasn't going to let him bully me into something I didn't want. I honestly didn't think paying for me to go to college was what he really wanted either, especially when beauty school was so much cheaper than university. I think this had more to do with Ron having something to brag about.

We'd just seen his family at Thanksgiving, and they'd been asking me and Ron's nephew (who was a high school senior too) which colleges we planned to apply to. Ron's nephew had listed several with reputable engineering programs he'd compare and decide between. Everyone had been impressed. But when I'd said I wanted to go to beauty school or see if New York City had a music or dance institute I could audition for, the entire family had laughed, as if my passions were the whims of a dimwit. My mother and Ron had shrunk back, embarrassed at having raised a flighty imbecile that thought she could make a living doing something she loved. I also noticed how ashamed I'd felt, for feeling like I didn't live up to whatever standards I should have, to make them proud of who I was.

"Believe me when I tell you that the last thing I want is to live under your frickin' roof," I said. "But please tell me, because I'd love to know, what you think I need to go to college for. Because I wanted to study music, but you said being in the Chicago Symphony Orchestra wasn't a real job. Then you decided to stop paying for my private lessons, which got me kicked out of orchestra altogether. Now, you're telling me I can't pursue a career in beauty, even though I'm doing really well at my job doing facials and makeup for weddings and models. So, please, enlighten us all with what you think I need to go to college for." I didn't even try to hide my sarcasm.

"Well . . ." Ron said, just to say something instead of the nothing he couldn't defend himself with.

"Exactly," I said. Then I walked out of the kitchen with a bag of chips, rolling my eyes as I passed Ron.

"You better go to that College Night, Dana!" I heard Ron call out behind me.

To shut him up, I went. I walked to the first table inside the door of the gymnasium, where a conservatively dressed young woman was eager to give her spiel.

"Here's some information about our different programs," she said as she handed me a thick folder with flyers and maps and pictures of happy twenty-year-olds holding armfuls of books. "Do you know what you're looking to study in college?"

"Uh, no," I said, rifling through the overwhelming quantity of papers. "I mean, I wasn't really thinking about college at all, to be honest."

"Well, DePaul University is a private institution based on the Catholic tenet of service, which welcomes and promotes cultural and intellectual diversity," she said, sounding like she'd over-rehearsed her pitch. I should have told her she'd had me at "private" and "Catholic." Both were fondly familiar to me, and both were quite expensive. "We offer various programs, including music and fine arts, business and finance, pre-law at our downtown Chicago campus—"

"Wait," I interrupted. "Pre-law?" I'd always felt inclined to help victims of abuse, specifically children like me who had no way out of families who didn't want them.

"Yes!" she said, happy to have intrigued me. "We have an entire college within the university, dedicated to preparing undergraduates for a career in law, politics—"

"And is the financial information in this folder? Like how much everything costs?"

"Yes, current tuition rates are detailed inside that packet, as well as financial aid information and the application for it. We offer a variety of options for—"

"Okay, thank you so much!" I said as I walked out of the event. I didn't mean to be rude, but I had all the information I needed to enact my revenge on Ron.

I'd overheard him talking at Thanksgiving about the incomparable affordability of state universities versus out-of-state and private institutions. So, if Ron was going to force me to go to college, I figured I'd make him pay for it, literally, by choosing this very expensive school. It couldn't be too hard to get into DePaul, being that I was Catholic, female, and half of a minority. I'd been told my pageant nomination would look good on my college applications too, so I supposed my agreement hadn't been for naught!

I filled out the application as soon as I returned home, wrote the required essays, and sent the package off for consideration.

The more I thought about it, the more I felt like going to college may not be as terrible an idea as I'd thought. No one else on my mother's side of the family had been able to pursue a higher education, aside from one cousin who'd gone to art school. So, if I could be one of the first to graduate with a degree, maybe then Mom could be proud of me for my accomplishment.

So, when an envelope from DePaul arrived just before Christmas, I scrambled to tear it open right inside the front door without pausing to remove my coat or my shoes.

The thick white stock with the blue collegiate logo at the top center read: *We are pleased to inform you that you have been accepted into an exclusive group which will comprise the Class of 1997.*

"Oh my god!" I squealed. "Mom! I got in!" I called out.

She came out of the kitchen, wiping her hands with a dish towel.

"I got in, Mom! To DePaul!" I declared with an ear-to-ear grin.

"What?" my mother asked.

I handed the letter to her and stood by, anxiously awaiting hugs and praise as she read it. I'd overheard classmates talk about how thrilled their parents were when they received acceptance letters. Some jumped up and down with their kids, told them they were proud of them for their achievement, and even took them to celebration dinners.

"Oh," she said as she handed the letter back. "Well, that's nice."

I stood in stunned paralysis when she returned to the kitchen. "Isn't this good news, Mom? Aren't you proud of me?" I asked, practically begging for some recognition as I followed.

"Yeah, Dane. But we'll have to wait and see what Ron says. I'm sure he'll want to weigh the options."

"Options?" I asked, feeling like I'd missed something. "*What* other options?"

"Well, we're not going to send you to the first place you get in," she said as if I should have known better. Apparently I didn't, because I hadn't applied anywhere else. "Ron has a clear idea of what we are able to spend on your education. So, we'll have to compare the costs of all the schools you're accepted at."

That was reasonable, except that these parameters hadn't been communicated to me before. I'd been told to go to college. And I'd gotten into one. So, regardless of affordability, I expected some props for having achieved the task.

"Okay," I said with a sigh, annoyed that Ron was the be-all and end-all of everything in our lives. "But it's good that I got in, right?" I prodded.

"Yeah," my mother said with the same flat tone she always spoke with.

I exhaled hard, deflating my body of the air my ego had flown high on for that short moment before. Then I spent half the next day in the counselor's office at school, thumbing through college pamphlets and filling out applications that the counselor promised to expedite to the college admissions offices for me.

An acceptance letter from Southern Illinois University arrived shortly after.

"You're not going to Southern Illinois," Ron dictated from his chair. "I've heard it's a party school."

"She doesn't need to go *there*, then," my mother agreed.

"I'm not paying for you to have fun. You need to go to a *serious* school," Ron continued.

I was standing right there listening to them speak of me as if I were a recovering addict with no self-control. Yet, I'd never once done drugs or smoked anything of any kind.

Anyway, DePaul *was* a serious school. Their real issue was with me. I wasn't good enough. Nothing I ever did would *be* good enough. I wasn't sure why I even tried anymore.

Like the Universal Dance Association trip to Paris, France, that I'd be leaving for soon, they refused to commend me for anything I did. Even after the local paper printed a whole story about the Paris trip, with pictures of me at pom practice, they didn't bring up Paris at all. It's like I wasn't travelling abroad for the holidays, or like I didn't even exist. Sometimes I wished I didn't, because it would be easier than feeling the burden of being.

"Same Ol' Situation"

*T*he box of uniforms and performance wear the Universal Dance Association required us all to wear in Paris arrived in due time for the trip. Everything was way too big, which I'd expected, since my mother had insisted on me ordering more than double my normal size. She'd said it was to ensure the garments would fit if I gained some extra holiday weight. I hadn't believed I could go from a junior's size three to nine in a month, especially when I'd increased the frequency and intensity of my morning workouts to start toning my body for the swimsuit portion of next summer's pageant. But I hadn't wanted to argue with Mom. And now it was too late to send the baggy clothes back. So, I resolved myself to fold the uniform skirt and warm-up pants over at the waist to prevent them from falling off.

As I assessed my frumpy reflection in my bedroom mirror, I wondered if my mother had intentionally misguided me to try to sabotage my trip. It sounded paranoid to think she would go to such extreme lengths to prevent the amazing experience of travelling abroad, and it was equally ridiculous for her to hope that an ill-fitting uniform would disqualify me from performing at all. I mean, I'm sure some other girl somewhere had a uniform that didn't fit. But it was nothing a swap or a sewing needle couldn't fix on the flight.

Anyway, I was glad to leave for Paris, like I had always been glad to leave for any camp or competition. Any time away from my mother and Ron was welcome, because I could breathe and just be, without the criticisms and judgments they used to subdue and demean me.

I gathered they were glad to get rid of me as well from the way I was dropped off at the international airport. I got out of the car at the curb at O'Hare, trying not to get run down by taxis recklessly racing by. People of all ages, sizes, and ethnic backgrounds rushed from here to there, none seeming to know exactly where they were going but bumping everyone around them with their suitcases on their way.

My mother got out of the car just as I heaved the large suitcase she'd let me borrow out of the trunk of her Dodge Daytona. Ron remained in the driver's seat, saying something to my mother.

"Come on, Dane," my mother ushered as Ron pulled away.

"Where's he going?" I asked as I muscled the humongous suitcase onto the safety of the curb. I worried he was leaving her behind, like she'd once done to him when she'd caught him eyeing an attractive woman dressed in head-to-toe spandex at the grocery store.

Pulling her coat tighter under her chin, my mother shuddered. "He didn't want to pay to park, so he's driving around for a few minutes while I take you in."

I barely heard her over the swoosh of the cars racing past and the horns of angry drivers urging others along. The thunder of airplanes taking off overhead added to the overwhelm and my increasing anxiety.

"Oh, okay," I said, relieved she'd thought to help me navigate the confusion all around us. I did see other girls dressed in the same purple tracksuit as me, with the "UDA" logo embroidered in white on the back. So, at least I knew we were in the vicinity of where I was supposed to be.

Through the automatic doors was a different sort of chaos. People still buzzed to and fro, muttering, directing, complaining, and bidding farewell. After checking my suitcase at the United Airlines counter, my mother did the same.

"You got your passport?" she asked.

I nodded and raised the dark-green leather cover Sonia had gifted me for Christmas to hold the legal document inside.

"And your boarding pass?" my mother asked. "You can't get on the plane without it!"

"Yeah, it's right here," I said, opening the passport to where I'd safely tucked the pass.

"Okay, good," my mother approved. "Well, I don't want to keep Ron waiting, so—"

"You can't stay just a little longer?" I pleaded. "Just until I board the plane?" Regardless of our relationship, I'd always hope my mom would make some attempt to soothe my fears.

"That's not for another couple hours, Dane!" my mother scolded. "Anyway, you'll be fine. Just go through security over there, then follow the signs to your gate."

I strained for breath as I scanned the place worriedly.

"If you get lost, just ask someone for directions. Okay?" she said.

I blew out a long breath, knowing she wasn't giving me a choice. "Yeah," I said, reminding myself I'd been lucky to have her with me this far.

"Okay, then. Have fun," she said in a monotone that didn't match. Then she gave me a weak hug.

"I will," I responded, clinging to her a little harder and longer than she seemed to be comfortable with. Fear of the unknown made me unwilling to release a woman I both hated and longed for, depending on the day.

"All right," she said, mustering the slightest closed-mouth smile as she released me. "We'll see you when you get back, then."

"Okay," I mumbled, feeling abandoned already.

"Be safe," she said as she turned to walk away.

"Will do," I said, though I doubted she'd heard me over all the other parents offering daughters sappier send-offs. Their longer and more emotional goodbyes *were* enviable, but I ignored them as I passed, since dwelling on what I lacked had served absolutely no purpose to me before.

After a stop in New York City to change planes, we arrived in Paris the next day. It was December twenty-seventh—my birthday, and by some strange irony, also my mother's.

Our birthday was probably the only thing we had in common. So, it was the one thing I made sure to acknowledge every year, even if she and Ron didn't always make a big deal of mine. Unfortunately, I couldn't call to wish her a happy birthday, because it was nighttime on the other side of the world. Plus, we were practically hurled into rehearsals and tours with no consideration for jet lag.

When we returned to the hotel at the end of the day, with just a short time to rest and change before dinner, there was a sticky note on the door of the room I shared with three other girls, indicating I had a message at the front desk. I went down to the front desk to retrieve it, thinking my mother had called to acknowledge the day. So, I was smiling when the French clerk handed me the small piece paper, and even happier to see eligible English letters written on it: *Happy Birthday, Dana! I love you. -Travis.*

I couldn't imagine how much it cost to call another country, after the way Ron griped about calls to the next town. That's probably why my mother hadn't called, I realized. But Travis had. Travis had wanted to ensure my special day was acknowledged. Travis had made the effort despite the expense. So, now I was rethinking my entire relationship, taking it much more seriously than I ever thought I would.

Travis was just supposed to be a stand-in to make Liam jealous and pass the time. This message, however, sent from halfway across the world, made me see Travis in a different light. It's like the vulgar and outrageous playboy he'd presented as at first was a front for the caring and considerate man he didn't want to be seen as. It reminded me of how Liam had denied his true feelings for me in front of his friends the day I was released from the mental health facility. So, maybe that was something all guys did, to protect their machismo or something. Not that it mattered now. I apparently had my guy. And I was apparently in love.

Knowing the depth of Travis's feelings for me gave me a sense of security and empowerment—not just in us as a couple but in who I was too. It was like someone finding value in me made me see that worthiness in myself, and I rode high on that euphoria.

So, I bought prepaid phone cards to call Travis whenever I could. No matter the time or what he was doing, he was excited to hear about my escapades abroad. I told him about the New Year's Day parade and performances, how small the original Mona Lisa really was, and how terrified I'd been at just the first tier of the Eiffel Tower. I told him how awestruck I'd been to walk the aisle of the Notre Dame Cathedral and how a gal from Wisconsin had tricked me into believing she'd seen the ghost that supposedly haunted the enormous opera house when we'd gotten lost inside.

I'd called my mother a couple times to share the same, but she was always too busy to listen, or it was the wrong time to have called at all.

It was just as well. Being away from the tensions at home was good for me. I didn't have the stomachaches and headaches that resulted from the constant upset. The strange freedom to be myself allowed me to connect with the girls I'd met through this experience more easily. They thought I was funny and that I was a good listener. They said I was smart and respected what I had to say. They complimented my talent, as well as my consideration. I carried myself with more confidence and esteem as a result, and I hoped that I could be *this* Dana when I returned home.

Then I got off the plane in Chicago.

Parents rushed towards their daughters excitedly, smiling and hugging and feeling glad for their girls' safe return. My mother and Ron, however, remained physically and emotionally unmoved from where they stood, wearing the same disapproving scowls as usual. And with each step I took towards them, fun and free "Paris Dana" became a more distant memory. I was a burden and a bother again, inconveniencing my parents with my need for a ride home.

"I'm Still Standing"

Early in 1993, I got a letter from the Miss Illinois Teen pageant office, officially welcoming me as the representative of my town in the state competition to be held in June. I couldn't believe it was actually happening! Then again, I couldn't believe anyone thought I was pretty enough to be in any kind of beauty contest, except the one in the board game "Monopoly."

My mother had never been very supportive of me modeling, though, so I didn't expect her to feel any better about this. Still, I had to tell her.

"Hey, Mom," I said as I sat at the kitchen table early that weekday evening. Ron hadn't come home with Jonathan yet, so it was an opportune time to have this discussion one-on-one.

"What are you doing?" she asked as casually as I was slumped back with my arm over the back of the chair.

"Well, actually, I have some news," I said then proceeded to explain how I'd been nominated for the pageant. Then I went over the list of what I needed for each of the four competitions comprising the whole of the pageant, thinking that including her in the process could potentially bond us in a way we hadn't been able to before. Plus, I could use her business savvy to help with raising the funds to pay the hefty entrance fee.

Instead of the surprise or excitement I'd hoped she'd express, Mom just stood there with her black T-shirt tucked into her belted blue jeans, staring out the window over the kitchen sink.

"Why would they pick *you*?" she finally asked, shaking her head.

The insult hurt, but I'd built some resistance to her as of late. "I guess they think I have a shot at the title?" Despite how it sounded, I wasn't trying to be a smart-ass.

"Do they know you were pregnant?"

Stunned at the audacity of her question, I opened my mouth, but nothing came out. She had no business bringing up a baby who would be on my hip right now if it weren't for her.

"I just think they'd take back their invitation if they knew you'd had an abortion," she justified. I hadn't thought I could resent my mother any more than I already did.

"No, Mom. I obviously did not volunteer that information," I said snottily. "But I don't think it has any bearing on who I am or how I look in a swimsuit or evening gown."

"Well—"

"Just forget it, okay?" I said, standing up to leave. I didn't need to hear any more reasons why I wasn't good enough for this, that, and whatever other accomplishments I achieved. "I was stupid to think you might actually be happy for me. Or that you might want to help me with all the stuff I have to do to prepare."

"What do you need other than money?" she accused.

"My mother! To support me in something for once!" I lashed back.

"I don't know how you want me to support you if it's not with money," she said.

"Everything always comes back to money with you and Ron!" I raised my voice while flinging my arms up at my sides.

I thought to show her the slew of information the pageant director had sent about how to approach local businesses about sponsoring me with a monetary donation in exchange for a small advertisement in the pageant program. She wouldn't listen, though, nor would she care. She would just find something else about the process to criticize or make me feel bad about instead. So, I collected the papers from my packet and got up.

"I just don't understand why you're doing this," my mother said as I started walking out. "You know you're not going to win, right?"

The insult halted me at the doorway. I was fully aware that the odds were that I wouldn't. But I wasn't participating in the pageant to win; I was doing it because I could. I'd never thought I'd be offered the opportunity, and I was excited about what doors it may open, or to simply feel like a princess for one small moment of my shitty fucking life.

Mom wouldn't understand that, though, because she refused to understand that I wasn't her. So, I took a deep breath. Then I proceeded up to my room, where I called Travis at work to tell him about the unpleasant interaction.

"Your biggest issue isn't her support, Dana," he said. "It's getting enough sponsors to pay for everything. So, I'll take up a collection here. All my workers like you. They'll be happy to help."

"Thank you," I said. "But where am I supposed to get the rest of the money? I spent all my savings on the Paris trip."

"You're resourceful. And you have a phone book," he said. "So, start making calls! And congratulations, by the way. That's huge."

"Thank you," I said, appreciating the acknowledgment, though it would have still been nice coming from my mother.

I spent the next afternoon calling various local businesses. Most told me they'd pass the information on to the owners, and the owners I spoke with said they'd think about it. I pressed on, attaining promises from a couple places I frequented who were glad to return the favor. It wasn't enough, but I wasn't giving up.

When a physical education teacher at school asked how the pageant process was going, I shared my stress about coming up with enough funds. Ms. Van Austen and I had developed a friendly relationship when I'd assisted her in counseling overweight teens who'd been physically incapable of participating in gym last semester. The next time I saw her, she gave me a personal check for a hundred dollars.

"Oh my god! Thank you!" I said, shocked at the unexpected contribution. Then I threw my arms around the petite blonde and squeezed her as tight as I could to show my gratefulness. "You really didn't have to do this."

"I'm happy to do it, Dana," she said when I released her. "I've always thought the world of you and would help you any way I can. Speaking of which . . ." She glanced around to ensure no one would hear. The gymnasium was empty, and only one other gym teacher was sitting inside their little office with caged windows. She pressed her lips together and impressed a stern stare into mine. "Some of us are a little worried about you."

"You are?"

"We talk in the teacher's lounge, you know. And we're noticing that you don't eat at lunch, that you often walk around with a box of cereal and snack out of it between classes," she said. "And with you needing money for the pageant, I'm just wondering . . . is your family *hurting* for money or something? Do you need help buying food?"

Surprised by the gross misperception, I shook my head anxiously. "No, not at all! My mom gives me fifty dollars a week to feed myself."

Creasing her brows as if it would help her to understand better, she said, "She does?"

"Yeah," I said nonchalantly. "I've found the money goes further if I buy food at the store instead of in the cafeteria, though. So, I usually buy Mini-Wheats because they're high in fiber, which I've read makes you feel fuller for longer, and the box lasts me a few days."

Ms. Van Austen stared into my eyes to gauge my honesty. She seemed to believe me but said, "Cereal isn't food, Dana. And it's not normal for parents to make their children fend for their basic needs."

I considered what she'd said. And I agreed. But my family dynamic wasn't normal. "My basic needs *are* being met," I reassured. Realistically, they were. Otherwise, Mom wouldn't harp on me to be more grateful to her and Ron for providing food, shelter, and clothing, and Ron wouldn't bitch about having to "pay for another man's child."

"Are you at least eating dinner at home every night?" she asked, as if it would make her feel better if I did.

I wanted to give her the answer she wanted to hear. I mean, few things made me as happy as sitting down to a family dinner with Kelly's parents and sisters on occasion, and then at Liam's (until his stepfather had unwelcomed me). However, I was a firm believer in telling the truth.

"My mom doesn't cook *every* night," I said, shrugging. "I mean, she always has dinner for my stepfather. And she makes sure my little brother eats. But he's only three, so he can't prepare his own food," I rambled. I realized too late that that didn't sound very good, though.

"But do *you* eat, Dana? Does your mother feed *you* every night?" she pressed.

Afraid I'd say something that would get my mom in trouble, and that I'd get in trouble as a consequence of misspeaking, I was nervous to say anything at all. But Ms. V's intense stare told me she wasn't letting me off the hook.

"Well . . . no . . . but she's busy working and taking care of my brother and the house. I do eat, though. I swear! Sometimes there's leftovers. Otherwise, I can make noodles or rice or toast if I want to cook for myself." My heart was racing a mile a minute now, hoping Ms. V would drop this. I needed to lose weight for the pageant, anyway.

She cast her eyes down, then looked back up and sighed. "It sounds like neglect, Dana."

"No," I refuted, desperate to make her see she was wrong. "I mean, my parents aren't *good* parents. Not to *me*, at least," I qualified. Ms. V's eyes widened. I cursed myself for having diarrhea of the mouth and felt compelled to elaborate. "They like my little brother a lot more, but that's because that's their child together. I'm just . . ." I didn't know how to sum up the sad story of my existence.

"Dana . . ." she said, prolonging my name.

"I swear I'm fine," I reassured her, even though I couldn't deny feeling glad she'd noticed that something was off about my life.

With her hand on my arm, she said, "Listen, if you ever need to talk . . ."

"I appreciate it," I politely replied before excusing myself to my next class.

I'd never come to her, though. Despite their best intentions, every other adult I'd trusted before—the cops, Child Services, Liam's parents, Mr. Fogel—had failed me in some way. So, it served no purpose to set myself up to be disappointed by yet another.

"Can't Buy Me Love"

By late spring, it seemed that the tides were finally turning in my favor. Ron decided I could go to DePaul in the fall. Then he took me for my driver's license test and gave me my mother's Dodge Daytona after I'd passed. She got a fancy new car out of the deal, so it was a win-win. With sponsorship money finally coming in from a few local businesses, I was able to focus on preparing for the pageant.

The cobalt one-piece swimsuit was as easy to choose as the simple ivory sheath I'd bought to wear for the judge's interviews. I got stumped on a costume that had to represent the state in some way but went with a Ziegfield Folly's dancer ensemble that the costume shop clerk had recommended. It was better than going as a corn on the cob.

All that remained then was the formal gown I needed for the evening gown competition. There was a special occasion dress shop nearby where the girl from poms told me she'd bought her dress when she'd competed for and won the state title. So, I made an appointment to try on dresses there, hoping they'd also have the clear plastic heels which only pageant princesses and strippers wore but were required nonetheless.

My mother was in the kitchen when I got home.

"Hey, Dane," she said as I walked to the refrigerator.

"Hey," I said in a dismal tone, immediately closing the refrigerator. I didn't need to put anything else in this "curvy" body, as the lady at the dress shop had so diplomatically referred to it.

"What are you up to?" she asked.

Ron hadn't come home with Jonathan yet, so I slumped into his kitchen

404

chair. "I was trying on dresses for the pageant. And I found one I really like."

"Oh, yeah?" my mother responded. I wasn't used to her being in a good mood. I had needed *this* mom so many times before, like at the dress appointment I'd just come from.

"Yeah, it's really pretty," I said before describing the floor-length black halter gown in detail.

"It sounds like something you'd wear," my mother affirmed.

"It is. But I think I'm going to have to keep looking," I said with a sigh.

"Why? If it's what you like . . .?"

"I stopped liking it once the lady told me the price," I said.

"How much is it?" my mother asked with scrunched brows.

"Eight hundred dollars," I admitted with a cringe. It was more than twice the cost of any other dress I'd ever worn to a dance or formal event.

"Eight hundred dollars?" my mother repeated with bulging eyes.

"Yeah," I said, grimacing. "*Before* alterations."

My mother huffed. "Where do you think you're gonna get *that* kind of money, Dane?"

"I don't know," I said. "I'm actually really stressed out about it."

"Well, you should be!" my mother snipped, instantly transforming into the "Mommy Dearest" I knew. Then she shook her head and said, "I still don't understand why you're doing this, when—"

I cut her off. "I know." I didn't need to hear her opinion a second time about how I wouldn't win. I was still recovering from the saleswoman's implication that my body wasn't like all the other girls' who competed in pageants. Apparently, stick figures were the expected norm. "I just wish you would stop saying things that make me feel bad about myself," I threw in as I got up to leave.

"I'm just trying to keep you grounded, Dana," my mother snarked behind me.

I turned back to my mother and crossed my arms. "Keeping your daughter grounded is one thing. But making your daughter feel like a worthless, ugly, undeserving piece of crap is another."

My mother rolled her eyes. "Why do you insist on using that language?!"

"Why do you always insist on diminishing me?" I said, throwing my arms up at my sides. "Jesus, Mom! Would it kill you to give me a compliment?

Or some encouragement?" I huffed and shook my head, fighting back the tears welling in my eyes.

My mother glared at me, as if I'd had some nerve speaking the truth. I held her stare, though, to show her I'd meant it.

After what had seemed like forever, she looked back at her dishes in the sink and said, "You wanna know why I don't compliment you, Dane?"

I could feel my body tense. Still, I responded with a reluctant nod.

"Because I don't want you to think you're more than what you are," she declared, impressing me with another intense stare. "It's a parenting method I read about in a book," she added, as if she was suddenly the authority of parental wisdom.

I looked at my mother disdainfully, wondering why she'd had to read a book about parenting at all. Why couldn't she just love me because of the simple fact that I was her daughter?

Then I went up to my bedroom and ruminated about what she'd said. The one thing my mother and I could agree on was that I wouldn't win this pageant. I certainly wasn't conceited to think I even had a chance. Still, it would have been nice for my mother to believe that I was worthy of the crown. Or at least be glad she'd birthed a daughter who others held to that higher regard.

A few nights later, I came down to the kitchen and saw the local newspaper sitting on the counter. It was folded open to an article titled, "Local Teen's Extra Energy May Help Win Pageant." The headshot the modeling agency had used to promote me a couple years before was smack-dab in the center. I was excited and embarrassed all at once.

"Oh, yeah," my mother said. I turned to see she'd just walked in, carrying some plastic toddler bowl Jonathan must have been snacking from. "An article about you was in the paper today," she said as unemotionally as ever, placing the empty dish in the sink.

I hadn't told her that a reporter from the local newspaper had come to my high school to interview me recently. I honestly hadn't thought she'd care. Plus, I didn't think it was that big of a deal. I'd been in the local paper before. The first time had been in eighth grade, showing me dancing to the song "Mony Mony" at a local event for teens. The last time had been a few months before, when I'd been interviewed about the trip to Paris and photographed practicing the routines.

"Thanks for saving it," I said.

"Yep," she said before returning to my little brother upstairs, who was calling out for her.

Leaning back against the counter, I scanned the small font, feeling weird reading what had been written about me based on an hour-long conversation.

It began: *All that Miss Teen Illinois contestant, Dana D., needs is a little help from her friends to compete with the crème de la crème from throughout Illinois. She seems to have everything else going for her.*

I thought that was a bit of a stretch, though I'd admit I'd felt a lot happier lately.

The 17-year-old high school senior is an honor roll student, accepted by DePaul University to begin her college career there this fall.

"I'm going to be a lawyer," I was quoted as saying when the reporter had asked what I planned to study there. It had always been my intent to help other victims of abuse get out of their situations, since I couldn't.

Dana, who not only performed with the Universal Dance Association in Paris, France, over Christmas vacation, also served as her school's pom squad secretary and treasurer.

After talking about my musical talents and previous affiliations with two symphonic orchestras, the article read, *Dana says people have asked her why her parents, who own their own business here in town, don't sponsor her in the pageant.*

I cringed.

"This is something I have to do myself," I'd said before explaining how local businesses could support me by donating items or money. I mentally high-fived myself for the diplomatic response. Still, I knew my mother had probably taken that as a shot.

The rest of the article explained the different competitions within the pageant and how I hoped to gain "invaluable experience" from it all, which also sounded like something a pageant contestant might have been coached to say.

Aside from the comment about my mother and Ron not sponsoring me, I thought the article was an accurate depiction of who I really was. All I could hope was that someone who owned a local business would be inspired to help me with a dress or shoes, or money for the rest of the items I needed. A part of me also hoped my dad might see it and secretly be proud.

The next night, my mother stopped me on my way out to meet Travis for dinner and handed me a check.

"What's this for?" I asked before noticing the amount.

"It's for your dress," she said with a sternness that didn't match the joyful surprise of the favor. "But don't tell Ron I gave it to you."

"No! I won't! I promise!" I said, shaking my head anxiously. "But—"

"I'm only doing it because I figure I'd have had to spend the money on a prom dress for you anyway," she said.

I wanted to believe her, but I knew better. This had something to do with the article. This wasn't the time to call her on it, though. I wasn't supposed to look a gift horse in the mouth or something like that.

"I'll just wear the dress to prom too, then!" I said, even though I'd had my heart set on a different dress I'd seen at the mall. "Will you come to the dress shop with me to order it? I wouldn't mind having your opinion on the dress, or maybe even trying on others for you."

"You said you'd found the dress you wanted, so I thought you just needed the money," she said. "I don't have time for that, anyway, between work and Jonathan and—"

I cut her off before hearing about all the other things in her life that took priority over me. "I know. I just thought . . ." *I'd make this last-ditch effort to ask for what I really wanted,* which was my mother, not her money. "Never mind," I said and went on my way.

"I'll Never Get Over You Getting Over Me"

I'd been so caught up in pageant preparations that I'd practically forgotten about senior prom. Or maybe I'd put the rite of passage out of my mind because it had been Liam's sparkly blues that I'd imagined gazing into while our bodies swayed to slow, romantic ballads—not Travis's.

Although things had been going well with Travis, prom wouldn't be what I'd hoped, at least not with him. He didn't go to my school, so he didn't belong to any friend groups that we could share a limo or take group pictures with. He was five years older and from a lower-class town in Michigan, so he didn't blend in with anyone I knew either. I'd asked Kelly and Miranda if they'd be willing to join us. Kelly was dating an older guy whose friend was dating another girl in our class, though, and they'd decided to keep to their foursome. Miranda already had plans to attend with another friend group, and there was no more room in their limo. So, I was the odd man out as usual.

Discouraged and dispirited that my vision of prom was turning out to be nothing like I'd thought, I went through the motions to prepare for it anyway, hoping for an unexpectedly pleasant outcome. I'd gone to the cosmetics store I worked at to apply my own makeup. The manicurist there painted my nails in a bright pink to match the fuchsia sequins on my dress. Then I walked across the mall corridor to the empty discount hair salon to have them do something with the mess of curls on my head. I left with a smoothed-out half-up do that didn't seem like anything special. It was better than anything I would have been able to do myself, though. So, I drove to Travis's apartment to dress and wait for him to get off work to do the same.

"You look amazing!" he said when he walked in and saw me all dolled up. He stood back to look me up and down, which momentarily lifted my spirits. "I guess I better get in the shower. I can't have you walking around like that without me!"

I smiled and then sank into his old couch to watch *Jeopardy* on TV. Travis emerged fifteen minutes later, wearing black tuxedo pants and a white button-up shirt that looked exactly like the work clothes he'd just removed a short time before.

"Ready?" he asked, fussing with the bow tie around his neck.

"Yeah," I said even though I wasn't mentally invested in the night. I couldn't shake the nagging feeling that I was no more important to any friends than I was to my mother or anyone else. I didn't want to piss on Travis's good mood, though, since he'd taken on the sole expense of ensuring this night was everything it should be for me.

"How do I look?" he said as he slid the tuxedo jacket on. He grinned broadly at his reflection in the mirror, exuding exactly the type of confidence a feather-haired hillbilly with a "flavor saver" would have when preparing to go to an elegant event where he probably didn't belong.

"Good," I feigned to be polite. I guessed I should have been glad he hadn't insisted on wearing his cowboy boots and wide-brimmed hat, like he usually did.

"I do look good, don't I?" he said as he checked himself out at different angles. "I still think I should have gotten the white tuxedo, though."

"This isn't the 1970s," I murmured as I went to the door. I'd seen the limousine he'd arranged for us pull up in the lot just outside his patio doors.

"All right! Let's go have some fun!" Travis said, raising his brows. I wished I had the same enthusiasm.

We stopped at my house on the way to the downtown Chicago hotel where prom was being held. I wanted my mother to see me in my dress and take pictures. Other girls had been talking about where they were meeting their friend groups with their parents, to capture fun memories before the night began. Since none of my friends thought to include us in their plans, standing on Ron's front lawn would have to do.

My mother answered the door. "Look at you, Dane!" she said with just about as much enthusiasm as ever.

Stunned at the positive regard, I stood on the stoop with a raised brow. "Thanks."

"Let me grab my camera. I'll be right out," she said through the screen door. Then she reappeared a moment later. "Hi, Travis," she said when she came outside.

"Hey, how are ya?" he acknowledged.

My mother didn't respond. She was more focused on inspecting my hair, which I thought odd, considering her inability to tame her much frizzier head of curls. I enjoyed her fussing regardless, particularly when she patted a spot on my head. It was attention and affection I didn't otherwise get.

"Why don't you two stand by the limo?" my mother instructed. We obliged. Then I mustered a couple more smiles for photos on the lawn, still failing to feel whatever magic my prom night was supposed to invoke.

Then, as soon as we arrived at the swanky hotel on the Magnificent Mile, the reason for my mood slapped me in the face. Liam had arrived just before us, looking even more handsome than I'd ever seen. The top of his white tuxedo shirt was unbuttoned, and his black bow tie hung undone from his neck. The black pants and jacket were slightly fitted, allowing notice of a muscular body he'd worked hard to achieve.

The exotic girl who'd replaced me was hanging on his arm. I gasped when I saw her wearing the exact dress that I had wanted to wear for the occasion. I just hadn't been able to afford it after buying the dress for the pageant.

The floor-length black gown hugged every luscious curve of her hips and bottom, and her ample bosom filled the halter, where several strands of gold chains joined the black collar to the sweetheart neckline above the chest. Her red curls and green eyes reflected off the gold accents, making every other girl in the place want to wither away at the sight of her natural beauty.

The perfect pair stood out, laughing and joking with friends as if oblivious to how delicious they both looked. Then they took pictures together and with their group, comfortable in the way they shared affection and adoring gazes. It's like I was watching that girl Julie live the fairy tale that was supposed to have been mine.

"Let's go find a table to sit at," I suggested to Travis to alleviate my torment. He agreed, so we entered the lavishly decorated ballroom.

Red-and-white balloon arches and floral centerpieces displaying the same school colors decorated the doorways and tables, while crystal chandeliers sparkled high above. The place was otherwise filled with girls in colorful tulle and sequin gowns, and penguin-suited boys with bows to match their date. I searched the room over to find anyone I knew and was glad when I spotted Miranda.

"Let's head over there," I told Travis above the loud music the DJ played. He nodded and followed.

"Hi, Miranda!" I said with a wave and a smile as we approached.

"Oh my god! Hi!" she said with so much enthusiasm that the dazzling facets of her hazel eyes reflected pretty blues and greens and every shade between.

"I love your dress!" I said after we'd hugged. The off-the-shoulder burgundy gown set off her long auburn hair beautifully.

"Yours is . . . ugh! You always look good!" she said with a wave of her hand. "I never understood how someone as pretty as you could always be so sad," she flippantly commented. The misplaced observation boggled me for a moment. But I had no time to explain that the two qualities didn't correlate before she asked, "So, where are you guys sitting?"

I looked around worriedly. "Um, I was actually hoping you might have two open spots at your table."

She cringed. "Sorry! We're full."

"That's okay," I smiled, trying to hide my disappointment.

"Let me know where you end up, though, okay?"

"Yeah," I said, nodding. Then Travis and I went out in search of seats again.

We asked about the empty spaces at a few other tables until we found two with untouched place settings that weren't already spoken for.

"Can we sit here?" I asked the girl who sat beside one of the open chairs.

"Yeah!" she said. I recognized her from the psychology class we took together. She'd also bought the lipstick she was wearing from the cosmetics store I worked at.

"That lipstick looks good on you!" I told her as we settled into our chairs.

"Thanks!" she said with a smile. Then she turned toward the person on the other side of her and engaged in a conversation with them. I tried not to take the act personally. It was hard not to, though.

I looked over at Travis for some attention or comfort or anything that would subdue the feelings of rejection that seemed to be triggered everywhere else I turned.

"Now, *that* girl knows how to have *fun!*" he said, pointing towards a girl who was waving her hands in the air and moving her body wildly on the dance floor.

Feeling like I wasn't the person Travis wanted to be there with either, I got up to leave. I wasn't sure where I'd go. I just didn't want to be there or anywhere where everyone's enviable connections to friends and partners were smothering me with what I didn't have.

"Where are you going?" Travis asked.

"The ladies' room," I politely answered. I was cramping, anyway, and wasn't sure if I had to go to the bathroom or if I was getting my period. I discovered it was the latter, which didn't help make the night any better.

When I returned to the table, I told Travis, "I wanna go."

"But we haven't even eaten yet. Or danced!" Travis complained.

"Well, I'm done," I said firmly. Although I'd put in a tampon a girl in the bathroom had given me, I just wanted to take this dress off before I bled all over it and wound up looking like Stephen King's Carrie on the pageant stage.

"What's going on with you?" Travis asked in an accusing tone as he followed me out.

It was a valid question. I knew I was being a pouty brat. I opted not to answer, though, because I didn't want to have to admit to my immature overreaction. It was bad enough that Miranda was right about my inability to be happy. This was a perfect example of that.

As we stepped onto the elevator that would take us down to the lobby, I caught a glimpse of Liam and Julie again. They were the last image I'd have of my senior prom, just before the doors closed.

"What's up with you?" Travis asked again, now that we were alone. "Why are you acting like this?"

I didn't know what to say. That I didn't realize how strongly I still felt about my ex? That it sucked to feel like I wasn't important enough to any of my friends for them to think to include us in the groups they'd arrived with, and doubly sucked to have to grovel like beggars for two spare seats at whatever table would withstand our company? That I didn't blame anyone for feeling the way they did about me when I didn't even like *myself*?

None of this was Travis's fault, though. I was the one who held back in friendships and relationships because I didn't trust people. I was the one who couldn't get past the past. I was the one who stifled my feelings about everything until they bubbled over like an unattended pot on a high flame.

"I just don't feel good," I said, opting for a half truth. "I got my period."

"Oh!" he said as if my answer explained everything.

He didn't say anything else after that. Neither did I. So, it was a long, quiet drive back to his apartment, where I showered, put on sweatpants and a sweatshirt, and went to sleep.

Travis was still sleeping when I left his apartment to go home the next morning. I didn't bother ruining his day by waking him so early to say goodbye, especially after how I'd ruined the night before.   "How was prom, Dane?" Mom asked as soon as I got home. "And the cruise at Navy Pier afterwards?"

"Awesome!" I lied with a fake smile. Then I rushed up to my bedroom and mourned the memories of what should have been. Alone. Like I always was.

"Don't Bring Me Down"

I graduated from high school in mid-June 1993. The most memorable part of the day was watching Michael Jordan lead the Chicago Bulls to their third consecutive NBA Championship win on the TV in the restaurant where we were supposed to be celebrating my educational achievement. It was just as well, as it distracted Ron from the diminishment he would have otherwise made me feel for having failed to graduate at the top of my class with whatever high honors he could have bragged about to friends and family.

It also distracted attention from the way I was pushing my food around my plate instead of eating it. The Miss Illinois Teen pageant was just a week away, and I was really nervous about how the slight bulge in my lower abdomen would look in the unflattering one-piece swimsuit. I'd tried it on so many times, hoping to eventually see a reflection I could tolerate better, but I never did. So, I'd ordered chicken, since 45 percent of its caloric content was used in digestion. But I was still worried about the other 55 percent I'd have to burn off.

When I awoke at five o'clock the next morning, I turned my stereo on as low as I could hear it without waking Ron. Then I pulled out the purple plastic platform Mom did step workouts on, and I did whatever kicks and lifts and jumps I could recall seeing her do. I figured this new exercise phenomenon was effective, since Mom was in my closet more, borrowing skirts and tops she would have never fit into before.

Despite exhausting myself with two similarly intense workouts daily and enduring headaches from skipping meals, by the morning of the pageant, my body looked exactly the same as it always had. I couldn't accept it without trying to change it, though. So, after packing everything I needed for the three days I'd be away, I went to the basement to burn some last-minute calories on my mother's exercise bike.

I turned on the oversized TV Ron had to have for the basement, finding only infomercials on every channel I switched to. So, I settled on a Thighmaster ad, hoping Suzanne Somers could teach me how to get that daylight I'd been looking for between my thighs, while I feverishly pedaled my way to nowhere.

My mother came down a few minutes later. She'd taken the morning off work to drive me to the hotel where the pageant and its contestants would be held. Ron hadn't seen fit for me to drive myself because he didn't trust that I wouldn't leave the hotel to do something I hadn't already done before.

"What're you doing, Dane?" my mother scolded.

"Exercising," I responded, hoping she didn't think I was being smart. She shook her head as she passed me on her way to the laundry room.

"I . . ." I started to explain, before pausing to take a breath. "I just wanna exercise as much as I can before—"

"Before what?" my mother interrupted, as if she didn't know.

Resenting the disregard, I withheld verbal response and glared at her instead.

"We need to head out so I can get to work," she said as she walked up the stairs, obliterating the significance of the pageant and the last-minute anxiety I had about being in it. Even my feet felt the defeat, succumbing to the slowing momentum of the pedals that carried them involuntarily until they finally stopped.

The car ride to the pageant was quiet other than the radio playing pop music between the DJ's enthusiastic mini monologues. I tended to clam up when upset, anxious, nervous, or hurt, and I was all those things right now. My stomach ached too, making me regret the coffee I'd had with my bird-like breakfast.

When we arrived at the hotel, which was located on the outskirts of the mall where Travis worked now, my anxiety peaked into straight-up panic. Teenage girls with perfectly coiffed hair and professionally applied makeup walked through the parking lot from every direction, each with a posse of mothers or friends or pageant coaches carrying their garment bags and suitcases. My nerves kicked me in the ass with self-deprecating reminders that my frizzy curls and insecure ego were nowhere near prepared to compete against these bubbly Barbies.

I looked over at my mother, who was oblivious to my inner turmoil. If she wasn't, then her silence was just cruel. I couldn't think straight enough to decipher her intentions, though. I worried more about calming myself before getting out of the car with the fake smile and positive candor every contestant was expected to display from what I could see. So, after my mother had finally parked, I plastered a fake Barbie-doll smile onto my face too while I dragged my bags into the hotel lobby. Then we stood in a long line, where my mother remained tight-lipped, waiting to check in and get my room assignment.

While we waited, I overheard other mothers giving their daughters pep talks and pageant coaches giving girls last-minute directions. I hadn't realized there was so much strategy involved in standing on a stage and smiling, which made me feel even more inept and out of place. So, I looked to my mother, hoping for any encouragement she could offer. Unable to decipher whether her stone-faced expression was one of displeasure or disinterest, I interpreted it as an indication that she didn't want to be there at all. So, I kept my mouth shut too, reminding myself to be glad she hadn't dropped me at the curb in her usual haste to be rid of me.

After checking in and receiving my room assignment, we were directed to the elevators. My mother piled the two garment bags she'd been holding onto everything else folded over my arm.

"You're leaving?" I asked her. I'd expected her to at least accompany me to my room, like the other mothers were doing.

"Well, yeah, Dane," my mother responded like a snarky teenager, implying I was stupid for asking. "I have to get to work."

"But—" I started but stopped when I realized I couldn't make my mother suddenly care that I was scared.

"I don't know what you want from me," she said with an annoyed huff. Except that she did, because I'd told her countless times before.

"Nothing, Mom," I said, forcing back tears. "I can find my way from here."

"Okay," she said. "I'll try to make it to Parent's Night tomorrow. I don't think Ron will be able to make it, though. He'll probably stay home with Jonathan."

Disappointed that I was a "maybe" instead of a priority, I pressed my lips together and inhaled deeply through my nose. When I exhaled, I said, "Yeah, of course. Well, I better get up to my room and change for my first rehearsal."

"Okay, I'll see you later, Dane," my mother said. And without a kiss, a hug, or a last-minute thought, she left me standing there with all my shit, and feeling like a piece of it too.

"Harden My Heart"

s I stumbled into my assigned room, managing my luggage and garment bags, I realized my roommate was already there. An old suitcase sat open on one of the queen beds, and a dress in dry-cleaner's plastic hung over the back of the desk chair.

"Hello?" I called out to announce my presence.

"Oh, hi!" I heard as a homely little thing with a slight southern drawl stepped out from what I assumed was the bathroom.

I couldn't help looking her up and down, because she looked nothing like all the girls I'd passed in the lobby. She wasn't wearing makeup. She hadn't done anything with her thin, straight blonde hair. In her too-small T-shirt and worn jean shorts, she didn't look like she was a pageant contestant at all.

"I'm sorry," I said, apologizing for the stare. "I'm Dana."

"I'm Laura Sue," she responded.

"Where are you from? South, obviously," I remarked, referring to her drawl.

She sat on her bed with the slumped shoulders of a bored child. "Alton. It's down by St. Louis, on the Mississippi."

"I know where that is," I said, though I didn't reveal that it was because I'd heard that Alton was also home to one of the most haunted locations in the state of Illinois. I kept my fascination with the paranormal to myself because people thought it was weird. "So, how did you end up *here*?"

"My mama heard about it and thought I should give it a go," she said. "What about you?"

As I hung my garment bags in the closet, I said, "I'm from a town just

419

north of Chicago. A girl I go to school with was Miss Teen Illinois two years ago, so the school nominated me, hoping for a repeat, I guess."

"Oh!" she said, her surprise being the first sign of emotion evoked from her very blah personality.

The more we chatted, though, the more I liked her. She was real. She wasn't trying to pass herself off as something she wasn't. She seemed to be as green and insecure as I was, too, which made me feel a whole lot better about being there myself. Plus, who knows what kind of tricks this little girl had in her back pocket? Maybe once she dolled herself up, she transformed into the beauty queen no one saw coming. Regardless, her untarnished small-town innocence was preferable to the snooty entitlement other girls our age tended to exhibit.

After chatting a little more, we had to report to performance group practice. Laura Sue wasn't in the group of advanced dancers I had been assigned to, so I only saw her in our room between grueling, non-stop rehearsals where we were taught multiple dance routines, practiced proper stage placement, and repeatedly ran through the sequence of events.

We weren't allowed contact with anyone outside of the pageant, so I was glad to have Laura Sue to talk to and pass the time with back in our room. Most of the other girls were career pageant contestants with egos as inflated as their poofy hairdos, making me appreciate my simple roommate even more. One girl bragged to everyone about the cosmetic surgery she'd had, hoping it would win her the crown this year.

My mother liked juicy gossip and inside information like that, so I was eager to tell her about that girl at the Parent's Night dinner, assuming she'd come. Despite our strained relationship, I'd do anything for some semblance of a connection, even if just for a moment, to feel like I had a mom.

The dinner was held the next night in the hotel's extravagant banquet room. Dimly lit brass chandeliers with teardrop crystals hung from the high ceilings of the expansive place. Ivory walls with ornate wood trim, burgundy carpet, and oval-shaped chairs added classic elegance to the space. With the hundreds of people buzzing in chatter as silverware and glasses clinked above it all, it looked like a wedding reception awaiting its guests of honor.

I walked into the lively atmosphere, feeling as hopeful and excited as I'd been in grade school when I'd look out into the gymnasium bleachers, hoping my mother had been able to make it to whatever musical performance I was in.

Among the sea of faces, I spotted her right away. Her employee Linda and my friend Patty were with her.

"Hi!" I said as I approached the table where they sat. "I didn't know you guys were coming!"

"Surprise!" Patty exclaimed as she stood to greet me.

She was a short Thai girl whom I'd befriended in seventh grade, when her family had moved to our area. I liked Patty because she was direct in a funny way and supported whatever I did. We squealed in excitement as we bounced in our embrace.

Then I went around to where my mother sat and gave her a weak hug before turning my attention to Linda, giving her a more enthusiastic embrace. I'm so glad you could make it!" I said as I smiled and squeezed Linda a little harder. She'd been working for my mother and Ron for about eight years. She seemed to be my mother's only friend, or at least the only person Mom saw in a social context on the rare occasion she had time.

"So, how's everything going here?" Patty asked as I sat beside her at the white-clothed table. Salads had already been placed before us, so my mother and Linda started eating.

"Good!" I responded. Then I told them all about it so far, from which songs I'd been rehearsing choreography for to how horrified I'd been the first time our plates had been inspected to ensure we'd eaten every bit before we could be excused. I shared gossip about the other contestants too, including the fifteen-year-old who'd had liposuction and a nose job to perfect her appearance.

"Are you serious?" Patty asked with a horrified expression.

"Totally," I responded. "The girl actually thinks she's going to win too. She's a snotty—"

"Bitch," Patty mumbled, finishing my sentence before taking a bite of her salad.

"Damnedest thing is she looks like a frickin' angel," I threw in.

I saw my mother roll her eyes. Linda smirked in response.

"What?" I asked my mother, wanting to know what the eyeroll had been about.

"Well, it's just that you tend to exaggerate things, Dane," my mother

421

stated like she was the supreme authority on my personality. Then she looked at Linda again for nonverbal agreement. Linda smirked again.

The pressure of the pageant made me less tolerant of my mother's demeaning. "What am I exaggerating?" I demanded, staring across the table at her. I noticed Patty and Linda lower their heads.

"I don't understand what you're getting so upset about, Dane," my mother said coolly. Then she looked at Linda and commented, "She's always been emotional, overreacting like this."

"How do you want me to feel, Mom?" I said a little too loudly, confronting her passive-aggression directly. Before she could answer, I justified, "I mean, you show up, which I appreciate, but then you cut me down like you always do! I never know if you love me or hate me or—"

"I wouldn't have come at all if I knew you were going to act like *this*," my mother snarked. Then she looked at Linda again. Linda raised her eyebrows and patted her mouth with her napkin to recuse herself from involvement.

"Act like what, Mom? Please tell me, because I never seem to do or say anything that meets your expectations of me." I noticed Patty lower her eyes and shift uncomfortably in her seat. I didn't care, though. I was sick of my mother treating me like everything I did was wrong!

My mother huffed. "Like *this*," she said with bulging eyes.

We all straightened up and quieted as servers brought our main dish. I was stewing, though, and ready to burst.

"I'm not hungry," I told a server as I stood and walked out despite the fact that I was starving. I was always starving, which was why I couldn't lose the weight I wanted to.

"Are you okay, Dana?" I heard behind me in the lobby. I turned to see Patty jogging to catch up to me.

"No!" I said, taking a deep breath to calm. "I don't understand why my mom can't see any good in me. Or at least be polite to me. I mean, if she doesn't want to be here, which she obviously doesn't, then why did she come?" I threw my arms up at my sides.

"I know. But she did come. And that's gotta count for something," she said.

"Well, it doesn't."

"You don't mean that," Patty said with carefulness not to scold.

"The hell I don't!" I said. "I mean, I want my mother here. But there's always some hidden slight in every gesture or word she says to me. If I address it with her, I'm 'sensitive.' It's like I'm not *allowed* to have feelings. So, I try to hold it all in, but—"

I stopped short when I saw my mother and Linda approaching.

"Since this is going nowhere, Dane, we're going to take off," my mother said.

"Of course you are," I responded with an out-of-place grin, shrug, and nod of my head.

She gave me a weak hug then, which I reluctantly accepted for the little it was worth. Then Linda and Patty wished me good luck before following my mother out. Linda glanced back, offering an apologetic closed-mouth smile. It wasn't her responsibility to make me feel better, though. It was my mother's, only she never took responsibility for anything that pertained to me. She pawned me off to anyone who'd take the brunt of me, leaving me to essentially fend for myself.

So, I returned to the banquet room and sat at the table reserved for the family I didn't have, hoping no one else noticed. I didn't want any attention on me, anyway. Being inconspicuous and insignificant is what I'd always counted on to protect myself from the abandonment and rejection that sent me down the rabbit hole I often found myself at the bottom of.

"A Little Respect"

*T*he two days of the pageant that followed didn't go much better than that dinner.

I'd awkwardly paraded down the runway of the stage in my Ziegfield Folly's dancer costume during the first night of the competition. Attempting to balance a two-and-a-half-foot-tall feathered headpiece hadn't been the problem, though; it was the super high stripper heels I'd clomped around the stage in like a Clydesdale horse learning how to walk.

Then the cobalt-blue one-piece I'd bought to wear in the swimsuit competition went missing in the couple minutes I'd been on stage in the Ziegfield costume. I ripped my bag apart looking for it, knowing all the while it had been there, because I'd double-checked before leaving the hotel room. I asked the girls around me if they'd accidentally taken it or seen someone messing with my things, but no one confessed. Under pressure to be back on stage, I had no choice but to wear the black leotard I'd worn for dance rehearsals, but because it wasn't a swimsuit, I received a lower score.

During the evening gown competition, I'd made it up and down the runway just fine in the sequined halter gown I'd worn to prom. As I took my place next to the other two girls who'd already done the same, I noticed one's lips quivering, like she was about to cry. So, I'd whispered, "Get your chin up and smile!" Then I flashed my pearly whites too. I was marked down for encouraging another contestant, instead of being praised for my selfless act.

I did score in the top five in the judge's interviews, though. The judges said they liked my personality, were impressed with my poise and presentation, and that my education and open perspectives were evident in my answers to their questions. That meant more than any physical comparison one could make, which really was subjective anyway.

But as my mother had predicted, I didn't win.

I was thrilled for the girl who did. Without a drop of makeup, a minute of exercise, or a second of coaching, her natural beauty beat out the repeat contestant who'd been intimidating everyone with her condescension and upturned (surgically altered) nose. I loved it when karma put people in their rightful place.

Most of all, however, I loved the reaction of the winner's father when she was declared Miss Teen Illinois. Wearing his dirty denim overalls, the short, rotund man stood from his chair, threw his grubby cap to the ground, and buried his scruffy-bearded face in his hands. When he looked back up to see his daughter adorned with the sparkly crown, he revealed tears of joy and disbelief. It brought tears to my eyes, because I'd never seen a man exhibit so much pride for his daughter. Every girl should have a father like that, or at least someone on her side, to be proud of her for who she was and all she accomplished.

I wished my dad could have been there, but Travis's presence sufficed. He was front and center in the audience every evening, waving to make sure I saw him and beaming proudly no matter how I performed. It was comforting to see a familiar face but to also know he was there to cheer me on for doing the best that I could without having to be the best overall.

Travis's mother was visiting from Michigan the following week. I'd met her once when I'd made a trip up there with Travis. However, we hadn't spent any significant amount of time together. I'd hoped to do that while she was here.

On her first day in, I drove to Travis's apartment after work. He was there with his parents and roommate, talking and catching up, when I arrived.

"How was the pageant?" Travis's mother asked when I sat beside her on the couch.

She had a warm smile that revealed the most beautiful straight white teeth, and short blonde hair that shimmered against her glowing tanned skin.

"Oh, you heard about that?" I asked, trying to act demure.

"It's all Travis has been talking about!" his dad said. "That he's dating a beauty queen!" I already knew that, but it still made me smile.

"Yes! It must have been quite an experience!" his mother said.

"That it was!" I said with a tinge of sarcasm. Then I told her about the girls who'd had plastic surgeries and how we'd been accompanied to the restroom after meals to make sure we weren't purging.

Everyone had their own commentary about my behind-the-scenes exploits. Then Travis's mom asked, "Did you take any pictures while you were there? Or weren't you allowed to do that either?"

"We weren't allowed to bring cameras," I said. "But I think Travis has the program booklet around here somewhere. All the contestants' headshots are in it."

I got up and searched through a pile of mail and other papers on the nearby dining table. The thick white program stood out from the rest. I returned to the couch and sat next to Travis's mom, who scooted her petite body closer to see.

"She did really good," Travis told his mother as I thumbed through the pages. I smiled up at him then continued my search for my headshot. "Oh, here it is!" I said, opening the program fully on our laps. My smile instantly dissipated when I saw Travis's handwriting on the page.

"What's the number you wrote by this other girl's headshot?" Travis's mother asked him. "Is that where she placed in the pageant? Nineteenth?"

"Um, no," Travis responded. I looked up at him and noticed his dad and roommate averting their eyes. I was keen on body language. This couldn't be good.

"What does it mean, then?" his mother asked, looking to me for a response.

I had an idea, so I began to explain. "Out of the hundred-plus girls, the first cut in the pageant reduced contestants to the top twenty."

"So, Travis marked the booklet with who he'd thought would make the cut?" his mother deduced as I flipped through the pages to determine my same guess. I saw various numbers in circles by other girls' pictures. All the numbers were under twenty.

I went back to my picture then, hoping I'd see a number this time.

"That's what it looks like," I mumbled, more to myself. I knew I hadn't been the prettiest or most talented girl there, but Travis hadn't thought I'd even make the top twenty?

With sorrowful eyes directed his way, I pleaded for an explanation that would alleviate the humiliation I felt to have his parents and friend witness this embarrassing revelation.

"I . . ." he said, stalling.

There was nothing he could say to take away the pain of his betrayal. I glared at him with trembling lips, desperate to escape before I erupted into tears. Then I stormed out of the apartment.

"I can't believe you did that, Travis!" I heard his mother scold just before the door closed behind me.

"What?" he responded like a snarky teenage boy. I could hear them from the hallway.

"Did you really think she wouldn't see that eventually?"

"I don't know!" he responded. "I was just there and figured I'd see if my predictions were correct in the end."

"This was a pageant, Travis, not the horse-racing track," his mother corrected. We went to the horse-racing track often. I liked the horses, and Travis liked betting on them.

"You need to go make sure she's okay," his mother said to him after a minute of muffled exchanges.

I heard his apartment door open and shut. So, I looked over from where I'd crumpled against the wall in the middle of the corridor.

"I'm sorry," he said, offering his hand to help me stand up. I didn't take it at first. I was so hurt by what he'd done but mostly that he didn't believe in me more. But then I did take it because no one else would want a loser like me. He took me into his arms and said, "I didn't mean anything by that."

I assumed that was an apology, though I wasn't inclined to believe it. His actions had proven that I wasn't pretty enough for him, so the damage had already been done.

"Eye of the Tiger"

I felt like I lost everything that summer. I didn't play viola or piano anymore. I didn't have dance lessons or recitals. I didn't have pom practice or marching band rehearsal. I didn't work at the cosmetics store anymore either. It wasn't that I didn't love it; I just couldn't think about moving out at eighteen if I was only making $4.25 an hour. So, I hopped from one job to the next, hating each more than the last.

Friends were moving away to college, making me wish I was moving away too. Instead, I would be commuting to DePaul, since Mom and Ron had determined I couldn't be trusted if I lived anywhere else. They wouldn't even agree to let me live in DePaul's dormitories because it was too close to home and Ron was too cheap to justify the expense.

So, while everyone else's life was changing, nothing changed in mine. And like every other morning, my first day at DePaul started off on the same wrong foot as all the others before it.

"I can't see it!" Jonathan whined. Ron caught the piece of toast Jonathan had rejected before it ended up on his lap or on the floor.

"Stop it," Ron scolded with one downward motion of his finger in Jonathan's face. I swore I was going to chop off that fucking finger in a rage like that which Lorena Bobbitt must have felt when she'd cut off her husband's dick.

"He just wants more butter on his toast," I said to Ron in a snotty tone. Then I walked over, took the toast, and sprayed more I Can't Believe It's Not Butter! on the bread until it glistened. If Jonathan couldn't see it, he really *didn't* believe there was "not butter" on his breakfast!

I returned the shiny square to Jonathan's plate at the table, and he took it up to his mouth happily. Then I went back to the opposite end of the galley kitchen and turned the radio to the country station Travis had turned me on to. The song "Trashy Women" was playing.

Jonathan bopped his head up and down to the hillbilly beat, giggling at his own silliness. It cracked me up too, which made him exaggerate his movements even more. He looked back and forth between me and Ron, to ensure his theatrics were soliciting the attention he sought.

"He doesn't need to be listening to that crap," Ron reproached.

"What crap?"

"This music," Ron responded.

Jonathan sensed the change in the energy around him and slowed to a stop. It pissed me off that his happiness, and now mine, had been brought to an end just because Ron had to assert his control over everyone and everything all the fucking time.

"Jesus Christ. It's just music," I snapped back.

"Don't you mouth off to me!"

Fed up with his constant demands, I turned back to him and said, "You know what? I'm so frickin' tired of you telling me what I can and can't do. Maybe if you just stopped treating me like a piece of shit, I wouldn't talk to you like you're one either!"

"What did you say?" Ron said as he stood from his chair. His squinty eyes made me nervous, but I stood just slightly taller and glared at him dead-on.

"You heard me," I asserted. "I'm tired of doing this with you every goddamn day!" I turned off the radio, put my coffee cup in the sink, and walked out to the foyer.

Jonathan came out of the kitchen and sat on the lowest step of the stairway to watch me put on my shoes. Ron came out after him.

"Get upstairs and get dressed!" he barked at Jonathan.

"No!" Jonathan said, crossing his arms and pouting.

"You . . ." Ron said as he raised a hand.

I immediately threw myself in between them, outstretched my arms, and turned my head from the expected impact, yelling "NO!"

When I didn't feel Ron's strike across my cheek, I peered at him sideways. I didn't move, though, worried he'd hit Jonathan like he used to hit me the second I moved out of the way. So, I glared at him, challenging him to dare me to a counterattack, until he slowly lowered his hand.

I stood tall again. Then, for the first time ever, I waved my finger in Ron's face. "Don't you dare lay a goddamn finger on my little brother!" I shrieked. Then I took Jonathan on my hip and went upstairs. Thankfully, the pounding footsteps I'd grown fearful of didn't follow us up.

After tearing the "scratchy" tag off the back collar of Jonathan's shirt, and then styling his hair straight because he didn't like his frizzy curls, I brought him back downstairs completely dressed and ready to go to school.

"You don't have to be an asshole to get a toddler to cooperate," I said as I set Jonathan down in front of Ron, who was sitting at the kitchen table, sipping his coffee.

Ron straightened up and scowled. Then he raised that pointy finger up to my face. "Don't you talk to me that way!" he seethed, huffing angrily out of his nose.

"I know. Because this is your house," I said, finishing his usual insult for him. Then I squatted in front of Jonathan, putting on a pretense of pleasant calm. "Have a good day, okay? Sissy loves you!"

Jonathan smiled as he threw his little arms around my neck and squeezed. I returned the affection. Then I regretfully left my little brother with a man I hated and distrusted even more now.

As much as I worried about Jonathan, I had to start taking care of me. I needed to focus on my education, so I could pursue a career and an income to create the stable home environment I'd always wanted. Then, if things were still bad at home, I could realistically think about bringing Jonathan to live with me, to extract him from the fate no one had chosen to save me from.

So, I immersed myself in my education and worked all the other days I didn't have classes, making as much money as I could and doubly avoiding being home if I didn't have to be.

The core classes at DePaul challenged me. Philosophy and religion professors told us to study and think and theorize but only rewarded the regurgitation of their own perspectives in papers and exams. It reminded me of the mass mind control the political science and journalism professors accused the media of, which was like the manipulative control I'd resisted all those years under Ron's roof.

Overall, college was basically reiterating to me what my mother had already demonstrated—that assimilation kept peace. But that didn't mean it was right, nor that I had to conform.

"Birthday"

$\mathcal{I}$ finally turned eighteen on December 27, 1993. I was legally an adult. I could legally come and go from Ron's house as I pleased. I didn't have to comply with whatever he dictated or demanded of me. I also had the upper hand on his abuse, now being able to press charges against him for assault if he were ever to lay a finger on me again. So, I was free, except that I had no place to go.

On my way out to meet Travis for my birthday dinner, I saw my mother, Ron, and Jonathan in the kitchen with a cake. My mother smiled as she cut into the red buttercream roses on the white frosted treat Ron had brought home to celebrate her happy day. It made me sad to see Jonathan sitting on Ron's lap, clapping and grabbing at the cake my mother plated for him, oblivious to the fact that it was my birthday too.

Suddenly aware I was in the foyer, my mother called out, "Where are you going, Dane?"

"Where I always go," I said dimly. "Anywhere but here."

She didn't respond but instead laughed at something Jonathan must have done. It's like I wasn't even there. So, I slipped out the front door to make her birthday wish come true.

The shrill sound of the telephone ringing at five o'clock the next morning startled me awake.

"Hello?" Travis asked when he answered the culprit on his nightstand. "Yeah, she's right here," he said before handing the phone to me.

"Who is it?" I whispered with my hand on the bottom end of the receiver.

"Your mother."

I sighed as I sat up then put the receiver to my ear. "Hello?"

"You didn't come home last night!" my mother said. She actually sounded worried.

"Obviously," I responded, rubbing the crusties out of my eyes.

"Do you know how scared I was when I woke up and saw that you weren't in your bed or anywhere in the house?!"

"I'm eighteen now, so I can legally do as I please. Anyway, you didn't seem too concerned about me when I left last night, so what does it matter where I slept?"

"We just assumed you had plans last night. But do you know how terrified I was to find your bedroom door open this morning and not see you in your bed?"

Although I heard a slight quiver in her voice, I didn't buy her worried mother act. "You didn't seem to care as much about my birthday yesterday," I told her.

"I wished you a happy birthday when I got home yesterday, Dane. Anyway, I can't be held accountable every time things don't go your way," she defended.

"You're right, Mom. I'm just being difficult," I said as sarcastically as ever.

She ignored my remark, saying, "Well, the next time you decide not to come home, I expect you to tell me, so I don't have to worry about you!"

"Duly noted," I said as I rubbed my forehead. "But just for the record—you're officially off the hook. You don't have to worry about me ever again."

"What's that supposed to mean?" she snarked.

"Whatever you want it to."

The sound of her annoyed huff annoyed me in turn but not as much as her saying, "Have a good day, then, whatever you decide to do over there."

I ignored her implication that there was some wild sexual encounter going on just because I was in the same bed as Travis. I mean, he was my boyfriend, and we did have sex, but not always, and not always in his bed. "I'm going back to sleep, but yeah. You too," I said. Then I hung up.

"Everything okay?" Travis muttered as I lay back down.

"I don't know. I guess," I said. "I mean, she noticed I was gone, so that's something. I just wish . . ." I stopped when I heard light snoring. My voice was apparently as invisible as I was in the darkness. So, there was no point wasting my breath on more deaf ears.

"Whose Bed Have Your Boots Been Under?"

Although I'd sworn I wouldn't live in Ron's house a day beyond my eighteenth birthday, I was having a hard time finding a place to live. No dorms were available at DePaul, nor could I afford them if they were. I couldn't find an affordable apartment, nor did I know anyone I could room with. So aside from staying at Patty's or Miranda's houses now and then if they happened to be home from college, I slept at Travis's a lot, just to avoid staying at Ron's.

"I don't know what to do," I complained when I called Travis between classes from a pay phone on campus. "I can't take one more second in that house!"

"What happened now?" Travis asked.

"Nothing," I said. "At least nothing that hasn't happened before."

"Ron's usual, then?"

"Yeah," I muttered. Then I imitated Ron, saying, "You're this and you're that, so if you don't like it here, then leave."

Travis chuckled at my summary of my life. "Well, you come to my apartment often enough. So, why don't you just stay here?" he suggested.

"Because!" I whined. "Your apartment is over an hour away from the city. That's too far of a drive from school and work."

"I guess you need to decide what's worse, then—sleeping at Ron's or driving back and forth?"

There was no doubt. However, moving in with Travis was a big step I wasn't sure I was ready to take.

"I don't work on the weekends," I thought out loud. "And I'm usually at your place anyway. So, maybe it wouldn't be a bad idea to just live with you from Friday through Sunday or Monday."

"You're welcome here whenever. You know that."

"You're sure your roommate won't mind?" I asked.

"No. He's always working or with his girlfriend."

"Well, then maybe . . ." I sort of agreed. "But only until I'm able to figure something else out."

"I'm saving for a down payment on a house, so maybe our next move will be to our own place," Travis remarked.

A *house?* I hadn't realized he'd been thinking about us in the long term. I could barely think beyond the next semester of school!

So, the permanence of his intention both excited and terrified me. On the one hand, I wanted to be with that one person who I could count on to never abandon me. So much so that I naively believed Travis's passionate rendition of the lyrics of Garth Brooks' "Shameless" when he sang, "I can walk away from anyone I ever knew, but I can't walk away from you." The problem was that I wasn't sure I wouldn't. I'd always been a runner, fleeing when I foresaw potential rejection, like when Travis had ranked other pageant contestants higher than me in his program.

Altogether, though, Travis was my constant. He was the one person who remained no matter what. I needed to hold on to that, on to him, because I feared what would happen if I didn't. So, I said, "Thank you." Then I released a long exhale of relief.

Living at Travis's on the weekends worked out really well. I had a warm bed to sleep in. I had free food to eat, whether I wanted to go to the restaurant Travis worked at or eat whatever he'd brought home from there the night before. No one was ever home, so I had a quiet space to study and write research papers. I cleaned and did laundry when I needed a break, which made me feel like I was earning my keep. Most of all, though, being there gave me peace.

Then, on a Saturday afternoon, I'd gone into the bedroom to look for a hair tie. My curly locks were preventing me from seeing the textbook I was hunched over. When I didn't see a hair tie on the dresser or nightstands, I knelt on the carpet to look under the bed, thinking one might have fallen and ended up down there. All I saw was a magazine and a lone black sock. I pulled them out, thinking I was tidying up.

My eyes widened at the sight of the large-breasted woman adorning the cover in her full naked glory. I'd heard of magazines like this but had never actually seen one. The closest I'd ever come to pornography was in 1983 when a bunch of us neighbor kids had gathered at an older kid's house to watch Prince and Apollonia have sex in his R-rated movie *Purple Rain*. We'd all gotten our butts whooped for that, after the girl's mom had found us and then called all of our parents to inform them of our crime.

Unable to ignore my curiosity, I opened the magazine to peek inside. Gorgeous women with no shame displayed their beautiful bodies in various positions and angles that might persuade heterosexual women like me to desire same-sex interactions with them. So, I couldn't be mad at Travis for appreciating the physical attributes of these women. In fact, I envied their beauty and their confidence even more. As for the sock . . . well, only a man could have invented them for the double duty of their usefulness.

I opened the top drawer of Travis's nightstand to shove the magazine and sock inside, when I saw a little black book lying on top of the other random items. At first glance, it appeared to be an address book. I wondered if it was one of those cliché "black books," where men kept lists of women whom they could count on having sex with at any given time. That was yet another item I'd never actually seen in real life. But this couldn't be one of those. Or could it? Curiosity compelled me to pick it up and take a look inside.

It was indeed an address book, just slightly larger than my hands. Travis had handwritten names and phone numbers on almost every alphabetically tabbed page. Some of the writing looked really old, like it had been there since Travis's teenage years. Some of it was newer, though. I could tell by the shade and clarity of the ink as well as the placements on the page.

Travis and I had been committed to each other for over a year, so I wondered why he had this. He knew what Liam had (almost) done to me. So, there was no way he'd cheat on me too. But then why hadn't he gotten rid of this? Unless he kept it just in case. I could have accepted that if he hadn't talked about buying a house for us. But regardless of where we were going, I expected monogamy now. And I expected that Travis's black book shouldn't have been sitting on top of everything else in his nightstand drawer.

Thinking it was a good time for a break anyway, I put the book away and went to visit my boyfriend at work. I had to find a way to induce the explanation and reassurance I needed that we were physically exclusive, at the very least.

"You lookin' for the boss?" a worker called out from the kitchen when I entered the pizza place through the back.

"Yeah. Do you know where he is?" I asked, looking over at the vacant metal desk where he usually was.

"He went to the bank, but he should be back pretty quick."

"Okay, thanks!" I said as the worker walked through the swinging door to the front of the restaurant. Then I sat in the desk chair to wait.

I looked around at the gray-and-white walls and the humongous dough mixer with the barrel of lard sitting next to it. It grossed me out to think people ate that, but the food was really good.

Bored and alone, I started thinking about that black book again and wondered what Travis might be hiding in *these* drawers. I looked around to make sure I was alone. Then I pulled open the top drawer on the right. Glaring back at me was a Polaroid picture of a woman who wasn't his sister or mom. I swore my heart stopped, because I stopped breathing altogether, until I gasped sharply to end my self-asphyxiation.

Who the hell was she? And why was her picture in my boyfriend's drawer? Worse yet, why was she on a bed, on all fours, with a seductive look on her flirty fucking face? I was starting to feel like a fool.

Just then, the worker came back through the swinging door and caught me with the Polaroid in my hand. He halted and stared, matching my open mouth and wide eyes. Then he cringed.

"What?" I asked in a panic. "What do you know?"

"I don't want to get in trouble with the boss," he said, shaking his head. He put his hands up like he was under arrest.

"Please tell me," I pleaded as my heart picked up its pace. "I swear I won't tell him how I found out. But please! I deserve to know whatever it is!"

The young man's head dropped. He closed his eyes as if wishing he weren't in this position. I inhaled deeply, feeling the same. Then he looked back up at me and said, "All I know is they talk on the phone pretty much every day."

What was left of my heart fell to the floor and shattered into pieces. I was stupid for thinking this womanizing hillbilly could be faithful to me when all he'd ever wanted was to put more notches in his belt. I should have known by the way he'd called me "jailbait" and bragged about dating a "pageant queen" that a young, pretty girl was all I was to him. And apparently all I'd ever be.

"I'm sorry," the worker said. "But from what Travis says about you, you're smart and talented and have a lot going for you. So, none of us can figure out why you'd want to be with a guy like him anyway."

I looked up at the young man and smiled weakly. It was sweet of him to try to console me. But I wasn't sure anything would do the trick right now. So, I got up to take my broken heart home, which, right now, was Travis's apartment.

"Thank you," I said, looking every bit of the defeat I felt. "Do me a favor, though, and don't tell him I was here. Okay?"

"Yeah, no problem," he said with upturned brows that expressed sorrow for my pain.

I wanted to talk to someone, but with my few friends away at college, I had no one to call but my mother. So, I called her as soon as I got back to Travis's apartment.

"Hello?" she answered.

"Hey, Mom. It's me," I said glumly.

"What's up, Dane?"

"I, uh . . . I just need to talk to someone. I'm not having the best day."

"What happened?" she asked, almost sounding concerned.

"Nothing really *happened*. It's just that I found a 'black book' in Travis's nightstand. Then I found a picture of woman in Travis's desk drawer at work. One of his coworkers said Travis talks to her on the phone all the time."

"Are you sure it isn't his sister or something?" my mother asked.

"I've met his sister, Mom. And sisters don't pose like that in pictures they give their brothers."

"Oh."

"Anyway, I'm starting to put other stuff together, like how he takes a toiletry bag with him to work on the nights he claims he has to close the restaurant."

"Maybe he likes to clean up before he comes home," my mother said.

"That's what I always thought," I acknowledged. "But I've found receipts from bars and those round coin-like things from a local casino in the bag. And *condoms*," I added, hinting that they weren't being used with me. I didn't clarify, though. I didn't need a lecture on unprotected sex right now. I'd already given *myself* one, anyway, especially if I wasn't the only girl he was . . .

"So, you think he's cheating, then?" she asked.

"Yeah. I mean, nothing else makes sense."

"I don't know what to say, Dane."

"And I don't know what to do. He's been flirting with girls right in front of me lately," I confessed, realizing that had been the beginning of the end with Liam. "Just last week, I went to visit him at work, and he gawked at a set of twins walking by, before calling out to them by name!"

"What did you do?"

"What was I supposed to do?" I said with a raised voice. "I let it go! I wasn't happy about it, but . . ." I felt tears of frustration building up because of the no-win circumstances I always seemed to find myself in.

After a long pause, my mother finally said, "It sounds to me like you've made up your mind to stay with him," she said. "And I think it's the right thing to do."

"Even if he's messing around on me?"

"You made a commitment to him, Dane. You need to honor it."

"You're making it sound like we're married!" I argued.

"Well, being in a committed relationship is like being married."

"I disagree," I asserted. "There is nothing legally holding me to him. I could walk away whenever I want. And if he's cheating, or if I'm not happy . . ."

"Relationships aren't about being happy, Dane," she said, shocking me with a seriousness that made me realize she actually believed that to be true.

I'd have thought a mother would *want* her daughter to be happy, though. Unless she was cryptically telling me *she* wasn't happy. And maybe misery really does love company.

"What are they about, then, Mom?" I begged, needing to know her perspective.

"They're about give and take," she said. "So, if someone can give you a nice place to live, comfort in knowing the bills will be paid and you have everything you need, then you take the rest."

That was really fucked-up advice. However, her skewed perspective made sense of her entire life with Ron, which thereby made sense of mine.

"Okay," I said, even though nothing she'd said was. "Well, I gotta get going. I have to get back to a paper I'm writing for political science."

I wasn't going anywhere, though. I was going to stay with Travis. I was going to ignore what I'd seen and pretend all was well. Like Mom, I would excuse and tolerate. Because if Travis and I broke up, I'd have nowhere to go, except back to where I would have to do the same with Ron.

"Goodbye Stranger"

⁓

Jonathan graduated from preschool in the late spring of 1994. It was a Thursday evening, so I'd changed at the house after that day's classes then rushed to Jonathan's preschool for the event.

There was standing room only, so my mother and I stood in the back of the room, smiling and laughing at the preschoolers as they shouted songs they were supposed to be singing and bopped to the (off)beat of the music.

Ron moved around the room with his expensive camera, pushing through people like a paparazzi anxious to get the money shot. People probably thought he *was* a professional photographer by the way he stood on his toes and then squatted to get certain angles. The elongated lens on the camera contributed to the whole charade. It annoyed me to no end that he always needed to be seen and perceived as more important than he really was.

After performing their last song and dance, the children were brought forward, one by one, to present the family pictures they'd drawn especially for this program. Each was cuter than the next, awkwardly explaining abstract crayon renditions of their moms and dads, siblings, and pets. The stick figures and analyses reminded me of my first session with Dr. Lehrfield, the child psychologist I'd been made to see just a few short years before.

"And next we have Jonathan, who will share a drawing of *his* family," the preschool teacher announced cheerily. Everyone clapped as my little brother stepped out to the front of the group with his deep dimples and toothy smile. Like his father, he loved being the center of attention.

"This is my family," he said loudly, holding up a large white paper. My smile immediately faded when I saw only three figures—a man, a woman, and a little boy.

I felt like I'd been stabbed in the gut, and the person holding the knife was smiling.

Jonathan was the one person in our house who I'd hoped considered me family, despite our half-blood relation. However, it wasn't his fault for thinking I wasn't. He only knew what he saw and heard. What he saw was our mother and Ron treat me as if I didn't matter, and I was sure he'd *heard* that I wasn't part of the family, from the asshole snapping pictures up front.

Given my lessened presence now that I lived with Travis half the time, I supposed part of Jonathan's perception was partially my fault too. Siblings usually lived at home *all* the time, at least according to a four-year-old.

So, despite the devastation of discovering I stood in no higher regard with my brother than I did with our parents, I stifled my upset in deference to Jonathan's presentation.

"This is my mommy," he announced, pointing to a vertical stick with four horizontal ones stemming out. The black squiggles on top accurately depicted her curly hair.

As the audience giggled, I glanced at my mother. Showing no emotion whatsoever, she stared straight ahead, blank-faced, with closed-mouth complacence. I couldn't tell whether she didn't want to acknowledge the uninvited attention or the obvious omission. Either way, she wouldn't look at me.

"This is me," Jonathan continued, pointing to a short, big-headed character with an equally large smile. "And this other guy is my dad."

My mother burst out laughing, like the rest of the room did. Jonathan's bluntness was almost as funny as the straight line he'd drawn for Ron's mouth.

Then, as Jonathan stepped back into line with his classmates, Ron stood in the front, facing the crowd as if taking credit for the explosive laughter and applause. Then he shrugged and cringed at the other parents and grandparents around him, making sure to ride the coattails of attention Jonathan had laid out for him.

I shook my head at the scene then glanced back at my mother. She pretended like everything was fine, like she had no clue of my justifiable offense. Then again, that's what she'd always done. She'd ignore any discomfort or sign of distress, hoping whatever it was would just go away. Better yet, she probably hoped *I* would go away, since I was the common denominator in every issue that seemed to arise within our family dynamic.

I did just as my mother did as the night went on, playing my role in the 'happy family' facade. We went to dinner to celebrate Jonathan's achievement, during which no one said a word about my exclusion from the family picture.

The following morning, Jonathan was trying to wrestle his chunky little body out of a shirt while Ron simultaneously tried to force it back on him.

"It's scratching me!" Jonathan screamed as he wriggled on the bottom stair.

"Stop it! Stop it right now!" Ron demanded at a louder decibel.

"No! I don't want to wear this scratchy shirt!" Jonathan shrieked even louder.

"GODDAMN IT!" I screamed at both of them at the top of my lungs. I was so tired of the constant argument in this house. Plus, it was the only way for them to hear me. "Just cut the fucking tag off his shirt, Ron, and then he'll put the damn thing on!"

Ron and Jonathan quieted instantly then stared as I yanked the tag off the back of Jonathan's shirt with quick ease.

"Fuck!" I said in frustration as I walked to the kitchen to throw the scratchy tag in the garbage.

Ron came in after me with that finger waving. "Don't you use that language in front of Jonathan!"

"Don't you fucking tell me what I can or can't say!" I lashed back for the millionth time. "Every fucking day of my life—every goddamn one—you're dictating and ordering and yelling about something."

"If you don't—"

"What, Ron?" I cut him off. "I mean, you obviously can't deal with children, so why the fuck did you *marry* a woman with a child and then have *another* one after? Jesus Christ!"

"Don't you—" he shouted, raising that finger in my face.

"No! Don't you!" I shouted back, raising my finger to his. "Goddamn it! I hate being in this fucking house," I grumbled to myself, instantly deciding to forego coffee so I could escape this tension. Then I went out to the foyer and slipped my feet into my ankle-high brown boots.

Ron followed me out, hollering, "If it's that bad, then there's the door!"

"You'd like that, wouldn't you?" I said as I stood.

"What?"

"For me to leave. For good," I said, stating the obvious. Then, before he could retort, I continued, "Well, guess what? Today's your lucky day. Because I'm fucking done." Then, in as calm a voice as I could muster, I squatted in front of Jonathan, who was playing with a toy on the foyer floor. "I love you, little brother. Have a good day, okay?"

Jonathan nodded and smiled. "Wuv you too, sissy!"

I squeezed my little brother like it might be the last time I would. Whether it was oblivion or forgiveness, however, Jonathan's demeanor permitted me to leave without feeling the guilt I'd felt in the past. He was theirs, so he was fine. I, on the other hand, was neither, and it was time for me to make my exit.

"All right," I said, choking back tears as I released my sweet sibling. "Never forget that sissy loves you. Okay?"

"Okay, sis," Jonathan said, refocusing his attention on the toy he had in his hands.

Then I walked out, closing the door firmly behind me.

It took the entirety of my drive to work to catch my breath, calm my nerves, and process the reality of what I'd just done. Fortunately, work was so busy that I didn't think about that morning again until my hour-long lunch break. Unsettled and upset still, I called my mother.

"I know you're at work and don't have much time to talk, but I need to talk to you, Mom. About Ron. I can't be in that house with him. I can't deal with the constant fighting and the hostility and tension and—"

"This again?" my mother asked with annoyance. "You know, Dane, I'm getting tired of all this too. You're always complaining about Ron, then he comes into work complaining about you. When will this ever end between you two?"

When you do something about it! I screamed at her in my mind. She never would, though. Her method of resolving conflict was not to resolve it at all. She preferred to act like nothing happened, so she could avoid accountability for whatever unpleasantness resulted. And if she had it her way, I'd keep my mouth shut, act like all was well, and forget about happiness altogether.

But I deserved better, even if she didn't believe that. So, I said, "I guess it ends now. If living there just a few days a week causes us all so much upset, then I just won't live there at all."

"Where're you going to live, then? Travis's?" she asked snidely.

"It's not like I have anywhere else to go!"

After a sharp sigh, she said, "I guess you've made up your mind, so . . ."

Tears welled in my eyes. I'd hoped she'd at least give me the decency of a weak plea to stay. Not that I would. It would have just made me feel like she loved me, even if just a little.

"I hope you're happy with your family," I said dismally. Then I hung up without a goodbye.

I went back to the house that evening, hoping to have a heart-to-heart. I also wanted to get some clothes and belongings to take to Travis's apartment, where I would apparently live from now on.

The house was dark aside from the headlights on Ron's newest sports car that switched off just as I pulled in behind it. Before shutting off mine, I saw Ron get out and glare at me to express my unwelcome. There was a time when he'd scared me, but that time had passed. So, I slowly emerged from my car, maintaining our mutual stare. Then I went into the house and scurried up the dark stairway two steps at a time, hurrying to get to my mother before Ron could bait me into an altercation.

Through the flashes of light coming from the master bedroom TV, I saw my mother sleeping from where I stood in her doorway. It hurt that she could after what had transpired that day.

As I looked upon this woman, cuddled into her blanket comfortably, I realized I couldn't convince her against a life she'd resigned herself to. I was the one who had to accept that she cared more about sustaining her socially appropriate pretense than she did about the consequences of her choices and how they affected me. So, I was the one who had to move on, to release us all from the burden of my unmet needs and to find the love I sought from her elsewhere. I just wished I could say goodbye, to feel some sense of closure.

With the light of the moon shining its silvery glow into my bedroom, I gathered some clothes and personal possessions without turning on the light. Making my final leave in the dark seemed appropriate to my mournful melancholy.

Over the blaring TV that had failed to keep my mother awake, I heard Ron's heavy feet coming up the steps. Triggered by memories of what followed those footsteps in the past, I suddenly felt like cornered prey. Stilled by panic, I was very aware of how loud my shallow breaths and racing heart sounded. Then I realized none of this stuff was worth my emotional or physical well-being. So, I threw the couple of bags over my shoulder and rushed out. The startle of the television flashing like lightning across Ron's scowling face halted me for a second, but then I stumbled down the stairs before this shadow of a man could do anything more than lurk.

As I sped away in my car, I glanced into my rearview mirror. The house was still and dark despite the horrors it held that would haunt my heart forever. I half expected to see Ron in the doorway, glaring from beneath the hood of a cloak, holding a sharp scythe that promised punishment for escaping the fate I'd been damned to.

Although I was glad that I'd finally left, I was sad to have lost my mother in the process. I wondered if she even *knew* I'd returned to beg for her love, though I couldn't comprehend why the inclination to love me wasn't as instinctive as it seemed to be for anyone else who'd ever given birth to a child. Then again, she had sold her soul to the devil—and mine too—to reap the benefits of the life she thought she couldn't have without him.

Aside from all the resentments and ill feelings, however, she was my mother. My stomach ached after having left at such odds. I wondered whether Ron would even inform her that I'd returned at all.

So, I decided to call her from Travis's apartment the next night. He wasn't home, anyway. He'd *said* he had to close the restaurant.

"Hello?" a tired voice answered after several discouraging rings.

"Mom?" my hopeful heart asked. I straightened my posture and kicked my feet like an excited little girl.

"Dane?" she responded, as if it had been years since we'd spoken.

"Yeah, it's me," I confirmed. "I just wanted to—"

"It's late," she interrupted. I glanced at the digital clock on the dark wood nightstand, whose ornate brass pulls outdated it even more. It was just after nine.

"I know, but—"

"We're trying to get Jonathan to sleep," she scolded.

"I'm sorry, Mom," I said, regretting having called at all. "I just thought—"

"Do you need something?" she asked, though the haste in her tone didn't expect it to matter.

I looked down at my feet, which had slowed their swing above the flattened carpet below. "No," I said, prolonging the word. "I just wanted to say goodnight, I guess."

During the long pause that followed, I wondered if my mother felt the same regret I did, for allowing a man to divide us. Then she broke the silence by snipping, "Well, you're the one who left, Dane."

I wiped the tears welling in my eyes. "You're right," I said. Then I gulped down my hurt feelings before they resurfaced to defend or avenge. "I'll let you go, then. I should get to bed, anyway."

"Okay, love you," she said, carrying on a lie she'd been telling me for years.

"Love you too," I muttered. Then I hung up.

After a long exhale, I switched off the light and crawled into the bed I'd made. Then I pulled up my knees and clutched the worn blue comforter under my chin. I'd always slept best in fetal position.

"Maybe Baby"

"You're quiet," Travis said, glancing over at me as he turned down the volume on the country music station he'd been singing along to. "Something wrong?"

It was August of 1994. We were on our way to his brother's condominium an hour away to see his mom and dad, who were visiting from Michigan. I'd have normally been anxious about making a decent impression on his family, whom I'd only been around a couple of times in the last two years. However, my mind had been plagued with worry about my period, which was a week late now. And I was *never* late, at least not since that first time with Liam.

"I'm fine," I said, curling up my lips enough to give the impression.

Travis tilted his head towards me and called "bullshit" on me with his high brows.

"Okay. You're right," I admitted with a one-shoulder shrug. "I've been kinda worried about something, but I didn't want to say anything unless I knew for sure, but—"

"Are you pregnant?" Travis asked with the wide-eyed enthusiasm and grin of a kid who'd just found out he'd won a Golden Ticket to visit the Willy Wonka Chocolate Factory.

"No!" I quickly refuted, as if doing so would erase the possibility.

"But you *might* be. Right?" Travis asked, holding on to a hope I didn't share.

"I don't know, Travis," I said with a tone that begged for him to stop pressing me. "I'm over a week late. But that doesn't necessarily mean I'm pregnant." At least I *hoped* not.

After the abortion, I'd sought out a local gynecologist who'd promised client/patient confidentiality when she'd prescribed me "the pill." My periods had come like clockwork since—except *this* one.

I'd thought of buying a pregnancy test, but I knew from having to take one before that more accurate results occurred when a period was further beyond a week late—something about hormone levels increasing and becoming more detectable. So, I was trying to stay calm and levelheaded for at least a few more days, to prevent a delay due to stress or a premature result that would still leave me in doubt.

Looking over at Travis to gauge his reaction, I should have been comforted by the closed-mouth smile of satisfaction radiating from underneath his scruffy 'stache. Most guys wouldn't be too thrilled to know they might have made a baby without meaning to. Travis's posture straightened into that of a proud papa, though, similar to a time I'd seen him holding my little brother on his hip. So, I guess I shouldn't have been surprised that he was happy. Still, I shrank down in my seat as Travis turned up the volume on the radio and serenaded me with George Strait's "I Cross My Heart," which just happened to be playing at that inopportune moment.

I offered Travis a weak smile every time he met my gaze with some dramatic expression of the lyrics coming from his mouth. I'd always loved that Travis enjoyed music and lyrics as much as I did. We'd shared a lot of laughs and romantic moments belting out classic rock and country tunes in the car together. It's just too bad I didn't love Travis with that same passion. It's not that I didn't want to. I couldn't help what I didn't feel, though.

So, I wanted to die when Travis blurted, "I might be a daddy," the second we got out of the car at his brother's. His mom and dad had come out to receive us, having no more of an idea than I did that they'd be greeted with the news that they might have their first grandchild.

"Oh, Travis! That's wonderful!" his mother said with an elegant enthusiasm that certainly hadn't come from the small, homely town they lived in. Then she turned to me and said, "Congratulations, honey!"

Shocked that Travis had come right out of the gate with an assumption he shouldn't have shared, I didn't know what to say. If I knew his parents better, I might have explained that it was just a missed period. But I barely knew his mom and didn't think it was appropriate to discuss my menstrual

cycle with his dad. So, I forced a half smile and attempted to subdue the worry and panic I really felt about the whole situation.

"Guess you two have been busy, huh?" his dad joked.

Normally, I would have chuckled at that. Instead, I averted my eyes to Travis, hoping he would dispel the dishonesty of his statement with an explanation. His wide grin and upright posture relished the moment instead. He really did want to be a dad, I realized. So much so that he was willing to pretend he was going to be and pull his parents into the fantasy world with him. So, I left well enough alone despite feeling like a liar by going along with it.

As we received more well wishes inside from his brother and his brother's long-time girlfriend, I awkwardly said, "Thank you." Then I tried to think myself into feeling happier about the possibility.

I mean, I was legally an adult now, so my mother and Ron had no legal say over me or my baby now. I had a job. I had an apartment. I even had a baby daddy whose family shared in his excitement and who would very happily welcome this baby without question. So, I should have been grateful.

Instead, I was disappointed that it wasn't Liam's. I was angry, almost, that *this* baby would get the life I'd wanted to give *that* one. It didn't seem fair. No matter what, though, I'd never let this baby know I hadn't wanted it as much as I had the other. I'd never let any another human feel what it was like to be me.

A few days later, I woke up with a terrible ache in my abdomen. Writing if off as whatever acid resulted from stress and caused my stomachaches, I went to the bathroom to pee. When I went to wipe and saw red-stained tissue, however, my spirits became just as bright. I released a long exhale of relief. Then an unconscious smile came across my face.

After suiting up with absorbent armor and taking a couple ibuprofen for the cramps, I went back to bed and shook Travis's shoulders lightly.

He squinted his eyes at me, clearly wanting to remain asleep. "You okay?" he asked with a dry rasp.

"Yeah," I said, trying not to sound *too* okay. "I just wanted you to know I got my period."

Looking as forlorn as expected with his sad mouth and upturned brows, Travis sat up and caressed my back. Then he pulled me in and held me, making me feel worse for feeling so glad.

"All This Time"

When the lease on Travis's apartment with his roommate expired in early 1995, we decided to get our own place together. Travis even surprised me with a fluffy white kitten that I instantly loved more than life. "Kitty" never left my side, forcing unconditional affection upon me, no matter my mood.

Travis and I were much more in love with the cat than we were with each other, though. We spent more time bouncing little foam balls against the wall for Kitty to catch in midair than spending quality time together. It was impossible to when he was always working and going to the casino with that black toiletry bag, and I was juggling a full-time job at a local real estate office with a full course load at DePaul.

So, he caught me off guard when he casually commented, "I put a deposit on an engagement ring!"

"What?" I asked as I abandoned the colorful cat-themed bathroom for the drably decorated bedroom adjacent and gaped at Travis from the doorway. He was sitting up in bed, wearing a ratty T-shirt, athletic shorts, and a satisfied smirk under the "flavor saver" that had never grown on me.

Any other girl would have been squealing with joy, jumping on the bed excitedly and throwing her arms around her soon-to-be fiancé. Any talk of an engagement between *us*, however, didn't make sense. Granted, we'd been together for two years now. But just last weekend, I'd cried my eyes out to a CD by the Judds when he hadn't come home to the romantic Sweetest Day dinner I'd cooked. When he'd returned the next morning, the condoms he'd had in his toiletry bag were missing. Yeah, I'd been checking. He just didn't know it.

"It's really pretty," he teased in a singsong tone.

My eyes darted around the room as if looking for an escape. I noticed the drawn shades preventing the sunlight from coming in and how much darker the nightstand and dresser appeared against the contrasting white walls. After zoning out for a minute, the weekend morning news anchor talking on the nineteen-inch TV in the corner distracted me back to where I was.

How do I tell Travis that he was misinterpreting my underwhelming reaction as surprise instead of the panic suddenly overcoming me, when I didn't know how to explain the panic without insulting him?

He was looking at me expectantly. So, I switched off the TV and sat beside him on the bed.

"Aren't you happy?" Travis asked.

After a long exhale, I said, "Yeah! I mean, that's huge! I never thought . . . I just—"

"It's what you want, isn't it?" His creased forehead expressed confusion for both of us. Whether he was referring to the engagement ring or the marriage, yes, I did! I just didn't know if I wanted those things with *Travis*.

"Well, yeah! But I'm only nineteen," I lamely excused to avoid hurting his feelings with the truth.

"And I'm twenty-five," he argued. "You know I want a wife and kids. It's not like we haven't talked about it!"

"I know, but . . ." I started, realizing I had no excuse for my engagement in those conversations.

"I don't understand, Dana," Travis said, shaking his head. "I thought we were on the same page."

"Well, I don't understand why we can't wait," I replied, fixing my eyes on Travis's blues.

"Because I don't to want to wait! I'm not getting any younger!" he protested.

My body tensed. He'd only raised his voice to me once before.

Just then, I recalled the exact point at which I realized that my relationship with Travis wouldn't last, at least not long term. I'd never talked to him about it, though, just like I'd never addressed his inability to be faithful to me.

After a deep breath to calm myself, I dropped my head then looked back up at him. "Remember when I missed my period last summer? And you got so excited that I might be pregnant that you were telling people you might be a dad?"

"Yeah?" he said, creasing his brow.

"Well, to be completely honest with you, I wasn't excited at all. I was actually relieved when my period finally came." I averted my eyes to avoid the shame he'd reflect to me in his.

"I don't understand. Don't you *want* to have kids?" he asked.

"I don't know," I half lied. The fear of treating any child like my mother and Ron had chosen to parent me *was* a deterrent.

The other half of my truth was that the possibility of being pregnant last year reinforced the regret that I'd never love Travis like I loved Liam. But how could I tell Travis he was just a "good enough for now" guy, instead of my forever ride-or-die?

"When were you going to tell me?" Travis murmured.

"Tell you what?"

"That this was going nowhere."

Travis's words sounded like the impending doom of the drums beating in the movie *Jumanji*, right before elephants stampeded through, destroying everything in their wake. My heartbeat picked up its pace as it hypothetically ran from the perceived threat.

"This isn't going nowhere, Travis," I said, desperate to hold on to the one constant in my life. "I'm a sophomore in college, though. I'm just trying to get through school, not get married and have babies! At least not yet, assuming that's what we even decide to do."

"Assuming?" Travis disputed.

"Yeah," I insisted. "We don't know where we'll be in a couple years. I might find a job in New York, and you might prefer to stay in Michigan. I don't know!" I shrugged.

Travis shook his head, refuting me without words. I reached for his hand to comfort him, but he crossed his arms instead.

"Don't pull away from me, Travis. This isn't my fault," I pleaded.

"It is, actually," he said with unusual sternness. Then he narrowed his eyes at me. "Because this has all been for nothing. It's all been a lie, hasn't it?"

I loathed liars. So, being accused of being one felt like a dagger to my heart. Yet, I was indefensible. It hadn't been my conscious intent to lead him on, but I felt shame nonetheless.

With a drooped head, focusing on my fingers fumbling in my lap, I whispered, "I wanted it to be you, Travis. I really did." He wasn't the one, though, and I didn't want to settle for someone whose infidelity would have to be tolerated. I had stayed with Travis regardless, because I was afraid to be alone.

At that, Travis got up and locked himself in the bathroom. I remained on the bed, trying to talk myself into accepting the one thing about him I couldn't get over. Travis was so good to me, so why couldn't I just be like my mother and grandmother and other women in my family who took the bad for the sake of the good?

Travis returned to the bedroom then, fully clothed. I watched in silence as he took his toiletry bag from the top of the dresser and walked out. The sound of the front door shutting firmly told me he was gone. My shoulders shook as I sobbed.

When I went to the leasing office to turn in my keys to the apartment a month later, I asked the lady if Travis had returned his. I was anxious to get my half of the security deposit back, to buy myself a bed for the more affordable apartment I'd moved into at the complex where I worked.

"Yeah, he came in with his son," she said with a smile. "Cute little boy!"

Travis didn't have a son. At least not a biological one. But I guess he'd found a built-in family with someone else, at a speed which made me certain that I'd been right to decline a future with him.

As dejected and depressed as I felt about the end of our relationship, I was proud of myself for refusing to settle. I shouldn't have to suppress who I was or sacrifice what I wanted in deference to someone else's desires and dreams. I'd already seen my mother do that. And I didn't want to be *anything* like my mother.

"After All"

"**D**ana?" I heard a man ask from the other end of my cell phone. It was May of 1997, and I was stuck in rush-hour traffic, trying to get out of the city.

"I'm sorry. Can I ask who this is?" I couldn't place the familiar voice.

"Oh! Yeah. It's Travis." My heart practically stopped. I hadn't heard from him since November of 1995, when I'd called him at work in a moment of anxious desperation, literally begging him to come back to me. Thankfully, he'd rejected me. "I just called to congratulate you. On your graduation from DePaul?" he asked with a tone questioning whether I had.

Still shocked to hear from this blast from the past, I was barely able to utter, "I didn't graduate. *Yet.*"

"You didn't drop out, did you?" he asked.

"No," I quickly refuted. Then I explained that I had to retake some classes I hadn't passed the first time, though I was still sore about how I'd tested high enough to end up in calculus in the first place.

"It's better to graduate a little late than not at all!" Travis said.

Although I was at peace with the fact that we'd been what the other needed at the time but would've been mistaken to force forever, I missed Travis's glass-half-full perspective. My current boyfriend was more of a glass-half-empty kind of guy.

"Yeah," I responded. "I worked too hard to quit now."

"Well, good! Because you're really smart, and that degree will take you places you'll never get without it," he said, sounding like a dad I didn't have. I'd thought to reconnect with mine but had yet to know what to say to excuse the half dozen years I'd been out of touch.

"Definitely," I said to fill the awkward silence.

"Everything else working out for you?" he asked.

What "else" was there unless he was probing my relationship status?

"Yeah, everything is good!" I lied. Then I anxiously ended the call with a "good to hear from you" and a "take care," to avoid more questions. I was aware of my tendency to overshare, and I didn't want to elicit unwelcome concern.

Travis and I weren't partners anymore, anyway. Nor were we friends. We were just two people who used to know each other. He didn't need to know that I wasn't happy with Darren—the guy I'd been with since just after our breakup. No one needed to know about how Darren had used a hockey stick and a crowbar and the silent treatment to assert his authority over me, nor how he'd violently shoved me up against a brick wall at his sister's wedding the month before.

The fear I'd had when Darren and I had run into Liam last week wasn't any of Travis's business either. I hadn't seen my high school sweetheart since senior prom, so the feelings I had for him came rushing back when we found ourselves at the same community theater production, which our young siblings had roles in. He'd gained more weight than I had but was otherwise exactly the same, as was my affection for him. So, Darren wasn't happy with me. He didn't have anything to worry about, though. Liam was still with that redheaded girl, who was as gorgeous as ever.

Telling Travis that nothing had changed with my mother and Ron was pointless too. Those heartaches were my burden to bear. So, he didn't get to be privy to how I'd felt when she'd recently given me a book that she'd originally bought for me in 1986.

To My Daughter, With Love had stood on the hutch of my bedroom dresser for years, taunting me with the lie of its premise. After I'd moved to Travis's, it had disappeared, which was just as well.

"I took it out of your room when we were remodeling it for Jonathan," Mom explained. "I thought I'd write some life advice in it for you, to give you when you graduated college. But since you're *not* graduating, I figured I'd just give it to you now."

Feeling like I had to defend the perceived failure, I'd insisted, "I *am* graduating, Mom. I just need more time to complete my courses." *And come* up with the money for them, since Ron decided that he didn't have to pay for my education beyond the four years it took everyone else to graduate.

"Well, just in case," she said, disbelieving and insulting me all at once.

I shook my head and almost asked just in case *what?* But I didn't want to get into a fight during what was supposed to be a sentimental moment. Instead, I placed the pink-and-powder-blue book on my lap and opened it to see what she'd written.

Inside the front cover, my mother had scribbled random tidbits, angled every which way: *Never go to bed upset. Say no to drugs. Brush. Floss. Smile a lot. Learn to cook one really great meal. Work. Have friends. Keep emergency numbers near your phone. Always look marvelous—it's better to look marvelous than to feel marvelous.*

I paused and sighed. But then a phrase on the bottom of the right page caught my eye.

It's okay to be a hypocrite.

I scrunched my brows, hoping I'd read it wrong. But I hadn't. And the atrocity of it made me wary of what she'd written inside the card taped to the middle of the interior cover.

Dear Dana,

I kept this book for a long time, believing I would come up with profound advice for living that would make a difference in your life. I didn't. Still, I have ideas: Decide to be happy. Weed out what goes through your mind. Keep the good, toss the bad. Stay honest. Save some of your money. Never make important decisions in haste. Usually, there is time. Never give in to an ultimatum. Treat others well. They'll most likely treat you well too. Have a hobby you can get consumed in. Always work on a self-image. Turn into the person you want others to see you as and love yourself as that person. Choose your mate carefully. Before you have kids, read about child-rearing. Have kids because you both truly want them. Sometimes life gets nuts. Learn to prioritize and forget about everything else while you take care of the really important tasks. Most of all, have a great life, and remember Sonia's famous quote: "Life's a beach and then you die."

Love, Mom

This "life advice," supposedly meant for me, seemed to be more reflective of my mother's regrets about hers. Because it wasn't "okay to be a hypocrite." It just needed to be okay for *her*.

So, I simply said, "Thanks, Mom," and closed the book.

© Jenny Taylor Boudoir Photography

A survivor of child abuse and an abusive marriage, Dana S. Diaz has made it her mission to serve as a voice for victims of narcissistic abuse. She has been featured on more than 200 podcasts and has been a guest speaker at conferences related to healing from trauma. Her experiences were the source of inspiration for both *Choking on Shame* and her first book, *Gasping for Air*.

Dana lives with her husband in Illinois and is currently working on the sequel to *Gasping for Air*.

Learn more about Dana at www.danasdiaz.com